Or Orwell

Or Orwell

Writing and Democratic Socialism

ALEX WOLOCH

HARVARD UNIVERSITY PRESS

Cambridge, Massachusetts / London, England

2016

First printing

Two stanzas from "Our Youth" as they appear as an epigraph from
The Tennis Court Oath: A Book of Poems by John Ashbery © 1977
published by Wesleyan University Press. Used by permission.

Library of Congress Cataloging-in-Publication Data

Woloch, Alex, 1970–
Or Orwell : writing and democratic socialism / Alex Woloch.
pages cm
Includes bibliographical references and index.
ISBN 978-0-674-28248-3
1. Orwell, George, 1903–1950—Criticism and interpretation. I. Title.
PR6029.R8Z89 2015
828'.91209—dc23
2015015042

For Karla

Contents

Prologue
Reagan and Theory

The Arabs took us. We knew
The dead horses. We were discovering coffee,
How it is to be drunk hot, with bare feet
In Canada. And the immortal music of Chopin

Which we had been discovering for several months
Since we were fourteen years old. And coffee grounds,
And the wonder of hands, and the wonder of the day
When the child discovers her first dead hand.

—JOHN ASHBERY, "Our Youth"

For our generation, he'll always be *the* president. After all, it might have been teenagers or even alert children who could understand best—which is to say who understood least—the cruel exclusions that defined this political era. Just as we were taking political reality in, we'd come up, time after time, against a government relentless at shutting real persons and experiences out. Who can say how deeply such impact rests? "[Y]ou have the cursed Jesuit strain in you, only it's injected the wrong way."[1] And so, growing up in the 1980s: Ed Meese and James Watt. Jeanne Kirkpatrick and Elliot Abrams. John Negroponte. These names are still with us, injected the wrong way. Waking up to the world, we discovered Reaganism, and Reagan will always limn the contours of discovery itself. Like first love—or heartbreak—the first government you learn to know stays with you.

On the one hand, then, we might have seen best—because we understood (rationalized, accepted, compromised) least. On the other hand, we came into conflict with this given world—the "mean season," as one group of social critics called it in 1987—precisely in relation to the development of our own world-conceptualizing faculties.[2] In this landscape, thought emerges haltingly—the very dynamics of discovery or immersion are strangely intertwined with rejection and withdrawal. Grasping the real, thought can only turn its back on the world. Discovery is shot through with bitterness, and the affirmation implicit in reasoning itself is resolved in other terms altogether: turning away, day-dreaming or abstraction, casting down eyes, cultivating various forms of detachment or retreat.

Strange combinations of action and inaction unfold in these crosscurrents. "Withdrawal in disgust is not the same as apathy," memorably proclaims one of the twenty-somethings from Richard Linklater's 1991 film *Slacker* (that low-key ethnography of, and from, the unhappy children of Reaganism and a film whose own meandering signals the same dilemmas that are faced by oppositional culture). Of course, withdrawal in disgust veers all too close to apathy; that's why this is a funny, biting line. It is hard to see any sustained radical thought of the Reagan years that is not marked, in part, by such disgusted withdrawal. And the exact limits of this are hard to trace. As the New Right ideology begins to saturate and limit a range of social institutions and political enterprises, the possibilities for coherent response rapidly decline. Thought, which draws on the world as much as breath draws on air ("promise-crammed"), is torn, in the 1980s, in an elaborate intertwining of rejection and engagement.

In the face of Reagan's popularity and the pervasive ideology of dismantling, progressive vocation of almost any kind confronted a set of trade-offs, paradoxes, or double binds. On the one hand, incremental contributions to embattled institutions—schools, hospitals, social work, local government—could easily serve in this period merely to mitigate, and even further propel, social retrenchment. As Republicans came to lean explicitly on the rhetoric of charity and volunteerism in the late 1980s ("a thousand points of light"), the tough logic of this was crystallized. For progressives relying intensively on the statistics which would measure the damage that cutbacks caused, individual effort, however resolute and energetic, could easily be turned against itself. Working harder with shrinking resources—as a doctor or nurse, as a teacher, in social services, relief organizations, or NGOs—might simply help to justify the draconian cuts, contributing to political conditions that forced more difficult work in the first place. Almost any ameliorative work could take on similar coloration in the 1980s. Often the left has been understandably critical of these institutions, with a critique that necessarily challenges—and even potentially undermines—many dedicated activists, immersed in the everyday world. But radical social-change and social-justice movements were equally precarious—often unable to achieve any substantial or meaningful progress, and, at worst, becoming a thorn in the side of reformists trying to improve, or simply defend, different institutions from within.

This same compounding of action and paralysis is one way to see the rise of academic literary theory, which reaches a politicized pitch during "the mean season," perhaps embodied in the success and influence, throughout the 1980s, of *The Political Unconscious,* Fredric Jameson's 1981 study subtitled "Narrative as a Socially Symbolic Act." Jameson's heady mixture of sublime thinking and symptomatic diagnosis offers one example of such alchemy, but these fundamental impulses are visible in many of the internal dynamics of the theoretical turn. The agency of the critic is often, in the energetic work of the 1980s, affirmed negatively, only against the reputed, now discredited, agency of cultural and literary texts. Numerous works in this period "split" in this way, at once mirroring a fallen or brutal world (in the thoroughly demystified textual object) and connoting a confident, aggressively critical capacity (in the theoretical agent him- or herself) that fed off the texts it deconstructed.[3] Two intertwined reactions to Reagan's ascendancy: despair and refusal, futility and escape.[4]

Like many other politically oriented critics, I'm interested in considering the history of the historicist and political turn in literary theory, as it is rooted in Anglo-American reaction, the era of Reagan and Thatcher, and the death of liberal intentionality in U.S. politics and culture. This is the period in which theory's dismissal of the "liberal subject" reached its most critical pitch but also when George Bush successfully stigmatized liberalism as a discredited and unspeakable taboo, "the L word," in the 1988 presidential campaign.[5] In a simple chronological sense, certainly, the turn toward Reagan and Thatcher overlaps the theoretical turn, which sees a fusion of linguistic and deconstructive paradigms (that develop throughout the 1970s) with ideological critique, critical theory, Marxist analysis, and New Historicism. These are the undeniable elements of a critical-theoretical firmament that defined the 1980s and, within the domain of literary criticism and literary history, transformed every field and specialization to one degree or another.

The Reagan–Thatcher ascendancy of the late 1970s and '80s gave underlying urgency and traction to this sweeping intellectual dynamic but also remained largely a blind spot for 1980s theory. Attuned in discerning ways to see history in every dimension of literature and culture (and "history is what hurts," Jameson famously writes in *The Political Unconscious* [102]), theory did not often confront or engage its own entwinement with a demoralizing set of historically specific political conditions. Certainly, the electoral blows of 1980, 1984 (most particularly), and 1988 were central to the lived experience of the intellectual and academic left. Artists, scholars, teachers, thinkers, and writers shared a lingua franca of despair—of bitter irony, disgust, disheartenment—that intersected with the rise of the New Right, the tangible popularity of Reagan, the harsh implications of his legislative agenda, the assault on organized labor, the growth of religious fundamentalism, the shift of the Supreme Court and federal judiciary ever further to the right, the rollback of civil rights, new levels of homelessness and urban despair, the AIDS crisis, a metastasized prison-industrial complex, and increased U.S. military spending and aggression. These policies and political turns punctuated the era with frustration, anger, and bewilderment for countless intellectuals: emotions not simply set in stone but churning out in relation to concrete, unfolding political developments and battles. If these battles were dispersed and multifaceted with competing and intricate temporalities, they were also grounded, above all, in the electoral cycles that facilitated the political power of the Republican Party and demarcated a shifting and retrenched ideological ground.

But these developments remained largely invisible in U.S. cultural criticism, despite its ever-intensifying politicization and deepening historicist inclination. The lack of connection defies our credulity, especially given criticism's heightened sensitivity toward the impingement of social and ideological conditions on literature, culture, and thinking. "History is what hurts," but criticism and theory from the late 1970s through the 1990s often seemed to avoid the painful political developments most close to home (even while ostensibly turning more politicized). One mechanism for this, of course, is the orthodox position that elides substantive difference between Reagan and the Democratic opposition, essentially cordoning off the entire sphere of electoral politics. In this worldview, of course, history is *not* constituted by the rise of the Republican New Right, and there is no particular reason for an intensifying sense of despondency or anger. This is an intellectual response that tended to cauterize the specific political wounds of this era.

Other critics—from a spectrum of different points on the left—have suggested that we need to scrutinize the relationship between the political turn in U.S. literary-critical theory of the 1980s and U.S. electoral politics in this same period. The political vigor of criticism in this moment doesn't emerge *ex nihilo;* like all other forms of thought, it is of its moment, and this is a moment of stark political frustration and numerous setbacks. Perhaps the earliest influential statement of this is David Bromwich's 1992 *Politics by Other Means,* which positions itself as a study of "ideologies in higher education, in the Reagan years" and points immediately to "a disparity between the self-contained (mostly left-wing) culture of the academy and the static (right-wing) political culture that dominates America today" (ix). Again, Bromwich begins the book proper: "I am concerned in these pages with two environments, a conservative political culture outside the academy and a radical political culture inside it. . . . The second culture thinks of itself as an antidote to the first, but it is not. It is part of the same disease" (3). What's notable here is the simple insistence on naming the regime: "the Reagan years," the "static (right-wing) political culture," the conservative "environment." Bromwich's central ambition is to identify the compensatory currents that structure such a relationship: this is a diagnostic criticism driven by terms of displacement, repression, substitution, the compensatory responses to intractable difficulties. In this sense, Bromwich's book draws on some of the same psychoanalytic energies mobilized in Jameson's idea of "the political unconscious." The two titles are indeed strikingly similar. What's repressed by the academic left, in Bromwich's view, is the full scale of political stasis, retreat, and corruption in society at large; as he writes at one point, "The guiding concern and solicitude of the academic system are felt to be obligatory *in exact proportion* to the absence of such helps in the organized system outside" (30, emphasis added). The emphasis is added by Bromwich himself in another passage, which also explicitly invokes this term of compensation: "Since the lapse of political argument in the mid-seventies, *the universities have existed in a compensatory relationship to the political culture outside them.* Absurdities are therefore countenanced in school . . . which would scarcely be allowed except for a belief that they somehow 'balance' absurdities of an opposite sort in the political culture outside school" (47). The italics are quite unusual for the book, and I point to them to underline the systematic, methodological nature of Bromwich's claim.

A more recent version of this argument, from a quite dissimilar left-wing position (and more sympathetic to some currents of contemporary theory) is Timothy Brennan's 2006 *Wars of Position: The Cultural Politics of Left and Right*. Here, too, we find a scathing critique of *sub rosa* political premises of 1980s theory that are connected to, rather than simply standing against, the rightward political turn that characterizes this era. Like Bromwich, Brennan begins by foregrounding the historicity of this political moment (what Bromwich calls "[t]he lapse of political argument in the mid-seventies"): "In writing this book," Brennan starts, "I found myself returning again and again to the same five-year period in American cultural life: 1975–1980, the period between the end of the Vietnam War and the beginning of the presidency of Ronald Reagan" (ix). Brennan argues that theory did not merely compensate for but (again: unconsciously) helped facilitate the rise of the New Right, by rejecting the specificity of politics as a legitimate category. As he puts it early on: "I explore how political belonging was ejected from the idea of identity. And . . . I examine the consequences of fleeing, as so many left intellectuals did in those years [the 1980s and 1990s], any politics seeking to enter or make claims on the state" (x). Most passionately, Brennan later says, "an entire generation has been taken out of politics" (25). And like Bromwich, Brennan insists that "theory is not the foil but the adjunct of American conservatism" (99).

Brennan and Bromwich are just two (quite different) examples of this critical effort, which angles to examine the political and social context of post-1970s academic thinking itself. But we need to be more pointed about this: "political and social context" is too neutral, failing to register the atmosphere of failure and political shock, the particularity of this congealed and narrow political moment. Reagan's ascendancy opens a period that makes hope difficult and can work, with ruthless alchemical dexterity, to transform pragmatism into insufficient compromise (co-optation, selling out) and principle into sectarian isolation. This is the air that critical theory—at the point of its institutional ascendancy—breathes. If there is intellectual progress in this period (and progress seems intrinsic to the self-definition of theory), it would seem to exempt itself from the very terms of historical conditioning that underlie the theoretical turn.

Both of these books worry about the dissonance between the radical energies of intellectual critique in this period (deriving, above all, from the deconstructive and historicist dynamics of criticism) and the demoralizing consolidation of right-wing power across U.S. political and social institutions outside the academy. And both sense that political despair, often not registered directly, produces unintended effects in intellectual life. Brennan's argument, for example, focuses on how often politics, as an aspirational enterprise, or the state, as an object that needs to be defended, can get dissolved, negated, or repudiated as legitimate categories in poststructural criticism. We could look, similarly, at forms of deconstructive ethics, wrested out of an abiding and often antipolitical skepticism, that veer into quasi-religious or spiritual frameworks. Or forms of Marxist analysis that take such a bird's-eye view of the long sweep of history, the nature of the human "subject," or the system of global capitalist relations as to blur away the political problems, and struggles, that are so evident at slightly closer scale.

Let me hazard one example of this effacement of partisan reality and then move on. I'm thinking here of Judith Butler's 1997 essay "Burning Acts, Injurious Speech" (published first in *Critical Inquiry* and then as part of her book *Excitable Speech*), which addresses, in large part, a divided Supreme Court decision from 1992, *R.A.V. v St Paul*, which struck down a Minnesota law prohibiting hate speech. Butler is an iconic figure for literary theory and criticism in the age of Reagan–Bush; she writes a series of deeply oppositional, skeptical, and galvanizing works in the late 1980s and throughout the 1990s, including *Subjects of Desire, Gender Trouble, Bodies that Matter,* and *Excitable Speech*. Significantly, Butler doesn't embrace an explicitly left-wing vocabulary in these early works, as she does in her co-authored volume *Contingency, Hegemony and Universality: Contemporary Dialogues on the Left* and other more recent writing. The misalignment between radical opposition (which draws, implicitly, on a left-wing framework) and concrete, embedded left politics is particularly evident in the "Burning Acts" essay because of its focus on the Supreme Court. Butler's rhetorical analysis of *R.A.V. v. St Paul* serves to dramatize the transportability of theoretical discourse into concrete political subject matter. Any analysis of Butler's essay would need to heed the significance of this gesture, and Butler's piece is quite explicit, at key points, that her essay is not meant merely as a critique of *this* decision but of the power of the Supreme Court more generally. Thus,

Butler writes (and we can notice how a searing criticism of the Court is embedded into an almost naturalized circuit of rhetorical analysis):

> Lastly, I want to suggest that the court's speech carries with it its *own* violence, and that the very institution that is invested with the authority to adjudicate the problem of hate speech recirculates and redirects that hatred in and as its own highly consequential speech, often by coopting the very language that it seeks to adjudicate. (54)

Butler's statement (reiterated in different ways throughout the essay) obliquely accuses the Supreme Court of perpetuating "violence" and "hatred" as it enacts its juridical power. On the one hand, it seems to me impossible to understand Butler's deployment of these terms outside of a specific, highly partisan battle over the federal judiciary and the Supreme Court in this period. It would be difficult, in other words, to imagine Butler characterizing the *pre*-Nixon court in this way. Right-wing attacks on the court and the struggle by both Democratic and Republican administrations to either preserve the constitutional legacy of the Warren Court or to hasten its demise occur across the entire span of Butler's work and, again, the more general period of high theory and reactionary politics. But while Butler's essay draws heavily on the projection of rhetorical analysis into this concrete, partisan, and deeply contested site of political power, the essay takes no explicit notice of the shifting, contingent nature of the Supreme Court at this historical moment. On the contrary, Butler maintains a studious poker face about this: "hatred" and "violence" do not emerge out of the *changing disposition* of the court—following the appointments of Rehnquist, Scalia, Thomas, Kennedy, O'Connor, and Souter by three Republican administrations—but rather seem to attach to the nature of the court as such. The two uses of "very" in this sentence ("the very institution," "the very language that it seeks to adjudicate"), insofar as they help to organize the core deconstructive work of Butler's analysis, function to generalize this circulation of power, as though it is the nature of any such institutionally sanctioned discourse, rather than the particular political bearing of the Rehnquist court, that catalyzes these dynamics. It's thus not surprising that Butler's analysis moves quickly from finding such rhetorical violence in Scalia's majority opinion to a more strained attack on Stevens's concurrence (which takes strong issues with key parts of the opinion). Certainly, Stevens's argument with Scalia is fair game (although the concrete analysis that Butler offers of Stevens's critique seems to me quite stilted).[6] But it is striking to the point of deliberate that Butler eschews any mention of partisanship, any gesture toward positioning this overarching analysis of the court in an historical and political context (even if only counterintuitively). In my view, the Olympian tone—which puts the critic, as a lone individual voice, at odds with the "very" power of the Court as a site of authority—implicitly relies on, but effectively works to obscure, this contingent, partisan context. In this attack on the Supreme Court, in general, the death of the Warren Court, in particular, goes untold (even as the painful, gradual constriction of the Warren Court's legacy arguably motivates the argument, and motors the *gesture,* of this piece). Strangely, but consistent with the period, Butler's piece is not only an intellectual rebellion but also a salve.

The rest of this book will be focused on a single, avowedly political writer. It won't return to the more contemporary context that I've invoked in this Prologue, just as this Prologue has not to this point mentioned George Orwell, the book's immediate object of attention. These opening pages, instead, have briefly put method—or a methodological atmosphere and desire—before object. This replaces one historical framework (Orwell, situated in the 1930s and 1940s) with another (the intellectual and political formation that underlies my own turn to and analysis of this writer). In one sense, of course, any work of literary history starts from (rather than merely moving closer toward or finally arriving at) a contemporary context. And in various ways, nearly every major literary author was both lost within *and* newly recognized through the theoretical matrix of the 1980s. But in this case, the loss—and, above all, the loss of attention to Orwell's intelligence, experimental energies, and critical ambition—is, I believe, particularly salient.

This book's opening wager, indeed, will be that the two terms "Orwell" and "theory" have, since the 1980s, continually worked to discredit, or efface, one another, and that such an entrenched opposition is worth unsettling.

There have been, in essence, only two choices here: to *accept* Orwell—to champion him and reread him—and then, as though of necessity, to cast a witheringly skeptical eye on literary theory; or to embrace theory, as a privileged way of knowing and even being, and to reject (or simply disregard) this politically passionate writer. Not just positioned on one side of the theoretical line, Orwell has been invoked to structure the boundary itself. James Miller, for example, writes in 2000: "Must one write clearly, as Orwell argued, or are thinkers who are truly radical and subversive compelled to write radically and subversively—or even opaquely, as if through a glass darkly. . . . If Orwell perfectly exemplifies the party of clarity . . . the German philosopher Theodor Adorno has come to represent the party of opacity" (34). This kind of comment is endemic in Orwell's post-1980s critical reception, and, crucially, it offers a frame that is often agreed upon by both "part[ies]" in this conflict. Thus Christopher Norris, in 1984, can invoke the *same* boundary line from the opposite direction: "Orwell's homespun empiricist outlook—his assumption that the truth was just there to be told in a straightforward, common-sense way—now seems not merely naïve but culpably self-deluding" (242). (With lightning-quick, 1980s speed, common sense here morphs into naïveté, naïveté into delusion, and delusion into guilt.)

Whether "culpabl[e]" or "exempl[ary]," Orwell has become a largely ritualized figure through which two warring entities—two modes of reading—seek to obliterate each other. I want to offer one further instance of such a division. First, from the opening of a 2014 review, by David Aaronovitch, in *New Statesman,* of Robert Colls's new study of Orwell:

> Since whoever we are (save for a few sad Leninists) we all agree with George Orwell, it usually follows that Orwell must agree with us. Whatever our 21st-century predilections, Tory or leftist, conservative or progressive, we discover blessings and endorsements somewhere in Orwell's words. We grab him for ourselves.

And from a 2000 piece in *New Literary History* by Eric Lott:

> [I]t's very hard to get the word "amateurish" out of my head when reading most of Rorty's published statements about politics (he actually likes *late* Orwell; do we really want to argue about this?). (674)

Like a pair of socks, these two comments, while pointed in opposite directions, bear a commanding resemblance. They "match" in their use of the first-person plural and even their parentheticals, which, by pathologizing the other perspective, lock the statements into a more profound intimacy, one of willed contradiction. Lott and Aaronovitch both insist not merely on affiliation or radical disaffiliation with Orwell but project this as a universal position, in the realm of second nature. There is a stark refusal here of the other camp—even as the countervailing comment, equally assured, suggests that this other camp is *not* so trivial or small after all. Orwell, on the one hand, should be (or already has been) ejected from the world of critical thinking: "do *we* really want to argue about this?" (emphasis added). On the other hand, he is utterly naturalized, the figure that, "whoever we are," we already agree with. He is internal to the point of non-definition or expelled absolutely. And while it is easy to conjure up writers who might occupy one of these two positions, it is more difficult to identify another figure who occupies both poles in this manner.

This is a contradiction that imposes itself on the mind, in an imperious and ultimately paralyzing way. It can stand in for many such contradictions in contemporary culture. In the pages that follow, I will offer a different reading of Orwell—in the hopes of breaking such paralysis. Ultimately, my study will come to rest on what Lott might stigmatize as "*late* Orwell"—and, more specifically, on the weekly columns, entitled "As I Please," that Orwell writes for the Socialist newspaper *Tribune*, between 1943 and 1947. But it will move through his body of work—pausing as well on key texts from 1931, 1937, and 1940—and aims to focus, above all, on the sheer activity of writing, the intricate, ongoing process of composition itself. In a basic sense, of course, this process underlies all of Orwell's varied work. Yet Orwell's writing—famously attentive to the politics of language—has not been fully engaged *in* its writerliness, and in the singular way that it calls attention to the (contingent) activity and (unstable) nature of writing. This focus opens onto a series of questions and quandaries—about thinking, hope, failure, political urgency, and political desire—that can resonate with this Prologue's opening discussion. To identify these quandaries, I believe, is to come to terms with—rather than to expose or to shatter—Orwell's politics, a self-consciously socialist political orientation which, not least in its contingency and instability, still has unfolding significance.

Or Orwell

Introduction

Orwell's Formalism, or A Theory of Socialist Writing

Poverty is what I am writing about. (*Down and Out in Paris and London* 9)

What books were *about* seemed so urgently important that the way they were written seemed almost insignificant. ("The Frontiers of Art and Propaganda" 12.486, Orwell's emphasis)

"And what are you going to write about, dear?" his aunt enquires. "My dear aunt," the youth replies crushingly, "one doesn't write *about* anything, one just *writes*." ... To admit that you liked or disliked a book because of its moral or religious tendency, even to admit noticing that it *had* a tendency, was too vulgar for words. ("Review of *The Novel To-day*" 10.533, Orwell's emphases)

Orwell and Political Intention

As much as any Anglophone writer, George Orwell occupies a strangely divided position: widely read and understood as an iconic political writer, he has been largely ignored or dismissed in academic literary theory and criticism—even as it has become more overtly political.[1] Orwell's contention in 1946 that "what I have most wanted to do throughout the past ten years is to make political writing into an art" ("Why I Write" 18.319), foregrounds the compelling question of literary intentionality.[2] Orwell rests near the canonical center of *deliberately* political twentieth-century writing, but the tendency of academic criticism when it turns to Orwell at all, since the 1970s, has been—as with so many writers—to uncover the political unconscious at work in his writing, which is to say its uglier, less controlled, more symptomatic ideological flaws and extrusions.

Orwell's writing identifies explicitly as democratic socialist, and such affiliation raises challenging questions for interpretation:

> Every line of serious work that I have written since 1936 has been written, directly or indirectly, *against* totalitarianism and *for* democratic Socialism, as I understand it. ("Why I Write" 18.319)

Contemporary criticism has fewer models for elaborating such explicit, stated politics ("*against* totalitarianism and *for* democratic Socialism") instead of amplifying or diagnosing the unintentional, perhaps only half-articulated, ideological currents or impulses of a text. Taking a book at face value, particularly in relation to its political aspirations, is unusual, even though the ideological vantage point of the literary critic him- or herself is often integral to the unfolding critical analysis. Skepticism toward intentional political belief can easily lead to an automatic mapping process in which the "guilt" of the author is commensurate with the innocence or righteousness of the critic, each intensifying the other.[3]

In the extensive scholarship on the key modernist writers who form the backdrop for Orwell's own literary productions, such guilt is certainly not always foregrounded, but the political investment (and thus assuredness) of this scholarship is often quite palpable. For example, much of the most persuasive and influential recent criticism on James Joyce has an orientation toward history, politics, or ethics—arguing either for or against the ideological currents of the text, the ethics and politics of Joyce's formal experimentation, or the ways in which his work fails at or succeeds in registering or representing historical forces. Criticism has developed keen skills at this kind of analysis, in which the historical or political subtexts and implications of form, genre, language, image, writing, discourse, etc. are teased out and magnified. But Joyce, of course, is a starkly different kind of writer than Orwell, and never seeks to be so explicit about the political ambitions or identification of his writing. It would be impossible to imagine Orwell's comment about "every line of serious work," or anything remotely like this comment, from Joyce. When Joyce, for example, complains about the Communist attacks on his work, the complaint is obviously tongue-in-cheek, ironic, and playful; when Orwell writes about his "serious work" or uses capital letters to assert that "my recent novel [*1984*] is NOT intended as an attack on socialism, or on the British Labour Party" (20.136),[4] he's obviously in full earnestness.

Such overt political "inten[t]" challenges an ingrained reflex of contemporary response, in which the taproot of critical energy consists in opening a text's internal contradictions and complexity to a sense of history that the writing bears witness to but does not intentionally grasp. Squarely political work might be, ironically, a major blind spot of the often subtle, politically articulated frameworks of contemporary criticism. In the strongest sense, we could say that criticism is born at the precise moment when the text's intentional politics (or political affiliation) ends. Orwell's writing poses this problem in particularly vivid and revealing form. We would be hard pressed to find a more iconic dramatization of an intention—from *within* the literary text itself—to engage political currents that contemporary criticism often understands itself to mediate (i.e., the intention "to make political writing into an art") or a more deliberate affiliation of such politically charged writing with a pronounced ideological perspective ("*for* democratic socialism, as I understand it").

"*For* Democratic Socialism"

Orwell's sentence about "every line" he has written since 1936 is crucial to this book for several reasons. The comment serves as a cue about the author's (political) intention that is unusually emphatic and specific. Few writers offer such a deliberate designation of their own work, particularly in these overt political terms. It is important to recognize (as many critics have noted) that Orwell does not here give much conceptual armature for his claim; this is not an effort to define democratic socialism or the relationship of writing to socialism. Rather than a rigorous delineation of his intent, Orwell's sentence dramatizes intentionality. It won't be clear from this passage what democratic socialism means to Orwell. But it is clear that Orwell wants to signal his affiliation with democratic socialism and (more oddly) wants to register his commitment *to* signaling this affiliation with socialism throughout his writing.

This distinction is worth underlining. Orwell's comment is an artful one. After all, we can't take this assertion as literal evidence that every line Orwell wrote between 1936 and 1946 was, indeed, "*for* democratic socialism" (and that Orwell—having written all this now securely defined work—is thus confirmed as a socialist). We also encounter this assertion, for lack of a better term, poetically—absorbing the qualities of the assertion itself (e.g., its hyperbole) and inferring, from these formal qualities, as well, the nature of Orwell's political commitment. When we think about it, the technique of this comment depends on the relative *in*accuracy of the statement, as it triggers a series of connected and unstated implications. First of all, we are surprised by such an emphatic assertion of the writer's political orientation, and surprised by the scope of the assertion ("every line"). Such magnitude stresses how keenly Orwell, in this instance, wants to express his political position. And this underlying sense of surprise suggests something else as well: that such continual, persistent affiliation—the writerly affiliation that this sentence imagines—would be *difficult*.

The emphasis, the surprise, the desire, the difficulty—none of this is expressly conveyed in Orwell's comment, but all of these implications are part of the intentionality that this line at once denotes (in regard to Orwell's earlier writing) and catalyzes (as a new act of writing itself). To mark the intention of this passage does not entail interjecting an external or biographical framework that then stabilizes or constrains the text. (It does not entail merely adjudicating whether Orwell's prose between 1936 and 1946 *is* so ideologically consistent.) What we might easily take as (quite insufficient) evidence of Orwell's socialist commitment is, rather, a contingent instance, and thus a dramatization, of such commitment—a dramatization that only unfolds, in fact, *against* the certainty of this statement. Such uncertainty is hidden in plain sight. "[D]irectly or indirectly," "as I understand it," "[e]very line of *serious* work" (emphasis added): Orwell's compact and memorably emphatic statement manages to contain all three of these complicating gestures. Each of them weakens Orwell's political claim in "Why I Write," if we take it as potential evidence of commitment. When we understand this comment instead as an action, an enactment of political intention, these same uncertainties only strengthen the effect.

"What Would Orwell Do?"

In a sure measure of the political desire always entangled with our reading of this author, Orwell has often been—and still continues to be—invoked anachronistically, producing relentless speculation and debate about what he would "do" or "think" about contemporary political conflicts and quandaries. What would Orwell have had to say about 9/11, the deceptions of the Bush administration, the Iraq War, the NSA, or, earlier, Vietnam? John Newsinger begins his important study of Orwell's politics by asking this kind of question while also noting its obvious shortcomings:

> The fall of Communism in Eastern Europe and the Soviet Union between 1989 and 1991 almost overnight changed the nature of the world we live in. In Poland, Hungary, East Germany, Czechoslovakia, Bulgaria, Romania, Yugoslavia, and in the Soviet Union itself, Communist rule collapsed with remarkably little bloodshed. . . . What would Orwell have thought of these developments? This is, of course, a dangerous question to ask. . . . Nevertheless, it is possible and worthwhile to suggest how the Orwell of the late 1940s, whose opinions we do know, would have responded. (ix)

And John Rodden, the leading critic of Orwell's complicated, proliferating reception, has even promoted the acronym WWGOD ("What Would George Orwell Do?") to characterize (and gently mock) this persistent meta-critical tendency.[5]

We might productively displace this question by posing a different hypothetical: what form of writing might Orwell have pursued in relation to any of these crises? The one thing that we could be certain Orwell would not have done, after all, would be to construct *another* animal fable or a second futuristic dystopia. Insofar as these frameworks are readily repeated or projected onto current political events (even if only through phrases that are culled from these two works), the political power of Orwell's writing gets lost *in* its putative re-articulation. Consider, just to begin with, that conjunction of *Animal Farm* and *1984*: two books written sequentially (after Orwell had ceased to write full-length books for several years), addressing shared or overlapping political crises, and both using explicitly bounded and stylized forms. If these two books reinforce each other in obvious ways, they also subtly interfere with one another, complicating what might otherwise be the simple convergence of either allegorical fable or dystopian projection with the political present. There is an almost embarrassing surplus of optics here, which would threaten to turn the "window pane" of engaged-prose into a kaleidoscope.

Not "what would Orwell say?," then, but "what form would Orwell use?" And, implicitly, what forms could we imagine using—and discarding—in relation to our own political world? This is perhaps the abiding question—or reorientation—that I want to provoke in this book, insofar as it would let us envision a writing at once topical and experimental. We can begin to consider Orwell's formalism, most simply, by foregrounding the wide variety of forms that his engaged writing takes. *Animal Farm* is aptly entitled a "fable" and can be considered an allegory, a satire, a tract, a version of historical reportage, a political intervention, or, in line with Orwell's next text, a dystopian fiction. *1984* obviously discards the "childish things" of *Animal Farm* while retaining many of its central concerns: it is, more evidently, a novel, at the boundary of science fiction (uniquely so in Orwell's work), an exercise in dystopian thinking, and, strangely, both naturalistic and futuristic. As I've suggested, these twinned texts make the problem of genre quite explicit, standing out against Orwell's 1930s novels, which are more generically unpronounced. But generic instability is the hallmark of a much wider swath of Orwell's writing in the 1930s and 1940s, which cuts through, and often troubles the boundaries of, autobiography, documentary, memoir, fiction, reportage, literary criticism, short-form journalism (most notably the newspaper column, titled "As I Please," that he writes in the mid-1940s for the socialist weekly *Tribune*), pamphleteering, and, of course, the multifarious possibilities of the essay.

Does this range in-and-of-itself make Orwell's writing "formal"? And what would such variety tell us about the political aesthetics at stake in the work? In exploring these questions, I want to resist three ways that criticism can explain (and often explain away) the kind of formal variety that marks Orwell's writing. I will call these the ornamental, pluralistic, and instrumental approaches. In the "ornamental" approach, formal variety is taken as epiphenomenal—as what adorns, without fundamentally disrupting, more unified concerns, or ingrained qualities, of the writer's work. (Form so often lends itself to this ornamental diminution, in ways large or small, explicit or implicit.) In the "pluralistic" approach, formal variety emanates out of a writer's wide-ranging *topical* interests. Moving from form to form, the writer demonstrates an eclectic and catholic sensibility. Changing forms register this changing mind, or, more basically, open-mindedness. In the third, "instrumental," approach, form is tactical. The writer *uses* varied forms for varied purposes, like a chef who wields an assortment of knives, ready-at-hand, for different tasks in the kitchen. Variety, no matter how manifest, is driven by function. And form's flexibility, no matter how conspicuous, finally marks the heuristic adjustment to such shifting functional needs.

These three frameworks—which come to understand formal variety as supplemental and decorative, or as an expression of (pluralistic) sensibility, or as a heuristic instrument—are not simply applicable to Orwell. They are categories that can be deployed, in many different contexts, to motivate or contain form. In pushing against these models of containment, we might begin by noting how Orwell's attachment to formal range is intertwined with a compulsive and sustained attachment to the praxis of writing itself. As the biographers Peter Stansky and William Abrahams suggestively put it, "For him a day without writing was not a good one. There were, effectively, no pauses in the process: if not a novel, then a review, or an essay, a letter, a diary, a shopping list" (180). Beneath variety, and powering Orwell's movement from genre to genre, is this underlying graphomanic drive: each change to a different form stems from, and thus also signals and reasserts, a core restlessness within the act of writing itself. And look at the trajectory here, shifting so swiftly from "novel" to "essay" to "letter" to "shopping list." The negativity of this sequence is important, suggesting that the movement between forms itself marks a kind of disintegration, leading inexorably back to writing's intrinsic fragility and contingency.

From any starting point, the momentum in reading Orwell is toward this scattering or dispersion of form. We need to register how strongly this compositional diffusion, and restlessness, runs against the ideal of "window pane" prose. The varied modes and genres that Orwell gravitates toward—his sustained investment in formal variety as such—suggests the limitations of any reading of Orwell, which imagines an unmediated ethical agency, as though there were a pith or essence to Orwell's ethical response that we could extract, like an elixir, from the writing and apply to current circumstances. The formal instability of Orwell's work militates against any view of his ethics or politics neatly detached from the concrete praxis of writing itself. In Orwell (if not Blair), no ethics without writing. And writing obeys its own logic, its own internal dynamics: the text moves not just in terms of ethical ideation but also in terms of writerly propulsion. This doesn't vitiate the political or ethical bases of Orwell's work. We can't find the political core of Orwell's work, however, in the mere expression or, again, ideational substance of the writing. It is misleading to see Orwell's writing practice as a hydraulic system for his ethical and political commitments. Instead, we need to align Orwell's politics with his expressed understanding of writing itself, his sense of its dynamics and vicissitudes, and his specific, strategic engagement with—and experiments in—writerly form. Far from trying to make writing into an unmediated instrument for political belief, Orwell's political agency is threaded through his exploration, and often his exacerbation, of writerly mediation. This exploration, as I hope to show in the course of this book, is in its own right self-consciously political.

Plain Style and Intention

Orwell's emphatic foregrounding in "Why I Write" of his political intention, as a socialist writer, is connected to another controversial dimension of his prose, which I've already touched on: the investment in plain style. This stylistic investment is manifested across the body of his work but also emphasized, like Orwell's socialist orientation, in several paradigmatic (more strictly aesthetic) comments, such as the lament, in "Politics and the English Language," that "[t]he whole tendency of modern prose is away from concreteness" (17.426) or, most famously, the dictum, once more in "Why I Write," that "[g]ood prose is like a window pane" (18.320). This view of language has elicited intense skepticism when Orwell falls into the ambit of recent or contemporary critical theory.[6] In particular, Orwell's comment about window pane prose rests at the center of his ongoing reception, and it is a comment I have already invoked and will return to throughout this book. Right now, however, I want to pause and consider the relationship between these two *kinds* of statements about writing: one set in which Orwell affiliates with a specific political aspiration ("to make political writing into an art," "*against* totalitarianism and *for* democratic socialism") and another in which Orwell affiliates with the ideal of linguistic transparency ("good prose is like a window pane," etc.). Orwell's work intertwines these two kinds of affiliation (or desire). And there are at least two ways to view this relationship. Most typically, sympathetic readers have taken Orwell's political values to prompt or underlie the investment in plain language. The prose style, *as* a chosen style of composition, connotes a set of values—such as accessibility, transparency, or ordinariness—that have political implications. An ideology would thus be indirectly suggested, and reinforced, through the plain-style medium of the prose.

My contention is almost the opposite. If the plain style connotes political values that we might align with Orwell's democratic socialism, one crucial motive for such plain style is, conversely, the sheer desire (both palpable and unfulfilled) to express his political orientation, directly and without distortion, in writing. The plain style is political, in other words, not merely because of how Orwell communicates (familiarly and, thus, democratically) but also because *what* Orwell aspires to communicate is explicitly a politics, a "political position" (19.86). This would be different from other writers of the period, who gravitated toward a simple or demotic style—writers such as Hemingway, Christopher Isherwood, or William Carlos Williams. All of these figures are concerned with the problem of plain style, and in each case, a set of political values, certainly, might be argued for or *inferred through* the plain style. But they do not use their writing, as insistently as Orwell does, to make their politics explicit. Orwell's valorization of the plain style, conversely, is often intertwined with the specificity of his political commitment, with a discrete and emphatic political orientation.

These two different paths by which we can connect the plain style and Orwell's (avowed) political commitments are worth distinguishing. The first direction suggests a happier, more harmonious relationship between language and politics. Political values would permeate the very operation of the plain style. (Orwell wants to write plainly, and this plainness, in-and-of-itself, is value-laden, infused with certain principles.) The second direction suggests a more anxious, unsettled relationship. Because it is so difficult adequately to develop, maintain, define, and communicate a politics, the writer aspires toward—rather than simply inhabiting—the plain style. (This would help explain, for example, the "struggle" and "effort" that Orwell often links to the plain style, including just before the key phrase in "Why I Write":

"Writing a book is a horrible, exhausting struggle, like a long bout of some painful illness. . . . And yet it is also true that one can write nothing readable unless one constantly struggles to efface one's own personality. Good prose is like a window pane" [18.320].[7] This struggle—never quite ending or over-come—would work against the effacement of personality that the passage invokes. Such "constant" effort at screening itself becomes highly visible.)

While I want to give credence to Orwell's intentional political affiliations, I don't want to claim that the expression of these commitments is simple or self-evident. On the contrary. This book grants an axiomatic validity (and coherence) to Orwell's political aspiration, centered on a vision of demo-cratic socialism, but also brings out his own sense of political writing as fun-damentally aspirational. In "Why I Write," Orwell avers, "what I have most *wanted* to do throughout the past ten years is to make political writing into an art," immediately linking this goal to a desire—and a desire that spurs an incessant and repeated form of action ("*throughout* the past ten years"). This same unremitting quality marks the exaggeration implicit in Orwell's polit-ical characterization of "every line of serious work" that he has written. Such rhetoric signals the unsatisfied quality of Orwell's political expression. In both these instances—in which Orwell imagines politics suffusing "every line" he has written, or spurring an emphatic ambition sustained, impos-sibly, "throughout" ten years of writing—political desire, precisely *as* it is unfulfilled, generates a compulsive and sustained attachment to the praxis of writing itself. "There were, effectively, no pauses in the process."

Intentions do not have to be met in order to be vivid and significant. And it is possible to take Orwell's paradigmatic comment about prose at face value, without naïvely mistaking his writing for a window pane, or even for writing that understands itself (naïvely) as a window pane. What's left of the iconic statement if we reject both of these alternatives? Orwell's work, in my account, *does* conceive itself as writing that, under the specific pressure of expressing political belief, strives to be like a window pane. But the striving, as we will see, is paramount. The representations articulated through the texts are never complete, and often work, deliberately, to produce and reg-ister aspiration, urgency, and impatience. In this light, Orwell's writing both expresses political intention and stages a dramatic complication of inten-tionality. This combination is more apparent still in another passage from "Why I Write," just preceding his dictum about the "window pane," that casts the desire that drives writing as structurally unfinalizable:

[O]f late years I have tried to write less picturesquely and more exactly. In any case I find that by the time you have perfected any style of writing, you have always outgrown it. *Animal Farm* was the first book in which I tried, with full consciousness of what I was doing, to fuse political purpose and artistic purpose into one whole. I have not written a novel for seven years, but I hope to write another fairly soon. It is bound to be a failure, every book is a failure, but I do know with some clarity what kind of book I want to write. (18.320)

In his claims of having "full consciousness of what [he] was doing" and, again, "know[ing] with some clarity" what he wants to do next, Orwell gives voice to that sense of purposeful intention, which is at odds with key critical tenets, both from New Criticism (as in Wimsatt and Beardsley's idea of the "intentional fallacy") and more recent theory (as in Jameson's idea of the "political unconscious").[8] The image of a writer who avows such "full consciousness" contradicts received ideas about artistic depth and autonomy, as it seems to constrain the free, open elaboration of the aesthetic within a prior, fixed set of extra-aesthetic (i.e., political) values or goals. This orientation is unmistakable. But Orwell also troubles this sense of clear intention. He does not profess to write less picturesquely and more exactly but only to have "tried to write less picturesquely and more exactly" and, again, to have "tried . . . to fuse political purpose and artistic purpose into one whole." He says, "I hope to write another book" and, echoing his initial comment about what he has "most wanted to do" over the preceding decade, suggests that he knows (with "clarity"!) what "kind of book I want to write." These verbs—"try," "hope," and "want"—strain against the direct purposefulness that Orwell espouses in these same passages (even as their linguistic simplicity simultaneously works to *reinforce* the plain style). They help recast such intention in terms of desire, not fulfillment.

Furthermore, Orwell incorporates two general claims in this passage, which also strain against the dominant, iconic figure of the window pane: "by the time you have perfected any style of writing you have always outgrown it" and "it is bound to be a failure, every book is a failure."[9] These two comments reinforce the aspirational quality already marked by the (more conventional) recurrence of verbs like "try," "want," and "hope." Insofar as any particular text will be a "failure," and, again, as any coherent "style" is outgrown as soon as it is perfected, writing continually falls short of its horizons and expectations, prompting the writer to "try" or "hope" more ardently, and to produce more furiously and prolifically. It is not just this or that specific piece of writing that fails, Orwell's passages suggest, but writing as such. This second comment, in particular, pushes toward an unforgiving structure within writing, a perpetual intercalation of success and failure, in which writing leads to more writing, and no sooner culminates (in that "perfect[ion]" of a "style") than it propels the writer both beyond and against the now already-written. Under this force of propulsion, writing remains in a state of restlessness, provoking and unsettling itself, in a potentially continuous process of internal differentiation.

Orwell and the Writerly

Orwell's aphorism that "good prose is like a window pane" proposes a definitive alignment between words and the stories they mean to convey, but both of these neighboring comments in "Why I Write" suggest that a pervasive misalignment is central to the rhythms and dynamics of writing. This is a Stendhalian economy of desire and regret—in which any consummated present is elided through the intricate cross-hatching of projective anticipation and ironic retrospection. Consider this passage from Orwell's 1949 notebook:

> It is now (1949) 16 years since my first book was published, & abt 21 years since I started publishing articles in the magazines. Throughout that time there has literally been not one day in which I did not feel that I was idling, that I was behind with the current job, & that my total output was miserably small. Even at the periods when I was working 10 hours a day on a book, or turning out 4 or 5 articles a week, I have never been able to get away from this neurotic feeling that I was wasting time. I can never get any sense of achievement out of the work that is actually in progress, because it always goes slower than I intend, & in any case I feel that a book or even an article does not exist until it is finished. But as soon as a book is finished, I begin, actually from the next day, worrying because the next one is not begun, & am haunted with the fear that there never will be [another one] a next one—that my impulse is exhausted for good & all. ("Notes from Last Literary Notebook" 20.204).

Orwell's comment presents two distinct but interlocking temporal rhythms within writing: any piece of writing feels impalpable and not yet of value before it is finished (even as the writing moves too "slow[ly]") but, then, all too quickly (from the very "next day") loses its significance after it is completed. The writer, unsatisfied, looks forward (since the text doesn't seem to yet "exist" as long as it is still incomplete) or backward (since "as soon as a book" *is* finished the writer feels "behind with the current job"). But he never, in this scheme, has a fully aligned relationship with the textual present.[10]

In *Homage to Catalonia*, describing Spain, Orwell writes: "As a general rule things happen too late, but just occasionally—just so that you shan't even be able to depend on their happening late—they happen too early" (13). "Too early" or "too late": this is the same predicament that Orwell, twelve years later, in the 1949 notebook, places at the core of his own experience as a writer. These are also the kinds of projection and retrospect suggested in the 1946 "Why I Write": on the one hand, the still-unfulfilled anticipation of an adequate writing ("I know with clarity what kind of book I *want* to write") and on the other hand, writing that, as soon as it is crystallized ("by the time you have perfected any style"), is immediately "outgrown," becoming a "failure," which prompts the writer to continue the "effort" or "struggle" of writing in another text.

Orwell's comment about being "early" or "late" in *Homage to Catalonia* sheds light on his civil war memoir as a whole, and I will return to it later in this book. Right now I'm using it to emphasize how an external situation, addressed by Orwell's writing, mirrors a condition that inheres within the act of writing itself. This bleed is significant. *Homage to Catalonia* will extend this jarring combination of being "too early" and "too late" both in terms of the discourse and the story. In one anecdote, Orwell dramatically incorporates the same double bind into a very specific problem faced by the Republican militias:

> Bombs were served out, three to a man. The Spanish Government had at last succeeded in producing a decent bomb. It was on the principle of a Mills bomb, but with two pins instead of one. After you had pulled the pins out there was an interval of seven seconds before the bomb exploded. Its chief disadvantage was that one pin was very stiff and the

other very loose, so that you had the choice of leaving both pins in place and being unable to pull the stiff one out in a moment of emergency, or pulling out the stiff one beforehand and being in a constant stew lest the thing should explode in your pocket. (*Homage to Catalonia* 86)

Here, at work within the world of the story (*not* in the writing itself), is a bomb that can fail in one of two ways. A soldier who "leav[es] both pins in place" might be unable to set the weapon off at all—or might set it off long after he needs to. But by taking the safety pin out in advance ("pulling out the stiff one beforehand"), he risks an explosion that goes off prematurely, "in [his] pocket," harming himself rather than the more distant enemy. The image offers a disturbingly precise reiteration of the way that something that tends to occur too late can also—"just so that you shan't even be able to depend on [it] happening late"—occur too early.

This external predicament—with its "seven second" interval and its risk of violent explosion—dramatizes the same temporal misalignment that Orwell's notebook entry attributes to his own experience in writing.[11] The parallel is a striking one. Writing, on the one hand, seeks to engage these processes, structures, and experiences in the actual world; on the other hand, writing needs to account for its *own* pervasive, disorienting rhythms and tempos. (Again, writing finds itself in a double bind, either unformulated and only reaching *toward* a sufficient construction or no sooner finished than potentially ossified.) This temporal misalignment ("too early"/"too late") connects to another distinct, if related, tension in the 1949 notebook entry—its uncanny combination of gradualness and suddenness. On the one hand, when the writer is at work, the incomplete writing "always goes slower" than anticipated. On the other hand, "as soon as" something is completed (no matter how gradual or painstaking the construction), it immediately fades from view. (That same sense of over-alacrity is implicit in the description from "Why I Write": "by the time you have perfected any style of writing [i.e., at that very instant], you have always outgrown it.") Again, this is not the first time that Orwell alights upon such a combination. As with that conjunction of "early" and "late," we can find a pointed externalization of these two compositional tempos (and thus of something that seems to proceed, strangely, at once too quickly and too slowly) in another notable, even paradigmatic, scene. I'm thinking of the eponymous description in "Shooting an Elephant" (written in 1936, thirteen years before the notebook entry):

> When I pulled the trigger I did not hear the bang or feel the kick—one never does when a shot goes home—but I heard the devilish roar of glee that went up from the crowd. In that instant, in too short a time, one would have thought, even for the bullet to get there, a mysterious, terrible changed had come over the elephant. He neither stirred nor fell, but every line of his body had altered. He looked suddenly stricken, shrunken, immensely old, as though the frightful impact of the bullet had paralysed him without knocking him down. At last, after what seemed a long time—it might have been five seconds, I dare say—he sagged flabbily to his knees. His mouth slobbered. An enormous senility seemed to have settled upon him. One could have imagined him thousands of years old. I fired again into the same spot. At the second shot he did not collapse but climbed with desperate slowness to his feet and stood weakly upright, with legs sagging and head drooping. I fired a third time. That was the shot that did for him. You could see the agony of it jolt his whole body and knock the last remnant of strength from his legs. But in falling he seemed for a moment to rise, for as his hind legs collapsed beneath him he seemed to tower upwards like a huge rock toppling, his trunk reaching skyward like a tree. (10.505)

The description (among other things) threads together the fast and the slow, offering an unsettling convergence of immediacy and gradualness. The elephant is "suddenly stricken" but also looks "immensely old." Even as the passage intertwines these two tempos, it edges each of them toward a boundary or extreme. In that "instant" the bullet doesn't just move very quickly, in contrast to the elephant, but with a speed that exceeds the capacities of the observer ("in too short a time, one would have thought, even for the bullet to get there"). Likewise, the "five seconds" that mark the elephant's slow response do not adequately convey the protracted sense of time as this delay is experienced. On the contrary, the elephant seems to have aged "a thousand years." The bullets can "jolt" the elephant's entire body but also make him move with "desperate slowness." The event passes in an instant and also seems to go on forever. And once more, this condition, attached to the depicted event that writing attempts to grasp, also resides at the troubled heart of writing itself. In short, at the core of the plain style there is an uneasy, jagged tempo. The formulation of a topic, idea, or argument in writing is shadowed by these dynamics of early, late, quick, and slow. Timing is difficult. We "struggle" to formulate an idea—until it *is* sufficiently formulated, of course, it remains incomplete; but once it *has* been formulated, it can quickly become inert.

"Parabola"

My goal in the previous section was to foreground certain events that are both represented within and reiterated by Orwell's writing. Tempos that Orwell finds "in the world" are echoed—and anticipated—by the tempos of writing itself. This blend is particularly important *because* of Orwell's commitment to a transparently plain style, attached, as I've been arguing, to an explicit and engaged political position. As my introduction proceeds, I want to connect this active sense of writing—of its medium specificity, we might say—to Orwell's manifest politics. I want to point now to an odd image that Orwell uses to describe writing. In two different passages from his work, Orwell presents a structurally similar frame for writing as a moving trajectory. First, in the 1940 essay "Charles Dickens," Orwell comments:

> What people always demand of a popular novelist is that he shall write the same book over and over again, forgetting that a man who would write the same book twice could not even write it once. Any writer who is not utterly lifeless moves upon a kind of parabola, and the downward curve is implied in the upward one. (*Inside the Whale and Other Essays* 80)

Six years later, one of his "As I Please" columns (the writing sequence at the structural center of my reading of Orwell) echoes and amplifies this idea:

> A novelist does not, any more than a boxer or a ballet dancer, last for ever. He has an initial impulse which is good for three or four books, perhaps even for a dozen, but which must exhaust itself sooner or later. Obviously one cannot lay down any rigid rule, but in many cases the

creative impulse seems to last for about 15 years: in a prose writer these 15 years would probably be between the ages of 30 and 45, or thereabouts. . . . Many writers, perhaps most, ought simply to stop writing when they reach middle age. Unfortunately our society will not let them stop. Most of them know no other way of earning a living, and writing, with all that goes with it—quarrels, rivalries, flattery, the sense of being a semi-public figure—is habit-forming. In a reasonable world a writer who had said his say would simply take up some other profession. In a competitive society he feels, just as a politician does, that retirement is death. ("As I Please" 64, 18.511)

When Orwell pens this passage in "As I Please," he is 43 years old. And, of course, his own incessant production ("no pauses in the process") begins—unusually—in his late twenties, after the long interregnum in Burma. The fifteen-year framework Orwell constructs thus has a pointedly self-critical dimension, as though, by this reflection on writing, in general, he were provoking a specific end to his own. The unnerving coincidence of Orwell's *particular* writing history with these harsh parameters contrasts with the casual tone of the comment: "one cannot lay down any rigid rule," "seems to last," "would probably be," "or thereabouts." On the one hand, the thought is lightly given and almost disavowed; on the other hand, Orwell seems stuck in the general framework he puts forward, like an insect caught on flypaper.

This strange rhetorical combination is typical of Orwell's writing. Two dissonant styles of thought—one exacting and compact, one familiar and diffuse—are intertwined. Such tension has particular salience here, however, as this unstable tonal meld also informs the more fundamental claims about writing that both of these parabolic images provoke. I want to foreground this image of the "parabola" as an important metaphor in Orwell's writing, and more specifically as a privileged figure for writing itself. In this way, we can cast it alongside Orwell's most famous description of prose, as "window pane." The two images of writing—as a static, unmoving pane of glass and as a restless, perpetually moving arc—are quite distinct. Both have a key place in Orwell's poetics, I would argue, and above all we can gain traction on his writing—and politics—by holding them in mind together.

We can begin by noting an uncertainty about where this motion that Orwell associates with writing resides or finishes. The passage from "As I

Please" configures such incessant movement on a biographical level, in the development of the author him- or herself. Like the boxer or the ballet dancer, the writer performs a discrete activity, but slowly the "creative impulse" that drives this activity attenuates or alters. The writer ages, and this inexorable aging process then bears on the writing: a writer, always growing older, needs to calibrate the way that he is changing with the activity he aims to perform. Already, though, such calibration suggests a complicated procedure that would flow into more intrinsic textual processes: the writer would need to keep one eye on the internal dynamics of the text—here equivalent to the boxing match or the performed dance itself—and one eye on his own unstable self. He would need to coordinate the demanding, yet highly constrained, movements of the performance with the gradual but inexorable "movement," through time, that constitutes his own aging. These are two quite different kinds of movement and the challenge of writing (or boxing, or dancing) would lie in their uneasy, imperfect reconciliation: as though a writer had to aim at quickly shifting targets from a slowly accelerating train.

This more interior dimension of writing is also suggested in the description of the parabola in "Charles Dickens." Most immediately, it is the author, again, who should move along a trajectory, developing and changing from book to book. None of these books, positioned within this mutable arc of the writer's development, should too closely resemble the others. But, as Orwell emphasizes, each *individual* book would also be "lifeless" if it were the kind of book that could be easily or mechanically reproduced. "[A] man who would write the same book twice could not even write it once." It is as though any repetitive impulse of the writer, from book to book, would take hold within each individual text, just as the movement that is the mark of a successful writer is not only traceable through the unfolding arc of his or her career but also drives each individual work: "the downward curve," Orwell thus notes parenthetically, "is implied in the upward." The full sweep of the parabola is discernible at each instant of its curve.

This emphasis on the doubleness of the curve (where the downward arc is "implied in" the upward, and vice versa) resonates with another aspect of that key scene in "Shooting an Elephant":

But in falling he seemed for a moment to rise, for as his hind legs collapsed beneath him he seemed to tower upward like a rock toppling, his trunk reaching skyward like a tree.

Here, too, the "falling" and "rise" of the wounded elephant—what would form the bend of the parabola in Orwell's later passage—are rendered simultaneously. This image of something that seems to rise even as it falls thus recurs in Orwell's work, first at the core of a crucial physical description and then as a figure for writing itself. In order to engage the poetics of Orwell's writing-practice, we need to hold on to the fundamental strangeness of this simultaneity, not rushing to abstract this configuration of an object that moves up ("reaching skyward") and down (with "legs collaps[ing] beneath") at the same time.

In its insistence on such simultaneity, the image of parabola hinges on a disorienting physical inversion that is in striking contrast to the transparency of the "window pane." (In a similar manner, as we've already seen, the description of the elephant conjoins the quick and the slow—"too short a time" and "what seemed a long time," "five seconds" and "a thousand years," etc.) Insofar as the curving parabola, or the double-motion of the wounded elephant, conflates such disparate movements—combining "up" with "down," and "ris[ing]" with "falling"—these images unfold in distinct tension with the oriented, coordinated logic of the plain style. Throughout this book I will draw on similar reversals that Orwell's prose adduces—moments that insist on tangling up elemental pairs of descriptors. "Quick" and "slow"; "up" and "down"; "near" and "far"; "early" and "late"; "inside" and "outside"; "empty" and "full"; and "back" and "front": as we will see, each of these obviously simple and "plain" oppositions, at different points in Orwell's work, is at once foregrounded and subjected to emphatic destabilization. (The simplicity of these terms is as important as the tension that Orwell elicits from them.)[12] And the accumulation of these moments—which will emerge inductively, in the course of my argument—is striking, since it suggests a quite disoriented, almost hallucinogenic, condition at the heart of the plain style.

Such reversals are not only a topical focus of Orwell's writing but, again, inhere within the dynamics of writing itself. (This is a basic but crucial point—and a key goal for me has been to begin this book about Orwell's writing by trying to distill his own reflective sense of writing as such.) Let me return, now, to the unsettling perspective on writing offered by these two—once more, rhetorically casual—comments in "Charles Dickens" and "As I Please." When Orwell figures the plain style in terms of a "window pane," he is emphasizing writing's desire to hold still, to freeze itself in a clear, discrete conceptual or ideational position. The writing would have a maximal correspondence with the substance it tries to express. The comments in "Charles Dickens" and "As I Please" point, instead, to a restless, agitated quality in writing, a sense of incessant, even compulsive, movement. If writing would be "lifeless" without this movement (as the passage in "Charles Dickens" suggests), such propulsion is also intertwined *with* aging (as the passage in "As I Please" suggests) and, implicitly, death. Such restlessness is both necessary to and at odds with writing's core desires—parabolic motion functions at once as the quickening pulse of writing and as a looming, exterior disruption. Motion enlivens and threatens writing. Orwell's competing images—writing as (frozen) "window pane" or (restless) "parabola"—establish a rich opposition between these two kinds of desire, as though writing, in its essential nature, strives to be both still and moving.

This opposition opens out onto large aesthetic and philosophical vistas. In any topically or conceptually oriented text, the sheer activity of the writing—the technical process of composition, the restless praxis of the writing itself—cannot be fully assimilated into the expressed idea. In this model, writing can never take its conceptual elaborations at face value; it can't "freeze" itself, as an expressed thought, in a sustained or integral way. Writing generates ideas, and its topical dimension is indeed crucial for Orwell. Writing can and should be "about" something, as the opening pages of *Down and Out* insist that the text is "about" poverty (9), but it can never rest in these terms, transmuting itself into pure ideation. Writing's inability to "catch up" with itself in this way, or to fully contain and account for its *own* elaboration, informs Orwell's image of parabolic movement. Writing propels itself, in this argument, because at any moment there is an unassimilated outside to the expressed thought: namely, the mode and fact of the expression itself. And as writing tries doggedly to "grasp" this outside, it can only generate further instances of it, like a swimmer trying to get ahead of the moving water pressure that her own strokes create. (Again, the plain style would not just be at odds with this process but could in fact function to intensify it.)

For Orwell, then, the desire for an author to "write the same book over and over again" connects to a pervasive, seductive tendency within writing. There is always a potential tension between the "interior" of writing—the thought, or ideational substance, that is at once advanced, sheltered, and communicated by the text—and the "exterior" of this expressed thought—an excess that inheres, most fundamentally, in the material nature of writing, its propulsive surface. And the serious problem posed by repetition, from one text to another, also pertains to dynamics within any single work. Just as the writer might lapse into such repetition ("writ[ing] the same book twice"), so any text can prompt a repetition or echoing of itself—insofar as it offers a stable, seemingly self-sufficient articulation of thought, detached securely from the movement of the writing—the sheer fact of the discourse—itself.

Orwell is wary about losing sight of these dynamic undercurrents of writing, and becoming transfixed on its static, ideational content. Over and again in his work, Orwell presents the lure of a phrase, image, thought, or idea that "extends" in this way. Here are three examples from his essay "How the Poor Die" (which describes the patients—and victims—of a public hospital in Paris), *The Road to Wigan Pier*, and "Revenge Is Sour" (a discussion of postwar Europe):

> One day his wife and daughter came to visit him. At sight of them the old man's bloated face lit up with a smile of surprising sweetness, and as his daughter, a pretty girl of about twenty, approached the bed I saw that his hand was slowly working its way from under the bedclothes. I seemed to see in advance the gesture that was coming—the girl kneeling beside the bed, the old man's hand laid on her head in his dying blessing. But no, he merely handed her the bedbottle, which she promptly took from him and emptied into the receptacle. ("How the Poor Die" 18.462)

> I have never travelled much more than a mile to the coal face; but often it is three miles, in which case I and most people other than coal-miners would never get there at all. This is the kind of point that one is always liable to miss. When you think of a coal-mine you think of depth, heat, darkness, blackened figures hacking at walls of coal; you don't think, necessarily, of those miles of creeping to and fro. (*The Road to Wigan Pier* 29)

> So the Nazi torturer of one's imagination, the monstrous figure against whom one had struggled for so many years, dwindled to this pitiful wretch, whose obvious need was not for punishment, but for some kind of psychological treatment. . . . Who would not have jumped for joy,

in 1940, at the thought of seeing S.S. officers kicked and humiliated? But when the thing becomes possible, it is merely pathetic and disgusting. It is said that when Mussolini's corpse was exhibited in public, an old woman drew a revolver and fired five shots into it, exclaiming, "Those are for my five sons!" It is the kind of story that the newspapers make up, but it might be true. I wonder how much satisfaction she got out of those five shots, which, doubtless, she had dreamed years earlier of firing. The condition of her being able to get near enough to Mussolini to shoot at him was that he should be a corpse. ("Revenge Is Sour" 17.362)

The crucial terms here for my argument are "to see in advance," to "think of," "imagination," "the thought of," and "dreamed years earlier of." These processes of thinking, imagining, and anticipating are, for Orwell, closely related to his core sense of writing's power and limitations and, finally, to its propulsive force. Writing expresses but also, and by its very nature, resists and exceeds consummated thought. In each of these cases, a conceptual impulse extends itself too effortlessly, or imperiously, and Orwell's texts develop various ways of putting pressure on this extension. The first example might be the simplest one, as the narrator's sentimental expectation is rebuffed by the actual, physical decrepitude of the elderly patient. But the empirical rejoinder that Orwell inscribes into this scene models an unstable process that his writing more insistently returns to (on the level of both story and discourse, substance and form). The tendency to "see in advance" speaks to central, and varied, concerns in Orwell's prose: how, once we arrive at a concept, it is perilously easy to stay with it; the dangers and resilience of overly stabilized definitions and categories; how we want to linger with what is familiar (or already-known); and more strictly psychological registers of these same dynamics. A set of distinct but overlapping processes—ideology, the ease of abstraction, the sway of convention, categorization, the shelter of familiarity, egotism—are at play in Orwell's writing, and they intersect around the basic process of thinking, the perils of thought (always in line with its galvanizing, seductive force). The predicament encapsulated in the last sentence of the excerpt from "Revenge Is Sour" thus has a broader resonance in Orwell's work.[13] "The condition of her being able to get near enough to Mussolini to shoot at him was that he should be a corpse." This strange "condition"—in which an object either eludes the individual's subjective

grasp (not "near enough") or seems to be fundamentally altered by proximity to it—is an essential one in Orwell's writing. In the most basic terms,
the thought that can seize an object in the world always risks—by the potentially static transformation of world *into* thought—losing the object as it
grabs hold of it. Thought can endlessly cover the world in its very capacities
and ambitions to uncover it: there are always points we are "liable to miss,"
not just through *lack* of thought (the things "you don't think of") but through
the animating force of thought itself (the things "you think of"). The paradigmatic double bind in "Revenge Is Sour" thus also echoes the unnerving
compositional quandary that I've already discussed. Like the work of the
writer, revenge can arise "too early," as a state of unfulfilled anticipation
("[w]ho would not have jumped for joy, in 1940, at the thought of seeing S.S.
officers kicked and humiliated?"), or be achieved "too late" ("[t]he condition
of her being able to get near enough to Mussolini to shoot at him was that he
should be a corpse").

Orwell's comment about the things we are "always liable to miss" will be
a crux for my reading of *The Road to Wigan Pier* in Chapter 2. And this tension—between what is unseen because unthought and what is (more
strangely) unseen because *thought*—is a hinge of this book's argument as a
whole. In fact, forms of absence, neglect, occlusion, and deprivation—and
the attendant paradoxes of such states—emerge at crucial points in each
chapter of this book. Orwell's focus on what we are "liable to miss" (in that
combination of thinking *and* not thinking) in *Wigan Pier* is thus echoed, as
we'll see, by his attention to "something missing" in *Down and Out,* to a
"bare" space in "A Hanging," to a "hole" in *Inside the Whale,* and to a per
son who "vanish[es]" in a key section of "As I Please." The pattern is striking. Against that plentitude we would associate with the plain style, this
book reveals a strange blankness, or emptiness, at the deliberate heart of
Orwell's work.[14]

Prolificacy

When we think about it, the plain style and prolificacy, of Orwell's kind, do
not go hand-in-hand. Such endless writing, almost on its face, erodes the
directness and topical stability of the plain style. After all, the plain style
seeks to cut short, to be efficient, to curtail linguistic mediation. Orwell's

prolific output—marked not merely by quantity but by that dynamic movement across genres—works in the opposite direction. Throughout this book I will seek to demonstrate that Orwell's image of writing as a window pane is persistently complicated (but *not* simply negated) by his own formal restlessness—or, more profoundly, by a formal drive that is a crucial element of all his work.

Orwell doesn't only write incessantly after 1930, he often reflects—in writing—on the incessant amount that he writes. The terms of this are ambivalent. Orwell seems both proud of and mortified by the quantity of material he produces. He valorizes the productivity of journalistic engagement but also frequently longs for silence, breaks, or intervals that would allow hesitation. And he understands his own furious efforts as both too much *and* too little, so that he will criticize his work in terms of over- and under-production. We've already seen an example of this in the passage in "Why I Write," when Orwell emphasizes, somewhat surprisingly, that he has "not written a novel for seven years." Shame or pride? Conversely, Peter Davison's *Collected Works* features one volume aptly titled "Smothered Under Journalism," a phrase taken from a 1946 letter Orwell writes to Dorothy Plowman: "I am anxious to get out of London for my own sake as well, because I am constantly smothered under journalism—at present I am doing 4 articles every week—and I want to write another book which is impossible unless I can get 6 months quiet" (18.115). The parenthetical elaboration—"at present I am doing 4 articles every week"—can't help but register some satisfaction in this prodigious output, straining against the compulsion, or "smother[ing]," it is meant to invoke. These tallies occur frequently in Orwell's work. One idiosyncratic but significant example of this, in *The Road to Wigan Pier*, vividly suggests the dueling impulses—both fantasy and nightmare—that can thread through such a materialized sense of writing. It is in Chapter 3, when Orwell is trying to gain conceptual traction for understanding the huge quantity of raw material that coal-miners extract:

Meanwhile, how much coal is the average miner producing?
The tonnage of coal raised yearly per person employed in mining rises steadily though rather slowly. In 1914 every mine-worker produced, on an average, 253 tons of coal; in 1934 he produced 280 tons.

> This of course is an average figure for mine-workers of all kinds; those
> actually working at the coal face extract an enormously greater
> amount—in many cases, probably, well over a thousand tons each. But
> taking 280 tons as a representative figure, it is worth noticing what a
> vast achievement this is. One gets the best idea of it by comparing
> a miner's lifework with somebody else's. If I live to be sixty I shall prob-
> ably have produced thirty novels, or enough to fill two medium-sized
> library shelves. In the same period the average miner produces 8,400
> tons of coal; enough coal to pave Trafalgar Square nearly two feet deep
> or to supply seven large families with fuel for over a hundred years. (43)

This projected inventory of his literary output obviously diminishes or
devalues Orwell's writing, both by the explicit results of the comparison
(how much less material a writer "makes" than a miner) and, more fundamentally, in the disquieting, even morbid, reduction of this material to the
physical space that it will occupy. But the same image also registers an out-
size ambition *within* its ostensibly diminutive results, as Orwell, from the
throes of a writerly identity still actively in formation (signaled everywhere
in the energetic text of *Wigan Pier*), reaches toward the future-perfect retrospect of a now-consummated authorial career. This ambition is further visible in the sheer magnitude of output ("thirty novels") that Orwell imagines
he will have written. In one sense, of course, Orwell presents this projected
authorial output as much too small. But the amount also seems, *Alice-in-
Wonderland*-like, conspicuously large. The energy of the passage thrives on
this core instability. (Thus, the gratuitous, strangely neutral detail: two
"medium-sized" shelves!)

This same ambivalence (about both under- *and* over-production) is at play
in a pair of letters that Orwell writes to Geoffrey Gorer on either side of the
composition of his 1940 *Inside the Whale*, Orwell's first volume of essays
(and another key "writing event" in my account of Orwell's work). After the
publication, Orwell writes:

> But I am trying very hard to join a Govt training centre & learn machine
> draughtsmanship, partly because I want a job, partly because I think it
> would interest me & as I fancy we are all going to be conscripted in one
> form or another within about a year I'd rather do something more or

less skilled. . . . I dare say we *could* get by if I stuck simply to writing, but at present I am very anxious to slow off & not hurry on with my next book, as I have now published 8 in 8 years which is too much. You didn't I suppose see my last *(Inside the Whale)* which came out a few weeks back. There is one essay in it that might interest you, on Boys' weekly papers, as it rather overlaps with your own researches. . . . There is an essay on Dickens that might interest you too. I find this kind of semi-sociological literary criticism very interesting & I'd like to do a lot of other writers, but unfortunately there's no money in it. All Gollancz would give me in advance on the book was £20! With novels it's easier to be sure of a sale, but I've now got an idea for a really big novel, I mean big in bulk, & I want to lie fallow before doing it. (12.137)

Before this letter, Orwell had already called the forthcoming book to Gorer's attention:

I began on another book, then I'm sorry to say my father died. . . . Then I got going on the book again & then the war threw me out of my stride, so in the end a very short book that was meant to take 4 months took me 6 or 7. It ought to come out in March & I think parts of it might interest you. . . . I want to lay off writing for a bit, I feel I have written myself out & ought to lie fallow. I am sort of incubating an enormous novel . . . only I don't want to begin it before I'm all set. It is frightfully bad for one, this feeling of the publisher's winged chariot hurrying near all the time. (12.6–7)

These two passages give a number of different, even conflicting, reasons for not writing. Some of these are in the realm of necessity, problems that encroach on and are clearly cast against the activity of writing: whether external disruption (the death of a parent), financial constraint (although, as Orwell points out, "we *could* get by if I stuck simply to writing"), or civic obligation (the impending draft). Others, on the contrary, suggest that an intrinsic dynamic of writing itself prompts Orwell to want to "[lie] fallow," "[lay] off writing for a bit," and "not begin before [he's] all set." Similarly, Orwell's quantification ("8 in 8 years is too much") echoes the mixed pride and embarrassment that we've seen in the passage from *The Road to Wigan Pier* ("thirty novels") and the letter to Dorothy Plowman ("4 articles every week"). More strikingly, we can trace a similar tension in Orwell's "anxious" desire to "slow off & not hurry," with its troubling suggestion that Orwell only experiences, or can describe, his desire to slow down through a quickening, or "anxious[ness]," directly counterpoised to it. (Even Orwell's ampersand seems to fuel the acceleration that he means to resist, as does the double negative.) Once again, around the scene of composition, Orwell intertwines the quick and the slow.[15]

Network

In adducing that parabolic image in Orwell, I juxtaposed three examples of how Orwell stigmatizes conceptual over-extension with the two descriptions, from "Charles Dickens" and "As I Please," of a restless movement within writing. This configuration of writing as a parabola also connects to Orwell's comments in "Why I Write," on the impossibility of remaining within any "perfected" style and on the way in which "every book" is a "failure." (Both of these comments occur just before Orwell's iconic description of "good prose" as "like a window pane.") This reading of Orwell's sense of writing's mobility, then, has itself moved through six different texts— "How the Poor Die," "Revenge Is Sour," "Why I Write," *The Road to Wigan Pier*, "Charles Dickens," and "As I Please"—all written between 1937 and 1946, and each of which is experimental in its own right. *None* of these six pieces, in fact, has an entirely stable relationship to a determinate genre. And none of them line up with each other, in their combination of urgency, speculation, concision, familiarity, anecdote, analysis, and self-reflection. These are all contingent and dramatic *acts* of writing, in my argument.

Versions of such movement are almost inevitable when reading Orwell. This book's focus will come to rest on only several texts of Orwell's: "A Hanging" (1931), *The Road to Wigan Pier* (1937), and *Inside the Whale and Other Essays* (1940) in Part One, and, most extensively, "As I Please" (1943–1947) in Part Two. But my discussion of these individual texts depends on the larger network of Orwell's textual production. In each case, I focus on how a particular text is caught within this field of writing, activating the formal tensions that I'm trying to give an overview of here. ("As I Please," which certainly has never been discussed so extensively before, is the crucial microcosm for this perspective on Orwell's writing: if all of his writing forms a politically productive field of texts, interconnected and overlapping, "As I Please," uniquely, stages this overflow within itself.) I see these four texts as particularly salient models of this poetic system, and, above all, of Orwell's effort to account for, and dramatize, the double nature of writing, as both ideational and material, referential and formally bounded.

My discussion of *Inside the Whale* (1940) thus focuses on how this single work is, in fact, a collection of three distinct texts, without a clear or settled relationship to one another. (Along with the eponymous "Inside the Whale," the book contains the extended study "Charles Dickens"—which we have already now encountered—and "Boys' Weeklies," a quite different kind of text in many ways.) It is the first time Orwell links discrete essays together into something larger. We've seen how Orwell's work, as it moves, restlessly, from "one book or even article" to "the next one," persistently juxtaposes texts of different kind, size, genre. The juxtapositions are as significant as (if perhaps more elusive than) the writing itself. *Inside the Whale* stages this friction *within* its own formal boundaries: the essay collection (emerging against, and in relation to, Orwell's other work) is only built out of three discrepant—and thus jostling—texts. In its tripartite structure, *Inside the Whale* frames, and thus, paradoxically, internalizes, the external friction that generates writing's parabolic force. In this way, a confusion of inside and outside—a confusion at the thematic center of the title essay's influential polemic about 1930s writing—also takes place on a formal level.

This play between writing's "inside" and "outside" (and between parts and wholes) is also formally evident in "As I Please," Orwell's weekly column for the Socialist newspaper *Tribune*. Orwell writes eighty of these columns between 1943 and 1947, and they are the central focus of Part Two. Indeed, Chapters 4 through 6 constitute one single case study, a close and extended reading of this writing project. (It is a corpus of writing that has often been cited, and admired, by Orwell scholars but never before taken as a major site of analysis.) How do we hold these eighty texts in mind? The weekly columns, already presenting the reader with an imposingly heterogeneous textual network, are almost uniformly (but not *quite* uniformly) divided into further subsections. As much as any writing by Orwell, "As I Please" thus makes such formal segmentation—and indeed dispersion—a transparent principle of composition. My deliberately extended reading of these short columns takes this phenomenon of dispersion as its (ironic) starting point. I begin to construct an overarching interpretation of the columns out of the fundamental (which is to say: structural) way that they work to exceed and resist coherent comprehension. When these transient, interlinked columns are placed at the center of Orwell's writing, they crystalize the active, formally restless conception of writing that runs through the range of his work.

Before considering "As I Please," however, this book pays most focused attention to *The Road to Wigan Pier* (1937), Orwell's daring account of the condition of employed and unemployed miners in northern England. It is this text that first makes the question of formal movement a *necessary* one within Orwell's work. Several years before his comment about the risks of "writing the same book over and over again," Orwell composes a book that refuses to be the same "even . . . once," instead splitting into two parts. As any reader of *Wigan Pier* will remember, the formal structure of this text is intimately intertwined with its political and ideological force. Politics almost, but *not quite* completely, motivates the stark division between Part One and Part Two. The undeniable residue of form—conspicuous, disruptive, and inassimilable—is the animating center of my reading. The two parts of *Wigan Pier* accord, as well, with the implications that I'm suggesting inhere within the parabolic image: roughly speaking, Part One is "window pane" prose, firmly grounded in its urgent topical orientation, while Part Two spins back to consider the writing of Part One, and the ideological orientation of the writer himself. Both formally—simply as an addition, a distraction, and a displacement away from the coal mines of *Wigan Pier*—and thematically, in its introspective and self-critical concerns, Part Two insists on a disruptive excess within writing, and, more specifically, within the topical representations that drive the beginning of the book.

"About"

To identify Orwell's writing as a privileged site of intentionality is not merely to note the obvious topicality of so much of his work. On the second page (though not the first!) of *Down and Out in Paris and London*, Orwell states "poverty is what I am writing about," establishing a topical explicitness evident in all of his major texts. *The Road to Wigan Pier* is "about" coal miners in northern England, *Homage to Catalonia* certainly about the Spanish Civil War, and the fictional codes of *Animal Farm* and *1984* fall short if the reader cannot understand the real events they are "about." (This is to take five indisputably major texts, the "kernels" of Orwell's propulsive writing practice.) My other epigraphs at the start of this introduction show two examples of Orwell pulling out this same preposition and resting attention upon it.[16] The sheer emphasis on such a quiet, colloquial term—now turned into an uncertain critical *category*—is telling. These passages suggest, once more, Orwell's interest in holding the reader's attention on the topical orientation of writing rather than merely on the topic itself. In the latter case, writing has a political intention. In the former, writing also is (oddly) "about" intentionality, "about" about-ness. It doesn't merely seek to transmit this intention but to dramatize it.

Throughout the 1940s, Orwell writes a series of essays that circle insistently around what we could call the "politics and literature question." The *circling* is important, as Orwell approaches the same set of problems in any number of his texts. For example, "Writers and Leviathan," "Politics vs. Literature: An Examination of *Gulliver's Travels*," and "The Prevention of Literature" all grapple, from the titles on, with the relationship between writing, art, and propaganda. These titles resonate, as well, with "The Frontiers of Art and Propaganda" and "Politics and the English Language." We could add numerous other texts. (On a different register: the 2008 collection of Orwell's critical essays is titled *All Art Is Propaganda*, while Davison's Volume 13 of the Complete Works is titled *All Propaganda is Lies*. Both phrases, of course, are culled from Orwell's work.[17])

I'm interested in Orwell's repeated movement toward this topic, in his work's (frequently) staged ambition to broach the relationship between "writing"—or "literature," "language," "art"—and politics. What can we make of the incessant returns to this question—apart from the content of the arguments that these different texts advance? There are a host of potential implications to such insistence. For instance, we could consider this a mark of pleasure on Orwell's part—a root inclination toward reopening the question, a pleasure *in* "writing" about "writing and politics." Alternatively, we could read this gravitation in terms of political obligation and compulsion, or perhaps in terms of cultural and professional identity—as though Orwell fulfills a generic or audience expectation by taking up this problem across so many different texts. However we would distribute the proportion of such motives—pleasure, political responsibility, authorial identity, compulsion, etc.—each works to make this series of texts stand out as a sequence of actions. Is it a meaningful or galvanizing sequence of actions for the reader? In asking this question, we can note another implication of Orwell's continual return to the interface of literature and politics. To the degree that this *is* a galvanizing action, the reader also accepts that it is a somewhat difficult one, as though part of Orwell's accomplishment rests in that mere reawakening of—rather than in the formulation of final answers for—the "literature and politics" question. The question is not self-evident. It might fade from view if it is not energetically reformulated, this sequence of essays suggests.

I'm highlighting this simple and obvious feature of Orwell's political writing—its incessant returns to that threshold between "literature" and "politics"—as an example of the second-order meaning that can attach to his work, not merely as idea but as action. It is often the case that engaged writers worry this line between literature and politics, as one might worry a thread. One key point of reference here would be Adorno's figure of "constellative" writing, and it is no coincidence that, as several Orwell critics have noted, early Lukács and Adorno offer a major theoretical articulation of the essay as a twentieth-century genre that resonates productively with Orwell's politically engaged writing.[18] The "constellation" suggests a nonlinear, noninstrumental form of argument, in which the conceptual substance of an idea cannot be dissociated from its dynamic elaboration. Similarly, this figure of constellation suggests a continual process of overflowing: one text leads into, or only completes itself in, another; no text stands out as fully self-sufficient, and thus no text can establish a stable or sealed identity between its form and its content. Each piece of writing is also an action, and this action, while of course *connected* to the ideational and topical ambit of the text, cannot be perfectly aligned with it. There is always a residual perspective, a position from which the text is written: the point of view of the writer, the fact and presence of language itself, the boundaries of genre. The two-part structure of *The Road to Wigan Pier* is (only) the most dramatic, and structurally evident, example of this emphasis in Orwell.

Yet Orwell's work, of course, is starkly different from Adorno's in its commitment to the plain style. Orwell's directness and simplicity would seem to work against this sense of constellative fragility and, more generally, against the displacement intrinsic to *any* second-order meaning. And in one important sense, my argument means to resist such second-order meaning as well—insofar as we take such displaced channels of meaning as a necessary rebuke to the intentional political purpose of Orwell's writing. Orwell's commitment to the plain style runs hand-in-hand with such political purpose. But we need to see Orwell's gravitation toward second-order meaning as *also* political. A materialist sense in Orwell's writing splits, continually, between a commitment to the plain style (which would bring the ideational substance of prose as close as possible to material reality) and an engagement with the materiality of language or writing itself (which would breach this ideational directness). Orwell aspires toward the plain style and cultivates its complications; he resists *and* gravitates toward second-order meaning. And both tendencies, I want to argue, are born out of the same democratic-socialist political orientation. Politics comes first—motivating both impulses in Orwell's work—so that we can take at face value the aspiration, as he says, "to make political writing into an art." In the following sections, I want to suggest how this split can itself be conceived on political—rather than ontological, linguistic, or aesthetic—grounds.

"Programme"

John Rodden's prolific work on Orwell in the past two decades would be one of the major exceptions to my claims about the ill fit between post-1980s literary theory and this engaged writer. Beginning with *The Politics of Literary Reputation,* Rodden has produced a canny sequence of criticism that never reads Orwell directly but rather reads him through the (varied, passionate, opinionated, compulsive) ways he has been read. Reviewing this work, Anna Vaninskaya suggests that a major strand of recent Orwell criticism is "more concerned with Orwell's reputation and relevance today than with his *oeuvre* as such" (597); and, indeed, that "[r]eception may well prove to be the native language of Orwell studies" (616), which seems "headed inexorably in th[is] direction" (615).[19] The reception theory (necessarily) refuses to take a specific ideological position or to identify a stable political center of the work itself. It moves easily between the ostensible political surface and other dimensions or levels of the text and thus can highlight rhetorical strategies and tensions on their own terms, without rooting them in a fixed ideological framework. There's no question that Orwell, at the core of his writerly enterprise, mobilizes different political registers. And Rodden's work has become a deserved cornerstone of Orwell scholarship. But this critical perspective also has marked limits. First, most obviously, it tends to diminish the concrete political force of the work. In such a reading, Orwell's adroit political rhetoric comes to transcend politics: Orwell's texts elicit and nurture (varied) ideological investments but in this varied effect necessarily lack any ideological definition. Second, and equally ironically, such attention to plurality can itself become a stable, even rigid, framework for understanding Orwell's work. Rather than conflating Orwell with one fixed ideology—and thus effacing his contradictions and tensions in the process—this view risks reducing Orwell to the (consistent) way that he triggers or accommodates inconsistent responses.[20]

The line of criticism that elevates Orwell as a uniquely composite political writer can easily neglect the generative instability of such compositeness. In a recent example of this, Geoffrey Wheatcroft writes:

> His politics were likewise sui generis. Although he called himself a democratic socialist, and served with a revolutionary-Marxist militia in Spain, he was in many ways an emotional and cultural conservative. The least doctrinaire of political writers, he had the gift of being able to transmute the Tory virtues of skepticism and pragmatism into a distinctive kind of radicalism. (27)

This description of Orwell as "in many ways . . . conservative," risks confusing two distinct political categories. Orwell's work might seek to disrupt entrenched lines of political opposition, in order to appeal to conservatives, but it doesn't concede policy grounds to the right. The policies that Orwell advocates are relatively explicit and consistent—while questions of tactics, political culture, and aesthetic processes of representation are all subjected, in Orwell's writing, to destabilization. Thus while Orwell participates in sustained ideological struggle on the left, he always understands this struggle as emanating out of—and never displacing him from—a democratic socialist political ground. His writing signals this distinction in a number of ways, and we have to actively disregard such signaling to construe the political project differently.

More specifically, Orwell's skepticism about different manifestations of political struggle (even when elaborated in his most heavy-handed, least convincing manner) doesn't vitiate a core set of socioeconomic principles that he adheres to. The aims of Orwell's political desire are relatively stable: it is only the means that are energetically questioned and destabilized, opening up lines of affiliation with what Wheatcroft calls conservative culture (or even emotion) and sites of conflict with different factions of the left. This affiliation doesn't soften the opposition to conservative policy, and to its positions on major economic and social questions such as education, taxes, social welfare, workers' rights, the power of economic elites, etc.But what remains, finally, if we refer to an "emotional or cultural conservatism" detached completely from such substantive or partisan grounds?

One of Orwell's most emphatic and programmatic statements about socialist policy, conversely, is easy to identify, since he calls attention to the passage, from *The Lion and the Unicorn,* in these terms:

> What is wanted is a simple, concrete programme of action, which can be given all possible publicity, and round which public opinion can group itself. I suggest that the following six-point programme is the kind of thing we need. The first three points deal with England's internal policy, the other three with the Empire and the world:

> 1. Nationalization of land, mines, railways, banks and major industries.
> 2. Limitation of incomes, on such a scale that the highest tax-free income in Britain does not exceed the lowest by more than ten to one.
> 3. Reform of the educational system along democratic lines.
> 4. Immediate Dominion status for India, with power to secede when the war is over.
> 5. Formation of an Imperial General Council, in which the coloured peoples are to be represented.
> 6. Declaration of formal alliance with China, Abyssinia and all other victims of the Fascist powers.

> The general tendency of this programme is unmistakable. It aims quite frankly at turning this war into a revolutionary war and England into

a Socialist democracy. I have deliberately included in it nothing that the simplest person could not understand and see the reason for. (12.422)

This comment forms an interesting crux in Orwell's work, as a consciously explicit, delimited catalogue of the policies that would underlie "Socialist democracy"—the political orientation animating (as he will claim in "Why I Write") "every line . . . I have written since 1936." [21] "Every line," perhaps; yet Orwell never repeats this kind of list: we'd be hard pressed to find a formal equivalent to this passage in all his work.[22] But he also doesn't modify or disavow these positions. To claim Orwell for even a "transmuted" version of "conservative" or "Tory" politics—when such a politics would, by definition, directly oppose these stated goals—subjects him to potential distortion.[23]

This list—in its emphatic specificity—thus sits uneasily with responses to Orwell's writing, which would emphasize the fluctuating, amorphous valences of his politics (or a resistance to politics *tout court*). It also weakens the case of critics who rebuke Orwell for a vague, indefinite socialism hinging on imprecise, abstract qualities such as "decency."[24] This list in "The Lion and the Unicorn," and most particularly the proposal to limit the gap in incomes to a "ten to one" ratio, functions quite differently. Any vagueness does not inhere in the policy proposal itself but rather in the necessary distance between this specific proposal and its potential enactment. There is a gulf, in other words, between the tangibility that Orwell lends to this set of policy prescriptions (a tangibility set off by the numbered list) and the diffuse, transformative ramifications that would flow from such a set of proposals, if they were to be realized. The ten-to-one ratio is thus, in one sense, conspicuously specific, but any reader in 1941 (or today) also would be forced to understand this specificity as merely provisional—something that only takes form, counterfactually, against the entrenched inequalities of a present-day world. Orwell invokes this sense of indefiniteness explicitly, a little further in the essay: "It is of course quite hopeless to expect the present government to pledge itself to any policy that implies turning this war into a revolutionary war. . . . Before such measures as limitation of incomes *become even thinkable,* there will have to be a complete shift of power away from the old ruling class" (17.426, emphasis added).[25]

This intrinsic provisionality might help cast light on the enigma of this passage within Orwell's work. Why would Orwell be impelled to foreground such a direct and explicit description in "The Lion and the Unicorn"—emphasized through its block presentation—and never formulate a similar account? Certainly this singularity speaks to Orwell's overarching aversion to repetition, particularly in relation to political writing.[26] While such repetition can characterize thinking or culture more broadly, the political implications of repetition also connect, more specifically, to Orwell's engagement with the dynamics of writing that I've been tracing. Why is repetition so pernicious? For Orwell, a text that repeats something already articulated by the writer is also potentially unaware of itself as an action. Such writing can settle too complacently into a position that has already been filled (by the previous writing)—and thus, more consequentially, risk not seeing itself as in a position at all (or seeing itself, in the terms I've been trying to establish, as all "thought" and no "form"). Repetition, in this sense, is one manifestation of writing's recurrent potential to forget its own (formally grounded) unfolding. Thus we might say, for example, that a repetitive conversationalist—someone who retells the same anecdotes—is a poor interlocutor not merely from bad memory (an internal process) but because he overlooks his *position* in relation to the weary listener who has already heard these stories. But this kind of faux pas is only the narrowest sense of such a "position"; Orwell's consciousness about this extends further, to the vexed nature of writing. Writing persistently can lead the reader into viewing it as both more *and* less of an action than is warranted. On the one hand, the projection inevitable in writing (and, particularly, politically engaged writing) can prompt us to confuse the act of representation with the represented world itself, or to confuse subjective agency with the objective sociopolitical realm. In this trajectory, we are caught up in and come to overemphasize the text's action potential. On the other hand, and following the course of this *same* trajectory: we can forget, or *under*-emphasize, the text's actual material basis, its compositional elaboration, or its position within a larger cultural and symbolic field. Orwell's commitment to form—and to writing as an ongoing "effort" or "struggle" at transparency—is grounded in his attentiveness to this problem of elaboration.

In my view, the political significance and force of "The Lion and the Unicorn," as a text within the highly variegated field of Orwell's writing, depends largely on the ballast of this numbered list (a ballast that is reiterated, in miniature, by the one particularly concrete detail *within* the catalogue).[27] The list thus functions not merely as a candid statement of Orwell's political orientation in 1941 but also as a dramatization of such candor. This dramatic quality is a key to Orwell's political transvaluation of the plain style, helping to recast such style as a site of aspiration rather than merely a controlling ideological position. The reader ironically senses an *achieved* (and thus fragile) directness—bound up with this egalitarian, "ten to one" impulse—that is forged through the dynamic working of the text. Such dynamic movement is explicitly signaled in this passage by Orwell's framing of the numbered catalogue. He wants this program to be "simple" and "concrete," for its tendency to be "unmistakeable," and he has "deliberately included in it nothing that the simplest person could not understand." This is not just direct prose but a deliberate and reflective *modeling* of directness (and, in this particular way, less direct than it might appear). Likewise, Orwell concludes the frame by commenting, "In the form which I have put it, it could be printed on the front page of the *Daily Mirror*. But for the purposes of this book a certain amount of amplification is needed" (422). Crucially, by the logic of Orwell's comment, the "amplifi[ed]" discussion that immediately follows at once elaborates the list (giving more of the details and consequences of each proposal) *and* negates it (by moving beyond the "simple" and "concrete" tone that is crystallized at this moment in the essay). Despite its proclaimed simplicity, then, this list is far from simple or transparently self-evident. On the contrary, the simplicity here, I've been arguing, is largely a matter of form. And it is a crucial mark of Orwell's formal restlessness that this list should present such a dramatic instance of writing, under the banner of an egalitarian impulse, that would—briefly but consequentially—coincide with itself: "simple," "concrete."

This discussion of the list in "The Lion and the Unicorn" could extend to the text as a whole, as one of numerous Orwell texts with an unstable generic identity. "The Lion and the Unicorn" isn't quite *like* anything else in Orwell's oeuvre (or outside it). As with many of Orwell's most important works, "The Lion and the Unicorn" presents a strange meld of novelty and familiarity. Its colloquial, informal tone easily works to elide just how strange the text is, generically speaking. (Once we pull back a little, it is harder to discount the text's formal originality—and even its quite experimental nature. But these qualities are elusive, delivering what Wordsworth calls "a gentle shock of mild surprise" rather than the more stable, conspicuous surprise of modernist form.) If Orwell doesn't repeat the numbered list lodged within "The Lion and the Unicorn," he doesn't repeat this *larger* mode of writing either.[28]

This introduction has considered how the plain style is intertwined, in Orwell, with the (unfulfilled) aspiration to express and define his politics. The "six-point programme" in "The Lion and the Unicorn" offers further intensification of this general process—first, as the list stands out, within Orwell's work, unrepeated; second, as the impulse *to* define is strong enough to generate this discrete formal device (the six-point list); and, third, as Orwell explicitly acknowledges, even while unfolding this concrete description, that the policies he advocates—because of the power of the ruling class—are still not "even thinkable."

"Political Position" (1)

This reading of Orwell insists that his ambiguities and intricacies (of which there is no shortage) can result from an embrace, rather than an eschewal, of action. His writing unfolds at the seam of an ideological crisis—the crisis of left-wing agency—precisely because it is so committed, in both obvious and subtle ways, to action. Before closing this introduction, I want to offer one further example of this more fixed, direct dimension of Orwell's prose. I'm thinking of two moments in Orwell's writing where he invokes the particular "political position" that he occupies:

> Men can only be happy when they do not assume that the object of life is happiness. . . . There is a well-marked hedonistic strain in his writings, and his failure to find a political position after breaking with Stalinism is a result of this. ("Arthur Koestler" 16.399)

> In this preface they will most likely expect me to say something of how *Animal Farm* originated but first I would like to say something about myself and the experiences by which I arrived at my political position. ("Preface to the Ukrainian Edition of *Animal Farm*" 19.86)

These two passages interest me because of the overlapping term "political position"—what Orwell claims that Koestler "fail[s] to find" and what Orwell himself must attain in order to write *Animal Farm*. Both of these passages emphasize the writer's active, and thus contingent, relationship to politics. In the Ukrainian preface, Orwell describes himself as "pro-Socialist" (87), as part of the "western Socialist movement" (87), and as a writer seeking a "revival of the Socialist movement" (88). Likewise, he casts himself, and his writing project, against the Soviet Union because it does *not* resemble "anything that one can truly call Socialism" (88) but has, instead, "contributed so much to the corruption of the original idea of Socialism" (88). Similarly, in "Arthur Koestler," Orwell associates Koestler's "failure to find a political position after breaking with Stalinism" (399) very precisely with his abandonment of Socialism (and not merely with an abandonment of politics more generally).[29] In both cases, then, the nature of Orwell's political position (now intimately connected to writing itself) is explicitly linked to socialism.

The two passages have an interest beyond serving as additional demonstrations of Orwell's socialist politics. On the one hand, the passage from "Arthur Koestler" details how easy it is to *abandon* socialism—or to abandon the "position" that Orwell himself occupies. On the other hand, the passage from the Ukrainian preface elevates this socialist perspective as the privileged source of writing. This priority of politics is striking because it is so explicit: quite simply, a set of extra-textual political commitments need to be "arrived at" before this literary work can "originat[e]." The political position is here a grounding source, or a cause, of writing. But in the same phrase— as the reader might have already noticed—Orwell also makes this textual cause (i.e., the cause of the text, of *Animal Farm*) an effect. *Animal Farm* might originate in, and thus rest upon, Orwell's "political position," but this politics rests upon an earlier sequence of Orwell's "experiences." This is the double catch hidden within Orwell's ostensibly plainspoken comment. Having read the sentence, we might reorganize these three phenomena into a coherent sequence: writing (*Animal Farm*); and before this, politics (Orwell's socialist views); and before *this*, experience (the chain of experiences the preface then goes on to summarize). But Orwell's work, I'd suggest, doesn't accommodate such a linear procedure. On the contrary, what is striking about this passage is the disorientation of the double catch, the feeling of a cause transmuting into an effect (and vice versa). In this light, the sentence works to give and take simultaneously. It gives us the strong idea of Orwell's "political position," resting behind the writing he wants to introduce, but, in the same breath, makes this position contingent upon a distended sequence of experiences.

I hope it is clear that, in my reading, such a double catch doesn't undermine the integrity or significance of "political position," as category, but, on the contrary, is part of Orwell's effort to define and engage this category as more than merely ideational. A further reading of Orwell's preface quickly brings out more disruptions of cause and effect. Most evidently, the privileged "experiences" that Orwell then goes on to recount are linked to his own earlier writing, further complicating any temporal priority of experience over writing. Here are some excerpts:

> I was born in India in 1903. . . . Shortly after I left school (I wasn't quite twenty years old then) I went to Burma and joined the Indian Imperial Police. . . . I stayed five years in the service. It did not suit me and made me hate imperialism. . . . (19.86)

> In 1928–9 I lived in Paris and wrote short stories and novels that nobody would print (I have since destroyed them all). In the following years I lived mostly from hand to mouth, and went hungry on several occasions. It was only from 1934 onwards that I was able to live on what I earned from my writing. In the meantime I sometimes lived for months on end amongst the poor and half-criminal elements who inhabit the worst parts of the poorer quarters, or take to the streets, begging and stealing. At that time I associated with them through lack of money, but later their way of life interested me very much for its own sake. (19.86–87)

> I spent many months (more systematically this time) studying the conditions of the miners in the north of England. Up to 1930 I did not on the whole look upon myself as a Socialist. . . . I became pro-Socialist more out of disgust with the way the poorer section of the industrial workers were oppressed and neglected than out of any theoretical admiration for a planned society. (19.87)

> In 1936 I got married. In almost the same week the civil war broke out in Spain. . . . Through a series of accidents I joined not the International Brigades like the majority of foreigners, but the POUM militia. . . . (19.87)

There is much packed in here. When Orwell writes, "[i]n the meantime I sometimes lived for months on end amongst the poor and half-criminal elements," the knowledgeable reader must immediately associate this statement with both the topic *and* the text, or composition, of *Down and Out in Paris and London*. And when he writes, "I spent many months (more systematically this time) studying the conditions of the miners in the north of England," we as easily put this in relation to *The Road to Wigan Pier*.[30] In this way, the "experiences" that precede Orwell's writing of *Animal Farm*—or, more precisely, precede the "political position" that precedes and motivates *Animal Farm*—turn out themselves to be largely constituted as writing. (This recursion to writing is important because of the weight that this comment puts on experience as the grounds *for* political belief, which is in turn depicted as the grounds for writing. Writing is at the end of a causal chain but also embedded within this chain.) As so often in Orwell, experience and reflection are thus intricately coiled around one another—just as the political stance that drives *Animal Farm* is poised between being cause and effect, and thus between its interior, ideational force and its exteriority. Having a political position is tricky—and not just in terms of distilling the values that orient it.

So far I've emphasized three things in the Ukrainian preface: that Orwell associates his "political position," explicitly, with Socialism; that he gestures toward the priority of politics over text; and that he complicates this sense of priority, insisting on his position as both a cause (of writing) *and* an effect (of experience). As in my earlier reading of other Orwell passages—the "six-point programme" and the comment about "every line of serious work"—I want to consider how these complications distill rather than merely dilute the emphatic avowal of political commitment here. Orwell understands this gesture of avowal, in other words, *as* a gesture, or an action—one with reverberating and thus incomplete significance. To stake out any political position has meaning that extends beyond the ideological substance of the position. (Why? Because the action of "staking out" the position is itself a process that intersects with this ideological substance.)

Rather than either debunking or taking Orwell's declaration for granted (in its very explicitness), or pausing only to fill out the exact ideological contours of the position that Orwell avows, we might focus on the term itself as a textual crux. What does Orwell mean, then, by "political position"? We can only, by definition, have *a* (i.e., one) "political position"—it is constituted as the intentional totality of our politics. There is little relation between taking a particular stance on a discrete political question and this more overarching sense of "position." On the contrary, the political position for Orwell is a terminus, a resting point that knits together all of one's political beliefs and affiliations—all such stances—into a coherent and sufficient unity. Orwell understands democratic socialism in this way. If such coherent totality is illusory, then so is the very term "position"; this is the first key point I want to stress. But, just as necessarily, our "political position" is formed in relation to other inassimilable positions at work in the political world. A political position is by definition contested. Structurally, it can only emerge, *despite* its projected coherence, in opposition to, and thus alongside of, these countervailing positions. This lends the term a specifically active sense: the political position is cast in conflicted relation with other positions in the world. It also, conversely, lends the term a pessimistic sense: to culti-vate a political position—unlike a set of political values *tout court*—is to confront its relative inefficacy. Any "position" that was *fully* efficacious—agreed to, actualized, or victorious—would, in this efficacy, cease to be a position at all. This is the second key point. If a "political position" is less than total, it ceases to be a position. If it is fully realized, it ceases to be a position. Both of these limiting pressures are crucial to Orwell's sense of socialist politics. Here, in this combined condition, politics is under a form of maximal stress—but not negated or disconfirmed. If we understand the "political position" in this way—as at once (willfully) coherent and self-disrupting—we can see how the term resonates with Orwell's particular commitments and intricacies as a writer. Orwell's writing hinges on the uncanny combination of immediacy and mediation, urgency and delay, reflection and immersion. These tensions are also, I want to argue, imma-nent to Orwell's engagement with this political category of "position." The political position, like that "parabolic" sense of writing that I have been focusing on, is fundamentally divided. By its very nature it is not secure, autonomous, or self-sufficient, but neither, in the face of this contingency, can we understand it as ultimately fragmented by the pressures of the external. (Once again, a "political position," as Orwell understands it, *neces-sarily* posits itself as a unified position: "socialism" is always in the singular.)

"Political Position" (2)

Orwell's preface to *Animal Farm* suggests the aesthetic importance of having a "political position" (in that assertion of the radical priority of politics over text). The argument with Koestler emphasizes the difficulty of maintaining one. Orwell's 1944 essay focuses on a literary-political ally, and for this reason the critique of Koestler takes on greater significance. One way into this significance is by the recurrence of this term across this text and the Ukrainian preface. In fact, "Arthur Koestler" touches on many other pieces by Orwell, exceeding its ostensible, generic limitations as a critical review. It is a text imbricated into his prolific, propulsive writing practice. This excess of the text—as an urgent, and thus generically open-ended exercise in writing—is quickly registered *within* the text, in Orwell's initial discussion of "political writing, or pamphleteering" as a mode that transcends or transgresses genre. Orwell situates Koestler's writing within this more general framework, as part of a "special class of literature" defined, ironically, by the way that it breaks across the typical classifications we would apply to literature:

> I mean by this the special class of literature that has arisen out of the European political struggle since the rise of Fascism. Under this heading novels, autobiographies, books of "reportage," sociological treatises and plain pamphlets can all be lumped together, all of them having a common origin and to a great extent the same emotional atmosphere. (16.392)

It is hard to ignore the self-reflective implications of this expansive comment, since the formal categories that Orwell invokes and confounds here relate so clearly to, even as they don't coincide exactly with, his own cross-generic writing. This echoing effect is important. Orwell's discussion of Koestler's writing is also an act of writing—with its own ambitious, uncertain generic status—even as Orwell's exploration of Koestler's (ultimately failed) political position is also part of his ongoing articulation of an active political stance. These two qualities run together, as the formal instability of Orwell's critical review is amplified because he is taking strong issue with a political position that largely overlaps his own. It is the extent of Orwell's proximity to Koestler that lends the polemical critique of Koestler more significance and urgency. And the heightened stakes of the text—emerging out of this unstable combination of political proximity and distance—help to motivate, in turn, its generic volatility, as a piece of writing, like so much of Orwell's work, that breaks out of its delimited place as criticism or essay.

Here is another intertextual shard that emerges out of the Koestler essay: if Orwell claims, as we have seen, that "every book is failure" in "Why I Write" (just before making the case for "good prose . . . like a window pane"), in "Arthur Koestler," he writes: "All revolutions are failures, but they are not all the same failure" (400). Juxtaposing these two shorthand comments, we confront an odd equivalency between all writing (or at least all "book[s]") and all revolutions. This found equivalency obviously intensifies a sense of Orwell's pessimism, by inscribing failure across these two different registers—except for its implicit suggestion that revolution and writing are one and the same (and that Orwell, someone undoubtedly committed *to* writing, is also, through a kind of transitive logic, committed to revolution, or to revolutionary desire).

This combination of pessimism and hopefulness is important, and indeed touches on the way that intertextuality itself functions in Orwell's writing (including this very doubling of "failure" between "Arthur Koestler" and "Why I Write"). As we've seen, Orwell's prolific, generically restless network of writing dramatizes a vivid, unstable interplay between process and meaning, form and idea, what a text *is* and what it is "about." In this interplay, hope and pessimism are built into the basic formal procedure of Orwell's work. (To put this another way: The plain style always expresses the *hope* that an idea will come across directly, fully actualized in one particular, specific event of writing. But Orwell's prodigious, formally shifting work sweeps up all such actualized moments into a much larger, and thus less finalized, textual field.) This is particularly pertinent to the Arthur Koestler essay, because of its ambivalent position toward its subject. Koestler is both the focus of Orwell's polemical disagreement and a figure of proximity and political affiliation. Despite their proximity, Orwell criticizes Koestler's inability to find (against his own ambition to "arrive" at) a "political position" (i.e., socialism). But Koestler's inability strikes close to home. And, indeed, to have a political position for Orwell isn't only to be committed but, precisely, to be at risk—to be vulnerable to abandoning it.

Orwell's great innovation is this active, exposed sense of holding a political position, not as merely an ideational process but as a dynamic, experiential one, almost like a form of intimacy in which attachment is paradoxically connected to fragility, commitment to volatility.[31]

This vulnerability has, as I've been arguing, a specific cause as well: political inefficacy. This point cannot be stressed enough. While Orwell's stance toward "political position" has a restlessly inward dimension (hence the strong current of autobiography throughout his writing), it is not quietist. On the contrary, Orwell considers "political position" only in an active sense. As he says, for example, in "Arthur Koestler": "actions have consequences, irrespective of their motives" (398). (Once again, this is specifically in relation to socialism; Orwell is here arguing against what he takes as Koestler's overly psychological diagnosis of left-wing commitment.) Politics will be experienced inwardly, but it is premised categorically on action. And the activist's relationship to writing begins out of urgency and impatience. As Orwell writes in 1937: "It is not possible for any thinking person to live in such a society as our own without wanting to change it." (11.168). This comment, from "Why I Join the I.L.P.," links thought and desire (i.e., "thinking," and "wanting"). To reflect at all, in a political sense, is to be cast into a desiring role. This desire for change, though natural and even equivalent to thought as such, cannot easily satisfy itself. "For perhaps ten years past," Orwell immediately continues in the 1937 piece, "I have had some grasp of the real nature of Capitalist society" (11.168). The long period of time that Orwell gestures at here doesn't only mark the extended, and thus more realized, nature of his opposition to capitalism but *also* the extended, and thus more unsatisfied, nature of his desire. This unsatisfied political desire—now stretched eight years further, into 1946—is a key to the Koestler essay as well. "The Russian Revolution, the central event in Koestler's life, started out with high hopes. We forget these things now, but a quarter of a century ago it was confidently expected that the Russian Revolution would lead to Utopia. Obviously this has not happened" (400).[32] The "failure" of the Russian Revolution, in Orwell's perspective, is implicated in the more wideranging failure of political desire to realize itself.

Orwell is witheringly critical about the potential of thought (born from the desire for political change) to transcend or internally resolve this failure. Desire gives wing to thought, but while every "thinking person" desires change, thought is always at risk of over-substantializing itself, mistaking its own unfolding for the object it conceives of, and not simply substituting ideals for reality but short-circuiting the protracted temporality in which political action takes place.[33] "There is one way of avoiding thoughts," Orwell begins a 1937 critique of Ortega y Gasset's reactionary essays on Spain, "and that is to think too deeply" (11.104). We could take this as an easy paradox, a rhetorical sleight of hand, a logical non sequitur, or an instance of Orwell's reflexive anti-intellectualism.[34] I take it instead as a meaningful idea, an idea about thinking itself. Orwell wants to emplace a principle of self-disruption into the core activity of thought. The Ortega review is titled "The Lure of Profundity," and it is this "lure"—generated by the momentum and seductive texture *of* thought—that Orwell means to stigmatize. (In this essay, significantly, Orwell aligns such momentum with Ortega's insistent evasions of "the central trouble in Spain . . . the frightful contrast of wealth and poverty" [105].)

We've already seen a few examples of how the process of thinking arises, and is foregrounded, in Orwell's work. Thought is necessary to *and* continually imperiled by writing: this doubled sense is a key to Orwell's work. The contrast between the "thinking person," in "Why I Join the I.L.P.," and "*avoiding* thought" by "think[ing] too deeply," in "The Lure of Profundity," echoes Orwell's emphasis in *The Road to Wigan Pier* on the (deceptively apparent) things that "you think of"—and thus the things you "miss," or "don't think of"—when "you think of a coal-mine." The quiet term "to think," as I'll have more chances to demonstrate in the course of this book, rests near the center of Orwell's writing, and also near the center of his conception *of* writing. "Thought" works its way into several titles—"Some Thoughts on the Common Toad," "Second Thoughts on James Burnham"—and the chief impulse of these phrases, which is to divide the focus *between* process and object, means and end, is reiterated in other titles as well: "Reflections on Gandhi," "Notes on Nationalism," "Looking Back on the Spanish War." In fact, the double gesture of these five titles is a good example of the way that Orwell both employs and disrupts the plain style. These titles certainly hold out the ideal of an *unambiguous* focus or topic of inquiry: quite simply "James Burnham," "Gandhi," "nationalism," "the Spanish [Civil] War," or "the common toad." At the same time, as we can see most easily, perhaps, in that last example ("Some Thoughts on the Common Toad"), each of these topics is partially displaced in the title. The foregrounded "thoughts" float free of their object, slightly unmoored, comical and extravagant. This whimsical, understated dissonance carries over to less sanguine pieces, like "Notes on Nationalism," where the provisional nature of Orwell's thinking is a crucial part of what is thought. In each case—whether by "thought," "reflection," "notes," or "looking back"—these titles, despite their explicitness, are fundamentally divided: half view, half window; half topic, half process.

In this section, I want to connect such incompleteness of thought back to the political context of action, urgency, and (relative) inefficacy that I've been highlighting. A sense of inefficacy rests at the heart of Orwell's commitment to what he identifies as a specifically *democratic* socialism. Most simply, we can understand this residual inefficacy as part of Orwell's resistance to any complacent form of ideological projection. Such projection always risks eliding the difficulty and unpredictability of democratically-grounded political actualization. Orwell's writing carries this tension into the core of thought itself. As we've seen, the thought that can inadvertently unthink itself (in "The Lure of Profundity"), by too confidently extending, is not easily dissociable from a thinking that is intrinsic to political desire (in "Why I Join the I.L.P.") "[T]o make life livable is a much bigger problem than it recently seemed," Orwell writes in "Arthur Koestler" (399). As the larger context makes clear, this "problem" has grown bigger, in Orwell's view, not merely because social conditions have worsened but because *the modality of change* is more imperiled and less teleologically secure:

Recently he described himself as a "short-term pessimist." Every kind of horror is blowing up over the horizon, but somehow it will all come right in the end. This outlook is probably gaining ground among thinking people: it results from the very great difficulty, once one has abandoned orthodox religious belief, of accepting life on earth as inherently miserable, and on the other hand from the realisation that to make life livable is a much bigger problem than it recently seemed. Since about 1930 the world has given no reason for optimism whatever. Nothing is in sight except a welter of lies, hatred, cruelty and ignorance, and beyond our present troubles loom vaster ones which are only now entering into the European consciousness. It is quite possible that man's major problems will *never* be solved. But it is also unthinkable! Who is there who dares to look at the world of today and say to himself, "It will always be like this: even in a million years it cannot get appreciably better?" So you get the quasi-mystical belief that for the present there is no remedy, all political action is useless, but that somehow, somewhere in space and time, human life will cease to be the miserable brutish thing it now is. (16.399)

"Since about 1930," Orwell writes. In the Ukrainian preface, we've seen, he suggests this same date as the origin of his own socialist position. ("Up to 1930 I did not on the whole look upon myself as a Socialist" [19.87].) Here, on the contrary, 1930 marks the decline of the Russian Revolution as a source of "hope," or as an event that could work to realize such urgent political desire. It is telling that Orwell, across these two pieces, would conflate his own *origin* as a Socialist with the same year that the failure of the Russian Revolution transforms the nature of political hope. This failure is not the death-knell of democratic-socialist aspiration but, oddly, its source.

Immediately after his comment on how "a quarter of a century ago it was confidently expected that the Russian Revolution would lead to Utopia. Obviously this has not happened," Orwell continues: "Koestler is too acute not to see this, and too sensitive not to remember the original objective" (400). The combination is striking. "[A]cute[ness]" is a mark of recognizing current realities; "sensitiv[ity]" the capacity not just to "remember" but to remember an "original objective"—or, in other words, to feel and to sustain a desire. Koestler can hold onto such a desire—unlike the culture at large, which "forget[s] these things now"—and in this capacity intensifies the "acute[ness]" of his recognition. Again, what's crucial here is that maximal pressure. For Orwell, socialist desire (also known simply as "thought") pro-duces above all urgency and impatience—such urgency, indeed, is the reason why Orwell, Koestler, or "any thinking person," enters into the sphere of politics, or aspires to inhabit an effective "political position."

What would be an example of socialist thinking that gives up on this kind of pressure (and, thus, even in its very thoughtfulness, curtails its own con-ceptual potential—or, put differently, fails to recognize the urgency of its own desire)? About six months before the Koestler essay, Orwell writes a brief, unpublished piece that is worth considering in this context: a review of

Harold Laski's *Faith, Reason and Civilisation*. (The review was solicited by the *Manchester Evening News* and then rejected, Orwell suggested to Dwight Macdonald, for its "anti-Stalinist implications" [16.298].) Laski comes up in the conclusion of "Arthur Koestler" as well, directly after the description of Koestler's unusual capacity to be both "acute" and "sensitive." Orwell continues, now returning to the opening premise of the essay:

> Koestler is too acute not to see this, and too sensitive not to remember the original objective. Moreover, from his European angle he can see such things as purges and mass deportations for what they are: he is not, like Shaw or Laski, looking at them through the wrong end of the telescope. (400)

In this image of the "wrong end of the telescope," we might note, once more, that an instrument of observation and a process of distortion are intertwined rather than simply opposed. Orwell repeats this metaphor in several other texts—yet another competing optical image to the clarity of the window pane.[35] (Orwell is interested here in optical distortion but also inversion. Turning around the telescope makes the viewer cognizant of *two* registers of distortion: the strangely distanced figures, suddenly recessed and contracted by the reversed telescope, also bring out the *commensurate* magnification that occurs when the telescope is the right way round.) Orwell's unpublished review takes Laski to task for using "'the Russian idea' and 'Socialism' interchangeably." It is thus another example of Orwell's investment in differentiating "Socialism" from—rather than collapsing it with—"the Russian idea."[36] And in his conclusion, Orwell makes explicit that Laski's conflation of these terms is rooted in the impatience that necessarily accompanies socialist desire (and that is shared by Orwell and Koestler both):

> And certainly the dilemma is a painful one. To work all your life for Socialism, to see at last a state definitely describable as Socialist arise and triumphantly hold its own amid a hostile world, and then to have to admit that it too has its failings—that needs courage. But we expect courage of Professor Laski, and he would write a better book if he would occasionally take the risk of giving ammunition to the reactionaries. (16.123)

We can see the key relation to the Koestler essay. Orwell once more doesn't want to insist merely that social problems have gotten worse but also that the modality of change, in the wake of revolutionary failure, is more precarious. "[T]o make life livable is a much bigger problem than it recently seemed." What is "painful" to Laski is equally intolerable to Koestler (and Orwell). Koestler's pessimism is produced by his unhappy position between "acute [ness]" of recognition and "sensitiv[ity]" of memory—and thus desire. Lasky's less anguished intellectual perspective, in Orwell's view, comes at the cost of softening this tension. "[I]nstead of warning his readers against [the despotism of the USSR], Professor Laski has chosen to assume that it does not exist" (123). Orwell's image of this in his Laski review suggests that thought is almost a kind of lubricant:

> At that time [with Laski's previous book] there were unmistakeable signs of uneasiness in Professor Laski's mind. There were even passages in his book which called up irresistibly the picture of a child swallowing castor oil. Now, however, Professor Laski has found out the right method of dealing with castor oil. Squirt a little lemon and brandy on top of it, hold your nose, shut your eyes, gulp the stuff down, follow it up immediately with a lump of chocolate, and really the experience becomes almost bearable.
>
> What is this castor oil with which Professor Laski used once to have difficulties? It is the authoritarian element in Russian Socialism: more broadly, it is the extreme danger of using dictatorship as a road to democracy. (16.122)

Again, the new ease that Orwell sees in Laski, I'm arguing, is the comfort or "lure" of thought itself. (And once more, this "lure"—of thought happily extending itself—is linked to a political aspiration that jumps too quickly toward an image of its fulfillment.) Laski's neglect of despotism in the USSR isn't the result of not wanting to think but, on the contrary, of *wanting* to think. (The "lemon," brandy," and "chocolate" here would be Laski's sheer intellectual expansiveness.) As Orwell points out, the book hinges on an extended analogy between the USSR and the early Christian church; what Orwell calls "a false analogy as it happens, but evidently a *comforting* one for the time being" (122, emphasis added). Orwell doesn't accept the substance of the analogy but also distrusts this "comforting" procedure of analogization, or "interchangeab[ility]." His own brief review thus centers on first identifying and then putting internal pressure on Laski's device (that palliative, by way of analogy, that would make Stalinism "almost bearable"):

> Look a little more closely at this analogy, and you can see that it is false in every particular. To begin with, Christian doctrine was formed at a time when the Church had no power. The early Christians were a hunted sect, largely consisting of slaves: the Russian government rules over a sixth of the earth. Secondly, in spite of heresies and controversies, Christian doctrine was relatively stable. Communist doctrine changes so often and so drastically that to continue believing in it is almost incompatible with mental integrity. Professor Laski ignores both of these differences. (16.123)

Each of the two "differences" that Orwell identifies, embedded within the analogy, are major concerns for his writing in this period. Furthermore, each touches on the fact of difference as such. As we will see, Orwell returns frequently to the formal sway of the status quo—the tendency of thinking to conform to, or valorize, what is already powerful or given. His insistence on distinguishing between the ideological formation that was "hunted" and the one that "rules" is thus an (egalitarian) rebuke to Laski's comfortable method of analogization. It inscribes a stark social difference, the difference between power and powerlessness, at the seam of the revolutionary parallelism. Orwell is also fascinated and frustrated by the "instability" of Stalinist doctrine.[37] Such instability depends, again, on the denial of differences, on ignoring sudden lurches and reversals in a government's policy in order to maintain a consistent ideological identity.

The critique of Laski thus briskly ties together "comfort," thinking, analogy, and the effacement of difference. On the other hand, Koestler's "short-term pessimism," in Orwell's view, gives up on thought too easily. In an important line, Orwell writes, *contra* Koestler: "[t]o take a rational decision one must have a picture of the future"(16.399). Projection here is connected to, rather than being placed in opposition with, reason or the "rational." But if a "picture of the future," in this way, underlies political thought, there is a perennial risk of collapsing this picture into any image of the present. Such a collapse (of the present into the future, and thus of political desire into actualization) marks the very effacement of democracy from within socialism. Democratic thought, by contrast, is *uncomfortable* thought, always aware of its inability to project itself smoothly into the future. Such discomfort must be nurtured, and is only intensified by the urgency intrinsic to socialist critique and aspiration. The picture of the future—enabling a "rational political decision"—is not a comfort to thought but a lash, to an already exacerbated, unsatisfied desire. The "picture," though necessary, can't be disentangled *from* the future; its future tense is never forgotten. "Every book is a failure."

Conclusion

In this introduction I've tried to foreground an internal tension, and drama, within Orwell's writing practice: between writing as (consummated) idea and as (propulsive) form. In many ways, of course, this is a constitutive division of writing: no writing can be entirely *un*realized as thought, or else it would become indistinguishable from merely graphic marks, and yet no writing can resolve itself as entirely equivalent to the thought it works to express.[38] Orwell's work, I want to suggest, develops this tension in singular and significant ways. Above all, his politically grounded investment *in* the plain style, in the ideal of writing that would be "like a window pane," works at many crucial points to intensify and amplify this tension. Form is so interesting in Orwell because Orwell—unlike many writers who intermix fiction and non-fiction, or who move restlessly between different genres—is also so resistant *to* form. And, likewise, the ironic mediation that often emerges from this formal drive takes on particular coloration in Orwell because of an ideological commitment that is quite starkly opposed—indeed mounts a kind of implacable (but never fully effectual) resistance—to it.

The criticism in this book is thus tension driven. But I also want to argue that Orwell's writing catches this tension, knitting it back into an intentional political poetics. Intention survives: transformed, more intricate, more circuitous, perhaps more canny, but not shattered or effaced. This book's governing hypothesis is thus threefold. First, Orwell is committed to (what he understands as) a discrete, coherent set of political values ("democratic Socialism"). Second, in writing—even in turning *to* writing, with his penname—he develops a theory of composition that is, despite what we might assume from the famous window pane comment, radically skeptical of any final, stable, or permanent expression of political belief. Third, this skepticism is not a negation, or even a dilution, of his democratic-socialist commitments—even as it obviously makes the expression of these commitments more intricate and complicated—but a manifestation of them.

At the center of this threefold process is a pervasive, stubborn skepticism about what we might call consummated expression. This skepticism manifests itself in many ways within Orwell's writing and writerly choices, from the seemingly casual statement that we've looked at—"every book is a failure"—in "Why I Write," to the conspicuous division of *Wigan Pier,* to the fundamentally negative perspectives of *Animal Farm* and *1984* (when viewed as part of a socialist corpus). In the previous sections I've tried to illustrate the formal—rather than merely ideological, or emotional and psychological—grounds of this skepticism: a perspective on form that, for example, drives Orwell's image of writing as a parabolic arc. In the chapters that follow, I will look at specific ways that Orwell holds the reader at the cusp of this kind of resolution. A series of formal questions anchor these readings: Orwell's initial engagement with (and radicalization of) the plain style in "A Hanging"; the conspicuous division of *Wigan Pier* into two linked but clashing parts; a similar, if more muted, tension between parts in Orwell's first essay collection, *Inside the Whale;* and, most pointedly, the constraints of weekly column writing that produce the imposingly heterogeneous sequence of "As I Please."

What underlies Orwell's resistance to such consummated expression, to writing that takes itself as adequate, finished, or perfected? There are a number of answers to this question, but we can schematize them in terms of two distinct problems, each grounded in his larger political perspective. I'll call these mimetic and sociological, respectively. (I've already sketched this division in my discussion of how writing, from Orwell's perspective, can simultaneously appear as "more" of an action *and* "less" of an action than it is.) First, there is a referential or representational concern. Orwell frequently returns to the risk—a risk courted most intensely in politically engaged, or topically focused writing—that the reader might take literary representation too literally, take the representation of the world, in brief, for the world itself. Much of Orwell's early work centers, of course, on explicit, referentially grounded topics: poverty *(Down and Out in Paris and London)*, industrial labor *(The Road to Wigan Pier)*, imperialist violence ("A Hanging" and "Shooting an Elephant"), and war *(Homage to Catalonia)*. In each case, as Chapters 1 and 2 will discuss in more detail, Orwell is wary that the textual representation might be taken as a sufficient substitute for—and thus function as a potential displacement of—these subjects.

Orwell's persistent confusion of fiction and nonfiction is one strong signal of his concerns and skepticism about this process. To put this schematically, we might say that the "nonfictional" text, as such, is always in danger of being the most deceptive (because we take it too easily at face value) and thus, in one sense, the *most* fictional, while the fictional text—by reminding the reader of its status as fiction—is directly transparent and indeed accurate about its own status, and in this sense completely *nonfictional*. This would be one way to explain, for example, the generic indeterminacy of "A Hanging," the factual uncertainty that hovers over "Shooting an Elephant," the acknowledged distortions of *Down and Out in Paris and London,* and the conspicuous formal division of *Wigan Pier*—as well as, conversely, the filtering, and transmutation, of historically marked violence and injustice into the form of a child-like fable in *Animal Farm*. This confusion of nonfiction and fiction as categories is amplified, as well, by Orwell's use of a pseudonym—something that, on its face, cuts *against* the commitment to the plain style and also complicates (even while intensifying) the pervasive autobiographical dimension of Orwell's work.

In Chapter 3 I'll consider Orwell's key comment in his 1940 essay "Charles Dickens," which offers another hinge for these concerns: "if you look for the working-classes in fiction, and especially English fiction, all you find is a hole" (12.21). Insofar as there is such a massive elision—a mimetic "hole," in most fiction, that engulfs the bulk of the British population—the risks of literary representation run very high indeed. In this process, the novel, as a literary form that is intrinsically connected *to* the project of social representation, risks knitting together a coherent, but fundamentally deceptive, world—one organized around a principle of exclusion. Orwell's position is not original; this idea of culture is intrinsic to Marxist analysis, and is one of the many perspectives, actively present in Orwell's work, that, as Philip Bounds has recently argued, draws on larger currents of Marxist and Anglo-Marxist thought. What is *more* original here is Orwell's formulation of this perspective: so blunt, emphatic, and authoritative, yet also curiously intimate and tactile. This is another crux in Orwell's writing and, once more, something that we can productively counterpose to his comment that "good prose is like a window pane." To find a gap of this magnitude—the British novel, *as a whole*, occluding the working class, as a whole—suggests something quite different from a window pane, no matter how dusty.[39] (Again, the plainspoken tone of the comment, by working *against* this mediation, also functions to intensify it.) And because the condition, as Orwell identifies it, is so general, it is not easily contained as a counterexample: as though Orwell merely meant to valorize his own work, or the work of a small group of contemporaries, against the pervasive negation, or elision, that he is here identifying (or, in his more tactile language, "find[ing]").

Orwell's second form of skepticism about consummated expression is more sociological, and directed at the position of the writer rather than the aesthetic nature of the text. Expression is not cost free. The sheer act of writing has a social force and significance that is not easily controlled by the writer him- or herself. (As we've seen, writing's parabolic trajectory, for Orwell, is produced by its inevitably external, or material, dimensions, no matter how conceptually actualized, or topically grounded, it might be.) To put this in the crudest terms, we could say that Orwell is highly aware that most people in any society are not professional writers. And he feels that this is not a problem—no matter how self-evident it might seem—that should be brushed aside by the left. One of the starkest expressions of this perspective occurs in "The Art of Donald McGill," though we need to constellate this memorable passage with a comment from "Why I Write," as well:

> And this reflects, on a comic level, the working-class outlook which takes it as a matter of course that youth and adventure—almost, indeed, individual life—end with marriage. One of the few authentic class-differences, as opposed to class-distinctions, still existing in England is that the working classes age very much earlier. They do not live less long, provided that they survive their childhood, nor do they lose their physical activity earlier, but they do lose very early their youthful appearance. . . . It is usual to attribute this to the harder lives that the working classes have to live, but it is doubtful whether any such difference now exists that would account for it. More probably the truth is

that the working classes reach middle age earlier because they accept it earlier. For to look young after, say, thirty is largely a matter of wanting to do so. (13.27)

This is an important passage in Orwell's work for three interrelated reasons. First, it illustrates the egalitarianism that informs so much of his work. This passage hinges on Orwell's wager that inequality extends far beyond mere material possessions: for example, to how people age, how people experience "youth" and "adventure," and even to the nature of "individual life." Second, this wager draws on the fact that such a manifestation of inequality is at once profound and relatively unnoticed. Orwell is drawn to unnoticed forms of inequality and, often, as in this passage, he seems to suggest an inverse proportioning: as though the more pernicious the consequence of inequality, the *less* it is noticed—and vice versa. Finally, this interest in not merely depicting inequality but in confronting how inequality is hidden and recessed, or persistently underdepicted, connects back to the problematic position of the writer (the "depicter") himself. Orwell writes outside the working-class perspective that he considers here—and the sheer fact *that* he writes, including his production of this essay, and even of this very insight, can both signal and produce this distance. Thus Orwell's comment in "Donald McGill" connects most explicitly to this passage from "Why I Write," where he is adumbrating reasons for writing:

i) Sheer egoism. Desire to seem clever, to be talked about, to be remembered after death, to get your own back on grown-ups who snubbed you in childhood, etc., etc. It is humbug to pretend that this is not a motive, and a strong one. Writers share this characteristic with scientists, artists, politicians, lawyers, soldiers, successful business men—in short, with the whole top crust of humanity. The great mass of human beings are not acutely selfish. After the age of about thirty they abandon individual ambition—in many cases, indeed, they almost abandon the sense of being individuals at all—and live chiefly for others, or are simply smothered under drudgery. But there is also the minority of gifted, willful people who are determined to live their own lives to the end, and writers belong in this class. (18.318)

Once again, this is a crucial passage in Orwell's work, particularly in conjunction with its sibling from "Donald McGill" (written about five years earlier). What Orwell describes as "individual life" in "Donald McGill" is rephrased as "individual ambition" in "Why I Write," and narrowed to the activity of writing itself. Conversely, the somewhat general division between an elite (a "top crust") and "the great mass of human beings" in "Why I Write" is identified, more pointedly, as an entrenched "class difference" in "Donald McGill." The combination of these two passages produces a serious and even tragic perspective on writing, and this is the perspective my book will seek to elaborate. Writing—necessarily the expression of interior thought—is at once a means of self-actualization (to "live [one's] own [life] to the end") and an activity almost fatally entangled with larger, external currents of inequality. Put differently, we could say that a responsibility of the writer, never fully accounted for, is to confront as completely as possible what the (act of) writing *makes him into,* as well as what he makes out of writing. This again points to a form of excess within writing, though now in a more strictly sociological sense—to "write" is to be a writer, and to be a writer is to join, and potentially to become engulfed in, an entrenched (and crucially: privileged) social class. This is, needless to say, a materialist perspective on the matter. No writer—no matter how noble, wise, or energetic— can opt *completely* out of this system. Orwell is not claiming, however, that writing can't be noble, wise, or energetic but only that these qualities will never be transcendent of the condition of writing—and often, on the contrary, writing will be most ignoble, foolish, or lazy when it is too confident of avoiding this condition.

PART ONE

Paradoxes of the Plain Style

The 1930s

1

"Quite Bare"

("A Hanging")

Orwell's "Power"

The political scientist Stephen Ingle grounds his important recent study of Orwell in the need to consider him as a writer rather than merely a political thinker, but he stops surprisingly short at the actual prose. Despite his stated goal—of "shifting the traditional focus of Orwell studies more squarely onto Orwell the writer" (23)—Ingle's analysis repeatedly glances off the burnished surface of Orwell's plain style, as though there were little to say about the texts as texts. His descriptions of the qualities of the writing, while glowing, thus tend to be both brief and almost tautological. Orwell's political impact, Ingle avers in his concluding remarks, rests in "the sheer power of his prose" (170). And again, at the end of his book: "[a]s a writer of exceptional power and an exponent of lucid prose, he was unsurpassed" (181). (Transposing "exceptional" and "unsurpassed" here, we can quickly see the circular shape of this praise.) An equally circular structure informs the first discussion of specific works. "A Hanging," Ingle claims, "is told with force and an economy of style" (36); "Shooting an Elephant," he remarks in the next paragraph, is "*just as* forcefully written" as the earlier text (36, emphasis added).[1]

What constitutes the "power" or the "force" that, in each of these comments, distinguishes Orwell's prose? On this in Ingle there is essentially "dead silence" (to quote a central phrase from "A Hanging" [10.209]). Such silence, I want to argue, is not the product of one critic's neglect but is solicited by the terms of Orwell's writing itself. "Powerful" is a recurrent adjective in readings of Orwell, and of the early text "A Hanging" in particular. It is a descriptor that simultaneously seems to encapsulate the text's core qualities and, ironically, to block or stall the critical analysis. "Powerful"—in this way perhaps like "beautiful," "interesting," or "great"—is a seductive resting point for critical evaluation, and one that often produces a tautological sufficiency. Many of Orwell's biographers praise and slight "A Hanging" in a similar manner, each discussion both drawn to and suspended by the plain-style power of the text. Gordon Bowker—comparing Orwell's text to an earlier Somerset Maugham short story—calls "A Hanging" a "far more *powerful* and effective piece of writing," "sharply observed" and "remarkable for its freshness" and "its vividness" (89). Michael Shelden describes "a riveting piece whose emotional *power* comes from a slow but steady accumulation of details" (121). Bernard Crick introduces it as "the first piece of writing that shows the distinctive style and *powers* of Orwell," full of "the precise, mundane observation of a Sickert" (151). The ubiquitous recourse to this term of praise—here by Shelden, Crick, Bowker, and Ingle—registers a crucial quality of Orwell's text. But lined up in this way, such repetition also inevitably feels like a loss. Not just as it travels from one critical response to another, but intrinsically, this evaluative assessment can lose hold of the object that it means to recognize.

This play of recognition and resistance is significant and worth considering. Even Ingle's minimal terms give the reader something to work with. The power of Orwell's prose, in Ingle's encapsulation, consists largely of its "lucidity," which in turn is rooted in its sparseness or "economy." "Force," linguistic clarity, and formal compression are thus aligned here. Orwell's aesthetic "power" is intertwined with a circumspection that is noted by but also echoed in his critical refraction. The economy of the text would be diminished if it were further elaborated, its "force" diluted. Ironically, Orwell's simple or plain prose is inapproachable, resistant to critical interpretation. The meaning of such a text, welded to the concise language through which it is conveyed ("vivid," "sharp," and "precise"), cannot be amplified without losing these core qualities: in this way, the "plainspoken" text is sealed into itself, even verging on meaninglessness. The "sheer power" of Orwell's crystalline prose leaves it enigmatic: "A Hanging," as we'll see, invokes the "unspeakable" (208) as well as "dead silence," at its core.[2]

Reading Plain Style: "It," "Bare," "Plank"

What is so striking about "A Hanging," particularly when we remember its status as such an early Orwell text (still signed "Eric A. Blair"), is how fully it inhabits and *knows* this condition of the plain style. The opening paragraph makes clear the strange negativity that underlies the economy and lucidity of the prose. A critique of the style is hidden in plain view in this Orwell text—somewhat like the violence of the execution in the story itself—and evident already at the start.

> It was in Burma, a sodden morning of the rains. A sickly light, like yellow tinfoil, was slanting over the high walls into the jail yard. We were waiting outside the condemned cells, a row of sheds fronted with double bars, like small animal cages. Each cell measured about ten feet by ten and was quite bare within except for a plank bed and a pot for drinking water. In some of them brown silent men were squatting at the inner bars, with their blankets draped round them. These were the condemned men, due to be hanged within the next week or two.
>
> One prisoner had been brought out of his cell. He was a Hindu, a puny wisp of a man. . . . (10.207)

What I'd first call attention to in this opening description is one term that could be deployed *on* the description: not lucid, economic, or forceful but "bare." In 1937, for example, Victor Gollancz's important foreword to *The Road to Wigan Pier* praises the documentary component of Orwell's text for the way that it "lays bare" the terrible social and working conditions of the coal-mining areas of northern England (xxii). This paragraph, too, strives to be "quite bare": shorn of ornament, extraneousness, or distortion. Other descriptive terms, applied belatedly by critics to "A Hanging" ("force," "economy"), do not appear already in the opening of the text, but "bare" does. Viewed in this light, the opening paragraph conveys an unexpected sense of self-consciousness, as though it weren't only narrating the story to the reader—as directly as possible—but also functioning, conversely, as a commentary or reflection on itself.[3]

If we want to ignore this salient word, the text makes that difficult. "Bare" is repeated twice more in the text:

> I watched the bare brown back of the prisoner marching in front of me. (208)

> The superintendent reached out with his stick and poked the bare brown body; it oscillated slightly. (209)

These subsequent occurrences heighten the ironic import of "bare," in its first use, as a term that also reflects back on the text in which it appears.[4] The opening paragraph itself aspires both to "lay bare," as Gollancz would say (directly presenting the referenced world, as in the sequence of denotative phrases, "[i]t was in Burma," "we were waiting outside," "these were the prisoners") and to attain a condition of bareness, with language stripped down to its least ornate form. This sense of linguistic austerity runs through the paragraph but takes on its most "realized" (i.e., bluntest) form in the sentence that actually includes this term: "Each cell measured about ten feet by ten and was quite bare within except for a plank bed and a pot for drinking water." The shorn prose is at its *most* minimal—and thus, paradoxically, most extreme—here. It aims for, and projects, efficiency, external precision ("ten feet by ten") and tactile directness. The adjective, "plank," is a crucial one for this crystallization of the plain style—not just phonetically but also semantically. A plank bed is a bed on the verge of being merely a slab of wood (and not a bed at all). The blunt description "plank bed" succeeds at conveying the materiality of the room (its hard surfaces) and, ironically, the inappropriateness of this materiality (a bed should be more *than* simply a piece of wood). In other words, the plain style at once exploits and registers a dissent against such stark materiality.

This is more than effective reportage. The prose relies on the same deprivation it condemns in order to amplify its own stylistic integrity.[5] This sentence, I've argued, ratchets up the plainness of the "plain style." The spare, material sense of the phrase "plank bed" signals the efficacy of the language, its desire to accurately convey this bare world. As a term, "plank bed" wants to be, and seems to be, static free. But as a *thing*, the plank bed, because of this same bare quality, is glaringly inadequate. The simple phrase pushes the reader into a monstrous, almost oxymoronic world: a world where the material that should constitute an (instrumentally defined) object threatens to simply overwhelm the object. That there is something disturbing about the description, as it confers *more* stylistic valence (on the writing) in inverse proportion to the deprivation it registers (in the story), is reinforced by other aspects of the plain-style opening. A jarring sense already is triggered by the subtly off-kilter opening sentence and phrase: "It was in Burma, a sodden morning of the rains." (The correct, or more syntactically seamed, version of this opening would simply read: "It was a sodden morning of the rains in Burma"). Instead, Orwell begins with a latent sentence fragment that foregrounds, but also isolates, the initial pronoun. The "it" here is again ostensibly "bare," shorn of ornament or extension, direct and simple. ("It" and "bare" have a particularly intimate relationship in the opening.) But the opening word is also, of course, enigmatic and imprecise. (*What* was in Burma?) "It" points to a thingness but not yet to a specific thing. The pronoun conveys neutrality and thus reliability, yet also seems problematically remote.

As we've already seen, the same quiet term, "it," is deployed in a charged and disturbing manner later in the text (where "it" is once again conjoined with "bare"):

The superintendent reached out with his stick and poked the bare brown body; it oscillated slightly. (19)

Here the pronoun marks the conversion of a person into a "body," and a body into a thing. "It" replaces "he." When Orwell writes of the prisoner, now become a corpse, that "it oscillated slightly," the three words (set off as a freestanding phrase) rehearse the essential brutality that underlies the text. In this process the pronoun's own semantic nature shifts: pushed beyond an instrumental role, within a channeled system of meaning, "it" becomes a disconcertingly focal point of attention. This reframing of the term at once strains against the subordinate function of *any* pronoun and brings out the strange materiality of this particular, impersonal pronoun ("it"), which here loses an instrumental sense and forces our attention in and of itself (even as the woodenness of the "plank bed" puts it on the brink of not being a bed at all). Of course, this same unnerving emphasis is also apparent in the opening phrase, as Orwell—already playing on the semantic instability of this thing-like pronoun—gives us the hint of a sentence fragment, and thus a hint of this same arrest. From the *very* start of this early text, Orwell makes the stakes, and intricacies, of the plain style explicit.

Empty and Full: "Each Cell Was . . . Quite Bare"

My reading of Orwell begins by highlighting these simple words—"it," "plank," and "bare"—in the opening paragraph of his very early text. With this focus, I mean to emphasize the curious combination of directness and obstruction entailed by the intensification of the plain style. Despite and because of being so absolute, the style also seems both unnerving and deficient. The text registers not only the aspirations but the costs of such plainness. The insufficiencies of this orientation constellate around a telling trick that the opening plays on the reader, at the hinge of its plainspokenness: the description first empties the cells of persons (the rooms are "quite bare" except for bed and drinking water) and only *then* notices or inscribes the prisoners. The cells are *not,* we quickly discover, so bare. This delayed representation of the prisoners might be brief, but the effect of this delay—the misleading, momentary "emptying" of the cells—is pivotal to the opening's style.

Such a delay works to put what I'm considering the "bare" orientation of this style on an almost inhuman register of description. This register doesn't so much deliberately or maliciously elide the prisoners who are contained within the cell as (perhaps more disturbingly) fail to discern the distinctively human against mere organic or material form. The opening of "A Hanging" plays with this point of view—a view that would be so remote from a human perspective that it couldn't draw distinctions between animals, persons, and things. (This is somewhat like the disorienting perspective conjured up in the opening of Dickens's *Bleak House,* which features an impersonal narrative attached so closely to the unnatural duration of legal time that it miniaturizes the scale of a human life: "The little plaintiff or defendant who was promised a new rocking-horse when Jarndyce and Jarndyce should be settled has grown up, possessed himself of a real horse, and trotted away into the other world" [16].)

In the rest of this chapter I'm going to focus on this lapse—pressing the analysis in a way that might seem inordinately elaborated in relation to such a small moment. The inversion at the opening of "A Hanging" is an important crux in Orwell. I want to insist on this device—this deception—and foreground its privileged place at the start of Orwell's first major piece of writing. The deception doesn't only pose an aesthetics of withholding as an alternative or supplement to Orwell's empirically committed plain style but places such withholding at the center of this style, even in its earliest manifestation. (All the texts I look at in this book will bear a resonance with the poetics of exclusion—and thus with this particular moment—at the opening of "A Hanging.")

Couldn't Orwell simply have meant to do a physical inventory, and not intended the description of the empty cells to carry over to the human population? I want to offer several registers of evidence for the deliberateness of this dissonant reversal (where what is initially described as bare is then reversed to become full). We can point first to the other, more explicit deception of the opening: its postponement of the first-person voice. The self-consciously "bare" introduction does not only elide the *object* of the text (i.e., the prisoners) but also the narrating subject. There are two things hidden at the start of the story, each reinforcing the other. The reader thus has to reframe the opening two sentences of the essay, which seem as though they are in the third person, after the belated introduction of an anonymous (and *still* not fully individuated) narrator:

It was in Burma, a sodden morning of the rains. A sickly light, like yellow tinfoil, was slanting over the high walls into the jail yard. *We* were waiting outside the condemned cells. (emphasis added)

The two forms of reversal—momentarily concealing, respectively, the subject and the object of the narrative—make space for one another within the tight bounds of the plain style, each providing further motivation for and amplification of the *other* deviation, like facing mirrors in a small room.[6]

Second, I'd point to a brief passage in *Down and Out in Paris and London* that suggestively echoes the opening deception in "A Hanging":

The cell measured eight feet by five by eight high, was made of stone, and had a tiny barred window high up in the wall and a spyhole in the door, just like a cell in a prison. In it were six blankets, a chamber-pot, a hot water pipe, and nothing else whatever. I looked round the cell with a vague feeling that there was something missing. Then, with a shock of surprise, I realized what it was and exclaimed: "But I say, damn it, where are the beds?" (146)

This passage is important in its own right (and I will return to it later in this book) but also provocatively close to the description in "A Hanging," both in the blunt, physical terms of the description and as it weaves that "shock of surprise" into its crystallization of the plain style ("quite bare," "nothing else whatever"). Returning to the stark location that opens "A Hanging," and to the stylistic register of this early text, this passage explicitly *depicts* the double-take that the "bare" opening of "A Hanging" (in that elision of the prisoners) implicitly provokes. The dramatization of such a reversal in this passage from *Down and Out* offers further evidence for the significance of this elision, as a conscious and disturbing strategy, at the opening of "A Hanging."

Third, a series of other verbal strategies in the opening of "A Hanging" amplify this structurally grounded instance of withholding. I've already suggested that a similar, more muted version of this tension, between lack and amplitude, can be teased out of the plainspoken term "plank bed" (as a term that points to the empty world but also functions to intensify the stylistic cohesion of the writing itself). Likewise, once the prisoners *are* inscribed into the scene (so that we might recoil from the denomination of the cells as "quite bare"), the emptiness is not negated: human beings are only in "some of" the cells. In this way the initial image of a bare (unpeopled) cell lingers on, even after it has ostensibly been surpassed. More crucially, the structural inversion is extended by the troubling, inadequate description of the cells' inhabitants ("brown silent men"). This phrase, coming *after* the startling reversal in which the "quite bare" cells turn out to be peopled, immediately reinforces the radicalized (or structural) sense of dehumanization that has just been enacted. Before this, indeed, the terms of human and nonhuman have already been confused, as the cramped sheds with double bars are compared to "small animal cages." Thus the momentary, but consequential, "emptying" of the prisoners from the cells is embedded within a more sustained textual process and not simply reversed or transcended.

We've already seen that the subsequent occurrences of "bare" are connected both to the *thingness* of the executed corpse (now turned into an "it") and twice to "brown." These repeated terms work to tie together a series of charged but also deliberately plain phrases (including several in the opening paragraph): "[i]t was in Burma;" "quite *bare*;" "*brown silent* men;" "*bare brown* back;" "*bare brown* body; *it* oscillated slowly." Brown is forced into relation with "bare," "silent," and "it," and these are the terms through which the text both depicts and enacts a dehumanization that climaxes in the actual execution of the prisoner but is grounded in this more pervasive logic of racial distinction. The prisoners are, in other words, not just portrayed as "silent" in, but actively silenced by, the blunt opening. And this silencing—which can turn a person into a thing (or an "it") and thus *can* make a populated room "quite bare"—is threaded into the basic terms of the plain style.

If this death, or silencing, is woven quite implacably into the plain-style prose, it also forms the topic and plot of the text: the execution of the prisoner, who is led from the condemned cells to the gallows, where another Burmese prisoner, at the command of the British superintendent, pulls a lever that drops the platform out from under him, causing death by strangulation:

> Suddenly the superintendent made up his mind. Throwing up his head he made a swift motion with his stick, "Chalo!" he shouted almost fiercely.
> There was a clanking noise, and then dead silence. The prisoner had vanished, and the rope was twisting on itself. I let go of the dog and it galloped immediately to the back of the gallows. . . . (209)

The phrase "dead silence" links and confuses adjective and noun, in a morose pun. Death is made equivalent to silence here: both manifested as and the result of it. Such an equivalence underscores the brutality of the *initial* linked phrase ("brown silent men") and confirms, as it were, the deadly logic of the connection that this phrase provokes (where to be "brown" is to be "silent"). The reiteration extends the network of plain terms that I'm tracing: "it," "bare," "brown," "silent," and now "dead." None of these terms, as the texts unfolds, can be pulled away from the others; each reoccurs, and all are linked together in shifting permutations.

Five Ways of Looking at the "Bare" Cell

1 and 2: Immediacy and Mediation

This reading interlocks the textual effect of the first plain-style paragraph (as it eerily depopulates the prison cells) and the plotted event of execution toward which the story moves. I've already suggested some of the ways in which the "bare" description in "A Hanging" is problematically connected to the deadly conditions that it depicts. I'm making a case here for how the plain style—marked so explicitly, at the beginning of this text, *as a style*—implicates itself oddly in the process of dehumanization that it bears witness to. This sense of the violence of language would seem to be foreign to Orwell's political and aesthetic perspective, which is so invested in words meaning what they say (no more, no less); in clear prose, discernible facts, and the possibility of lucid description. The deception in the opening of "A Hanging" (connected so directly *to* the plain style) is important for this reason. It is the first, paradigmatic thing that is "hidden" within Orwell's writing and an ironic amplification of how the plain style, in Orwell's initial text, revolves around an act of hiding.

I have highlighted several distinct registers of evidence for the presence of this elision at the opening of Orwell's early text. I now want to consider the varied implications of this strategic deception on the text as a whole. My aim here is to go "all in" and to consider the full range of implications that are activated or lurk in potential. In the most pragmatic terms, the text leads the reader to first envision the cells as bare of persons and only then, after a brief but consequential hesitation, inscribes the prisoners back into this space. They were there all the time, but the reader and the text briefly missed them. The dual presentation of the cells—as both populated and "quite bare"—is a strikingly literary conceit, creating a sense of doubleness that is not easily assimilable to any strict empirical or rational framework. What could the text mean by leading us to imagine a cell block populated with condemned prisoners as empty—and then compelling us, almost immediately, to notice this mistake, overlaying this initial image of the empty room with an incommensurate image of the populated cells? What is the potential gain in this doubled image, insofar as the text refuses then simply to absorb the bare, empty cells into our sense of them as populated?

This process cannot be reduced, immediately, to only one register of meaning. I want to consider, instead, five distinct (sometimes overlapping, sometimes antithetical) ways in which to understand this opening elision, all of them relevant to the significance and "power" of "A Hanging." The aesthetic technique at play here is quite different from our received sense of Orwell, hinging as it does on irony, reversal, and deception. The text's opening, *because* of its commitment to the plain style, intensifies all these qualities. The irony turns on the term "bare," a term that also signals the text's reflection on its own austere style. As I've already suggested, there is a complicated working-through of the empirical imagination here. The tactile detail of this opening passage—its very aspiration toward precision and transparency—culminates in absence and negation: to grasp the material reality of the world also, potentially, is to empty this now-denuded world of significance. The "bare[ness]" of the cell would stem, in this first sense, from the sheer effort of looking directly at physical reality, on its own terms, outside of any mediating human consciousness. In "Art as Device," Victor Shklovsky famously describes the technique of defamiliarization, which differentiates literary language from more empirical forms of discourse, as the ability to "make a stone feel stony" (6). The opening of Orwell's text offers a darker, more negative version of this process. We feel the tactile intensity of the material world—with its "double bars," "plank bed," and the "pot for drinking water"—only in relation to the elision of persons themselves. (Later on, and working from the associated terms "brown silent men," and "dead silence," "A Hanging" refers to the prisoner as "dead as a stone" [209].) The drive toward an unmediated relationship with the referenced world ("to make the plank feel planky," as it were) leads paradoxically to this omission.

This is not the only way, however, to understand the image of emptiness at the center of the opening paragraph. If this bareness marks the text's desire for empirical immediacy, another, almost inverted way to understand this emptiness is as an assertion of mediating form, as though the text had internalized, and were ironically amplifying, its limited (and *non*material) nature as a written account. Orwell's writing often gravitates toward this kind of puncturing or hollowing out of language, provoking sudden reminders, in the midst of its urgent effort to connect words and things, that words are only words. For instance, the first third of *Homage to Catalonia*, even while emphasizing how Orwell seeks to abandon writing *for* action ("I had come to Spain with some notion of writing newspaper articles, but I had joined the militia almost immediately, because at that time and in that atmosphere it seemed the only conceivable thing to do" [4]), lingers on the difference between the melodramatic anticipation of war and its actual, mostly tedious, nature. Thus, Orwell writes, for example:

> According to my ideas of trench warfare the Fascists would be fifty or a hundred yards away. I could see nothing—seemingly their trenches were very well concealed. Then with a shock of dismay I saw where Benjamin was pointing; on the opposite hill-top, beyond the ravine, seven hundred metres away at the very least, the tiny outline of a parapet and a red-and-yellow flag—the Fascist position. I was indescribably disappointed. At that range our rifles were completely useless. . . . (21)

And again:

> I ought to say in passing that all the time I was in Spain I saw very little fighting. I was on the Aragon front from January to May, and between January and late March little or nothing happened on that front, except at Teruel. . . . Up here, in the hills round Zaragoza, it was simply the mingled boredom and discomfort of stationary warfare. A life as uneventful as a city clerk's, and almost as regular. Sentry-go, patrols, digging; digging, patrols, sentry-go. . . . Often I used to gaze round the wintry landscape and marvel at the futility of it all. The inconclusiveness of such a kind of war! (23–24)

The two passages insist on a range of deflationary terms. "[L]ittle or nothing happen[s]," the rifles are "completely useless," Orwell experiences "very little fighting," "sees nothing," and suffers only "boredom and discomfort," while remaining "stationary" and peering out at a frozen "wintry landscape." Ironically, this accumulation of "inconclusiveness," "uneventful[ness]," and "futility" prompts Orwell to "*marvel*," provoking "a *shock* of dismay" and "*indescribable* disappointment."[7] Similar kinds of deflation help to organize the (incomplete) encounter with poverty in *Down and Out* and with industrial labor in *The Road to Wigan Pier*. In all of these texts, Orwell's writing often pulls itself up short, suddenly reminding the reader of the distance between a written representation, however topically grounded, and the thing itself. "I do not feel that I have seen more than the fringe of poverty," Orwell writes in the penultimate paragraph of *Down and Out* (213). And, at the hinge of *The Road to Wigan Pier,* he characterizes the searing documentary mode that he is now abandoning as only "a rather fragmentary account of various things I saw" (121). This description of one text as merely encompassing the "fringe" of its ostensible focus ("poverty is what I am writing about," Orwell insists early in *Down and Out* [9]) and another as offering only a "fragmentary" depiction of *its* focus are crucial, because structurally evident, examples of how Orwell's writing often works to deflate not the objects of representation—poverty itself, or industrial hardship—but the mediated, incomplete refraction of these objects. ("Words are such feeble things," as Orwell earlier writes in *Wigan Pier* [57].)

The opening of "A Hanging" can also be understood in this way, as crystallizing the sense of a basic emptiness that lurks within any representation (an emptiness that we can sometimes feel *more* vividly against the very plenitude of realist affect). The stated bareness of the cells functions, on this register, as an ironic imaging of the hollowness of linguistic representation. It is a projection, within the story-world itself, of our nagging awareness that even the most topically grounded or referentially charged language is nothing but a tissue of words, if not lies. This skein of language would be like the hoax gift, constituted only by its elaborate wrapping paper, imagined by Georges Perec in *W, or The Memory of Childhood*: "a gigantic parcel made of wrapping upon wrapping and containing, as its sole and ultimate gift, a carrot. [*un paquet gigantesque qui n'était fait que d'emballages superposés renfermant, comme ultime et seul présent, une carotte*]" (155). I should be clear on this point: it would be impossible to view these empty cells only in this light. But this kind of self-reflexive "hollowing out" is not merely a process I want to impose upon the text (from a more postmodern perspective). It is most clearly evident on another textual level altogether—in the provocative *generic* uncertainty of "A Hanging." Is this text factual or fictional? Is it an "essay" or a "story"? Biographers and critics, for example, have called this text Orwell's "first distinctive work" (Meyers 69), "a brilliant early essay" (Bowker 88), "the first of his great essays" (Crick 193), "a brilliantly artful short story" (Crick 151–152), and one of "his best documentary sketches"

(Shelden 161). As these descriptions suggest, the text has an unstable quality—an amorphous status between "documentary," "essay," "sketch," "story," or perhaps merely "work"—which, in and of itself, complicates the referential coherence of the piece. Intertwined with this generic question is another simple, yet vexed, ontological one, that has long engaged Orwell criticism: did the execution that "A Hanging" recounts actually occur in Burma, under Eric Blair's watch (so that the language of the text refers—however artfully—to a real physical and historical event), or is this language, on the simplest level, referring to events that never took place?[8]

The text's indeterminate status between imagination and fact signals an implicit rejection of normative journalistic discourse. There is no reason to write such fiction, or to write a text that calls attention to its own elusiveness and unreliability, if the same events could be simply and easily communicated *as* factual. The very existence of this composite text—not exactly a documentary account, a story, a sketch, or an essay—works to discredit each of these more stable categories of writing. Much of Orwell's subsequent "documentary" work is suspended in this quasi-factual mode. In *The Road to Wigan Pier*, Orwell thus memorably reviews some of the experiences that led to his composition of *Down and Out in Paris and London* and parenthetically notes: "nearly all the incidents described there actually happened, though they have been rearranged" (152). It is important that we can read this statement almost exactly opposite the way it is ostensibly oriented (i.e., as acknowledging that some of the incidents described in *Down and Out* definitely did *not* happen), and that this ontological instability is then intertwined with a more strictly, and pervasively, compositional one: the "rearrange[ments]," which allow for condensation, elision, and temporal discontinuity (putting something in a different order from where it occurs, skipping over things, combining two or more incidents into something new, etc.).

Suspended between the categories of fact and fiction, "A Hanging" does *negative* work, in other words, not just offering another representation that can be added to our cultural stockpile but disrupting and troubling the social mechanisms of representation. The text throws a spanner into the works. This aim of hollowing out different kinds of discourse about colonial violence—part of the deep skepticism of Orwell's text—is also something we can put in relation to the opening image of emptiness that I've been emphasizing. It, too, offers a challenge to rational, factual discourse (which would smoothly and definitively reject the inaccurate image of such bare cells) and to the integrity of linguistic representation (as it suggests a commensurate hollowness within writing itself, only furthered by the text's uncertain generic status).

3 and 4: Absent Person and Absent View

If the provocative image of emptiness functions in this way as a block (suggesting that we can't see what the text is showing us, or even that what the text shows us is partially or wholly duplicitous), the same image is, conversely, motivated by the violence that Orwell's text intends to focus on. In one specific sense, after all, this image of emptiness is all too accurate (and thus mimetically grounded): these "condemned" prisoners are each facing imminent execution, the same destruction that the unnamed narrator will go on to elaborate, for one prisoner, in the rest of the text. The initial rendition of the cells as "quite bare" effectively anticipates this destruction, insofar as all these specific persons, who fill the space that we briefly take to be empty, *will* soon be gone—not just moved from this space but permanently and absolutely extinguished. This approaching destruction of the soon-to-be-hanged prisoners suggests a third, more narrowly motivated but equally valid way to understand the repudiated image of the "quite bare" cells. It is as though the text is already mindful of the impending disappearance of these doomed men, and the elision is simply an artful method of foreshadowing. The (future of the) story is translated back into the (present style of the) discourse.

Crucially, however, the "bare[ness]" in the opening paragraph—in its absoluteness—doesn't only implicate the looming destruction of these persons as objects of observation or contemplation. It also broaches a still-more-troubling non-perspective, which would be all that follows in the wake of this destruction. No "view" of the cells, as inhabited, is possible outside of the individual who would make this observation—and in the (impending) absence of *this* observing subject, we might say that the cells, even while still peopled, would be "quite bare." This idea of an extinguished point of view—and a simultaneously emptied "world," no longer apprehended through the individual point of view—might seem like an overly elaborate way to explain the jarring elision we're considering. But it is an idea that is crucial to "A Hanging," raised most explicitly at what is often taken as the key moment in the narrative:

> And once, in spite of the men who gripped him by each shoulder, he stepped slightly aside to avoid a puddle on the path.
>
> It is curious, but till that moment I had never realized what it means to destroy a healthy, conscious man. When I saw the prisoner step aside to avoid the puddle, I saw the mystery, the unspeakable wrongness, of cutting a life short when it is in full tide. This man was not dying, he was alive just as we were alive. All the organs of his body were working— bowels digesting food, skin renewing itself, nails growing, tissues forming—all toiling away in solemn foolery. His nails would still be growing when he stood on the drop, when he was falling through the air with a tenth-of-a-second to live. His eyes saw the yellow gravel and the grey walls, and his brain still remembered, foresaw, reasoned— reasoned even about puddles. He and we were a party of men walking together, seeing, hearing, feeling, understanding the same world; and in two minutes, with a sudden snap, one of us would be gone—one mind less, one world less. (10.208–209)

Any interpretation of "A Hanging" needs to engage this memorable passage and, more specifically, needs to account for the condensed implications of the final clause. This nearly tautological clause, both collapsing and estranging the two terms ("one mind" and "one world"), suggests the same confusion of subject and object that I also want to argue for in the opening paragraph.[9] And the tenuousness of the narrator's observation leading into this passage (as his insight is rooted in the "slight" movement of the unnamed prisoner), connects to the difficulty of keeping this particular distinction in mind: the difficulty of understanding the destruction of a single prisoner in terms of a vanished "world" (the entire world that the prisoner himself had also "see[n]," "hear[d]," "fe[lt]," and "understood") rather than *merely* a vanished "mind." It is almost impossible to keep this distinction in mind—to imagine, within one's own embodied comprehension of this "same world" (as the text pointedly calls it), the absolute, and permanent, destruction of another view on the world. In the most mundane sense, our point of view,

able to move wonderfully across the range and span of the world, is blocked
only at this: at recognizing the absolute destruction of point of view itself. In
different terms, it is almost impossible for any person to understand the execution of another person as the destruction of a subject, with a defined and
integral perspective (on the world at large), rather than simply the destruction of an object (of one's own observation and understanding).

"A Hanging" foregrounds the contingent nature of the narrator's observation, when it connects his most wide-ranging insight to the very slight movement of the prisoner. Orwell's decision to ground the key recognition scene
in this deliberately minor event ("stepp[ing] slightly aside to avoid a puddle
in the path") has always been understood to carry a suggestive ethical, and
aesthetic, force. But I want to argue for the precision of this narrative
choice—not merely as it touches on the precariousness of recognition in
general, but as it elaborates this more specific and pressing tension between
"mind" and "world," or between the subjective and objective dimensions of
the destruction that the narrator witnesses and the narrative recounts. In
this reading, the "slight[ness]" of the prisoner's movement (which paradoxically triggers his recognition) anticipates a particular epistemological instability lodged at the heart of this recognition and summarized by the *almost*
tautological phrase "one mind less, one world less." The difference between a
vanished "mind" and a vanished "world" is both absolute and also disturbingly "slight," in two distinct senses: in a temporal sense, as an extinguished
world is always the immediate consequence of the extinguished mind, and
in an epistemological sense, as anyone else's understanding of such a vanished world—by the sheer, ongoing force of subjectivity itself—is impossible
to sustain or stabilize.

In its talismanic phrase ("one mind less, one world less"), Orwell's early
text centers on this destruction of a subjective viewpoint. "A Hanging" goes
out of its way to exacerbate both the difference and the relationship between
the disappearance of an object (of perception) and the disappearance of a
subjective perspective or point of view itself. Just as the disappearance of an
object (of perception) takes place only *within* the world (a world that is necessarily apprehended, and constituted, from one's own point of view), so,
conversely, the disappearance of any single point of view, "A Hanging"
insists, annihilates the "world" as such. It is quite fitting, then, that the image
of a bare cell in the opening of "A Hanging" is also both brief *and*

absolute—a flickering (or "slight") moment within the reading process (which we understand only as it ends) that nevertheless broaches on a disturbingly permanent or total sense of absence. (The quick erasure of the bare cells is not merely a correction, in this sense, so much as a way of registering the remarkable difficulty of holding such bareness in mind, for more than an instant.)

We can see a careful reiteration of this same problem in a passage that I've already cited depicting the scene of execution, which explicitly invokes the terms I'm foregrounding:

> There was a clanking noise, and then dead silence. The prisoner had vanished, and the rope was twisting on itself. I let go of the dog and it galloped immediately to the back of the gallows. (209)

This description suggests both that the prisoner has plunged beneath the platform, temporarily disappearing from view, and also that he has "vanished" into materiality, becoming, in the same instance of execution, a mere corpse, or thing, like the rope that twists back on itself. The "vanish[ing]" is thus, as with those "bare" cells in the opening paragraph, *both* permanent and ostensibly quite brief, as the narrator almost immediately continues:

> The prisoner had vanished, and the rope was twisting on itself. I let go of the dog, and *it galloped immediately to the back of the gallows;* but when it got there it stopped short, barked, and then retreated into a corner of the yard, where it stood among the weeds, looking timorously out at us. *We went round the gallows to inspect the prisoner's body.* He was dangling with his toes pointed straight downwards, very slowly revolving, as dead as a stone. (209, emphases added)

In this description, the reader is forced to confront two different registers. We're led to understand the idea of the prisoner vanishing in absolute terms: the body remains (for our observation), but the subjective perspective of the prisoner has been permanently extinguished. He has exactly as little personhood, as little capacity to observe the world, as that piece of rope that winds back upon itself. This twisting rope—by emptily miming the doubled motion of consciousness—is a crucial image for the text: an absolute image of reflectiveness extinguished. At the same time, however, the narrative insists on the more literal, limited meaning of "vanished": the body itself has only momentarily disappeared from view, and the essay lingers on the details of its reemergence (as first the dog and then the executing party go around to the other side of the gallows and find the corpse beneath the drop). If we struggle to "see" this event from the point of view of the prisoner, the disappearance is permanent; if we see it from an outside point of view, and thus (necessarily) understand the prisoner himself as an external object, the disappearance is only momentary.[10]

This is another trick, then, that the text plays on the reader. Even the sheer mechanics of such a ruse reinforces (and provides further evidence for) the opening paragraph's initial deception. All such tricks, of course, take on particular salience—and even pathos—within the ostensibly direct, plain-style orientation of "A Hanging". The two tricks are related to each other, as well, since the brief elision of the prisoners, in the first paragraph, also presses on the distinction (both "slight" and absolute) between persons and things, or mind and world, tarrying with an apocalyptic perspective that would comprehend a person only in terms of a pure, subsuming materiality. The "blink" in the opening of this text—in which the reader (quickly) notices that he or she has (momentarily) *missed* the human beings within the cell— thus anticipates the bitter rending between these two forms of "vanishing": one absolute and permanent, one temporary and contingent. (Similarly, the opening paragraph no sooner *reveals* the prisoners, within the "quite bare" cells, than it masks them again, as "brown silent men.")

5: Unseeing

This chapter has had two major purposes so far: to specify the nature of Orwell's ethical intervention in "A Hanging" (an intervention that has often been noticed but not concretely elaborated) and to connect this with the dynamics of the plain style. This is in some sense a very deconstructive reading, since it focuses on the aspirations and ironies of the plain style as an expression of writing that aims to directly yield a referenced world. This is part of what is at stake in my effort to identify a (very pointed) center to Orwell's plain style: the opening paragraph of "A Hanging" (as it is *more* distilled and impersonal than the rest of the text); the core, descriptive sentence within this opening (*more* tactile and austere than the rest of the paragraph); and, finally, the "bare[ness]" at the center of this sentence. "Bare" is such an important qualifier here because its opposed potential meanings—"exposed" *or* "empty"—crystallize the tensions of the plain style. Orwell's text insists on this paradoxical relationship between the tactile and the desolate senses of "bare," and it connects this paradox to a more sweeping tension—between "mind" and "world" vanishing—at the core of the prisoner's violent execution.

I've traced several diverging implications of the emptied cells in the opening paragraph of "A Hanging" and suggested how they each are entangled with, and reflect back upon, the intensified plain style of Orwell's early text. We can understand the jarring, deceptive elision that is embedded in the "bare[ness]" of the opening in these competing, associated ways: as a radicalization of the text's materialist drive ("to make the plank feel planky"); as an inscription of the text's sheer textuality and thus its fundamental a-materiality; as a foreshadowing of the impending destruction of these persons within the represented world (as soon-to-be-executed prisoners); or as a method of momentarily registering the absolute non–point of view, the obliterated perspective, that will be the hidden consequence of this destruction. Orwell's text puts these implications into play with one another, creating an unusually resonant structure (unusual precisely as such resonance works in concert with the austere stylistics of the opening).

I've already suggested a fifth "way of looking" at these bare cells: as another manifestation of the racialized discourse that pervades the opening of the text and underlies the brutality at its center. Here the text's elision would *not* be a means of registering that absolute loss of a person's point of view but rather an enactment of the imperialist point of view that has ceased to recognize the Burmese prisoners, in particular, as persons. This returns us to the narrative's impoverished description of the "squatting" prisoners as "brown silent men" in the first paragraph. From its opening, the language of "A Hanging" generates the same kind of distortions that underlie and are produced through the violence of the British disciplinary system. That is why it is so important that the text no sooner acknowledges the prisoners who are within the bare cells than it works to corrode this knowledge (only "some of" the cells are occupied; they are occupied by prisoners described as merely "brown silent men;" the men—in these "small animal cages"—are "squatting" like animals [i.e., nonpersons] might).

This final sense of the passage is crucial, and arguably it is distinct not just in degree but in kind. The same narrative device works to register the destructive effects of dehumanization and functions as a cause or rhetorical buttress of such dehumanization. Even as the text elevates point of view, in the manner we've seen, it also brutally critiques point of view, as instantiated by the (unreliable) first-person narrative itself. This is a remarkable effect of "A Hanging": to combine its rebellious representation of point of view as foundational to any "world" (in the submerged person of the prisoner) with its dramatization of the stark limits, and incompleteness, of point of view (in the privileged person of the narrator).

In line with the intensification that governs this text—an intensification we can find not just in that strangely absolute image of the "quite bare" cells but, for example, in the desolate afterimage of the rope "twisting on itself"— "A Hanging" doesn't only distill this incompleteness in terms of the narrating first-person character but, more essentially, in terms of the act of narration as such. In narrating, or writing about, this violent event, Orwell's text, of course, necessarily contains a point of view that survives, and thus negates, the destruction it registers. The first-person narrator in the text (also emerging, only partially, through the opening paragraph) *is* emphatically depicted in a complicitous state, half-in and half-out of the proceedings that he recounts. And this complicity—an obvious and striking feature of the text—manifests itself in terms of both story and discourse. In the discourse, as we have briefly seen, the first-person voice only gradually emerges—first masked *as* third-person and then hidden with an imprecise first-person plural ("we were waiting" [207], "[w]e set out for the gallows" [208], etc.). The transition to first-person singular is incremental, conspicuous and jarring. On the level of action or content (story), we see that the narrator remains among the party of executioners. His exact role is unclear, but he doesn't obstruct or in any way protest against the proceedings that he observes. More than this, he obliquely participates in, rather than simply observing, these proceedings. He points to a picture (as narrator) but also seems to be part of the picture himself (as character). He restrains the dog (though barely acknowledges this fact)[11]. He partakes in the celebration that occurs after the execution, joins in the collective laughter, and also "[finds himself] laughing" (210) at a crucial point.

Here it is important to remember the status of "A Hanging" as an early and also a foundationally autobiographical text for Orwell. Orwell's writing begins from within this structure of complicity, and we can't stabilize the terms of this complicity too quickly. The complicity that Orwell describes is not merely unethical—though "A Hanging" certainly forces us to connect the dispiriting actions (and non-actions) of the narrator as character in the story and the muted, unstable voice of the narrator in the discourse. At the same time, this complicity is (still more disturbingly) entwined with the text's ethical aspirations—in the strong claim that it is necessary to occupy an uncomfortable, unstable position half-in and half-out of the imperialist system. One clear mark of Orwell's investment in the complicitous position of the narrator in "A Hanging" is how dramatically he foregrounds this position in the opening sentence of "Shooting an Elephant," written six years later and with an obvious relationship to "A Hanging":

> In Moulmein, in Lower Burma, I was hated by large numbers of people—the only time in my life I have been important enough for this to happen to me. (10.501)

Both "A Hanging" and "Shooting an Elephant" are determined not to allow the articulation of an imperialist critique to rest confidently or assuredly outside the system they indict. Both embed the events of the text in the experience, and perspective, of the younger "Blair," who is explicitly a collaborator with imperialism. But both also make clear that we can't easily separate this collaboration from the present-day writing of the text itself.

"A Hanging" presents a bracing version of this, for example, in the withholding of any information about the prisoner's "crime." (I put this in quotation marks because we get the strong sense, from the story as a whole, that the "crime" could be quite arbitrarily imposed on the prisoner, from within the depths of a violently unjust imperial administration of punishment.) We never learn the reason for the execution. On the one hand, Orwell's refusal to enter into the details of the prisoner's past demonstrates the hollowness of these contingent circumstances, as a sophistic mask of the violent execution. Only when the hanging is delinked, in this absolute way, from any specific "crime" of this individual prisoner, can it be revealed for what it truly (or more structurally) is: a contributing instance and violent effect of a racialized regime that systematically dehumanizes the subject population of Burma. On the other hand, the lack of attention to the prisoner, which turns him into a cipher, is also another sign *of* this dehumanization.

This double-edged withholding helps us access the structural force of that network of terms—"it," "bare," "brown," "silent"—which circulate through the text. The prisoner, of course, is just "*one* prisoner" (207, emphasis added), one of the "condemned men" (plural) or the "brown silent men" (plural) who are "squatting at the inner bars," in a "row of sheds," which the narrator likens to "small animal cages."[12] His anonymity in "A Hanging" is intimately tied to this structural condition, but it is difficult to say whether the text renders the prisoner's obscuring or merely obscures him. Rather than simply bear witness to this structure, from an outside position, the text sets it (again) in motion and remains suspended in its terms. This distinction is crucial because only such immanence allows the text to register the structure *as* a structure—active, pervasive, overwhelming—rather than as an (externalized, delimited) object. To read "A Hanging" is to feel that grip of the structure around you.

This dynamic is reinforced by several passages describing the anonymous prisoner, activating various registers of compression, diminution, or distortion. For example, the narrator writes, in the second paragraph:

> They crowded very close about him, with their hands always on him in a careful, caressing grip, as though all the while feeling him to make sure he was there. It was like men handling a fish which is still alive and may jump back into the water. But he stood quite unresisting, yielding his arms limply to the ropes, as though he hardly noticed what was happening. (207)

It is not clear here if the narrator is imposing, critiquing, or attributing to others this comparison of the prisoner to "a fish"—a comparison that we can't help but understand in the same terms of dehumanization that we've been tracing (and that appears in the paragraph that follows "small animal cages" and "brown silent men were squatting"). The desperate condition of the man, who is being marched to his death, does resemble the actual

condition of a fish on land (only just "still alive"). But that condition is ultimately caused by the prisoner's treatment *as* an animal, even as the analogy
itself derives from the perspective of the guards (who want to keep the slip-
pery fish from jumping back into the sea). The analogy thus works both to
register and reproduce this desperate condition. Unlike the struggling fish,
the prisoner responds by "yielding his arms limply," but of course this "limp"
motion of the prisoner associates uncomfortably closely *with* the fish, even
as the concluding phrase, "as though he hardly noticed what was happening," works to evacuate the prisoner of consciousness, diminishing
rather than reinforcing a sense of his humanity. In a similar way this initial
description of the victim begins: "One prisoner had been brought out of his
cell. He was a Hindu, a puny wisp of a man, with a shaven head and vague
liquid eyes" (207). In these descriptions, the slightness of the person—
"limp," "puny," disinterested (and later "look[ing] on incuriously" [208])—is
hard to disentangle from the externalized perspective that has difficulty
identifying with, or expressively realizing, the prisoner's own subjective perspective. This externalized perspective binds the prisoner to the same racialized categories that underlie his precarious, and now doomed, position. "He
walked clumsily with his bound arms, but quite steadily, with that bobbing
gait of the Indian who never straightens his knees" (208). Just as he is anonymous, and only "one" of the group of "silent brown men," the narrative ties
its parsimonious descriptions of him, as an individual, to a prefabricated,
racially marked image. In a similar way, the narrator's description of the
prisoner moves toward a detached (and thus derealized) image in the
opening: "He had a thick, sprouting mustache, absurdly too big for his body,
rather like the moustache of a comic man in the films" (207). Finally, when
the prisoner, on the gallows, does speak—breaking from the "silen[ce]" and
impassivity that has characterized him—the utterance is also bounded and
non-expressive, reduced, in the perspective of the narrator (and all the other
participants), to a repeated ("steady") "sound" or "noise":

> And then, when the noose was fixed, the prisoner began crying out on
> his god. It was a high, reiterated cry of "Ram! Ram! Ram! Ram!" *not
> urgent and fearful like a prayer or a cry for help,* but steady, rhythmical,
> almost like the tolling of a bell. The dog answered *the sound* with a
> whine. The hangman, still standing on the gallows, produced a small

cotton bag like a flour bag and drew it down over the prisoner's face. But *the sound, muffled* by the cloth, still persisted, over and over again: "Ram! Ram! Ram! Ram! Ram!" . . . Minutes seemed to pass. The *steady, muffled crying* from the prisoner went on and on, "Ram! Ram! Ram!" never faltering for an instant. . . . We looked at the lashed, hooded man on the drop, and listened to his cries—each cry another second of life; the same thought was in all our minds: oh, kill him quickly, get it over, stop that *abominable noise!* (209, emphases added)

I read these different verbal strategies (of elision, distortion, caricature, generalization, externalization, etc.) as rooted to the larger structural dynamics of the text, just as I'm reading the opening paragraph in structural terms. I thus don't view these forms of misrepresentation (eliding the prisoner, or diminishing him) as simply political lapses, by Orwell or the narrator, but also as part of the effort to instantiate the force of structure, to realize it immanently, from within its pervasive unfolding, rather than from the outside (as a closed, static, potentially contained or sentimentalized object of knowledge).

"A Hanging" as Early Text

This bleak immanence is the structural posture that "Shooting an Elephant" (1936) famously gravitates toward, as it narrates the younger Blair's growing consciousness not just of the hideous realities of the imperialist system but of his own constrained and compromised position within that system. The moment of realization produces a paradigmatic dissociation, in which Blair continues to act and also watches himself act, neither free to break *from* the action (and realize himself only on the level of his thoughts, his critical self-awareness) nor to inhabit the realm of his actions happily:

And suddenly I realized that I should have to shoot the elephant after all. The people expected it of me and I had got to do it; I could feel their two thousand wills pressing me forward, irresistibly. And it was at this moment, as I stood there with the rifle in my hands, that I first grasped the hollowness, the futility of the white man's dominion in the East. Here was I, the white man with his gun, standing in front of the unarmed native crowd—seemingly the leading actor of the piece; but in reality I was only an absurd puppet pushed to and fro by the will of those yellow faces behind. I perceived in this moment that when the white man turns tyrant it is his own freedom that he destroys. . . . He wears a mask, and his face grows to fit it. I had got to shoot the elephant. I had committed myself to doing it when I sent for the rifle. . . . But I did not want to shoot the elephant. I watched him beating his bunch of grass against his knees, with the preoccupied grandmotherly air that elephants have. It seemed to me that it would be murder to shoot him. . . . (10.504)

In this passage, the essay would seem to dramatize a movement of con-sciousness—a before and after within thinking. "*Suddenly* I realized," Orwell writes; and again, "it was *at this moment,* as I stood there with the rifle in my hand, that I *first* grasped;" and yet again, "I perceived *in this moment*" (all emphases added). But (as these repetitions might suggest) it is hardly accurate to call "Shooting an Elephant" a conversion narrative. As with "A Hanging," the essay remains suspended in the terms that it cri-tiques. Even in this passage, the phrase "yellow faces" strikes a dissonant note, and the text relies throughout on similar terms, which cannot be easily displaced onto the discredited perspective of the narrator-as-character. Thought does not propel the observing figure outside of the situation he grasps.

The structural relationship to imperialism is evident from the opening of "A Hanging," conditioning the stark terms of its elaboration. "Shooting an Elephant" is an important companion piece to "A Hanging" in part because it foregrounds, and explicitly topicalizes, a complicity that is already inter-twined with the "plain style" in this earlier essay. Orwell continues to under-stand his experience in Burma in quite structural terms, terms that overwhelm any grounded, clearly discrete, observational, or empirical sub-jective capacity. The second part of *The Road to Wigan Pier* (written just before "Shooting an Elephant" and six years after "a Hanging") contains his most extended "recollections" of these events and continually marks the experience as enveloping, as something that surrounds him, and impacts him, before he can fully fathom or comprehend its nature:

I was in the Indian Police five years, and by the end of that time I hated the imperialism I was serving with a bitterness which I probably cannot make clear. In the free air of England that kind of thing is not fully intelligible. In order to hate imperialism you have got to be part of it. Seen from the outside the British rule in India appears—indeed, it *is*—benevolent and even necessary; and so no doubt are the French rule in Morocco and the Dutch rule in Borneo, for people usually govern foreigners better than they govern themselves. But it is not possible to be part of such a system without recognizing it as an unjustifiable tyranny. (143–144, Orwell's emphasis)

I had begun to have an indescribable loathing of the whole machinery of so-called justice. . . . The wretched prisoners squatting in the reeking cages of the lock-ups, the grey cowed faces of the long-term convicts, the scarred buttocks of the men who had been flogged with bamboos, the women and children howling when their menfolk were led away under arrest—things like these are beyond bearing when you are in any way directly responsible for them. I watched a man hanged once; it seemed to me worse than a thousand murders. (146)

For five years I had been part of an oppressive system, and it had left me with a bad conscience. Innumerable remembered faces—faces of prisoners in the dock, of men waiting in the condemned cells, of subordinates I had bullied and aged peasants I had snubbed, of servants and coolies I had hit with my fists in moments of rage (nearly everyone does these things in the East, at any rate occasionally: orientals can be very provoking)—haunted me intolerably. . . . I wanted to submerge myself, to get right down among the oppressed, to be one of them and on their side against their tyrants. And, chiefly because I had had to think everything out in solitude, I had carried my hatred of oppression to extraordinary lengths. (147–148)

As we can see from these selections, the account in *Wigan Pier* insists on the overwhelming nature of imperialism's impress: it generates experiences that are "intolerable" and "beyond bearing," and provokes "an indescribable loathing," a bitterness, "which [Orwell] cannot make clear." The excess is both extensive and intensive. In the paradoxical image of "innumerable remembered faces," it is the multiplicity of incidents that disrupts the faculty of representation. (Each "face" is "remembered," but their accumulation is disturbing and impossible to hold in mind.) Conversely, the single execution rests beyond description, and Orwell can only gesture at the magnitude of this one event through the amplifying metaphor *of* multiplicity ("worse than a thousand murders"). Orwell's recourse to this self-defeating quantitative comparison sounds a troubling depth, and it's crucial in this light that "A Hanging," his earlier narrative of this putatively singular event, goes out of its way to frame the execution as only one of many. The impact of imperialism is intertwined with this confusion, or crisscrossing, between the singular and the multiple—and we can understand the narrator's unstable, complicitous position in "A Hanging" in relation to this confusion as well.

Orwell's passages in *Wigan Pier* also conflate a deeply psychological process—his paralysis in the face of what is "intolerable," "haunting," or "beyond bearing" for him—with a representational one, what's "indescribable" or impossible for the writing to "make clear" to the *reader*. There is a tension between these two processes. The latter problem is an essentially rhetorical one, in which the communicating writer has a clear sense of what he wants to describe but is frustrated by the imperfections of the medium. In the former case, the writer himself is also confused and disoriented. This brings us to another conspicuous aspect of these selections from *Wigan Pier*. Even while emphasizing the overwhelming impress of imperialism (both extensively and intensively), these same comments subvert their own premises. In each of these passages, the writing punctures itself, refusing to convey or contain the totality of the experience it is ostensibly discussing. To see imperialism, Orwell insists, you have to be on the "inside," and any representation is already partially on the "outside." Writing itself forms a kind of crest or fault line. The language here deliberately makes the reader uncomfortable. It's almost impossible to accept the pivot of Orwell's abusive, parenthetical interjections in *Wigan Pier*. How can the writer contend, in the middle of his jeremiad, not only that imperialism "appears" but "indeed . . . is" benevolent? Or, more starkly still, break the momentum of his negative litany with the disorienting parenthetical, "nearly everyone does these things in the East, at any rate occasionally: orientals can be very provoking"? It is, again, easy to explain this dynamic in symptomatic, psychological, or ideological terms: these retreats can be read as signs of Orwell's lingering ethnic prejudice and complicity—a complicity that, after all, he has just confessed to. This is probably the consensus view of Orwell's relationship to imperialism, and the interpretation that can most easily account for the *recto* and *verso* of Orwell's text. But Orwell's writing on imperialism (an experience that, as the autobiographical sections of *Wigan Pier* again make clear, informs his very activation *as* a writer) deliberately means to create a "back" and "front" that cannot be reconciled from a detached, mastering perspective.[13] (We see this, for example, in that non-depiction of the "crime" in "A Hanging," at once a concealment and an exposure.) The explanations of Orwell's doubleness have always been somewhat unsatisfying in this sense. First, they suggest that Orwell is unaware of this pattern in his writing—unaware of the starkly dissonant swerves that his texts about imperialism consistently enact. Second, and related to this, the synthetic view of Orwell as an ideological composite doesn't tell us how the contradiction is actually enacted *in* writing, or, for instance, how it intersects with the orientation of the "plain style" or contributes to the "power" or "force" that critics often note. It doesn't tell us anything, in other words, about the poetics of Orwell's textuality, its vivid and concrete work *as* writing.

This is again not to say that writing trumps all else. On the contrary, it is in the wake of experiencing imperialism that Orwell is perhaps most explicit about the limitations of writing (even as the experience of imperialism underlies his decision to become a writer).[14] Precisely insofar as the relationship to imperialism was so "unbearable," and insofar as he senses the impossibility of adequately "describing" or "making clear" its pervasive, systematic brutality, Orwell comes to understand the core enterprise of writing differently. There is no direct expression of imperialism for Orwell. Imperialism goads him to write, and thus rests behind—not just within—the act of writing. "Every book is a failure," and if Orwell comes to inhabit successfully any mode of expression, this success immediately makes him more acutely restless: "by the time you have perfected any style you have already outgrown it." Such restlessness, in my argument, accounts for the tonal swerves that we can trace in the autobiographical section of *The Road to Wigan Pier*. I read these disturbing turns as self-correcting (and thus, simultaneously, self-sabotaging) impulses, designed to restrain the "force" of the writing, or, put differently, to foreground the systematic, mediated nature of writing, its belated relationship to a primary experience of imperialism that isn't simply recovered through, but generative of, the praxis of writing—imperfect, impatient, unsatisfactory. (As George Perec writes, and memorably illustrates in *W*, "the unsayable is not buried inside writing, it is what prompted it in the first place" [42].)

In its conspicuous focus on an execution (an execution, as we've seen, that already informs the opening lines and even the opening word of the text), "A Hanging" dramatically heightens these tensions: the mere act of survival, the thinking that is implicit in writing as such, inexorably belies and diminishes the destructive event that it attempts to record (or, more simply, to write). But what's crucial here is the position of this text at the very start of Orwell's prolific writing. The status of "A Hanging" as an originary event of writing complicates the explicit topical focus of the piece. The text puts together two unique events: the emergence of the author and the eponymous death of the victim, that same man whose hanging, Orwell avers in *The Road to Wigan Pier*, "seemed worse to me than a thousand murders." This combination is startling and troubling, as Orwell's own origin as a writer—dramatized and intensified in the opening of "A Hanging"—is linked to the violent destruction of another person. This uncanny relationship is neither muffled nor excused by Orwell, but emphasized. It underlies the strange way, as we've seen, that the plain-style opening of the text both bears witness to and elides the events it describes, at once direct and rebarbative, revealing and distorting. But, furthermore, Orwell's essay literalizes or inscribes this writerly emergence through the position of the first-person voice, marked by its troubling, undeniable complicity.

The World Asleep

Orwell's insistence, in this way, that there is no safe or certain space for reflection characterizes a central tendency—and accomplishment—of his writing more generally. It is a complicated and multifaceted position. Over and again, Orwell's writing gravitates—formally, thematically, topically, stylistically—toward an intermediate state of reflection: toward thought that is neither at home in the world nor secured in a stable manner outside of or against the world. Orwell's texts thus frequently present the spectacle of observation, or cognition, that runs into the world it is attempting to comprehend. As one instance of this, quite distinct from the status of reflection in "A Hanging," we could consider the set piece at the end of *Homage to Catalonia*, where Orwell enacts the disorienting trip from war-torn Spain back into England and then imagines English culture, as a whole, in a state of sleepfulness:

> And then England—southern England, probably the sleekest landscape in the world. It is difficult when you pass that way, especially when you are peacefully recovering from sea-sickness with the plush cushions of a boat-train carriage under your bum, to believe that anything is really happening anywhere. Earthquakes in Japan, famines in China, revolutions in Mexico? Don't worry, the milk will be on the doorstep tomorrow morning, the *New Statesman* will come out on Friday. The industrial towns were far away, a smudge of smoke and misery hidden by the curve of the earth's surface. Down here it was still the England I had known in my childhood: the railway-cuttings smothered in wild flowers, the deep meadows where the great shining horses browse and meditate, the slow-moving streams bordered by willows, the green bosoms of the elms, the larkspurs in the cottage gardens; and then the huge peaceful wilderness of outer London, the barges on the miry river, the familiar streets, the posters telling of cricket matches and Royal weddings, the men in bowler hats, the pigeons in Trafalgar Square, the red buses, the blue policemen—all sleeping the deep, deep sleep of England, from which I sometimes fear that we shall never wake till we are jerked out of it by the roar of bombs. (231–232)

What is the condition that Orwell writes against here? What is this state of sleepfulness, and what prompts it? The passage varies tremendously on this question: from a very particular state of privilege ("the plush cushions of a boat-train carriage under your bum"), to a much wider, shared constellation of Englishness ("the barges on the miry river, the familiar streets, the posters telling of cricket matches and Royal weddings"), to, most expansively, the size and omnipresent shape of the world ("a smudge of smoke and misery hidden by the curve of the earth's surface"). These interlocked frameworks suggest the pervasiveness of the condition that Orwell wants to foreground. This dulled sense, in which we lose our awareness of the world (while *in the* world), might manifest itself in idiosyncratic, psychological terms or as the effect of a particular social position, as a diffuse cultural sense of Englishness or even the constraining force of embodiment as such (as though the very curving of the earth itself, "visible" in every horizon-line, militated against sympathetic alertness). The "difficult[y]" that Orwell registers ("[i]t is difficult when you pass that way . . . to believe that anything is really happening anywhere") moves through all these frameworks, just as the sustaining comfort of national identity shifts easily between somatic and discursive levels (the milk on the doorstep and the *New Statesman* every Friday). (It is the same conjunction that appears in *Wigan Pier:* "I am a degenerate modern semi-intellectual who would die if I did not get my early morning cup of tea and my *New Statesman* every Friday" [210].) In a similar way, the passage confuses subject and object, shifting obliquely from the conditions that might draw an individual into this state of sleepfulness ("the England I had known in my childhood," "the deep meadows," "the familiar streets"— where such "de[pth]" and "familiar[ity]" lulls the returning Orwell into this unknowing state) to the other individuals who are in this state themselves (so that it's the "men in bowler hats" and the "blue policemen" who, like everyone else, Orwell included, are "*all* sleeping the deep, deep sleep of England"). They are at once the agents and the bearers of this condition. Orwell's reluctance to identify or limit the cause of this unawareness, and his proclivity to implicate himself so clearly in the problem he describes, to frame it in both general *and* intimate terms, in both physical and cultural terms, as an object of critique and of nostalgic sympathy: all of these tensions suggest how Orwell isn't thinking only of a certain condition of individual subjects but of a condition that rests more closely within subjectivity itself. (To *think,* for Orwell, is always to risk falling "asleep" in this way.) And, as in many other places in his work, Orwell is drawn to imagine (or to think about) thought's distance from the world and then—in the final, jarring image—to stage the unsettling collapse of this distance.

"Just out of Reach"

This disruption—being "jerked out" of "sleep"—is already anticipated in Orwell's early, initiatory text. It is at the core of the other famous set piece within "A Hanging" (alongside the prisoner's avoidance of the puddle), to which I want briefly to turn. (And any reader of "A Hanging" might be wondering, by now, what my argument has to say about this "dreadful" event, also known as a dog.)

> We set out for the gallows. Two warders marched on either side of the prisoner, with their rifles at the slope; two others marched close against him, gripping him by arm and shoulder, as though at once pushing and supporting him. The rest of us, magistrates and the like, followed behind. Suddenly, when we had gone ten yards, the procession stopped short without any order or warning. A dreadful thing had happened—a dog, come goodness knows whence, had appeared in the yard. It came bounding among us with a loud volley of barks, and leapt round us wagging its whole body, wild with glee at finding so many human beings together. It was a large woolly dog, half Airedale, half pariah. For a moment it pranced round us, and then, before anyone could stop it, it had made a dash for the prisoner, and jumping up tried to lick his face. Everyone stood aghast, too taken aback even to grab at the dog. (208)

In one sense, then, the dog, rushing in with that "volley of barks" is like the bombs that Orwell imagines at the end of *Homage to Catalonia*. Orwell draws vivid attention to the abruptness of this moment, or, to put this only slightly differently, to the impact of the event on the consciousness of the executing party. "Suddenly . . . stopped short without any order. . . . A dreadful thing . . . goodness knows whence . . . bounding among us . . . a loud volley . . . leapt round us . . . pranced round us . . . before anyone could stop it . . . taken aback." This "sudden[ness]" is *not* an objective description of the "thing" that happened, nor merely a subjective description, of the "dreadful" psychological state of the executing party. More narrowly and precisely, it dramatizes a threshold between interior and exterior. It registers the intersection of the "world" with the "mind[s]" of the executing party: an intersection characterized, structurally, both as sudden ("stopped short," "goodness knows," "bounding" "loud," "leapt," "taken aback") and as surrounding or overwhelming the perceiving self ("volley," "leapt *round* us," "pranced *round* us").

In essence, then, the interaction with the dog—despite one or two telling details ("half Airedale, half pariah")—is not presented on a realist register but a phenomenological one. The episode elaborates, in these precise ways, the "mind"/"world" dichotomy foregrounded in the puddle scene and also at play, as I've been arguing, in the opening's dialectical approach to the plain style. Orwell underlines this through the exaggerated terms by which he defines the event (and crystallizes its status as a discrete event): "A dreadful thing had happened." The narrative introduction of this "thing" mimes its impact, by delaying its definition: "Suddenly, when we had gone ten yards, the procession stopped short without any order or warning." The impact of the dog's intrusion is thus inscribed before its concrete presence can be defined, so that the process of surprise is foregrounded over the surprising thing.

I'm interested here in the reiteration of "suddenly" and "a dreadful thing" (echoed, as I've shown, by other terms in this paragraph—"without . . . warning," "bounding," "before anyone could stop it," "made a dash for," etc.). The amplification strikes at something essential about Orwell's approach to writing this early text (a text that, in turn, is essential to the larger network of his writing). Once again, as with the plain style of the opening paragraph, Orwell's text pushes to an extreme. The reiterations lend an absolute, or *structural,* quality to the otherwise anecdotal episode. The expressive form, heightened in this way, trumps the (simply paraphrased) referential content here: the "character" of the dog ("half Airedale, half pariah") who intrudes on the movement of the prisoner to the gallows. It's not enough to point out, as Paul Gilroy has perceptively noted, that the dog is placed here as a witness to this unjust procession. Gilroy writes:

> The grim proceedings are disrupted by the intrusion of a stray dog which . . . inadvertently humanizes the condemned man by refusing to respect the false gravity that Britain's remote government has invested in this exercise of its overarching power. Orwell's nameless dog—"half Airedale, half pariah"—rushes up to the prisoner and "jumping up tried to lick his face." The proximity of the canine brings some important dimensions of militant, anti-imperial humanity into focus. (77–78)

This thematic reading registers but doesn't dwell on the expression of the event and, most urgently, its intensification (that "jumping," "rush[ing]," or sense of "intrusion"). Orwell's text carries us, inexorably, to this formalized register. Gilroy is less interested in the impact of this event within the articulation of the text itself, connected, through the emphatic intensification of the dog's intrusion, to the subdued voice of the first-person narrator (and thus to the plain style). This passage, in fact, expands and foregrounds the unsettling first-person plural: beginning with "[w]e set out," the narrator continues, "[t]he rest of *us* . . . followed," "*we* had gone ten yards," "[i]t came bounding among *us*," "leapt round *us*," "pranced round *us*," "before *anyone* could stop it," "*everyone* stood aghast." Here the "us" of the passage (which privileges the perception of the narrator while muting his voice) is rooted, ultimately, to the mediated nature of written discourse, while the startling "dog" is rooted to the represented event, as such.

The first paragraph describing the dog, as we've seen, emphasizes shock and suddenness, the intrusion of an external "thing" onto consciousness, and the excessive nature of this object (as it encircles—"leap[ing] round" and "pranc[ing] round"—the group of officials). The second paragraph picks up on this relationship, describing the varied efforts to bring this threatening, volatile, elusive object into the grasp of subjective intention. It is as though the paragraph is describing the very effort of reflection to encompass the object that has intruded upon or disrupted it:

"Who let that bloody brute in here?" said the superintendent angrily. "Catch it, someone!"

A warder, detached from the escort, charged clumsily after the dog, but it danced and gambolled just out of his reach, taking everything as part of the game. A young Eurasian jailer picked up a handful of gravel and tried to stone the dog away, but it dodged the stones and came after us again. Its yaps echoed from the jail walls. . . . It was several minutes before someone managed to catch the dog. Then we put my handkerchief through its collar and moved off once more, with the dog still straining and whimpering. (208)

Crucially, the dog does not only reside outside such an effort but "just out of . . . reach," on the brink of the warder's grasp. The inconspicuous modifier "just" once again lends this description structural force. For me, this quiet adverb is as important as any other word in the essay. Only the "just" lends this passage its dialectical complexity and its phenomenological charge. By dialectical, I mean that this image (not "out of reach" but "*just* out of reach") invokes a continual tension between interior and exterior—an excess that is recurrently produced in thought's effort to grasp the external object. In this way, this key scene in "A Hanging" fits squarely into Orwell's larger concern with the dynamics of thinking and with writing's own ideational force. What's most important is the way that the dog hovers at this vibrant, unsettled edge of reflective mastery. Any thought, from this perspective, includes an element that is neither securely "inside" nor simply "outside" the thought, necessary to but not sufficiently contained by the reflection, its structuring ground. Every image of reflection is incomplete.

Last Words

This sense of incompleteness is reemphasized in the disturbing, and isolated, final sentence of "A Hanging," the only point in the text that returns to the bare style, and inhuman (non-)perspective, of the opening. The prisoner has been killed, and the party of executioners returns to the prison, retracing their initial route:

> I found that I was laughing quite loudly. Everyone was laughing. Even the superintendent grinned in a tolerant way. "You'd better all come out and have a drink," he said quite genially. "I've got a bottle of whisky in the car. We could do with it."
>
> We went through the big double gates of the prison, into the road. "Pulling at his legs!" exclaimed a Burmese magistrate suddenly, and burst into a loud chuckling. We all began laughing again. At that moment Francis' anecdote seemed extraordinarily funny. We all had a drink together, native and European alike, quite amicably. The dead man was a hundred yards away. (210)

The close of the essay sees Orwell reversing the narrative order he establishes at the outset, going *back* from the first-person singular ("I found that I was laughing quite loudly," the last time the narrator uses the "I"), to the first-person plural ("We went through the gates. . . . We all began laughing"), to a last sentence with no inflections that could distinguish it from the third person. In fact, this final sentence returns to both the inertness of the opening line ("It was in Burma") and the peculiar depersonalization of the opening description ("Each cell measured about ten by ten feet and was quite bare within except for a plank bed and a pot for drinking water."). First-personness, at the close, is caught in a paradigmatic dissociation, at once the object and the subject ("*I* found that *I* was laughing"), as though this self-observant laughter could go on forever, like the rope twisting around itself. Third-personness, on the other hand, is unburdened by such mediation but cast, once more, outside of any human point of view, so that it is unclear whether the demarcation of the corpse as "a hundred yards away" takes place from the perspective of the survivors ("native and European alike") against whom such separation must be defined or from a detached, bird's-eye perspective that alone would be able to gauge the distance between the executing party and the body. More important, however, is the grim irony that attaches to this outside perspective, a perspective that inexorably becomes affiliated with the distance or remoteness of the corpse from the circle of survivors. While the final line does place the narrator, and the reader, "away," outside, and detached from the amicability of the survivors (from the amicability of *narrative* itself), what marks the disturbing distance as distance is once again the non-perspective of the dead man. There is, of course, nothing—*absolutely* nothing—"a hundred yards away": no mind, no world. If "A Hanging" (and Orwell's own writing practice) begins by paradoxically casting the populated cells of the condemned men as "bare," it ends, appropriately enough, by focusing its final attention on a "man" who is not there.

Interlude

Between Texts

After "A Hanging": The Road to *Wigan Pier*

In Chapter 1, I built a reading of Orwell's early, initiatory text, "A Hanging," around the key phrase from his first paragraph: "quite bare." Chapter 2 will come to hinge on a brief phrase as well, from *The Road to Wigan Pier*: "getting to work." Once more, it is a very blunt, simple phrase (but also, as with "quite bare," an aspirational one). My interpretation of "A Hanging" also pivoted on the status of that text *as* an early text and thus a point of origin for Orwell's subsequent writing. As we've seen, Orwell's piece forces this novel activity—of authorship—into unhappy relation with destruction. The open landscape of textuality emerges in tandem with the untimely death that it represents. The end of the anonymous prisoner is coextensive with the origin of the writer.

While "A Hanging" is a new kind of action for this unknown author—and thus a galvanizing *event* of writing—it follows and depends on this earlier, brutal occurrence. And, indeed, Orwell's brief title—dangling so conspicuously between verb and noun—is etymologically linked with "depend."[1] Orwell's subsequent texts depend on, or we might say from, "A Hanging"—in the simple sense that they don't stand in and of themselves but proceed from (ever) earlier writing. All of his other texts, unlike "A Hanging," can be (and ultimately must be) read in relation to the writing that came before, just as "A Hanging" demands to be read in relation to the event that precedes it. Orwell's work foregrounds this mundane structural condition in at least two ways (and, in doing so, makes such dependency less mundane—contextualizing and dramatizing it). First, as I discuss in the Introduction, Orwell's work shifts restlessly between different forms, genres, and scales. Because of these shifts, even a relatively cursory encounter with his work brings the reader up against a stream of writing, branching off in new directions and provoking further permutations of itself. Second, and more idiosyncratically, Orwell's writing insists on a specific autobiographical sequence, often returning to and rehashing key events from his life. This recounted life is built into the unfolding work. And this autobiographical sequence, with its accumulating refractions of past experience, is embedded in the more general, intertextual sequence of the writing, as it offers accumulating refractions of past *texts*. (These two trajectories are tightly connected, but they are not identical. Rather, such autobiographical sequencing can function variously as an echo, a displacement, a framework for, or a potentially disconcerting concretization of this larger, intertextual drive.)

It is important, then, that Orwell doesn't merely revisit his life in multiple points of his writing but that he does this through a complicated sequence of generically varied texts. "Shooting an Elephant," for example, returns to the topical ground of "A Hanging." And *The Road to Wigan Pier,* as we've seen, reviews the Burmese experience described in both "Shooting an Elephant" and "A Hanging." *Wigan Pier* also discusses, at some autobiographical length, Orwell's earlier composition of *Down and Out in Paris and London.* (Of course, *Down and Out* itself draws on previous autobiographical events.)[2] Orwell's *Homage to Catalonia,* in turn, refers obliquely back to *The Road to Wigan Pier*—Orwell at one point addresses readers "who wrote to me about my last book" (210)—while numerous texts after 1937 refer back to *Homage to Catalonia*.[3] These coils—locking texts together; building "life" into the writing and then "writing" back into remembered and experienced life—are a crucial part of Orwell's art and of the particular way that his writing comes to define, and engage, the production of textual meaning. (And as with so many aspects of Orwell's work, these "coils" function in sometimes tense, unsettled relation to the plain style.)[4]

Let me offer one more detailed example. As almost any biography of Orwell tends to dramatize, *Homage to Catalonia* recounts events that take place just after he finishes writing *Wigan Pier.* The link between these two works is particularly intimate: indeed, it forms a meta-structure in Orwell criticism, and one that bridges texts and life.[5] Orwell departs for Barcelona days after submitting the manuscript of *Wigan Pier*. *Wigan Pier,* conversely, is published while Orwell is still fighting on the frontline outside Huesca. The texts are also roughly the same length (about 70,000 and 80,000 words, respectively). The crucial break between Parts One and Two in *Wigan Pier*— which I will discuss more extensively in Chapter Two—starts with this line, set off as a separate paragraph:

> The road from Mandalay to Wigan is a long one and the reasons for taking it are not immediately clear. (118)

Homage to Catalonia has nothing like this two-part structure. It is, for the most part, a determinedly continuous and temporally linear narrative.[6] But when Orwell returns to Barcelona near the center of the book (thus hinting at two potential stages within the narrative), we can find a reiteration of *Wigan Pier*'s structural break. Orwell begins Chapter 9, without warning:

> From Mandalay, in Upper Burma, you can travel by train to Maymyo, the principal hill-station of the province, on the edge of the Shan pla-teau. (108)

The echo is unmistakable. But despite the intersecting autobiographical *content* (Orwell's unexpected reference, in each text, to "Mandalay"), this overlap is secured only by the strange formal identification, as this out-of-place reference occupies the same structural position as the line in *Wigan Pier*. It is particularly strange, of course, because *Homage* otherwise eschews the bifurcation we find in *Wigan Pier*. Such an overlap thus pushes the reader's attention outside of *Homage to Catalonia*, back toward Orwell's previous text and toward the divided center of this preceding text. Here, at this moment in *Homage to Catalonia*, there is a ghostly residue of the decisive formal characteristic of *Wigan Pier*: its rupture. Of course the formal intimacy that drives this backward movement, from *Homage to Catalonia* to *Wigan Pier,* feeds as well on the texts' matching references to Burma. This is important because, in another embedded displacement, these two phrases, each at the center of a book, also recall the *opening* phrases in two earlier texts of Orwell:

It was in Burma, a sodden morning of the rains.

and:

In Moulmein, in Lower Burma, I was hated by large numbers of people—the only time in my life that I have been important enough for this to happen to me.

In Chapter 1 I discussed how these dual openings problematize, respectively, third- and first-person writing. The authority of what seems like a third-person voice, in this opening line of "A Hanging," results in both depersonalization and fragmentation. And the conspicuous priority of the first-person narrator, in the opening line of "Shooting an Elephant," is linked with both self-abnegation and self-division. In moving from the middle of *Homage to Catalonia* to the more conspicuous middle of *Wigan Pier*, the reader is cast still further back—toward these earlier texts; toward the unsettled *beginnings* of the earlier texts; and, through these openings, toward "Burma," itself, as the (still earlier) ground of Orwell's own biographical experience. The entire textual chain pulls back to this foundational, but displaced, experience. (By *displaced* I mean, most simply, that the experience is represented belatedly, and even as it works to ground Orwell's origination *as* a writer, it is accessible only through this writing.) Thus, as we've seen, the Burmese experience, for Orwell, must be understood not merely as an origin represented through writing—however imperfectly or partially—but also as what has generated writing, as an (ongoing) activity, in the first place. "Burma," in this particular sense, is the motive for the *formally* troubled opening lines.

"Behind every fortune is a great crime." This realist sensibility is enacted throughout Orwell's writing, but the "fortune" here is the fact of writing itself. And the "crime" is, most obviously, the experience in Burma, a radically preliminary event within Orwell's prolific writing—visible in one of his initiatory texts ("A Hanging"), in the opening line *of* this piece, and even in the stark first word of this opening. As we've seen, this "it" denotes both the event that "A Hanging" will recount *and* what is specifically unrecountable about this event, namely the transformation of a person into a corpse or thing. It is neutral and ominous, tactile and hollow, blunt and enigmatic. The "it," we could say, both inaugurates and seals, as in a sarcophagus, the plain-style orientation of Orwell's prose. (In this way, "A Hanging" instantly generates, on a semantic level, the same kind of displacement that I've been identifying as a key element of Orwell's intertextuality, more generally.) The narrator, partially, witnesses this event, but he is also, partially, responsible *for* it. And the execution, indeed, might not even have taken place. The only real "evidence" for the veracity of Orwell's text is his reiteration, in a later text (in *Wigan Pier*) that "I watched a man hanged once" (146). This is the final insult to the anonymous victim of "A Hanging": killed in the world, lost in the text, but perhaps nonexistent in the first place (or constituted only by that chain of writing).

My aim here isn't to fetishize the imperialist origins of Orwell's writing, as a compulsive source of repetition, but, on the contrary, to see the way that he manipulates these origins, in writing, as a self-conscious aesthetic, and political, strategy. The encounter with such searing injustice in Burma is neither a stable topic within nor something unconsciously outside of Orwell's writing practice, but at its deliberate threshold—"just out of reach," as Orwell characterizes the disruptive dog in "A Hanging." (This resonant detail is worth emphasizing because it speaks to Orwell's epistemological sensibility, in this way—and thus, relatedly, to his aesthetic sense of writing itself.) One crucial function of the autobiographical impulse in Orwell's work is the sense it conveys of *any* writing as part of an ongoing sequence that begins prior to, and thus extends outside of, the text's own ideational ambit. In this way, no writing can quite catch up with itself. There is *always* that dog at the threshold, we might say. As I highlight in the Introduction, this sense of writing's incessant, *and* incessantly defeated, reach is crucial to Orwell's work. "With suicide, as with murder," Orwell writes in his 1949 notebook, "the great difficulty, disposal of the body" (20.202). This odd thought, playful and distressing, hits at the same sense of outsidedness. It is a peculiarly Orwellian comment—not so much in terms of its content as in its ironic formal logic. The epigram is absurd because this is not merely a "great difficulty," "as with murder," but a paradox and impossibility: the suicidal body, of course, cannot "dispose" of itself. Even as we'd strive to eliminate ourselves—and this veers toward the *same* core paradox that "A Hanging" emphasizes, but from the other direction—our body would remain in the world.[7] In a similar vein, Orwell begins a 1940 book review for *The New Statesman and Nation*, "Professor Whitehead once remarked that every philosophy is coloured by a secret imaginative background which does not officially form part of its doctrines" (12.274). These two comments, otherwise so topically distinct, and separated by nine years, encapsulate the formal process that interests me. I want to connect the "body" that the suicide cannot dispose of and the "secret . . . background" that is inassimilable to the *inside* of any philosophy (i.e., to the wide, official terrain of its "doctrine"). This connection is a structural one. In the Introduction, and in the discussion of "A Hanging," I've linked this ironic sense to Orwell's engagement with the activity of writing itself. In the simplest terms, writing, too (like "suicide" or "philosophy," in Orwell's two aphorisms), generates an inassimilable outside through its own unfolding, producing implications and meanings that are attached to, but not fully contained by, itself. Here we're back to what I've called the "crest line" of writing, and the impact of the compositional process as such. These are two more brief instances in Orwell's work that we can constellate around such an orientation. The execution that Orwell witnesses *and* doesn't witness (remember that doubled "it") is one exemplary version of this outsidedness, one technique or strategy for making his writing stop short. Orwell's writing, in this sense, continually generates—or even invents—its own displaced origins. (This resonates, of course, with a more *literal* unreliability in Orwell's accounts of his formative political experience—in "A Hanging," "Shooting an Elephant," and *Down and Out*.)

"Stepping Over"

This Interlude, entitled "Between Texts," bridges my readings of "A Hanging" (in Chapter 1) and *The Road to Wigan Pier* (in Chapter 2). So the title emphasizes how this section, itself, takes place "in between" two text-centered chapters. (And, certainly, insofar as books of literary criticism are so often divided by chapters devoted to different texts, it could be a worthwhile enterprise to think about the blunt space "between chapters"—and what *happens,* or is prevented from happening, in those spaces.) But I also mean to emphasize, in this title, how Orwell's own writing moves "between texts" as well. This returns to the discussion, in the Introduction, of Orwell's work as graphomanic "network"—full of interconnecting, diverging, and overlapping texts. Here my concern is not primarily to analyze so much as to reenact some of that horizontal, associational movement from text to text, that compositional propulsion that works, so suggestively and counterintuitively, in tandem *with* the plain style (in all its ethical and political urgency).

To highlight this suspended quality of Orwell's prose—its anadiplostic momentum *as* writing, within an ongoing textual field—I want to look at one brief passage from much later in his writing career: another entry he makes in his 1949 literary notebook. To go from the opening of "A Hanging" to this notebook—which includes remarkable entries about Orwell's terminal illness—is to cross the chronological antipodes of Orwell's writing. In many ways, Orwell's 1948 and 1949 notebooks continue and extend aesthetic principles at work most visibly in the column "As I Please," which will be the focus of Part Two of this book. (In this sense, my own argument here will be amplified in Part Two, perhaps mirroring the spiraling, interconnected nature of Orwell's writing.) We'd be hard pressed to find a more formal manifestation of Orwell's work, as the notebooks resolutely embrace a principle of montage. Here, as with "As I Please," we encounter a conspicuous and often galvanizing variety that is difficult even to summarize, without diluting. The writing moves, restlessly, from topic to topic. And, more saliently, the notebook moves across different textual registers, freely traversing (and thus also accentuating) the fault line between first-order writing (including precisely dated journal entries that describe the substance of Orwell's thoughts and experience) and a strange concatenation of second-order writing including (but not limited to) quotations, press clippings, and catalogues of different words. One page, for example, simply lists, in vertical form, an untitled group of thirty-two political and military idioms (beginning with "Vanguard," "Lay the foundations," "Pave the way for," and "Spearhead" and ending with "Rally [the progressive forces]" and "Iron out"). Another page includes a similar list, now run together as a paragraph: "*Critical jargon:* Values. Alienated. Disoriented. Reductions. Frame of reference. Avant-garde. Kitsch. Motivation. Evaluate. Discrete. Dichotomy. Aesthetic (noun). Creativity. Criteria. Epigone. Psyche. Schizoid. Revaluation.

Modes. Significant. Artform. Perspectives" (20.209). (My book, indeed, might come close to using all these stigmatized terms!) There are numerous other, surprising examples.[8] The juxtapositions in these notebooks are crucial. Each side of this fault line—the quasi-Flaubertian exercises in extracting, listing, and thus ironizing words and the more intimate, confessional, though often also clinical passages about Orwell's own thoughts and experiences—works to destabilize the other.

The passage I want to touch on, written some nineteen years after "A Hanging," concludes one of the more substantive, diaristic entries that begins by relativizing the modern feeling that "the death of a child is the worst thing that most people are able to imagine" (20.202). Orwell speculates, in typically counterintuitive fashion, that "[o]ne great difference between the Victorians & ourselves was that they looked on the adult as more important than the child. In a family of ten or twelve it was almost inevitable that one or two should die in infancy, & though these deaths were sad, of course, they were soon forgotten, as there were always more children coming along" (20.202). Orwell's meditation on this problem then shifts quickly, moving from the "preposterous incident" in *Jude the Obscure* where "the eldest child hangs the two younger ones & then hangs itself," to a quite different context. The next part of the entry preserves the almost conversational tone of speculation—obviously connected, for Orwell, to the specific process of writing a journal entry—while veering toward a much more intensified, and urgent, topical register:

I read recently in the newspaper that in Shanghai (now full of refugees), abandoned children are becoming so common on the pavement that one no longer notices them. In the end, I suppose, the body of a dying child becomes simply a piece of refuse to be stepped over. Yet all these children started out with the expectation of being loved & protected, & with the conviction which one can see even in a very young child that the world is a splendid place & there are plenty of good times ahead.

Query: are you the same again if you have walked home stepping over the bodies of abandoned children, & not [even] succouring even one of them? (Even to take care not to tread on them is a sort of hypocrisy.) M[alcolm] M[uggeridge] says that anyone who has lived in Asia has in effect done this kind of thing already. Perhaps not quite true,

insomuch that when he & I lived in Asia we were young men who wd
hardly notice babies. (20.202)

This brief excursus conjures up, like "A Hanging" seventeen years before, an
absolute state of injustice. The injustice is absolute both in its sheer, intensive
quality—a child abandoned to die on the streets—and its extensiveness—
such children are "so common," as Orwell puts it, "that one no longer notices
them." If there weren't so *many* children, in this city now "full of refugees,"
they wouldn't be so mistreated. The number of such children and their dehu-
manized condition—like "refuse to be stepped over"—are mutually reinforcing. This is quite terrifying when we think about it. We saw this same
conjuncture in "A Hanging"—the prisoner who dies is one of a much larger
group of men, circulated through the condemned cells. In both texts (1931
and 1949), the mutual reinforcement, of extent and acuity, both anchors and
seals the catastrophe.

It is important, conversely, that Orwell inflects this as a newspaper article
he has "read recently." This is a very light touch to galvanize such absoluteness. It is almost as though the reader, with the mere flip of his hand (or
the notebook writer, with the stroke of the pen), has summoned the absoluteness that overwhelms him. This newspaper reader is like a strange,
modern-day Tantalus, not chasing pleasures just out of reach but eliciting
crises that, in their very intensity and urgency—their absoluteness—slip
away. This subjective sense is enhanced by the intimate, provisional nature
of such journal writing. Despite its urgent topical focus, and its relative compression, this is a shifting and tentative passage, at once speculative and self-
critical. Almost each sentence enacts such shifting, leading to the unsettling
deflation of the second paragraph, with its string of questions, doubts, and
rejoinders.

The jarring combination of absolute (event) and provisional (form) connects this passage to the aesthetics already at work in "A Hanging." "Are you
the same again," Orwell asks, "if you have walked home stepping over the
bodies of dead children and not even succouring one of them?" The answer
to this rhetorical question is, of course, no. Orwell wants to insist on such
differentiation, or self-loss. "You" are not the same person as you would have
been. Orwell is not Blair. Such self-loss is a generalized condition in Orwell's

view, since this catastrophe in Shanghai, while absolute (as we have seen), is by no means singular. As Orwell writes in "Arthur Koestler" (1944):

> Since about 1930 the world has given no reason for optimism whatever. Nothing is in sight except a welter of lies, hatred, cruelty and ignorance, and beyond our present troubles loom vaster ones which are only now entering into the European consciousness. (16.399)

This "welter of . . . troubles" is linked to the "compunction" that Orwell sees as a governing quality of modern culture. The term comes from an important passage in "Writers and Leviathan" (1948):

> Of course the invasion of literature by politics was bound to happen. It must have happened, even if the special problem of totalitarianism had never arisen, because we have developed a sort of compunction which our grandfathers did not have, an awareness of the enormous injustice and misery of the world. And a guilt-stricken feeling that one ought to be doing something about it, which makes a purely aesthetic attitude towards life impossible. (19.288–289)

Orwell derisively literalizes such compunction in the next, key sentence of the 1949 passage, that disturbing and self-puncturing parenthetical: "(Even to take care not to tread on them is a sort of hypocrisy)." To avoid causing further harm requires a positive alertness. The pedestrian has to mark the homeless body in order to sidestep it. The "care[ful]," deliberate movement shifts seamlessly into defensiveness and avoidance. Orwell, almost untowardly, imagines himself into this very strange moment, of mingled attention and neglect. (Thus notice the unforgiving drive of the passage: as it moves from "no longer notic[ing]" an unsheltered child, to "stepping over" the child, to "tread[ing] upon" the body.)

This awkward, imagined moment—of "tak[ing] care" not to "tread on" an abandoned child—reiterates a structural dissonance at play in Orwell's earliest, already ethically urgent, writing. Following from the absoluteness of this catastrophe, Orwell imagines an intractable form of complicity. The simple act of walking down a street entails stepping over, or on top of, half-formed corpses. Life and death are intermingled here—the mundane life of the pedestrian and the untimely death of the unsheltered refugee. This can remind us, once more, of the way that "A Hanging" (simply *as* early text) conjoins destruction and the creative event of writing itself. In this overlap, the movement of the pedestrian begins to blur with the writer, or with the movement of the writing itself. The pedestrian's complicity, indeed, echoes the universal complicity of the executing party in "A Hanging." As we've seen, the narrator concludes, in a sweeping gesture that encompasses himself: "*We all* had a drink together, native and European, quite amicably. The dead man was a hundred yards away" (10.210, emphasis added). And "A Hanging" also anticipates the 1949 notebook's guilty image of circulation, since the story, as a whole, is structured around the movement of the executing party from the prison to the gallows and back. This system of circulation—closely aligned with writing, and here shaping the fixed contours of the plot (back and forth from the gallows)—is counterpoised to the inassimilable violence of the execution itself.

Earth's Surface

There is a further echo of "A Hanging" in this 1949 passage. Orwell turns quickly to consider how "these children started out with the expectation of being loved & protected" and, from here, to "the conviction which one can see even in a young child that the world is a splendid place." We might remember the plainspoken hinge in "A Hanging": "one mind less, one world less" (10.209). The key term connecting these two passages is simply "world." With Orwell's darting emphasis on the child's perspective upon the world, this passage enacts the same phenomenological movement as "A Hanging." Mind and world are paradoxically dependent on one another. The obliteration of a single "mind" is also the (untold) obliteration of the entire world. And the "world" is just what contains all the "mind[s]" that, one by one, actualize it. The "world" in this account is, necessarily, an embedded series of worlds.

In both texts, then, the "world"—like writing itself for Orwell—is depicted as a tactile, sensuous threshold. This same phenomenological impulse, once we see it, pops up at other key points in Orwell's work, such as these two comments, from "Why I Write" and *Homage to Catalonia*:

So long as I remain alive and well I shall continue to feel strongly about prose style, to love the surface of the earth, and to take a pleasure in solid objects and scraps of useless information. It is no use trying to suppress that side of myself. (18.319–320)

And, as Orwell describes his mind after the bullet wound to his throat:

There must have been two minutes during which I assumed that I was killed. And that too was interesting—I mean it is interesting to know what your thoughts would be at such a time. My first thought, conventionally enough, was for my wife. My second was a violent resentment at having to leave this world which, when all is said and done, suits me so well. I had time to feel this very vividly. (186)

"[W]orld" and "earth," here, form a vibrant boundary. The four key phrases that I want to juxtapose, spanning across the arc of Orwell's career (so to speak), are: "[t]his world which . . . suits me so well" *(Homage),* to "love the surface of the earth" ("Why I Write"), "the conviction . . . that the world is a splendid place" ("1949 Literary Notebook"), and "we were a party of men walking together, seeing, hearing, feeling, understanding the same world" ("A Hanging").[9] Orwell's comment in "Why I Write" is particularly significant in this context, as this striking attachment to "the surface" of the earth is linked so emphatically, if counterintuitively, to "prose style" itself. I hope it is clear that, in my reading, this connection does not confirm Orwell's commitment to the mere "solid[ity]," or apparentness, of either language or world.[10] (This is obviously the ordinary way to understand Orwell's equation of "style," "the surface of the earth," and "solid objects.") On the contrary, turning prose itself *into* a "surface" emphasizes the unsettled perspective on writing that I've been putting forward, in which the propulsive action of writing can never be fully disentangled from (nor adequately conflated with) its ideational essence. Here attention would shift just slightly, for example, from the "pane of *glass*" to the "*pane* of glass" (thus another threshold), though what's crucial, of course, is that these two terms—"pane," "glass"— are almost diabolically indissociable. The point isn't *only* that the window is stubbornly there, distinct from any view that it allows, but also that this view, onto the depth of the world, is inextricably there as well, no matter how hard we try to see just the window itself. And to sum up the wager of this book: Orwell's specifically *democratic* socialist politics is located at this unstable juncture, in that intertwining and separation of "pane" and "glass," or "window" and "view." (After all, Orwell's iconic comment, so notable for its concision, could have been *more* concise still—but how different to write "good prose is like a window" instead of "good prose is like a windowpane.")

The sensuous, the tactile, the vibrant surface: this might seem to suggest a very happy version of Orwell—full of "love," "the conviction that the world is a splendid place," the "shared world," or that world that "suits [him] so well." The network of these phrases is, indeed, revealing and important. But this, of course, doesn't take full account of the pressure that gives rise to this tactile sense—of both writing *and* "world"—in Orwell's work. It is not just that these hopeful images can be brutally and swiftly negated (as is the case with the "shared world" in "A Hanging" or the sense of splendor in the 1949 notebook entry). The larger point, as the tension of "pane" and "glass" suggests, is that such a tactile impulse, in writing, emerges in tandem with an embattled and skeptical sense of writing's own delimited actuality; with Orwell's sense, as I discuss in the Introduction, of politically engaged writing as always potentially more and less of an action than it takes itself to be. Even the simple unfolding of such interconnected passages speaks to this more negative valence, as these signifying chains can work to hold the writing within itself, propelled backward and forward, stretched out in a sequence of connections and displacements, and thus unable to consummate itself as complete or adequate expression. (It is in this way that "A Hanging" functions as a degree zero for *both* the topical substance of Orwell's ongoing work and for the writerly network itself.) We thus need to juxtapose this cluster of passages with the numerous, sometimes overlapping, points in Orwell's writing that configure "the world," above all, in terms of an engulfing—or, again, absolute—ethical catastrophe. Here, as well, we could draw together four passages and scenes that I've already touched on: "the welter of lies, hatred, cruelty and ignorance" that Orwell describes in "Arthur Koestler"; the "enormous injustice and misery of the world" that he invokes in "Writers and Leviathan"; the single execution in "A Hanging" (because of the way this text establishes the "one prisoner" *as* part of a larger group of "the condemned men"); and "the body of a dying child" (remembering, again, the way such deaths "are becoming so common" in this city "full of refugees"). These are each, in different ways, pointed descriptions of a pervasive condition, "enormous" and ubiquitous. This encircling sense sweeps up any scale other than the world—and it is, indeed, a world affair. Orwell's memorable image of the contemporary world as a "welter" of troubles stresses the overwhelming nature of this, not just its sheer quantity. The impact of this unexpected term rests in the way that it simultaneously describes the scale of a problem and the limits of our confused response.

The Road to Wigan Pier—my focus in the next chapter—is squarely anchored within this constellation, another key act of writing that seeks to confront enormous "injustice and misery." Consider how the memorable conclusion of *Homage to Catalonia* that I discussed in Chapter 1, which tracks Orwell's movement back from Spain into England, inflects his earlier text into just one sentence within its catalogue description: "The industrial towns were far away, a smudge of smoke and misery hidden by the curve of the earth's surface" (231). This single sentence could also be—and indeed *was*—an entire book: i.e., Orwell's previous book. And this "smudge of smoke" hidden by the curve of the world is also a world itself, a "welter" of "misery and enormous injustice," what Orwell calls at the end of Chapter 1 in *Wigan Pier* "the filthy heart of civilization" (20).

There is an unstable, double inversion here: from book to sentence and from "world" to "smudge." If, in "Why I Write," the "surface of the earth" is aligned with "prose style" and "solid objects," here the "earth's surface" is much more negatively conceived, serving not as an emblem of tactile directness but as that which underlies the "far away," structuring distance, neglect and loss. At the same time, as I'm suggesting, this hard necessity is intertwined with writing's own inexorability. Compositional movement, from one text to another, drives the startling perspectivism here, in which the topical ambit of *Wigan Pier* shrinks from serving as the form-giving circumference of one book to a subordinated phrase within the next book. "A man who would write the same book twice could not even write it once."

Taking Aim

Landscape descriptions abound in *The Road to Wigan Pier*, and yet there is a strong sense throughout this text that the topic of *Wigan Pier*, its focus or what it is "about," is not defined by any geographical or loco-descriptive terms. We'd be hard pressed, in many ways, to find a more topical book than *The Road to Wigan Pier.* And at the same time, the book holds onto that self-conscious sense *of* topicality, of its "about-ness," that I discussed in the Introduction. As with *Homage to Catalonia,* there is a lot of attention in *Wigan Pier* to *aiming at* a target—and in this attention, a way that the target itself is not quite hit. Indeed, I want to approach this topical drive, in *The Road to Wigan Pier,* by first considering the sequence of misfires, inaccurate targets, and accidental wounds in *Homage to Catalonia* (particularly in the beginning of this text). Some examples (all emphases added):

1. The bomb burst over to the right, outside the parapet; fright had spoiled my aim. (90)

2. Benjamin grabbed the nearest man's rifle, took aim, and pulled the trigger. Click! A dud cartridge; I thought it a bad omen. (21)

3. There were also a few Winchester rifles. These were nice to shoot with, but they were wildly inaccurate. . . . (34)

4. According to my ideas of trench warfare the Fascists would be fifty or a hundred yards away. I could see nothing—seemingly their trenches were very well concealed. Then with a shock of dismay I saw where Benjamin was pointing; on the opposite hill-top, beyond the ravine, seven hundred metres away at the very least, the tiny outline of a parapet and a red-and-yellow flag—the Fascist position. . . . We were nowhere near them! At that range our rifles were completely useless. (21)

5. The difficult passwords which the army was using at this time were a minor source of danger. They were those tiresome double passwords in which one word has to be answered by another. Usually they were of an elevating and revolutionary nature, such as *Cultura-progreso,* or *Seremos-invencibles,* and it was often impossible to get illiterate sentries to remember these highfalutin words. One night, I remember, the password was *Cataluna-heroica,* and a moon-faced peasant lad named Jaime Domenech approached me, greatly puzzled, and asked me to explain.

"Heroica—what does heroica mean?"

I told him that it meant the same as valiente. A little while later he was stumbling up the trench in the darkness, and the sentry challenged him:

"Alto! Cataluna!"

"Valiente!" yelled Jaime, <u>certain that he was saying the right thing</u>

Bang!

However <u>the sentry missed him.</u> In this war everyone always did miss everyone else, when it was humanly possible. (36–37)

6. I was very anxious to learn how to use a machine-gun; it was a weapon I had never had a chance to handle. <u>To my dismay I found that we were taught nothing about the use of weapons.</u> The so-called instruction was simply parade-ground drill of the most antiquated, stupid kind. . . . <u>At the time I did not grasp</u> that this was because there were no weapons to be had. (9–10)

7. A little while later, however, a bullet <u>shot past my ear</u> with a vicious crack and banged into the parados behind. Alas! <u>I ducked. All my life I had sworn that I would not duck the first time a bullet passed over me;</u> but the movement appears to be instinctive. . . . (22)

8. [O]ne of the children of our company rushed back from the parapet with his face pouring blood. He had fired his rifle and had somehow managed to blow out the bolt; his scalp was torn to ribbons by the splinters of the burst cartridge-case. It was our first casualty, and, characteristically, <u>self-inflicted.</u> (20)

9. I could see the Fascists, tiny as ants, dodging to and fro behind their parapet, and sometimes a black dot which was a head would pause for a moment, impudently exposed. <u>It was obviously no use firing.</u> . . . I tried to explain that <u>at that range and with these rifles you could not hit a man except by accident.</u> But he was only a child, and he kept motioning with his rifle towards one of the dots. . . . Finally I put my sights up to seven hundred and let fly. The dot disappeared. I hope it went near enough to make him jump. It was the first time in my life that I had fired a gun at a human being. (21)

10. And all day and night <u>the meaningless bullets wandering across the empty valleys</u> and only by some rare improbable chance getting home on a human body. (24)

11. Once, rather later than this, I was photographing some machine-gunners with their gun, which was pointed directly towards me.
"Don't fire," I said half-jokingly, as <u>I focused the camera.</u>
"Oh, no, we won't fire."
The next moment there was a frightful roar and a stream of bullets tore past my face so close that my cheek was stung by grains of cordite. <u>It was unintentional,</u> but the machine-gunners considered it a great joke. Yet only a few days earlier they had seen a mule-driver <u>accidentally shot</u> by a political delegate who was playing the fool with an automatic pistol and had put five bullets in the mule-driver's lungs. (36)

12. I managed to take a rather <u>blurry photograph</u> which was stolen from me later. (17)

And, finally, this linked group of three passages:

13. <u>The thing I was after</u> was the machine-gun. . . . I flashed my torch inside the machine-gun nest. <u>A bitter disappointment! The gun was not there.</u> Its tripod was there, and various boxes of ammunition and spare parts, but the gun was gone. (93)

14. We flashed the torch through the window and instantly raised a cheer. A cylindrical object in a leather case, four feet high and six inches in diameter, was leaning against the wall. <u>Obviously the machine-gun barrel.</u> We dashed round and got in at the doorway, to find that the thing in the leather case was <u>not a machine-gun</u> but something which, in our weapon-starved army, was even more precious. <u>It was an enormous telescope,</u> probably of at least sixty or seventy magnifications, with a folding tripod. Such telescopes simply did not exist on our side of the line and they were desperately needed. (94)

15. <u>It was a great pity about the telescope.</u> The thought of losing that beautiful bit of loot worries me even now. (100)

Again, my rationale for listing this network of passages from *Homage to Catalonia* rests in the relationship between these activities, in the referenced world of the text—centered on various ways of *taking aim* at, and often missing, a target—and the topical drive of Orwell's writing, in and of itself. Writing "takes aim" as well. And, most particularly, *The Road to Wigan Pier* (Orwell's immediately proximate text) takes aim, at the "enormous misery and injustice" of the industrial north in England during the Slump.

The emphasis on taking aim is also one way to disrupt aim: a text's consciousness of itself, as topical, is one way in which its topical orientation can be partially deflected. This is a cumulative implication of this sequence from *Homage to Catalonia*. But these passages in *Homage to Catalonia* don't just deflate the process—of aiming and firing—as a series of errors. They also, conversely, draw our attention *to* this process, foregrounding it as an object of textual representation and holding the reader's focus on it. Taking aim is—paradigmatically—a means to an end. But in this network of passages, the means becomes an end in and of itself. This is precisely the aesthetic accomplishment of these passages.[11]

You have to miss a fair amount for this to be the case—otherwise, the firing of the gun would simply be absorbed into its instrumental purpose, into the target that it successfully reaches, or the enemy it successfully destroys. With this separation of aim and target, the figure of a gun and the figure of a window (so crucial in Orwell's work) are drawn strangely close to each other. Notice how the camera stands in for the gun in some of these passages (most evidently passage 11). A camera is half gun—pointed, and aimed at an object—and half window. If a weapon can be "wildly inaccurate" or, say, "burst over to the right," the photograph that Orwell takes is "rather blurry," and in the key passage, Orwell's effort to "[focus] the camera," is juxtaposed with the machine gun "pointed directly toward me." Camera and gun each "point" at the other here, radicalizing their equivalency; and the sudden, inadvertent discharge of the machine gun seems to occur simultaneously with, and even to act as a stand-in for, the snap of the photograph. ("Click!" as Orwell says in passage 2). Taking a photo, like firing a gun, is a matter of (imperfect) aim. The blurred photo that Orwell "manage[s] to take" in passage 12 is stolen and later Orwell notes, when he is briefly in a frontline hospital (or "casualty clearing station") that the "hospital assistants stole practically every valuable object I possessed, including my camera and all my photographs" (77). (Photographs can thus be blurred or lost—two different kinds of "failure.") In a similar way, the last three passages displace gun with telescope, once more veering closer, in this substitution, toward the mechanics of representation itself. The telescope is abandoned as well; the loss "worries [Orwell] even now" (i.e., as he writes).

There are two final points I'd like to note about this sequence of passages. First, it should be clear how misfiring, or *missing* a target, is intertwined with hitting an object unintentionally. On a more general level, we might say, deflation is intertwined with—not merely juxtaposed against—shock. The bullet that flies past Orwell ("with a vicious crack") is too frightening for him *not* to duck (or, in other words, for him to recognize how far away it really is). If one rifle has a "dud cartridge," another one blows up in the soldier's hands (so that he "rush[es] back" with "his face pouring blood"). While "meaningless bullets wander" across the divide between Republican and Fascist troops in passage 10, the gun that is "accidentally shot" in passage 11 "had put five bullets in the mule-driver's lungs." The mishandled machine guns, as we've seen, graze Orwell's cheek with cordite.[12] In passage 5, Orwell sets up an elaborate double negation (thus building, as well, on the face-off between camera and gun): the soldiers should never have fired at Jaime Domenech, but if they *had* to fire, they should never have missed. "Bang!" Though harrowing, such compounded error (simultaneously a gun that didn't need to be fired and a target that couldn't be hit) results in uneasy equilibrium, as though the password had just been successfully communicated.[13] But the effect of this mutual cancellation, once more, is not merely to diminish but also to suspend, and thus foreground, both mistakes, dissociating error from its absorption into consequence.

The doubled inversion here is one more sign that Orwell is up to something more than just factual reporting. This sequence of mistakes and disappointments with pistols, rifles, and grenades is, of course, fundamentally ironic. Irony is the device ("the means") through which these events are narrated. Simultaneously, these represented events work to give palpable substance to the text's own ironic structure. (They are a representation of irony itself.) The final point I want to note is how assiduously Orwell draws himself, or more precisely his writing, into this process. He layers his own mistakes—of perception, cognition, judgment—into the sequence of external mistakes that the narrative records. (Again, and crucially, the act of misfiring is a general one; it takes place on multiple levels of the text.) We can see this, for example, in the flashes of directly conveyed but erroneous thought in several passages, as when Orwell describes his false inference in passage 4, "seemingly their trenches were well-concealed" (in fact, he is looking for these trenches in the wrong place), or his overly hasty projection in this clipped, emphatic sentence from passage 14: "Obviously the machine-gun barrel" (in fact, he is looking at the telescope, not the machine gun). In both cases, these snippets of prose carry us from indirect description to a more immediate enactment of Orwell's thoughts. The language starts to mime Orwell's thinking (as it was occurring at the time of the recollected past, rather than as it occurs in the present of the narration itself). But this intensified transparency seems directly connected to the ironic puncturing—a neat illustration of the plain style's double-valence in Orwell, threading between immediacy and displacement. Likewise, after noting his dismay in passage 6—"I found that we were taught nothing about the use of weapons"—Orwell deflates his own ironic indignation, adding, "At the time I did not grasp that this was because there were no weapons to be had." Crucially, this correction doesn't erase the dismay, or, in other words, mute the primary irony. This description of the soldiers' "so-called instruction" is still a part of that network of passages revolving around how guns are mishandled, targets missed, aim is off, etc. But it does demonstrate how this irony is continually internalized: irony pivots, rather relentlessly, from these inaccurate guns to Orwell's own inaccuracies—and in, further, toward the writing itself. It is on this note of irony, and its potential relationship to political commitment, that I want to turn now to my reading of *Wigan Pier*.

2

"Getting to Work"
(The Road to Wigan Pier)

Irony and Socialism

Irony and socialism. The two terms are meant to suggest a disjunction that structures much of twentieth-century radical culture. While the pressure of Stalinism threatens to make socialism a commitment that blunts skeptical and critical consciousness, the ironic sensibility of high modernism too often disables action and solidarity. Much of Orwell's work takes place within the structure and terms of this choice. His writing can be interpreted as an ongoing effort to engage—rather than to either transcend or acquiesce to—this profound cultural tension. In this chapter, I want to trace how the conceptual framework of Orwell's democratic socialism helps motivate a specific articulation of literary irony. Raymond Williams, discussing *Homage to Catalonia*, aptly summarizes Orwell's double politics as "bitter hostility at once to the capitalist order and to orthodox communism" (60). This negotiation between two failed extremes fits Michael Denning's modeling, in a different context, of the cultural field emerging out of the American Popular Front. Denning writes: "The heart of the Popular Front as a social movement lay among those who were non-Communist socialists and independent leftists, working with Communists and liberals, but marking out a culture that was neither a Party nor a liberal New Deal culture" (5). This is a fine description, but we should note its unstable, paradoxical quality. The "heart" of socialist politics in this period is not fixed and cannot be precisely located; it exists only as the double negation of two more stable poles. Such an indeterminate position between political extremes—the troubled location of democratic socialism—can motivate a literary doubleness as well. Orwell—like other authors of the democratic left—resists two extremes that shape the theoretical categories of literature in the 1930s and '40s: high modernism or socialist realism; hyper-formalism or ideological reduction; writing as purely language or as pure propaganda. Such double opposition demands a fluidity of thought, a capacity for critical self-negation that resembles—but also transvalues—the kind of ironic cognition more typically associated with New Criticism and deconstruction.

I'm thinking in particular of that wide, powerful tradition of twentieth-century literary theory that configures modern irony as distinctly negative or unstable. M. H. Abrams summarizes this perspective: "unstable irony . . . offers no fixed standpoint which is not undercut by further ironies. At an extreme . . . there is an endless regress of ironic understandings; such works suggest a negation of any secure evaluative standpoint" (92). This kind of ironic "undercut[ting]," "negation," or "regress," so central to twentieth-century literary aesthetics and theory, can easily frustrate or corrode polit-ical engagement. As Franco Moretti polemically avers, "[t]here is a complicity between modernist irony and indifference to history" (247). Moretti, echoing any number of key critics of modernism, goes on to define modernist irony as a shift of attention away from "what happens, the logic of events and deci-sions" toward "our unmotivated . . . subjective reactions" to events.

The gap between an event and the consciousness of an event—between observed reality and the subjective observer—also underlies Paul de Man's influential essay "The Rhetoric of Temporality," which equates the negativity of Romantic and post-Romantic irony with literariness in general. This essay works as both a sweeping formulation of, and a terminal point for, New Criticism's theory of negative irony. For de Man, irony's disjoining of actual and literal meaning exemplifies the way that *all* modern literary language differentiates itself from simple communicative language:

> The relationship between sign and meaning is discontinuous . . . the sign points to something that differs from its literal meaning and has for its function the thematization of this difference. . . . The ironic, twofold self that the writer or philosopher constitutes by his language seems able to come into being only at the expense of his empirical

self. . . . [I]ronic language splits the subject into an empirical self that exists in a state of inauthenticity and a self that exists only in the form of a language that asserts the knowledge of this inauthenticity. (214)

I would call attention particularly to de Man's phrase "at the expense of." The "writer[ly]" self comes into being "at the expense of [the] empirical self." Here we have that gulf between irony and social engagement, which we could schematize through a series of unpleasant and yet familiar choices: self-righteousness *or* cynicism; naïveté or insincerity; commitment or awareness; in M. H. Abrams's terms, a "fixed standpoint" or an "endless regress."

The most obvious way that we might approach Orwell's politically engaged irony, and distinguish it from this tradition, is to take it as predominantly instrumental: a means of expression rather than a mode of cognition. This is the perspective that Wayne Booth puts forward in *The Rhetoric of Irony*. Rejecting the primacy of unstable or negative irony, Booth deliberately spends most of his attention on what he considers the undervalued "positive" kind of irony: where one statement is undercut in order to make another, specific claim. Booth argues that you *can* use irony from within a particular "standpoint," and that an ironic statement usually has a fixed, referential ground. This is a rhetorical perspective that would seem particularly relevant to irony within political or polemical discourse. But Orwell, in fact, is often quite a negative ironist. He does not use irony simply as a stylistic tool, employed within a rhetorical arsenal, in order to make effective political points. Rather, negative irony is central to Orwell's political cognition. Orwell *thinks* ironically, even as he thinks politically. In this chapter, I want to consider how the negative irony stressed by critics like Abrams and de Man, revolving around the division between stable, empirically grounded observations and an authentic writing self, is suggestively resonant with the irony that saturates *The Road to Wigan Pier,* a text of decidedly political engagement.

The Road to Wigan Pier was distributed by the Left Book Club, an ambitious organization in England co-founded by Orwell's publisher Victor Gollancz. Samuel Hynes describes the Left Book Club as Gollancz's "experiment in political education":

His plan was to issue to his members each month selected political books on current subjects, at prices that could be kept low because the market would be predictable. . . . In its best years . . . in the last three years of the 'thirties, the Club flourished and grew far beyond anyone's expectations. . . . [I]n the autumn of 1937 it reached more than fifty thousand members, a level which it maintained until the end of the decade. . . . For its members the LBC was clearly a haven, a collective something for the depressed and scattered Left to belong to. (208–211)

At that time, Orwell was best known for his early account of poverty in England and France, *Down and Out in Paris and London,* which was published by Gollancz in 1933. Orwell moved to northern England for about two months in early 1936, and his collected essays include an extensive journal from this period that provides much of the raw material, as it were, for *The Road to Wigan Pier.* The book was published, as we've seen, soon after Orwell left for Spain, where he joined the POUM militia and was eventually shot in the throat. He returned to England and wrote *Homage to Catalonia,* his other 1930s masterpiece and a text that builds on many of the stylistic achievements of *The Road to Wigan Pier.*

Both *The Road to Wigan Pier* and *Homage to Catalonia* put pressure on the documentary form by calling attention to the presence of the inscribed observer. Raymond Williams has limned this crucial aspect of the 1930s texts, arguing:

The unity of Orwell's documentary and imaginative writing is the very first thing to notice. . . . [W]hat is created in the book is an isolated independent observer and the objects of his observation. . . . All of Orwell's writing until 1937 is, then, a series of works and experiments around a common problem. Instead of dividing them into "fiction" and "documentaries" we should see them as sketches toward the creation of his most successful character, "Orwell." (60)

This tension between the "isolated . . . observer" and the "objects of his observation" is especially acute in *The Road to Wigan Pier.* Orwell foregrounds the fallibility of his empirical observations of working-class life, as the text hovers between describing the social conditions that Orwell sees and describing how to see (and how easy it is to miss seeing) social conditions. The position from which Orwell observes events is continually integrated into, and ironically disrupts, the observations themselves. Thus the book opens with a little ironic jab, set off as a paragraph, which highlights the gap between the experience of the working class and the observations of the middle-class writer: "The first sound in the mornings was the clumping of the mill-girls' clogs down the cobbled street. Earlier than that, I suppose, there were factory whistles which I was never awake to hear" (5). Orwell is still sleeping when the factory whistles start; he is woken by the actions he is supposed to witness and describe.

The Road to Wigan Pier's insistently ironic tone often does point to this kind of gap; a range of effects are generated by the ways in which Orwell misses the full experience of the working class. If this tension between observer and experience informs the opening paragraph—like a kind of warning at the entryway of the essay—it is most notably reflected in the structure of the work as a whole, which gets divided into two parts when Orwell changes topics, swerving away from the workers in northern England to write about how the class divide poses problems for Socialist intellectuals. This shift—which is, indisputably, the most striking and essential feature of the book—calls attention to the increasing weight of Orwell's self-consciousness as an observer: empirically grounded observation gives way to self-reflection, to Orwell's much more introspective focus on his own "subjective reactions." As Orwell writes:

> In the earlier chapters of this book I have given a rather fragmentary account of various things I saw in the coal areas of Lancashire and Yorkshire. . . . Here I shall have to digress and explain how my own attitude towards the class question was developed. Obviously this involves writing a certain amount of autobiography. . . . (121)

This need to pull back into himself seems to confirm—and lend a structural ballast to—the negative weight of Orwell's ironic consciousness. The writer despairs of giving more than a "fragmentary account" of what he observes around him, as a fully coherent picture is disrupted by his autobiographical reflection—an almost unwelcome "digress[ion]" that now becomes the orienting interest of the text.

Yet the essay is Orwell's first and most explicit engagement with socialism, and the most direct statement about socialism's importance for the book occurs at this point, in the seam of the essay's major division. Orwell inscribes the *raison d'être* of the essay within this ironic turning point, as he shifts from "the coal areas of Lancashire and Yorkshire" to autobiography. The passage in full reads:

> In the earlier chapters of this book I have given a rather fragmentary account of various things I saw in the coal areas of Lancashire and Yorkshire. I went there partly because I wanted to see what mass-unemployment is like at its worst, partly in order to see the most typical section of the English working class at close quarters. This was necessary to me as part of my approach to Socialism. For before you can be sure whether you are genuinely in favor of Socialism, you have got to decide whether things at present are tolerable or not tolerable, and you have to take up a definite attitude on the terribly difficult issue of class. Here I shall have to digress. . . . (121)

The text redescribes itself as part of an "approach to Socialism" just as it is veering away from the empirical description of social life. In this way, the structural irony of the essay—Orwell's shift from social observations to a focus on the position of the observer—is implicated in the essay's explicit turn toward socialism. (The term "Socialism," repeated 112 times in Part Two of *Wigan Pier,* does not occur in Part One.) By conflating what could be two quite separate moments of his book—its ironic pivot and this announcement of topicality—Orwell suggests that the text's identity, as an engagement with socialism, is formed in the disjunction of its two parts. It is as though this fissure were, indeed, part of the very "approach" that is described.

"Impossible to See"

In the rest of this chapter, I want to consider how *The Road to Wigan Pier* develops this relationship between "approach[ing] . . . Socialism" and negative irony, understood, most essentially, as the estrangement of the writing self from the events that are written. The most common way to read the political significance of Orwell's swerve toward introspection in Part Two is as part of his insistence, as a now self-identified socialist, that the Left must be highly self-critical. Orwell's critique of his own vestigial class consciousness gets developed into a polemic against the middle-class biases of Socialism in England, so that, as Orwell writes later in the essay, "in order to defend Socialism it is necessary to start by attacking it" (172). Alex Zwerdling has traced how this strand of "internal criticism" structures much of Orwell's writing and politics, and takes on particular intensity in the second part of *Wigan Pier*:

> His critique of socialism could be savage, particularly in *The Road to Wigan Pier*, which Richard Rovere has called "perhaps the most rigorous examination that any doctrine has ever received at the hands of an adherent." Yet this criticism was always designed as internal; it was precisely Orwell's unquestioning fidelity to the ideals of the movement that, in his mind, justified his uncompromising criticism of some its theories, tactics, and leaders. (5)

In this sense it is fitting that *Wigan Pier* would define itself as an "approach to Socialism" only at its ironic hinge, since Orwell's self-reflectiveness—more generally—helps constitute a space for internal criticism that he understands as vital to the democratic left.

The divided nature of *Wigan Pier* is certainly its most important structural feature, and it can be viewed, in this light, as enabling a discrete epistemological process.[1] The autobiographical turn enacts a puncturing—a moment of quite explicit, and critical, self-reflection—that Orwell views as necessary to socialism. There is always a risk, however, that this process will be abruptly halted, if the ironic tension between the two sections becomes so strong that we no longer hold the essay together as a coherent structure. Certainly we can see this instability in the essay's reception, as it gets unraveled back into two constitutive parts: the "socialist" Part One (straightforward documentary) and the "critical" Part Two (ironic and introspective). Such a divided reception of the book is, in one important sense, actually built *into* the book, through the fascinating foreword that Victor Gollancz, stung by Orwell's polemical attack, added to the Left Book Club edition.

This foreword parses the book's two parts: while the opening section "is a terrible record of evil conditions" (11) that "lays bare" (xxii) the "vileness" (xxii) of industrial exploitation, the second section causes Gollancz to mark "well over a hundred minor passages about which [he] thought [he] should like to argue with Mr. Orwell in this Foreword" (xii). This kind of separation is also evident in reviews that are more favorable toward the second part, such as the 1958 discussion in *The Nation:* "Having written this much to fulfill his obligation to Gollancz and Co., Orwell started right over again on a companion tract to fulfill an obligation to himself. The second half of the manuscript he turned in to the Left Book Club is a sweeping attack on professional Socialism and theoretical socialism" (Hatch, 114).

Orwell certainly separates the two parts of his text, but this separation, I have suggested, elaborates—on a structural level—an ironic perspective that informs the text as a whole. We should be wary of too rigidly distinguishing the "internal criticism" that drives Part Two of *Wigan Pier* from the more straightforward documentary in Part One. Besides diminishing the ironic complexity in Part One, this kind of analysis can risk a political misreading, if it too quickly separates empirical engagement from critique.[2] The "internal criticism" that emerges in Part Two is actually necessary to the documentary recording of social ills in Part One—just as, we might argue more generally, Orwell's irony is an intrinsic part of his socialist commitment. Returning to the documentary half of *The Road to Wigan Pier,* I want to suggest other ways that negative irony—with its problematic fracturing of reference—is drawn into relation with socialism (beyond Zwerdling's important point about internal critique). First, *Wigan Pier* historicizes this kind of epistemological and linguistic tension. Second, and this will explain the title of this chapter, the text shows how intensification *of* the dissonance between experience and observation can actually facilitate an original, and specific, kind of engagement with labor's alienation.

The motivation for Orwell's turn toward the self in Part Two centers on the "terribly difficult issue of class." Class difference ties together the two sections of *Wigan Pier* and produces the disjunctive movement from Part One to Part Two.[3] More specifically, Orwell insists that a tension between language and referent (an irony culminating—as I've been suggesting—in the text's own divided form) is itself a product of the class structure. He does not claim that words are inevitably nonreferential but, more specifically, that middle-class words cannot accurately represent working-class reality. As one memorable passage describes:

> Watching coal miners at work, you realize momentarily what different universes different people inhabit. Down there where coal is dug it is a sort of world apart which one can quite easily go through life without ever hearing about. Probably a majority of people would even prefer not to hear about it. Yet it is the absolutely necessary counterpart of our world above. (33)

This social gap extends to Orwell's representation of language itself, as the book's most explicit criticism of its own inability to linguistically represent reality is couched in specifically material terms:

> But mere notes like these are only valuable as reminders to myself. To me as I read them they bring back what I have seen, but they cannot in themselves give much idea of what conditions are like in those fearful northern slums. Words are such feeble things. What is the use of a brief phrase like "roof leaks" or "four beds for eight people"? It is the kind of thing your eye slides over, registering nothing. And yet what a wealth of misery it can cover. (57)

This passage is typical of the continuing reflections on language that, as many critics have noted, form a central part of Orwell's writing (most famously realized in "Politics and the English Language" and the extended representation of "Newspeak" in *1984*). The relation between these "feeble" words and the misery that they "cover"—or both hide *and* abstractly comprehend—is a linguistic equivalent to that relation between the extracted coal that is necessary to the English economy (to "the world above"), and the labor that is hidden "down there"—literally underneath the ground, but, more pervasively, obscured *beneath* its own furious production. Orwell actually takes this analogy further, as he elaborates the specific social facts that these words—otherwise chosen in a seemingly casual way—"cover":

> Take the question of overcrowding, for instance. Quite often you have eight or even ten people living in a three-roomed house. One of these

rooms is a living-room, and as it probably measures about a dozen feet square and contains, besides the kitchen range and the sink, a table, some chairs and a dresser there is no room in it for a bed. So there are eight or ten people sleeping in two small rooms, probably in at most four beds.

The "three-roomed" house cannot accommodate the human beings it is meant to contain, just as Orwell's own phrase does not fully encompass (or, again, "cover") the experience that it refers to. In both cases, the actual human beings are crowded into a structure—the "small rooms," the "brief phrase"—that is inadequate.

This perspective on the insufficiency of his words provides a sociological context for the tension between language and reference that *The Road to Wigan Pier* more continually both generates and foregrounds. If Orwell's text, in many ways, cannot adequately represent working-class experience, its failure to do so also illustrates divisions that underlie working-class life in the first place. A stubborn, entrenched social gap—between the (fraught) production and the (pervasive) use of coal—stands behind and, in this sense, conditions *Wigan Pier's* incomplete linguistic representations, grounding an irony that could otherwise be taken as absolute or intrinsic to language as such.

But Orwell's essay does not just situate the ironic division between observation and self—which would seem to estrange "mind" from "world"—within a concrete social context. The ironic sensibility that "fragment[s]" Orwell's descent into the coal mines also allows him to see things in new ways. We have seen how Orwell highlights, in that oversleeping that ironically begins the book, the distance between his consciousness and the objects of his perception. This gap between his own middle-class observation and working-class life increases as he approaches the actual location of work, reaching a climax in Chapters 2 and 3 (the only chapters actually set in the mines). Descriptions of the mines build on the tension between observation and obscurity that is itself rooted in class difference. Thus Orwell writes, "The time to go there is when the machines are roaring and the air is black with coal dust, and when you can actually see what the miners have to do" (21). Tellingly, he can only "see" the actual work of coal mining when his vision will be essentially blocked because the "air is black with coal dust."

Orwell twice repeats this gesture of making the working conditions that he sets out to describe come in the way of the description itself:

> Nowadays, the preliminary work is done by an electrically-driven coal-cutter, which in principle is an immensely tough and powerful band-saw. . . . [I]t makes one of the most awful noises I have ever heard, and sends forth clouds of coal dust which make it impossible to see more than two or three feet and almost impossible to breathe. (30)

> The first impression of all, overmastering everything else for a while, is the frightful, deafening din from the conveyor belt which carries the coal away. You cannot see very far, because the fog of coal dust throws back the beam of your lamp, but you can see on either side of you the line of half-naked kneeling men, one to every four or five yards, driving their shovels under the fallen coal and flinging it swiftly over their left shoulder. (22)

Here the very work that the writer attempts to observe gets in the way of these observations. Orwell can "actually see what the miners have to do" at the same time that he "cannot see very far" and looks through "clouds of coal dust which make it impossible to see." Putting himself in the position of observation ironically distorts what he is seeing: "Probably you have to go down several coal-mines before you can get much grasp of the processes that are going on round you. This is chiefly because the mere effort of getting from place to place makes it difficult to notice anything else" (24). Orwell then seems stuck "getting from place to place"—approaching the miners' work, without ever being able to arrive at the observations he is after. (The beam of light is "thrown back" on itself, in the face of this situation, just as the observing self, writ large, is thrown back upon its own reflective consciousness in the autobiographical turn of Part Two.)

We might compare this to a paradigmatically ironic episode that Geoffrey Hartman identifies in Book 6 of *The Prelude*, which narrates Wordsworth's ascent and crossing of the Alps. (I'm choosing this example because it is so central to the definition of negative Romantic irony that I discussed above. The crossing of Simplon Pass is a crux of Hartman's extensive book, even as Hartman's study was a cornerstone of early deconstruction, in its most sophisticated and literary manifestation.) Attempting to reach the mountain's summit, the apex of nature, the poet realizes that he has passed the summit only after he is already descending; and the force of this shock reveals the independence of the poetic imagination from nature. As Hartman describes this scene: "[The poet's] mind, desperately and unself-knowingly in search of a nature adequate to deep childhood impressions, finds instead itself, and has to acknowledge that nature is no longer its proper subject or home" (39). (Note how the tone of this self-reflective movement—the mind finding itself "instead" of the nature it seeks—echoes de Man's depiction of self-consciousness arising "at the expense of" empirical grounding.) We can see something important by superimposing this scene of crossing—and the epistemological structure it yields—over Orwell's strenuous movement in the mines. We might read Orwell's "descent" into this underground space through Wordsworth's failed mountainous ascent and use the dialectic between nature and imagination as a framework through which to understand the dialectic between work and observation so central to 1930s literary culture. And Orwell's turn toward his own observing self in Part Two of *The Road to Wigan Pier*—a turn whose motivation I am locating *in* the difficult trip to the coal face in Part One—is akin to this literal turning point in *The Prelude*. As Hartman writes, "The poet is forced to discover the autonomy of his imagination, its independence from present joy, from strong outward stimuli . . . this discovery . . . means a passing of the initiative from nature to imagination" (41).

In Hartman's reading of the Simplon Pass episode, crucially, Wordsworth is led back *into* nature through the unfortunate way that he misses nature; the shattered relationship between "nature" and the "imagination" that is evidenced by the shocking elision of the mountain summit finally comes to produce a growth in the imaginative faculties, which, in turn, will expand the poet's comprehension of nature itself. Now the independent mind of the poet *converges* upon nature, as "a stream/That flowed into a kindred stream" (60, Hartman quoting *The Prelude* 6.743–744), rather than projecting a more absolute, symbolic unity with nature. In a similar way, Orwell registers something crucial about exploitation from within the disjunctions that occur as he attempts to approach the experience of the miners. Unsuccessfully trying to "get to work"—and thus to bridge the epistemological gap between the middle and working class—Orwell does "see," and what he sees, ironically, is how difficult it is for *miners* to travel to work. In a crucial artistic decision, Orwell deliberately spends more time in Chapter 2 discussing the commute, the process of "*getting* to work," than the actual work of mining itself. The five-page passage that focuses on this commute begins:

> What *is* surprising, on the other hand, is the immense horizontal distances that have to be traveled underground. Before I had been down a mine I had vaguely imagined the miner stepping out of the cage and getting to work on a ledge of coal a few yards away. I had not realized that before he even gets to his work he may have to creep through passages as long as from London Bridge to Oxford Circus. (25)

After a memorable five-page description of traveling through these tunnels, Orwell concludes (in a passage I've already touched on in the Introduction):

> But what I want to emphasize is this. Here is this frightful business of crawling to and fro, which to any normal person is a hard day's work in itself; and it is not part of the miner's work at all, it is merely an extra, like the City man's daily ride in the Tube. The miner does that journey to and fro, and sandwiched in between there are seven and a half hours of savage work. I have never traveled much more than a mile to the coal face; but often it is three miles, in which case I and most people other than coal-miners would never get there at all. *This is the kind of point that one is always liable to miss.* When you think of a coal-mine you think of depth, heat, darkness, blackened figures hacking at walls of coal; you don't think, necessarily, of those miles of creeping to and fro. (29, emphasis added)

In that key generalization—"this is the kind of point that one is always liable to miss"—Orwell suggests that even while (and effectively because) he was unable to directly see the work he was trying to approach, he has grasped a crucial point about work, that people have been always liable to miss. Namely: that the full meaning of work—from the perspective and experience of the laborer—will exceed its social definition. Here we can see the theoretical significance of Orwell's "fragmentary account." Attention to the difficult commute provides a brilliant image for a much more general process: the inevitable disjunction between a worker's experience of labor and the abstract definition of this labor under capitalism. The experience *of* work cannot be contained within the (wage) definition of this work by capital.

Exploitation is, in this terrible but simple sense, "ironic." The most basic linguistic definition of irony is when literal or stated meaning contrasts with actual meaning. In capitalism, analogously, the only "literal" meaning of work (namely: the monetary definition of this labor through a wage) contrasts with the actual meaning of work (i.e., the full experience of this labor from the point of view of the worker). Capitalism can systematically produce this gap—which is why it is a point "one is always liable to miss."

The achievement of *The Road to Wigan Pier* lies in its startling conflation of two kinds of ironic gaps: the gap between middle-class writing and working-class life and the gap between the alienated experience of the laborer and capital's definition of this labor. In one necessary sense, as we've seen, these are opposed to each other. But both kinds of irony converge around the same situation: *getting to work*. The writer's difficulty in "getting to work"—or of representing the working class—converges upon (but is not equated with) the miner's efforts to get to work, understood as one of the many aspects of labor that are rendered invisible by capitalism. The essay thus travels from experience that can be only partially recorded—we remember how Orwell calls Part One of the essay a "*fragmentary* account"— to a general, conceptual model: "the kind of point one is *always* liable to miss" (emphases added). At the place of fissure between observer and work, Orwell reaches a social insight, transforming a negation into a possibility.

If these extended tunnels provide a point of intersection between Orwell's ironic account of his own problems in representation and the experience of the miners, they also stand in for a governing concern of writing in the 1930s.[4] After all, "getting to work" is one colloquial way to describe and encapsulate the central project for so much political narrative in this period (and after): from socialist realism, with its accounts of factory and agricultural life to the debates over proletarian literature (which Orwell addresses directly in Part Two of *The Road to Wigan Pier* and in numerous other texts). The long tunnels that Orwell calls attention to in *Wigan Pier* are, in this crucial sense, at once figurative and literal: reiterating the social distance between middle-class words and working-class experience but also grounded in the actual commute of the workers themselves. The commute is a particularly rich figure to structure the text's own epistemology because it is located so clearly in the realm of everyday, working-class life. The commute functions in the essay, then, as both symbol and material ground: as a mark of the imposing distance between actual labor and its written representation and as the all-too-real distance built into the experience of labor itself. It is only at this particular juncture that irony and solidarity converge: in the underground mine tunnels that, in fact, form a "road" beneath the road that stands above ground and appears in the text's own title. (Orwell pushes the juxtaposition in at least one striking passage: "You could quite easily drive a car right across the north of England and never once remember that hundreds of feet below the road you are on the miners are hacking at the coal. Yet in a sense it is the miners who are driving your car forward" [34].)

The intricacy of this episode in *The Road to Wigan Pier* makes it one of the great literary representations of "the commute" (a category, of course, that we might not have thought to deploy until seeing this account). If other texts might dramatize the ennui or burden of "getting to work" more acutely, Orwell's essay registers the experience of the commute by turning it not into a mere object of representation but also the conceptual ground *for* representation itself. The solidarity of this passage does not just consist in the way that anyone who has experienced a long, and unrewarded, commute might recognize his or her own experience in these pages—the forceful registering of an experience that by its very nature remains hidden (i.e., unpaid). Orwell further uses the commute as a more general, but still socially grounded, model for the hidden experience that constitutes exploited labor as such. Here, as the miners crawl through the same tunnels they have (previously) built to arrive at the ore they will mine, is activity intrinsic to their labor, inseparable from their labor, but not constituted as, or recognized as, work. Perhaps the very premise of socialism is that this misrecognition, or exclusion of experience, also is intrinsic to the wage relationship itself, which systematically grants workers back *only a part* of the value they have constituted through their work. In other words, part of the work that the miners perform when they *get* to the end of the tunnel is as invisible, unrewarded (or unrecognized) as the difficult and unpaid commute itself.

This is why Orwell's irony cannot, finally, be like Booth's. The writing doesn't strive simply to make the reader translate the irony and see the miner's work but, more intricately: to see some of the miner's labor; to recognize, in this insight, how aspects of this work hadn't been seen; and to see, most urgently, that all of what constitutes this work has still not been registered. It is the residual irony in Orwell's choice of his paradigmatic site (the tunnels rather than the coal extraction itself) that transforms the grasping of exploitation into a "convergence" that can never be finalized. We might say, to use the language of more contemporary theory, that Orwell here *decenters* exploitation in a way that will not be fully articulated until the political theories of the New Left—with their attention to the multiple sites of social identity—are fully developed.

"Into the Cage"

To trace this out, I want to examine the way that Orwell's interest in the commute as displacement in no way stops at this passage. Rather, a series of displacements, grounded in this representation of the mine tunnels, proliferates in Part One of *The Road to Wigan Pier*. Once we have grasped this scene's ironic form of insight, we can locate other examples of experiences that are systematically produced but not registered by capitalist labor—and are produced, in large part, by the way that they are not registered. Like the commute, these experiences can be best engaged through an ironic framework that continually accounts for the gap between writing and experience (a framework that itself is encapsulated by the structure of the commute that it helps to bring to light). A second major example in Orwell's essay is the problem of injuries in the mines, one of the great injustices of industrial capitalism. Injuries, like the commute, have become a component part of labor but are not included in the "literal" definition of labor. Rather, they exist as an ironic residue of capitalist production. Orwell writes:

> Of the five pay-checks I mentioned above, no less than three are rubber-stamped with the words "death stoppage." When a miner is killed at work it is usual for the other miners to make up a subscription, generally of a shilling each, for his widow, and this is collected by the colliery company and automatically deducted from their wages. The significant detail here is the *rubber stamp*. (43–44)

Once again, this passage simultaneously represents a social fact and represents the process of social observation, as the narrator self-consciously points to the act of finding the "significant detail" in the passage. This paragraph is typical of Orwell's subtlety: the passage makes logical sense, but is more intricate than we might see at first glance. The rubber stamp is a "significant detail," superficially, because it points to the terrible quantity of injuries in the mines. But, less obviously, the detail is significant because it captures the qualitative disjunction between the event as it is uniquely experienced by the individual and the social reproduction and representation of the event. The inadequacy of the rubber stamp—*as* a signifier—is now deployed to cast light on the horrific nature of these repeated deaths. This is why Orwell puts a sentence in between the first mention of the rubber stamp and its revealed importance. The additional sentence drives the irony of the passage. Part of the shock in this depiction of the scene is precisely that the reader does *not* see the "significan[ce]" of the rubber stamp until it is pointed out, so that this disjunction is incorporated into the reading experience itself.

The "significant detail" of the rubber stamp (another "feeble," inadequate form of representation) is soon followed by a related episode, when the discussion returns to injuries involved not in the work itself but, again, in the activity that precedes and follows work—on the dangerous elevator shafts that sometimes collapse. The paragraph begins precisely within the ironic framework that Orwell has constructed, with one of the points that we are always "liable to miss" or not consider: *not* the actual injury (which is more accessible to the imagination) but the ordeal of getting a worker to safety after he has been injured:

> When a miner is hurt it is of course impossible to attend to him immediately. He lies crushed under several hundredweight of stone in some dreadful cranny underground, and even after he has been extricated it is necessary to drag his body a mile or more, perhaps through galleries where nobody can stand upright. (46)

The difficulty of the ordinary commute to work—which I've identified as an epistemological crux of the essay—is now magnified in the horrific process of returning the injured coal miner *from* work. In this way, Orwell combines two "residual" aspects of labor that he has identified (the commute to and from work, and accidents that take place during work) into a third experience (i.e., the "commute" of the injured worker himself) that is even more likely to be overlooked. This residuum of a residuum suggests an ongoing process, a potentially endless series of displacements that are driven by the worker's own actual displaced relation to his labor. (Here we can see the endlessness, or recursiveness, so strongly associated with negative irony—but now transvalued.) In each case, Orwell does not convey the essential injustice of work directly but through the worker's approach to and flight from the location of work itself.

The consideration of the difficult travel involved after an injury then leads, through an associational logic that's typical of *Wigan Pier,* into injuries that can occur during the travel *to* work and, more specifically, injuries that take place on the elevator shaft (i.e., on the device that goes into the tunnels that the miners must *then* traverse to get to work). The passage continues as follows, beginning with another reference to Orwell's own status as an observer (a status that revolves around his own efforts to "get to work"):

> Usually when you talk to a man who has been injured you find that it was a couple of hours or so before they got him to the surface. Sometimes, of course, there are accidents in the cage. The cage is shooting several hundred yards up or down at the speed of an express train, and it is operated by somebody on the surface who cannot see what is happening. He has very delicate indicators to tell him how far the cage has got, but it is possible for him to make a mistake, and there have been cases of the cage crashing into the pit-bottom at its very maximum speed. (47)

The cause of injuries here is the difference between really "see[ing]" things and looking at them from the outside, through "indicators" that can mistranslate the actual speed and lead to a mistake. In other words, the injuries are caused by the same kind of distance, between observer and worker, that Orwell—taking "aim," as a writer, at industrial, working-class experience— is trying to overcome by stepping into the elevator cage in the first place. This description of the elevator cage in fact directly recalls the start of Orwell's traversal into work in Chapter 2, which begins at the same location:

In some ways it is even disappointing, or at least is unlike what you have expected. You get into the cage, which is a steel box about as wide as a telephone box and two or three times as long. It holds ten men, but they pack it like pilchards in a tin, and a tall man cannot stand upright in it. The steel door shuts upon you, and somebody working the winding gear above drops you into the void. You have the usual momentary qualm in your belly and a bursting sensation in the ears, but not much sensation of movement till you get near the bottom, when the cage slows down so abruptly that you could swear it is going upwards again. (24)

As the injury passage (in Chapter 3) continues, Orwell once again incompletely registers what the worker might experience.

This seems to me a dreadful way to die. For as that tiny steel box whizzes through the blackness there must come a moment when the ten men who are locked inside it *know* that something has gone wrong; and the remaining seconds before they are smashed to pieces hardly bears thinking about. A miner told me he was once in a cage in which something went wrong. It did not slow up when it should have done, and they thought the cable must have snapped. As it happened they got to the bottom safely, but when he stepped out he found that he had broken a tooth; he had been clenching his teeth so hard in expectation of that frightful crash. (47)

When Orwell tries to identify with the terrified worker, he is basing his account on his actual experience of going down this elevator. The imaginative projection comes to focus on the most inaccessible aspect of consciousness: that dilated moment of time, "the few remaining seconds" that get ripped out of any objective temporal framework (just as Orwell's own trip down the elevator confused his sense of "up" and "down"). At first the observer seems unable to grasp this—as Orwell writes, these instances "hardly bear thinking about." But, once again, the inability of the observer to fully think the experience of the worker as he is about to be injured leads into the worker's own "expectation of that frightful crash." It is, in fact, the fear of grave injury—*not* the actual crash—that produces an injury, a minor injury that emerges ironically from fear of the major one.

This passage encapsulates Orwell's political perspective in *The Road to Wigan Pier*. The broken tooth would not even be accounted as an injury—all the statistical indicators, the rubber stamps of accidental death, are not finely tuned enough to include this incident. It is another of the details "one is always liable to miss": a horizon of experience that we cannot fully arrive at but that we can always move toward. It is easier to grasp the tragic significance of a miner's death but more difficult, and meaningful, to approach the *fear* of death, or of significant injury, that the miner more continually experiences. Conceptualizing exploitation entails persistently converging on the actual experience of singular persons stuck in oppressive structures; the ramifications of this structure (unlike the structure itself) cannot be fully articulated. One challenge of socialist theory is to make sure that the power of its explanatory mechanism doesn't generate a concept of exploitation that facilitates another distortion of this singularity. There is always more to exploitation than meets the eye; or more than the projection we make onto, the generalization that we make out of, alienated work. Orwell's irony situates the experience of alienated labor in a kind of Chinese box series—behind and within work are life-threatening accidents; behind accidental death is the fear of fatal injury; behind the fear of fatal injury is a broken tooth; behind the injured tooth is, perhaps, the difficulty of getting proper medical attention—in a way that encapsulates the essential structure of alienation more powerfully and cogently than any "direct" representation could. In the controlled failure of representation, experience actually comes rushing in.

"One Tends to Think"

Consider these passages from Part One of *The Road to Wigan Pier*, all lingering on a similar kind of abstraction and misprision:

1. It is a great mistake to think of a miner's working day as being only seven and a half hours. Seven and a half hours is the time spent actually on the job, but, as I have already explained, one has got to add on to this time taken up in "travelling," which is seldom less than an hour and may often be three hours. In addition most miners have to spend a considerable time in getting to and from the pit. . . . (38)

2. Before I had been in the coal areas I shared the widespread illusion that miners are comparatively well paid. One hears it loosely stated that a miner is paid ten or eleven shillings a shift; and one does a small multiplication sum and concludes that every miner is earning round about £3 a week or £150 a year. (40)

3. The great mining disasters, which happen from time to time, in which several hundred men are killed, are usually caused by explosions; hence one tends to think of explosions as the chief danger of mining. Actually, the great majority of accidents are due to the normal every-day dangers of the pit; in particular, to falls of roof. (45–46)

4. I found—one might expect it, perhaps—that the small landlords are usually the worst. It goes against the grain to say this, but one can see why it should be so. Ideally, the worst type of slum landlord is a fat wicked man, preferably a bishop, who is drawing an immense income from extortionate rents. Actually, it is a poor old woman who has invested her life's savings in three slum houses, inhabits one of them and tries to live on the rent of the other two—never, in consequence, having any money for repairs. (57)

5. When you see the unemployment figures quoted at two millions, it is fatally easy to take this as meaning that two million people are out of work and the rest of the population is comparatively comfortable. I admit that till recently I was in the habit of doing so myself. I used to calculate that if you put the registered unemployed at round about two millions and threw in the destitute and those who for one reason and another were not registered, you might take the number of underfed people in England (for *everyone* on the dole or thereabouts is underfed) as being, at the very most, five millions.
   This is an enormous underestimate. . . . (75)

6. How many of these caravan-colonies exist throughout the industrial areas it would be difficult to discover with any accuracy. The local authorities are reticent about them and the census report of 1931 seems to have decided to ignore them. . . . The probability is that throughout the north of England there are some thousands, perhaps

tens of thousands of *families* (not individuals) who have no home except a fixed caravan.

But the word "caravan" is very misleading. It calls up a picture of a cosy gypsy-encampment (in fine weather, of course) with wood fires crackling and children picking blackberries and many-coloured washing fluttering on the lines. (61)

In each of these passages, Orwell first proposes and then rejects an idea, a figure, a term, or a conclusion. *Wigan Pier* repeats this gesture enough that we can understand it as a systematic one, with theoretical bearing. And these passages all echo the text's paradigmatic distinction between the work one might "imagine," and thus hold in mind, and the neglected commute, or movement *to* this site of labor. We might say, with this set of examples, that the text carries such displacement—the displacement of the commute—into the texture of its own thinking. In this way, *Wigan Pier* subtly intertwines an imperfect, fluid process of thought (or representation) with the object that thought attempts to comprehend. I want to conclude on this point of overlap, discussing these scenes within *Wigan Pier* in which Orwell deliberately pauses on, and details, the act of thinking itself.

All of these passages point to the ease with which reflection can undermine itself: whether through the internal momentum of abstraction or as the (inevitably) hardened image of a represented object works to corrode engagement with the actual object. This is *not* simply a matter of stigmatizing sanguine beliefs. While some of these examples are marked by such sanguinity, diminishing the real difficulties that the miner faces (the "caravans" that blunt how bad housing is, or the figures on unemployment), others disproportionately *magnify* these difficulties (as in the images of the selfish landlord or the catastrophic accident). Crucially, thought can lose its object (here, the condition of labor in the industrial areas) in either of these inverse ways. This doubleness is so significant because it is only here—in the interlocked potential both to diminish *and* to exaggerate social suffering— that Orwell's work at once insists on an authentic and legitimate object of representation (in the reality that can be missed) and refuses to ever equate writing with this object (because of the inevitable pitfalls of exaggeration).

Exaggeration here is more than an emotional mistake—it is a potential implicit within the momentum of thinking. This can return us to the discussion in the Introduction, and Orwell's wariness, in "The Lure of Profundity," about "avoiding thoughts" by "think[ing] too deeply" (11.104). Several of these examples hinge on the deceptively simple verb "think," amplifying, once more, the key discussion of the commute: "when you *think* of a coalmine you *think* of depth, heat, darkness, blackened figures hacking at walls of coal; you don't *think*, necessarily, of those miles of creeping to and fro" (29, emphases added). Thus, Orwell writes, "it is a great mistake to *think* of a miner's day as being only seven and a half hours," and, again, "one *tends to think* of explosions as the chief danger of mining" (emphases added). I want to insist that the sheer process of thinking—rather than a particularly mistaken category of thoughts—is a problem here,[5] even while the first sentence of Chapter 2 (which in many ways reopens the book) suggests that the topic that engages *The Road to Wigan Pier* is available only through a conscious and discrete act of thought: "Our civilization, *pace* Chesterton, *is* founded on coal, more completely than one realizes until one stops to think about it" (21, Orwell's emphases).

The quiet, colloquial term, "one stops to think," is important. The phrase itself, we might say, is worth stopping to think about. Here, at the opening of Chapter 2, deliberate reflection is necessary in order to grasp the implications of how—and even the bare fact that—"our civilisation . . . is founded upon coal." *Wigan Pier*—the book as a whole—depends on this act of deliberate reflection. But thinking also leads toward those mistakes that Orwell repeatedly stigmatizes. While reflection takes place by "stop[ping]," it also (perhaps *in* this very halt) creates a movement or "tend[ency]" of its own. "[O]ne *tends to think* of explosions as the chief danger of mining" (passage 2, emphasis added). This sense of tendency—not as the substance of a particular (or lazy) thought but as a momentum intrinsic to thinking—is implied, as well, when Orwell describes how it is "fatally easy" to take a numerical figure as definitive (as in the "unemployment figures" in passage 5) or how a word "calls up" a problematically fixed image ("caravan," in passage 6). In combination, these passages, ranging across Part One of *Wigan Pier*, suggest how almost *any* thought has the potential to oversubstantialize itself.[6] This *precarious* condition of thinking—thought's capacity to undermine itself through its very momentum—is crucial to Orwell's work. (We will pick up the same question—or drama—most explicitly in Chapter Four, when I turn to his weekly column "As I Please." But it is visible in Orwell's writing more generally and a central interest of this book.)

We've seen that this process can lead to a mediated diminishment of social suffering but also—more surprisingly—to its distorted magnification. The stakes here are high, as Orwell, at different points in *Wigan Pier*, critiques the "mythical figure" of the proletarian and also the idea of a pure, or authentic, proletarian writing.[7] These two critiques are closely related to one another, and they both speak to Orwell's underlying, almost technical, concern with writing. Writing deludes itself if it conjures up an absolute "object" that underlies its expression or an authentic and stably grounded writing subject: in each case, whether the worker takes his place as the final, legitimating focus of written representation, or as an initial, grounding source of writing, it can serve to bolster an overly idealized confidence in writing, as such, which would now, in some fundamental sense, seem frictionless and unmediated.

Likewise, just as Orwell considers the way that thought can both diminish *and* magnify its object, his critique is not aimed only at what is "vaguely imagined" or "loosely stated" but also at how we can extend and bolster an idea through "calculat[ion]" (passage 5). Calculation is a process we might have opposed to such vagueness and looseness. In this example, Orwell tallies up different categories of persons in order to estimate how many people might be in poverty. Similarly, in passage 2, Orwell writes, "one does a small multiplication sum and concludes that every miner is earning £3 a week." The multiplication that Orwell highlights might be "small," but he is intent on foregrounding it, as a discrete conceptual action (separate from but leading to a subsequent "conclu[sion]"). *Wigan Pier* lingers on such discrete, interlinked steps of thinking—on the small-scale calculations that form the tissue of sequential reasoning. It is an intimate approach to the process and texture of thought. And here such reasoning is implicated *in*, not cast against, the "widespread" and "loosely stated" "illusion" he's criticizing. Orwell describes these very calculations, indeed, as a "habit" that he was prone to (passage 5). Thought, which is necessary in order to break habit or unawareness (no text of *Wigan Pier* unless we first "stop to think" about that foundational role of coal), can reproduce these states from within its own immanent unfolding. This is crucial because it qualitatively changes the terms of Orwell's own conceptual posture.

In my reading, this "small" but deliberately highlighted act of ratiocination stands in for the seductive capacity, and thus momentum, of reasoning or "thinking" as such. In the rest of the paragraph Orwell puts a *series* of modifications up against this conclusion ("that every miner is earning round about £3 a week or £150 a year"). This level of pay only applies to the coal "getter," not to the workers employed on subsidiary jobs (like "fillers"). Many laborers are "paid piecework" (40) and so depend on the variable qualities of the mine. Most crucially, miners are not always called to work, and this "average calculation" of their annual pay (by multiplying a weekly wage) "takes no account of blank days" (40). The varied additions suggest, again, that Orwell is more interested in demonstrating the ongoing process of generating such disruptive counterexamples than in simply formulating an alternative total. This process hinges on a sequence of displacements, amplifying, once more, the displacement at the experiential core of working in the mines. And Orwell uses this same sense of "addition"—as disruptive supplement rather than as "sum" or synthesis—twice in the opening example: "as I have already explained one has got to *add on* to this time taken up in 'travelling,' . . . *In addition* most miners have to spend a considerable time getting to and from the pit" (38, emphases added). Here, on the topical register as well, we are back to the commute and to the distended process of getting to work. (We can note that Orwell, in fact, expands the terms of this commute in this passage—now incorporating the initial, aboveground travel "to and from the pit," thus anticipating his longer discussion of housing conditions and slum clearance in Chapter 4 [51–74].) In this way, even while showing how writing can never be equated with the object of its engagement, Orwell's text draws the procedure of his own writing, and thinking, closer to the real displacements that drive this "fragmentary account."

3

"Semi-Sociological"
(Inside the Whale)

1 + 1 + 1 = 1

Inside the Whale and Other Essays, published by Victor Gollancz in March 1940, contains three essays: "Charles Dickens," "Boys' Weeklies," and the title work, "Inside the Whale," ostensibly a consideration of Henry Miller's *Tropic of Cancer.* These three pieces have all enjoyed continued attention but have rarely been viewed together. On the contrary, each of them has migrated into recycled editions, collections, and anthologies, beginning with the inclusion of both "Charles Dickens" and "Boys' Weeklies" in the edition of *Critical Essays* published in 1946. This proliferation of Orwell's essays, circulated through and lodged within many different host forms, marks at once their appeal and ephemerality. *Inside the Whale* is from a moment when the author is still trying to gain a (pen)name for himself. The ensuing success of all three pieces heralds Orwell's emergent status as "a major essayist" (Crick 260). But the essays' very mobility also carries with it a price, signaling the potentially transient nature of so much of Orwell's engaged, spontaneous, occasional writing.

There is a tension, in other words, between the survival of the essays and the demise of the book. I want to recover the book itself, not in order to argue for its privileged or durable status but, on the contrary, to focus more attention on the contingent nature of Orwell's writing. This slender book has a problematic form to start with. Such a small sample is not really a "collection" of essays at all. (With one less text, Orwell would have had to change the title to *Inside the Whale and Other Essay!*) Such limitation calls more attention to the convergences, and divergences, between the three parts. But when critics confront the original source of these distinct texts, they usually read it as a mere framework for its three subjects, all construed, in a very general sense, as "literary criticism."[1] Biographers might note a common thread or, on the contrary, point to the book's heterogeneity. Meyers, for example, claims that "all three essays are subtly autobiographical" (204). Crick argues, conversely, that Orwell's text "show[s] the full range of his interest" (260). Both points are fair enough. But quickly settling on either unity or range, as the governing quality of the collection, can overlook the hesitation that is provoked by the essays' uncertain proximity.

What holds *Inside the Whale* together? Do we view the book as three distinct parts (privileging their diversity)? Or do we fuse these parts together into a single, more significant whole (privileging the essays' commonality)? The text offers us little help in answering these questions. We find no preface, head notes, afterword, or other textual matter that would stand outside of (or above) the three essays—and no explicit references in any of the pieces to each other. While Orwell injects himself into each individual essay, in a conspicuous show of subjective sensibility, he is as consistently reticent in displaying himself as the organizing hand of the essays as a whole. Any connection between the three texts thus does not emerge through the expressed comments of the author but only through an engagement with the more silent rigors of formal structure itself.

I want to focus attention on this *structural condition* of each essay in Orwell's collection. If the essays are transparent, their concatenation is enigmatic. While each essay points us "out," toward the larger world, the book holds us "in," comparing and juxtaposing its different parts. In this fundamental sense, form creates a threshold effect. Any number of formally divided works might function in this manner. *Inside the Whale* heightens this effect, as its blunt stylistic surface would militate against—and thus ironically increases the force of—such "holding" action. The combination of divided structure and plain style drives the reader in opposing directions. And, of course, Orwell's essay collection, from the title on, very much concerns the opposition between an "inside" and "outside." In this way, the underlying structural condition is reiterated and amplified thematically (or vice versa).

Inside and outside, boundaries and thresholds: Orwell's title foregrounds these categories. The structural logic of the text, as tripartite collection, foregrounds them as well. And *Inside the Whale* comes to suggest that "literary criticism"—which is, in a fundamental sense, writing "about" writing and thus always incipiently self-reflective writing—also foregrounds this division. In his letter to Geoffrey Gorer (which I discussed briefly in the Introduction), Orwell uses the term "semi-sociological" to describe the book. It is a striking neologism and one that reinforces that sense of *Inside the Whale*'s fundamental intermediateness:

> There is an essay on Dickens that might interest you too. I find this kind of semi-sociological literary criticism very interesting & I'd like to do a lot of other writers, but unfortunately there's no money in it. (12.137)

It is a curious term for Orwell to use, one that causes a sort of jamming that might take place so quickly as to go unnoticed (but not unfelt). By the logic of syntax itself, the additional prefix "semi-" *extends* the technical nature of the phrase. In this light, the term is more schematized, more methodological even than "sociology"—or the already affix-burdened "sociological"—freestanding. But semantically, of course, Orwell means the prefix to *puncture* such disciplinary arrogation, suggesting that this criticism is only reluctantly or intermittently "sociological." (This tension, between the syntactic and semantic nature of the word, wouldn't confront the reader so sharply if Orwell had written, for instance, "partly sociological" or even "semi-social.")

The neologism thus hovers between technicality and familiarity, providing—if only by its alliterative, internally rhyming phonetic structure—a kind of bump in Orwell's famously plain style. It is both whimsical and serious. Looking just at the surrounding phrases, we can see quite clearly how the word stands out. This jamming is caused most simply, of course, by the introduction of a more technical and abstract term into the plain style (like a polysyllabic black sheep caught in a crowd of shorter words). But Orwell is not just creating a conflict between this one complicated term and the rest of the prose. As we have seen, there is a tension between abstraction and familiarity built into the term itself. This is a tension produced by the crosscurrents of sound, meaning, tone, and syntax that run through the ambitious, elusive word. At the same time, of course, the adjective raises more strictly conceptual problems and concerns. What are the stakes of a *purely* sociological approach to literature, or of a "literary criticism" that fails to be sociological altogether? Can criticism successfully inhabit the threshold between an intrinsic and a historical relationship to the literary object? Can it stay on the "inside" and the "outside"?

Orwell ends the book by foregrounding the *"impossibility"* of writing in the (present-day) world, finishing his long evaluation of *Tropic of Cancer:*

> [I]t will probably be admitted that Miller is a writer out of the ordinary, worth more than a single glance; and, after all, he is a completely nega-tive, unconstructive, amoral writer, a mere Jonah, a passive accepter of evil, a sort of Whitman among the corpses. Symptomatically, that is more significant than the mere fact that five thousand novels are pub-lished in England every year and four thousand nine hundred of them are tripe. It is a demonstration of the *impossibility* of any major litera-ture until the world has shaken itself into its new shape. (187–188, Orwell's emphasis)[2]

Orwell's italicized use of the term "impossibility" is important. The emphasis turns what might be a difficulty into an absolute, and categorical, crisis. What form of writing can adequately comprehend history, and, in moments of political crisis and tumult, what purchase can writing have? As with his fracturing of *The Road to Wigan Pier,* Orwell turns this problem of writing's "impossibility" back in toward his *own* writerly efforts and, more specifi-cally, toward the "semi-sociological" literary-critical writing that he is here embarking on. It is no coincidence that this description of impossibility ends Orwell's own book as well. *Inside the Whale* is a project that will turn out to be the last of eight volumes that Orwell writes in as many years and also the *first* collection of essays he has written. It is tempting to see a rela-tionship between this biographical fact and the gloomy final words of the book—as though Orwell's own work soon comes to register the "impossi-bility" he invokes, by the temporary abandonment of book-length projects in favor of more contingent, provisional forms of journalism (that ultimately will secure his own reputation as an essayist).

If *Inside the Whale* functions as such a pivot within Orwell's writing trajectory, it would suggest that a negativity inheres in the essay form itself, as Orwell conceives of it. The essay, as the most contingent form of writing, might always reflect its own transience—its own formal inadequacy—no matter how expressive, direct, or powerful its rhetorical and topical achievement. This ironic sense of reflexivity takes a specific form in *Inside the Whale*, as Orwell's inaugural essay collection is focused strictly on the literary-critical, and includes no political or topical pieces. It is all words about words. Despite the bluff, conversational tone that runs through the book, this also makes for a quite inward-looking work—an inwardness further provoked and sustained by the enigmatic relationship between the three parts. The problem of methodology (always potentially a *reflective,* or inward-looking, problem) is foregrounded in *Inside the Whale,* as the three essays—shadowed by that concluding sense of writing's "impossibility"—suggest distinct kinds of literary analysis. It is not at all self-evident, in reading this collection, what the ideal scope or scale of criticism should be. The first two pieces contrast popular but canonical literature (Dickens's novels) and nearly anonymous mass culture ("the so-called penny dreadful"[123]). They also juxtapose the focus on a single author with a more extensive analysis of an entire genre. "Charles Dickens," is, furthermore, divided into two different approaches to its object, as Orwell self-consciously interrupts the flow of the essay to comment:

> By this time anyone who is a lover of Dickens, and who has read as far as this, will probably be angry with me.
> I have been discussing Dickens simply in terms of his "message," and almost ignoring his literary qualities. . . . Why does anyone care about Dickens? Why do *I* care about Dickens? (66)

Likewise, the final essay, "Inside the Whale," dramatizes this kind of shift by arguing that the consideration of a single object—here Henry Miller's *Tropic of Cancer*—necessitates a much wider examination of an entire period of social and intellectual history. Orwell stages this movement, from (single) object to (broader) context, at the crucial hinge of the essay: "It is worth trying to discover just what this escape from the current literary fashion means. But to do that one has got to see it against its background—that is, against the general development of English literature in the twenty years since the Great War" (146).

Reading the three essays in *Inside the Whale* as one book thus provokes lingering questions about what constitutes both the object and the method of literary analysis. Is it better to focus on a text's ideological "message" or on its aesthetic "qualit[y]"? How can we consider any single literary work *without* engaging—and perhaps getting lost in—"its background"? Do we understand texts as part of a literary or a popular culture, in terms of an author or a genre?[3] These tensions arise within each essay—most conspicuously at those hinges in "Charles Dickens" and "Inside the Whale"—but also as the reader moves between the essays. In order to see these tensions (which are vividly presented by each piece), we need to posit the potential autonomy of the book, *Inside the Whale,* as a unified object. Only such integrity would render the strained relationship between the three essays as meaningful or even visible. But in this way, one of the critical problems that Orwell's book raises—the contested status of any literary text *as* an integral or autonomous object—doubles back into the book itself.

Synthesis and Abstracting ("Boys' Weeklies")

The overarching formal question of *Inside the Whale* as a book—what holds these three disparate essays together?—is indeed echoed in the essays themselves. Each of the three texts is engaged, and troubled, by the conceptual problem of putting parts together. Consider, for example, this passage from early in "Boys' Weeklies":

> The *Gem* and *Magnet* are sister-papers (characters out of one paper frequently appear in the other), and were both started more than thirty years ago. At that time, together with *Chums* and the old *B[oy's] O[wn] P[aper]*, they were the leading papers for boys, and they remained dominant till quite recently. Each of them carries every week a fifteen- or twenty-thousand word school story, complete in itself, but usually more or less connected with the story of the week before. The *Gem* in addition to its school-story carries one or more adventure-serials. Otherwise the two papers are so much alike that they can be treated as one, though

the *Magnet* has always been the better known of the two, probably because it possesses a really first-rate character in the fat boy, Billy Bunter. (91–92)

This paragraph—so blunt and commonsensical—might look like a strange one to single out. Orwell seems to be making unmediated claims about an object, as though his conversational language aims to express thoughts so simply that there would be nothing to see or discover about thinking itself.[4] Yet Orwell also calls attention here to a specific moment within the thinking process: we see him defining the object that will then focus his discussion. In the crucial line of the paragraph, Orwell writes, "Otherwise the two journals are so much alike that they can be treated as one." This is mundane—and yet structurally emphatic: an odd combination that is typical of *Inside the Whale*. The author is actively formulating the object that he will consider—combining the "two" magazines into "one" larger, more abstract, entity. And here is an explicit analogue to that problem faced by the reader of the essay—whether the three parts of *Inside the Whale* can be "treated as one." Tellingly, Orwell modifies this synthetic assertion on either end. The "[o]therwise" and "though" point forward and backward to two ways in which the basic object that Orwell is constructing—by that conceptual fusion of the *Gem* and the *Magnet*—can devolve back into its component parts. Right before his claim, Orwell points out that the *Gem* uniquely carries adventure stories in addition to school stories (and only "otherwise" might be considered equivalent to the *Magnet*). Right after, he notes that the *Magnet*, alone, has a character who *doesn't* reappear in the other magazine and is particularly popular. With these caveats—and more through the force of syntax than evidence—Orwell suggests that his own synthetic abstraction is vulnerable.

This *connotation* of vulnerability is more significant than the particular details that are offered here. A similar sense is conveyed by the parentheses in the first sentence: "(characters out of one paper frequently appear in another)." This also comes across as an unimportant, even laborious, addition, catching the reader up with what the writer already knows or has already thought through. The writer needs to pause, and the parentheses, ostensibly subordinating this extra piece of evidence, also suggest—or dramatize—displeasure at the delay. The piece is taking us through the writer's thought process, in other words, and specifically how he has conceived of the two papers as one. (Such a movement, to take "two" objects and treat them as "one," is the raw matter of thinking.)

This is particularly important to the essay at hand. The underlying axiom of "Boys' Weeklies" might be that studying popular culture *requires* a foundational gesture of abstraction, in which we reframe something that seems to be manifold or variegated as systematic and coherently organized. As many critics have noted, "Boys' Weeklies" is the most prominent in a series of influential essays that Orwell writes on British popular culture, anticipating the fusion of literary and cultural studies in later critics such as Raymond Williams.[5] "Boys' Weeklies," as a freestanding essay, has a pride of place in Orwell's prescient attention to mass culture. It also has a specific place in *this* book between the two other strikingly different essays. The methodological implications of this essay are pronounced, and stand out in sharper relief by the study's juxtaposition to the more explicitly literary analyses that surround it.[6]

Orwell begins "Boys' Weeklies" by dramatizing the thought process that we have seen played out above:

> You never walk far through any poor quarter in any big town without coming upon a small news agent's shop. The general appearance of these shops is always very much the same: a few posters for the *Daily Mail* and the *News of the World* outside, a poky little window with sweet-bottles and packets of Players, and a dark interior smelling of liquorice allsorts and festooned from floor to ceiling with vilely-printed twopenny papers, most of them with lurid cover-illustrations in three colours. (89)

This description immediately anticipates the cognitive act of abstraction that Orwell later develops. Like the two journals that can be treated as one, the shops in these many "poor quarter[s]"—even while crammed with an abundance of material—are all "very much the same." Orwell begins by depicting this conceptual movement as a literal encounter—the essay imagines the embodied reader "coming upon" what will turn out to be its own object of (intellectual) inquiry.

Orwell's impulse is to physicalize the thinking process. This is a suggestive opening for what is, after all, an act of criticism (and thus of reflection). We could argue, of course, that the beginning of "Boys' Weeklies" is a symptomatic example of the plain style's ideology. Before we even get to thought itself, we have its negation. Orwell is uncomfortable with pure abstraction; he tries to weigh down thought, to naturalize it. But the relationship that Orwell establishes here is fundamentally open ended: it moves in both directions. The essay also can be seen as subtly calling attention *to* thought, to its own reflective processes. The bluffer the tone, the more uncanny these inscribed processes become. The opening is crucial to this effect. Its dramatization of thinking (in these physical terms) is reiterated when the essay later refers, as it were, to its own composition. Discussing the sensationalism common to the journals, Orwell abruptly breaks the frame to write:

> Merely looking at the cover-illustrations of the papers which I have on the table in front of me, here are some of the things I see. On one a cowboy is clinging by his toes to the wing of an aeroplane in mid-air and shooting down another aeroplane with his revolver. On another a Chinaman is swimming for his life down a sewer with a swarm of ravenous-looking rats swimming after him. On another an engineer. . . . (112)

The magazines piled across Orwell's writing surface ("on the table in front of me") echo the physical chaos of the news shop. But they are now almost at the point of transmutation *into* the conceptual evidence that underlies the argument we are reading. A similar turn occurs near the beginning of Orwell's other most prominent study of popular culture, "The Art of Donald McGill." Orwell writes:

> [T]he special value of his postcards is that they are so completely typical. They represent, as it were, the norm of the comic postcard. Without being in the least imitative, they are exactly what comic postcards have been any time these last forty years, and from them the meaning and purpose of the whole *genre* can be inferred.

> Get hold of a dozen of these things, preferably McGill's—if you pick out from a pile the ones that seem to you funniest, you will probably find that most of them are McGill's—and spread them out on a table. What do you see? (13.24)

Even that simple action of "spread[ing] . . . out" these postcards militates against the reduction implicit in seizing on the postcards as "typical" or the "norm," or as encompassing "the meaning and purpose of the whole genre." And as with the passages we're examining in "Boys' Weeklies," a specific trajectory has been enacted, from the outside to the inside, from the "pile" of postcards in the store ("the 'comics' of the cheap stationers' windows . . . they are on sale everywhere" [13.23]) to the table at home, the distinct sheltered space of writing—and implicitly of thinking itself.

These set pieces suggest that the aim of Orwell's essays is not merely to secure the messiness or chaos of the outside (i.e., these objects of popular culture) *within* the privacy and safety of writing or thought but rather to externalize the activities of writing and thinking, now rendered strangely visible. Consider the trajectory of opening lines in each of the first five paragraphs in "Boys' Weeklies":

> You never walk through any poor quarter in any big town without coming upon a small newsagent's shop. The general appearance of these shops is always very much the same. (89)

> Except for the daily and evening papers, the stock of these shops hardly overlaps at all with that of the big newsagents. Their main selling line is the twopenny weekly, and the number and variety of these are almost unbelievable. Every hobby and pastime—cage-birds, fretwork, carpentering, bees, carrier pigeons, home conjuring, philately, chess—has at least one paper devoted to it, and generally several. (89)

> Probably the contents of these shops is the best available indication of what the mass of the English people really feels and thinks. (90)

> Here I am only dealing with a single series of papers, the boys' twopenny weeklies, often inaccurately described as "penny dreadfuls." Falling strictly within this class there are at present ten papers, the *Gem*,

Magnet, Modern Boy, Triumph and *Champion*, all own by the Amalgamated Press, and the *Wizard, Rover, Skipper, Hotspur* and *Adventure,* all owned by D.C. Thomson & Co. (90–91)

The *Gem* and *Magnet* are sister-papers (characters out of one paper frequently appear in the other), and were both started more than thirty years ago. (91)

Orwell manipulates the paragraph breaks (formalized markings of thought within an essay) to circle insistently around the vagaries of conceptual synthesis: categorical thinking ("falling strictly within this class"); typicality ("always very much the same," "sister-papers"); taxonomic distinction ("the stock of these shops hardly overlaps at all with that of the big newsagents"); synecdoche ("the content of these shops is the best available indication of what the mass of the English people really feels and thinks"). The opening of "Boys' Weeklies" shows just a little bit more work than it has to; we can feel its conceptual pulse.

In this sense, Orwell's essay doesn't merely synthesize a mass-cultural genre but represents the process and the intricacies of synthesizing. This is another crucial threshold effect in *Inside the Whale*. Because of this procedural residue, thought doesn't meld securely onto the object. This incomplete relationship to the material at hand is not merely formal but is connected to the sociological status of these texts as popular culture. These boys' weeklies—like Donald McGill's vulgar seaside postcards—are distinct *objects* for critical analysis. In one sense, of course, the point is to see these things that typically have not been seen—seen, that is, within critical analysis. (No previous article in *Horizon,* for example, where "Boys' Weeklies" first appeared, had focused on anything like this topic.)[7] But in another equally crucial sense, the point is also to not "see" them too well: to *not* translate them, too securely or smoothly, into the interiority of critical reflection. They must remain as discrete, tangible objects: as something outside the mind that encounters and refracts them. As we have seen, Orwell calls these papers "the best available indication of what the mass of the English people really feels and thinks." If such texts are the best (or "best available") means of accessing the reality of mass social life, they still serve as an imperfect "indication." The goal of abstraction in "Boys' Weeklies" is explicitly to grasp at this mass reality—but the essay also works to suggest how this comprehension will always be limited. To see (i.e., to critically reflect upon) the objects of popular culture also means, for Orwell, to cross a sociological divide. By necessity, the critic writes from a different position, from *elsewhere*. In this sense, criticism that is turned toward popular culture is at once empirical (tactile, precise, observant) and sociological; it involves a seeing and a crossing.

This horizon of social class helps further explain why Orwell initially physicalizes the act of synthesis that will sustain the essay. Orwell glosses reading as strolling. When he later tells the reader that "you would find something like them in every chapter of every number"(94), it echoes how the essay *begins* by telling the reader that "you never walk far through any poor quarter in any big town without coming upon" newsagents' shops that are "all of the same general appearance." In both statements, an encounter ("coming upon" "find[ing]") fuels generalization ("every . . . every" "any . . . any"). In this way, the essay actually connects an event that takes place on the "outside," in physical, social space (walking in a new city), and something that takes place "inside," as part of the conceptual activity of reading and interpretation. At the same time, the opening of the essay is specifically configured as an encounter across a divide or threshold (or from "outside" *to* "inside"). The vocabulary of the opening paragraph draws on social, and epistemological, processes explored by the essay as a whole: "walk through," "come upon," "poor," "general appearance," "posters," "little window," "cover-illustrations" (these last three all different kinds of frames), "outside," "dark interior," "vile," "lurid." Much of the analytic sensibility in the essay as a whole is dramatized in this passage, which configures representation *both* as an act of framing (the window, the posters, the covers) and as a problematic encounter where "coming upon" entails crossing a threshold (separating "outside" and "interior") toward the "lurid," "vile," and "poor."

This vocabulary of frames, thresholds, social typicality, physical detail, and class division is reminiscent of the proto-novelistic sketches of early Dickens, which themselves are a foundation for nineteenth-century realist stylistics. For example, "The Pawnbroker's Shop" opens:

> Of all the numerous receptacles for misery and distress with which the streets of London unhappily abound, there are, perhaps, none which

present such striking scenes of vice and poverty as the pawnbroker's shops. . . . The subject may appear, at first sight, to be anything but an inviting one, but we venture on it nevertheless. . . . We have selected one for our purpose, and will endeavour to describe it.

The pawnbroker's shop is situated near Drury-lane, at the corner of a court, which affords a side entrance for the accommodation of such customers as may be desirous of avoiding the observation of the passers-by, or the chance of recognition in the public street. It is a low, dirty-looking, dusty shop, the door of which stands always doubtfully, a little way open, half inviting, half repelling the hesitating visitor, who, if he be as yet uninitiated, examines one of the old garnet brooches in the window for a minute or two with affected eagerness, as if he contemplated making the purchase; and then looking cautiously round to ascertain that no one watches him, hastily slinks in: the door closing of itself after him, to just its former width. . . . [T]he plate and jewels would seem to have disappeared . . . for the articles of stock, which are displayed in some profusion in the window, do not include any very valuable luxuries of either kind. A few old china cups, some modern vases adorned with paltry painting of three Spanish cavaliers playing three Spanish guitars, or a party of boors carousing: each boor with one leg painfully elevated in the air, by way of expressing his perfect freedom and gaiety; several sets of chessmen, two or three flutes, a few fiddles, a round-eyed portrait staring in astonishment from a very dark ground; some gaudily-bound prayer-books and testaments, two rows of silver watches quite as clumsy and almost as large as Ferguson's first; numerous old-fashioned table and tea spoons displayed, fan-like, in half-dozens; strings of coral with great broad gilt snaps; cards of rings and brooches, fastened and labelled separately, like the insects in the British Museum; cheap silver penholders and snuff-boxes, with a Masonic star, complete the jewelry department; while five or six beds in smeary clouded ticks, strings of blankets and sheets, silk and cotton handkerchiefs, and wearing apparel of every description, form the more useful, though even less ornamental, part of the articles exposed for sale. (220–223)

Dickens obviously dwells on the threshold to the shop, lingering on that moment of transition *from* inside to outside. The key point is that this represented action also gives us an image of representation itself. The entrance into the pawnshop, disproportionately foregrounded, serves as an emblem for the sketches' own process of transmuting the reality of London social life. The textual push-and-pull between generality and particularity in this, and other Boz sketches, helps to motivate such a focus on the threshold. "The Pawnbroker's Shop" (like the *Sketches* as a whole) works as a hinge between larger abstractions (here "selected" to illuminate "*all* the numerous receptacles for misery and distress" in London) and much smaller particularities (down to "each boor with one leg painfully elevated in the air"). The threshold, so common a *topos* in realist poetics, is not merely an imagined space of crossing (within the story) but also reflects on this fraught balance, within realist representation itself, between detail and abstraction.[8] To focus too strictly on details risks rendering social life as an unorganized, random, and chaotic mess of social facts; to work too confidently on the level of generality risks subsuming all social experience into schematic conceptual abstraction. As we have seen, Orwell's essay engages a similar dialectical process: the relationship between detail and type within realist art might parallel the interplay of example and claim within an essay. (And, of course, "Boys' Weeklies" is preceded by Orwell's own sustained examination of Dickens in *Inside the Whale*—an analysis that hinges, as I will discuss below, on trade-offs inherent to social representation.)

Orwell's artistic decision to begin this generally light-hearted essay on the threshold, and in the second person (unlike the other two essays in the collection) is important. It frames the self that is both at stake and at work in the essay as particularly fragile and insecure: someone staring across a boundary separating inside from outside, self from world. By opening "Boys' Weeklies" with this physical, socially marked image for the act of interpretation, Orwell suggests the estrangement that the abstracting self experiences in its encounter with the material of popular culture. This sense of estrangement, clustering around images of thresholds and dividing lines, is always in tension with the comfort, whimsy, and familiarity of the essay. It is an estrangement that mirrors what Orwell will call the "dividing line" that structures British culture itself:

The most definite dividing line between the petite-bourgeoisie and the working class is that the former pay for their education, and within the bourgeoisie there is another unbridgeable gulf between the "public" school and the "private" school. It is quite clear that there are tens and scores of thousands of people to whom every detail of life at a "posh" public school is wildly thrilling and romantic. (99)

This passage, in combination with the essay's opening, generates a number of resonant, overlapping terms: "best available indication," "coming upon," "dividing line," "unbridgeable gulf." We can only grasp social reality through the "best available indication" because of these relationships that are structured around such an "unbridgeable gulf." If Orwell says "it is quite clear" that many look across this social divide at a public-school life that they can never attain, his imprecise description of "tens and scores of thousands of people" suggests, simultaneously, the extensiveness of this mass and the way that its size is *not* perfectly "clear" or precisely legible. This lack of precision is not merely quantitative; it stems from the gulf that Orwell, in this essay itself, is attempting to look across (but also to acknowledge or see in and of itself). Peering out at what he takes as mass culture ("the contents of these shops is the best available indication of what the mass of the English people really feels and thinks"), Orwell encounters these "tens and scores of thousands of people" peering *into* what they take as elite culture—imagining the "thrilling and romantic" life at a "'posh' public school." This is a crucial point in Orwell's essay, since it is where the initial focus of inquiry—"the mass of the English people"—resurfaces in specific relation to the analysis of the *Gem* and the *Magnet*.

Mimesis, Doubled ("Charles Dickens")

A similar concern for, and leeriness about the abstraction of, "the mass of the English people" recurs in the other two essays of *Inside the Whale*. In "Inside the Whale," Orwell focuses on the ironic way that left-wing writers' very commitment to the political aspect of literature risks estranging them from everyday life:

[T]he truth is that many ordinary people, perhaps an actual majority, do speak and behave in just the way that is recorded here [in Miller's *Tropic of Cancer*]. . . . For the ordinary man is also passive. . . . During the past ten years literature has involved itself more and more deeply in politics, with the result that there is now less room in it for the ordinary man than at any time during the past two centuries. . . . I do not mean that the people Miller is writing about constitute a majority, still less that he is writing about proletarians. No English or American novelist has as yet seriously attempted that. (137–138, 144–145)

And, in his analysis of Dickens, Orwell, discussing "[h]is descriptions of the London slums," concludes:

There are many similar passages in Dickens. From them one gets the impression of whole submerged populations whom he regards as being beyond the pale. In rather the same way the modern doctrinaire Socialist contemptuously writes off a large block of the population as "lumpenproletariat." (43)

"Ordinary people," "a large block of the population," "proletarians," "the mass of the English people," "whole submerged populations"—this social horizon informs all three of the essays. This last passage explicitly brings the "submerged populations" that rest uncomprehended in Dickens's nineteenth-century fiction closer to a contemporary example of the "doctrinaire" who likewise "writes off a large block of the population." But I would argue for a further, oblique echo of this same process, in Orwell's own purely *textual* compression of "many similar passages" into a single example. If "Boys' Weeklies" shows (rather than merely relies on) that process of fusing discrete objects into a single conceptual whole, "Charles Dickens" subtly emphasizes, alongside Orwell's general claims about Dickens's novels, the process of generalizing about a novel. It is a process that hinges on the pivot between selective quotation from and overarching analysis of the literary text. For example, if at one point Orwell casually asserts that "there are similar passages scattered all through Thackeray's works" (which he is using as a point of comparison with Dickens), he can also suggest, after another exemplary, and truncated, quotation: "The passage I have abridged above ought to be read in full. It and others like it show how deep was Dickens's horror of revolutionary hysteria" (23, 40).

These are more than rhetorical flourishes. Reading a novel can create a tension between connecting a diffuse series of "scattered" passages that run through the work and seizing on isolated, particular passages "in full." In forging such connections and adducing the "similar," we necessarily "abridge." The almost technically methodological question raised here—how many examples need to be registered in order to demonstrate (or even to construct) an interpretive claim about a novel?—flows into the larger tensions we have been examining. Like the comment in "Boys' Weeklies" ("otherwise the two journals are so alike that they can be treated as one"), Orwell's assertion that "there are many similar passages in Dickens" is deceptively transparent. Finding those "similar passages" is not such an easy thing to do, and it is certainly a process that takes time (and readerly agency). It takes immersion *in* the object (here, a novelistic oeuvre) but also detachment from this object. Once again, these are only "semi-sociological" essays, half-in and half-out. In fact, throughout "Charles Dickens," Orwell gestures to a long history of reading that informs but cannot be *fully* integrated into the argument. In the most basic sense—and it is crucial to register this basic fact— Orwell's extended essay on Dickens presupposes a long, extended immersion, as reader, in Dickens's work. Orwell's immersive reading is, of course, centered on Dickens but also registered in a series of comparisons to other writers like Thackeray or Charles Reade. Thus, for example, Orwell writes: "If one wants a modern equivalent, the nearest would be H. G. Wells. . . . Anyone who has *studied Wells's novels in detail* will have noticed that though he hates the aristocrat like poison, he has no particular objection to the plutocrat, and no enthusiasm for the proletarian" (33, emphasis added). In comments like this, Orwell gradually widens the ambit of reading that lies behind his argument. And he subtly highlights the movement between a reading that has taken place, as he says, "in detail" and the distillation of such reading into a short "abstract."

These compressed evaluations of different authors (driven always by earlier, more extended encounters with their work) dramatize the interpretive choice that underlies the essay as a whole: the synthetic, immersive focus on a single author's work, a novelistic oeuvre. And a striking feature of the readerly synthesis that drives Orwell's interpretation of Dickens is the way that his generalized statements come to elevate the place of detail within Dickens's work. "[I]t is fatal for a caricaturist to see too much" (36), Orwell writes, and his analysis turns repeatedly to the "part," "episode," or "detail" in Dickens, as with these two notable examples:

> Dickens is obviously a writer whose parts are greater than his wholes. He is all fragments, all details—rotten architecture, but wonderful gargoyles. (75)

> The outstanding, unmistakable mark of Dickens's writing is the *unnecessary detail*. Here is an example of what I mean. The story given below is not particularly funny, but there is one phrase in it that is as individual as a fingerprint. (69, Orwell's emphasis)

The italics here are important. They signal—as they often do for Orwell—a heightening of conceptuality itself.[9] In this case, they mark that strange point where reading "in detail" can get transmogrified into one general, overarching claim. Here the generalization ironically centers on detail itself. By making his abstraction of Dickens come to focus on the use of detail (each one "individual as a fingerprint"), Orwell seems to lead abstraction to a place beyond itself.

This double-edged relationship between details and abstraction is mediated in part through the length of Orwell's own essay—a lengthiness that takes form only against the shorter trajectories, but more extensive topics, of "Boys' Weeklies" and "Inside the Whale." ("Charles Dickens," at over 20,000 words, is twice the length of "Boys' Weeklies" and a length-and-a-third of the title essay, which runs about 15,000 words.) The size of the essay, I want to suggest, stands as a formal correlative to Orwell's immersion in Dickens (and, more peripherally, a host of other novelists: Wells, Thackeray, etc.). This unevenness is important: any such nonstandard segmentation can call attention to the lengthiness—or brevity—of specific sections (think of a music album with one particularly long song) and reinforce this length as a *willed* formal decision of the author. In other words, variety in length once again calls attention to the contingent "writerliness" of Orwell's work, a writerliness that unfolds, as I've argued throughout this book, in unresolved tension with the plain style. Variety in length (more than length in and of itself) signals contingency, choice, freedom—and also can provoke reverberating unease. If *this* text, section, or song can extend in such a way, does it mean that other sections also might be further elaborated? Or truncated? What is the justification for any of these lengths? Why *should* a song be three minutes or a chapter thirty pages? At the limit, such variety corrodes any authority that would justify this particular unit of composition and ultimately justify the act of composition itself—one reason standardization of length is so often the norm. Without such standardization, every text, out of its own resources, would have to motivate and justify its particular duration, to both define and defend its own form.[10]

"Charles Dickens" is the longest essay in *Inside the Whale* (and, indeed, the longest critical essay in all of Orwell's work). Its length shadows its argument, and is intertwined, specifically, with the focus on, or immersion in, a single writer. While Orwell expresses concern that he is concentrating only on the ideological "message" rather than the aesthetic value of Dickens, the sheer formal position of the essay within *Inside the Whale* confers distinction onto the author. Part of the argument about Dickens is elaborated through this extension, through Orwell's willingness, within such "semi-sociological literary criticism," to linger disproportionately on one figure. (This formal cathexis is signaled in other ways as well, perhaps most conspicuously by Orwell's famous attention to the writer's imagined "face" at the end of the essay [85].) The anomalous length of "Charles Dickens" is thus another way in which *Inside the Whale* tends to underline (both thematically and formally) the *unsettled* practice of literary criticism. The collection provokes reverberating questions, clustered around the precarious boundary of subject and object in any literary-critical argument. What should a topic be? How can we pull out one particular strand of writing from the much larger culture? What does it *mean* to consider someone at length? How should we use textual examples? And, in the final analysis, how do our own acts of writing and thinking—our own effort to put thoughts into words—correspond with the object, the words and thoughts, that we are writing and thinking about?

I've mentioned the peculiar way that detail itself emerges as the overarching quality that Orwell distills, or "abstracts," from Dickens's work. The loss implicit in abstraction (in that sense in which an editor might present the condensed "abstract" of a novel or book) connects as well with an even more crucial feature of Orwell's reading of Dickens: its striking negativity. If Orwell will claim that Dickens himself has a "rather negative attitude towards society" (62), he begins his own analysis with an explicitly negative question: "Where exactly does he stand, socially, morally and politically? As usual, one can define his position more easily if one starts by deciding what he was *not*" (11, Orwell's emphasis). Orwell assiduously delineates Dickens's power of social and artistic comprehension against the background of what Dickens fails to see. On the one hand, Orwell continually makes large (and general) claims for Dickens, arguing, for example that "he attacked English institutions with a ferocity that has never since been approached" (10) or that "in the power of evoking visual images he has probably never been equaled" (57). On the other hand, the essay is punctuated, and driven forward, by all the aspects of experience that are missing from Dickens's novels. Thus: "he does not write about the proletariat" (11); "he displays no consciousness that the *structure* of society can be changed" (18); "[t]here are large areas of the human mind that he never touches" (78); "[i]t is noticeable that Dickens hardly ever writes of war, even to denounce it" (41); "he is not mechanically minded" (59); "[o]ne can see Dickens's utter lack of an educational theory" (30); "[h]e is hostile to the feudal, agricultural past and not in real touch with the industrial present . . . the future (meaning science, 'progress' and so forth) . . . hardly enters into his thoughts" (60); "[h]owever much Dickens may admire the working classes, he does not wish to resemble them" (45); "[w]hat he does not noticeably write about, however, is *work*" (54).

"Not . . . no . . . never . . . hardly ever . . . not . . . utter lack . . . not in real touch . . . hardly ever . . . not . . . not noticeably": there is an energy of negation here that goes well beyond the mere tactic of "defin[ing Dickens's] position more easily." Indeed, this essay could have a secure place within that long tradition of left-wing literary criticism that emphasizes a dialectical approach to artistic vision, focusing on how the accomplishments and limitations of a text are intertwined (and both shaped by historical currents). The thunderous "no" of Orwell's essay focuses specifically, like "Boys' Weeklies," on the radical outsidedness of the working class, not just to Dickens's novels but perhaps to writing as such. In the essay's most significant line, Orwell distills his negative perspective and extends it well beyond Dickens's texts: "If you look for the working classes in fiction, and especially English fiction, all you find is a hole" (11). The absence of the working class connects to the "submerged populations" and to "the mass of the English people" that Orwell inscribes as the horizon of his analysis in "Boys' Weeklies." In different ways, both essays concern the problem of mass observation, to use the talismanic 1930s formulation.

This sentence hovers once more between tactile simplicity and structural amplification. Again, we could choose to see this as a purely rhetorical strategy, a mechanism for conveying an abstraction as though it were a tangible observation. In its negativity, as well as in this precarious balance of structural reach and colloquial tone, the comment resembles the paradigmatic statement we considered from *Wigan Pier*: "This is the kind of point one is always liable to miss" (29). Physicalizing his abstraction, Orwell formulates a paradoxical action: to "find" a hole is once more to see something that *isn't* there—as when Orwell initially fails to "see" the beds that are missing from the spike in *Down and Out*. (I will return to this scene, which I briefly touched on in my reading of "A Hanging," in Part Two.) The point that we always miss; the missing beds (themselves initially "missed") in *Down and Out*; the "quite bare" cell in Orwell's earlier text "A Hanging": all of these examples resonate with the "hole" that Orwell puts at the center of British fiction. It is worth looking at this passage "in full":

> To begin with, he does not write about the proletariat, in which he merely resembles the overwhelming majority of novelists, past and present. If you look for the working classes in fiction, and especially English fiction, all you find is a hole. This statement needs qualifying, perhaps. For reasons that are easy enough to see, the agricultural labourer (in England a proletarian) gets a fairly good showing in fiction, and a great deal has been written about criminals, derelicts and, more recently, the working-class intelligentsia. But the ordinary town proletariat, the people who make the wheels go round, have always been ignored by novelists. When they do find their way between the covers of a book, it is nearly always as objects of pity or as comic relief. . . . If you ask any ordinary reader which of Dickens's proletarian characters he can remember, the three he is almost certain to mention are Bill Sikes, Sam Weller and Mrs. Gamp. A burglar, a valet and a drunken midwife—not exactly a representative cross-section of the English working class. (11–12)

"This statement needs qualifying, perhaps." We can recognize, again, the odd way that Orwell puts forth this kind of *methodological* point so brusquely, with such casual language, that he both obscures and intensifies its conceptual force. Such tonal simplicity can highlight the procedure of thought, over and above the assertion. Such an effect is crystallized in this example, as the sentence—one of the most concise, minimal phrases in *Inside the Whale*—concerns nothing other than a call for conceptual elaboration. It is a blunt call for less bluntness. (And the concluding "perhaps" that qualifies this blunt imperative *to* qualify merely ties the slipknot of the paradox.) In fact, Orwell offers a number of "qualifi[cations]" to his central claim—a claim that focuses on the same threshold of social division so central to the analysis in "Boys' Weeklies." Orwell's qualifications don't diminish the sense of a social reality resting outside of written discourse but, on the contrary, begin to show the specific (and varied) displacements that occur when writing attempts to comprehend this outside world. These displacements can take a number of forms: geographical (from the troubling city to the valorized countryside), characterological (the servants or thieves who stand in for the working class), or *generic* (the shift to comedy or pathos under the pressure of observing the working class). Remembering the preposition in Orwell's title ("Inside"), we can discern the complex aesthetic idea that is so simply presented under the trope of working-class characters who "find their way between the covers of a book" only as "objects of pity or as comic relief." The play between inclusion and exclusion here is a basic part of how the novels work and reflects on the fact of social submersion itself, or the subordination, in the actual world, of "the people who make the wheels go round." Orwell's reading calls attention to how external reality is registered in writing, how it is distorted, and how such distortions are part of (and can point us toward) the world that has not been sufficiently comprehended.

This list of displacements is not exhaustive. There could be (and, in fact, are) other examples that Orwell raises to show the distortions or transformations that can occur when this "submerged population"—that forms the outside of novelistic writing—"finds its way" into the closed structure of a book. We need to see these examples as methodological rather than simply as taxonomic. In fact, they suggest a specific model of mimesis: the characters that are refracted in this way—by the substitution of the proletariat with the figure of an agricultural laborer, or the configuration of the worker through the specific syntax of comedy—are *not* entirely disconnected from the working-class reality that rests outside the form. Orwell's analysis of the "hole" in English fiction does not vitiate the relationship between the written and working-class reality but suggests its intricacy, and suggests, further, that by confronting this intricacy, we can gain a more vital sense of the reality that is comprehended—and occluded—through the literary text. Thus Orwell's comment that "the narrowness of vision is in one way a great advantage to [Dickens], because it is fatal for a caricaturist to see too much" is another emblematic statement about the relationship between representation (the powerfully original "caricature" that Dickens achieves) and constraint (the "unseen" that is necessary to such caricature). To read in this way entails attending to what a form of writing registers and to what we miss in—and also *through*—the written text (or what we can miss in and through our own act of reading). Orwell chooses Dickens not because he exemplifies a lack of vision (which would motivate searching for "what he is *not*") but, on the contrary: as this method applies even to a writer with such social passion and power, it approaches something that might be intrinsic not merely to "the overwhelming majority of novelists, past and present," but to the act of literary representation itself.

In the first essay of *Inside the Whale*, Orwell projects this "impossibility" of writing back, to the nineteenth-century, and out, across the entire tradition of the English novel. (We've seen that Orwell ends the essay collection on this note of literature's "impossibility," and we can get well into the particular nature of *Inside the Whale* by connecting this radicalized sense of difficulty to the working-class "hole" that we find in "Charles Dickens.") At the same time, Orwell grapples with the quite specific accomplishments— and limits—of Dickens's work. The essay doesn't simply prosecute the literary text (or the category of literariness) for its "holes" and occlusions. Despite the catalogue of omissions, the essay insists on the irreducible social and aesthetic power of Dickens's text and links this power, or artistic vision, to the negativity that so much of the essay traces. "Wonderfully as he can describe an *appearance*, Dickens does not often describe a *process*" (57, Orwell's emphasis). The trade-off between "appearance" and "process" (like that between abstraction and particularity) is a dynamic one: the vividness of Dickensian description is contingent upon its lack of attention to process or structure, which is why Orwell can argue that it is "fatal for a caricaturist to see too much." Nor is the emphasis on particularity merely formal in Orwell; as his characterization of the detail ("as individual as a fingerprint") might suggest, Dickens's descriptions have a social meaning as well. So, for example, after commenting that "Dickens sees human beings with the most intense vividness," Orwell laments the way that "even people like Squeers and Micawber get sucked into the machinery" of a melodramatic plot structure (56). Vividness is abolished, detail flattened by the "machinery" of the plot; here we can see the process of submergence itself, even if the novels cannot account for the "submerged population" who "make the wheels go round."[11]

Many twentieth-century Dickens critics after Orwell (especially those self-consciously positioned on the left) have been drawn to the strange cross-hatching of radical energy and conservative reflex in Dickens's novels. The best criticism of this kind sees the partitions of the work as unsettled and fluid, the "displacements" discussed above as always potentially able to generate social meaning, often in oblique or surprising ways. Even in Orwell's own essay, we can see a counterintuitive recuperation of the "happy ending" in Dickens, that feature of narrative syntax that, more than any other, has been most easily identified with the blindness, sentimentality, or conservatism of Dickens's novels. Orwell's essay develops this idea, arguing that the inheritances that so often play a large role in these endings function to problematically secure (on the level of *plot*) the absenting of work that has already taken place so profoundly on the levels of description, structure, and character. As Orwell introduces his discussion of Dickens's endings:

> With the doubtful exception of David Copperfield (merely Dickens himself), one cannot point to a single one of his central characters who is primarily interested in his job. His heroes work in order to make a living and to marry the heroine, not because they feel a passionate interest in one particular subject. . . . In any case, in the typical Dickens novel, the *deus ex machina* enters with a bag of gold in the last chapter and the hero is absolved from further struggle. (61)

Here, the logic of the happy ending is introduced entirely in terms of our main problem, the detachment of all (central) characters in Dickens from work. However, Orwell continues the discussion. Precisely because these endings are *so* evacuated of real social content, they also heighten a vacuity that is rooted in the negative drive of Dickens's work in the first place. Orwell is most explicit about this theme in this same passage, which continues:

> [Dickens] himself, as is well known, worked like a slave and believed in his work as few novelists have ever done. But there seems to be no calling except novel-writing (and perhaps acting) towards which he can imagine this kind of devotion. *And, after all, it is natural enough, considering his rather negative attitude towards society* [my emphasis] . . . When Martin Chuzzlewitt had made it up with his uncle, when Nicholas Nickleby had married money, when John Harmon had been enriched by Boffin—what did they *do?* The answer evidently is that they did nothing. . . . That is the spirit in which most of Dickens's books end—a sort of radiant idleness. (62)

In this more complicated reading of the "happy ending," the fury of Dickens's own writing, a fury born out of his "rather negative attitude toward society," produces an idleness that seems, at first glance, to obscure both the sheer work and the negative attitude that underlie it. "[T]hey did nothing," and such "nothing[ness]" functions (almost as in Bourdieu's reading of *Sentimental Education*)[12] to gloss the negative activity of writing itself. (Later, in a pseudonymous essay titled "Can Socialists Be Happy?" that I will discuss in Part Two, Orwell returns to the topic of Dickens's happy endings and comes up with another, different reading of their social and aesthetic meaning.)

Orwell's interpretation of Dickens links Dickens's writerly achievement closely to its limitations. But Orwell's essay also resists stabilizing such a tension by invoking the knowledge of criticism against the misprisions of literature. As we have seen in "Boys' Weeklies," the essays, by dramatizing the act of abstraction itself, work against such stability, enfolding the dynamics of literary representation (as it negotiates between detail and structure, appearance and process, the particular and the abstract) into the evidentiary and conceptual elaboration of the critical essay. In Orwell's essay collection, basic procedures of literary criticism resonate with—or shadow—the political and literary problems with which he is grappling. Juxtaposing the power of abstraction (mostly simply expressed through the linking of "many similar passages") and the limits of excerption, Orwell subtly recasts the dynamics of literary mimesis within the unfolding of his own critical analysis. Since Orwell is concerned, ultimately, with the social realist tradition in literature, these essays establish an important parallel between literary criticism and literature itself, as Orwell relocates key processes and problems of realism—the crossing of a threshold, the encounter with a messy, multitudinous reality, the play between detail and type—within the process of criticism. This doubling up of mimesis is the political "background" for the divided structure of *Inside the Whale,* as the problem of synthesis that is dramatized within each essay is reiterated in terms of the essay collection itself. Put differently, by keeping us partially "inside" his own collection (juxtaposing the different parts of *Inside the Whale*), Orwell continues to question what constitutes the "inside" and the "outside" of writing more generally.

With this in mind, I want to return to that passage in "Charles Dickens" that draws parallels between the compression of critical abstraction (the "many" passages that one selected episode stands in for), the novels' own elision of social reality (the mass of persons "submerged" within both city and story), and the distortions of *contemporary* ideology ("In rather the same way the modern doctrinaire Socialist contemptuously writes off a large block of the population as 'lumpenproletariat.'") This last is important not just as a means of scoring partisan political points. In his most extended act of historical literary criticism, Orwell wants to avoid the traps of a "presentism" that asserts its own knowingness through the errors of the past. These different levels of dialectical tension (between the object and the subject, the past and the present, the critic and the writer) are apparent from the opening sentences of Orwell's essay, which are set off as a separate paragraph:

> Dickens is one of those writers who are well worth stealing. Even the burial of his body in Westminster Abbey was a species of theft, if you come to think of it. (9)

Note the simultaneous devaluation of object *and* method here: while literary criticism is reduced to a kind of thieving, Dickens himself is depicted, first off, as a corpse. The second paragraph immediately works to specify this—moving from the institutionalization of Dickens (the burial in Westminster Abbey presumably places him "inside" rather than "outside" the British status quo) to contemporary Dickens criticism. Discussing Chesterton, the Marxist critic T. A. Jackson, and Lenin himself, Orwell writes that "The Marxist claims [Dickens] as 'almost' a Marxist, the Catholic claims him as 'almost' a Catholic," while Lenin, "found Dickens's 'middle-class sentimentality' so intolerable that he walked out in the middle" of a dramatization of *The Cricket on the Hearth* (9). This is the beginning of a number of contemporary references that center around the problem of revolutionary politics—as introduced by the theorist (Jackson) and practitioner (Lenin). Consider these three comments:

> It is said that Macaulay refused to review *Hard Times* because he disapproved of its "sullen Socialism." Obviously Macaulay is here using the word "Socialism" in the same sense in which, twenty years ago, a vegetarian meal or a Cubist picture used to be referred to as "Bolshevism." There is not a line in the book that can properly be called Socialistic. (14)

> In the chapters [in *Barnaby Rudge*] dealing with the riots Dickens shows a most profound horror of mob violence. . . . These chapters are of great psychological interest, because they show how deeply he had brooded on the subject. . . . Here is one of the descriptions, for instance. . . . You might almost think you were reading a description of "Red" Spain by a partisan of General Franco. (19–20)

> [N]ever anywhere does he indulge in the typical English boasting, the "island race," "bulldog breed," "right little, tight little island" style of talk. . . . The one place where he seems to display a normal hatred of foreigners is in the American chapters of *Martin Chuzzlewit*. This, however, is simply the reaction of a generous mind against cant. If Dickens were alive today he would make a trip to Soviet Russia and come back with a book rather like Gide's *Retour de l'URSS*. (40)

Rather than use a present-day political stance as a secure ground for judging Dickens, Orwell instead puts into play a series of conflicts, of misprisions and transvaluations. Structurally, of course, all three analogies are almost ornamental—"in the same way as which," "you might almost think," "rather like." (Remember that "if you come to think of it" in the opening lines.) But by focusing on the methodological ground of the essay itself (i.e., Socialist and Left ideology), these analogies have more than a decorative function. In each case, the analogy rests on an interpretive conflict: the mischaracterization of counterculture sentiment as "Bolshevist," the propaganda about Communism by Fascist ideology, or Gide's own landmark in political disillusionment *about* Communism. At the same time, these passages offer conflicting senses of Dickens himself—a writer who misdescribes the Gordon riots but *avoids* the misdescriptions of the "foreign" that plague his period. What's crucial to note is that Orwell accesses the contradictions in Dickens not through a stable ground of political clarity but in relation to the contradictions and difficulties of his own contemporary moment. The first passage thus draws a line of historical continuity *through* error—from the overgeneralization of "Socialism" in the 1860s to the overgeneralization of Bolshevism "twenty years ago."

This use of the present once again illustrates the fragile nature of self-reflexivity in "Charles Dickens" and *Inside the Whale* as a whole. There is a model here for the critic who, in judging history, also is embedded within history—just as the criticism that addresses writing is also a form of writing itself. Especially in the context of the essays as a whole, Orwell is attempting something ambitious: an emphatically historicized reading of Dickens that, nevertheless, also puts Dickens in vital, unsettled relationship with the contemporary. Not just rendering a judgment on Dickens from the vantage point of the present, Orwell's essay reminds us both of the historicity of the present itself and of our inability to fully escape from the present *into* history (by making such secure judgments about the limits of the past).

This sense of the "escape" that might be latent within *all* critical writing is merely a part of that more insistent way in which the three essays register how the experience depicted inside the world of literature, writing, and culture can never adequately account for the world *outside* of literature (or, more precisely, for the outside of writing itself). An important demonstration of this before *Inside the Whale* is the provocatively materialistic approach to writing that underlies Orwell's 1936 novel *Keep the Aspidistra*

Flying. The novel might be the most pertinent intertext with *Inside the Whale*, if only as Orwell's version of a fictional genre that he stigmatizes in "Charles Dickens," when he comments on how "a writer nowadays is so hopelessly isolated that the typical modern novel is a novel about a novelist" (54). *Keep the Aspidistra Flying* at once enacts and bristles against this kind of self-reflexivity, focusing on the material conditions behind the career of a writer—and bookstore worker—who is himself obsessed with the relationship of poverty to culture. In a key moment for Orwell, the novel describes Gordon Comstock trying to "get to work" on his overwritten and never-finished long poem:

> Money again, always money! Lack of money means discomfort, means squalid worries, means shortage of tobacco, means ever-present consciousness of failure—above all, it means loneliness. How can you be anything but lonely on two quid a week? And in loneliness no decent book was ever written. It was quite certain that *London Pleasures* would never be the poem he had conceived—it was quite certain, indeed, that it would never even be finished. And in the moments when he faced facts Gordon himself was aware of this.
>
> Yet all the same, and all the more for that very reason, he went on with it. . . . And after all, there were times when the mood of creation returned, or seemed to return. It returned to-night, for just a little while—just as long as it takes to smoke two cigarettes. With smoke tickling his lungs, he abstracted himself from the mean and actual world. (31–32)

This is a peculiar version of self-reflexivity, and Orwell's insistent attention in *Keep the Aspidistra Flying* to the *materiality* of literature (from the money that underlies culture generally to the protagonist's subsistence work turning books into commodities to the sheer physicality of pen, ink, and paper) resonates with the "materialist" or "realist" sense of writing in *Inside the Whale*—as the essays work to externalize the act of comprehension that allows writing to take in the world. In order to grasp the world through writing, we risk displacing ourselves from the world, but this displacement is, itself, utterly worldly. Any abstraction of the "mean and actual world" can

risk turning into abstraction "from . . . the world," and Orwell's transvaluation of the term captures something essential about both the power and
danger of writing.

Abstracting of the world or abstraction from the world: all three essays of
Inside the Whale draw a connection between the self-reflexivity of writing
and the confrontation with class division. Self-reflection in *Inside the Whale*
is grounded in our starting point—the three essays' enigmatic division. This
division both turns our attention to the internal relationship of the three
essays and foregrounds the limits of each text's contrasting methodological
framework (or its means of comprehending the external). If self-reflection is
the essential trope of a writing that plunges us in, to the text itself, Orwell's
attention to the frame calls equal attention to a world that—never entirely
grasped—still lies outside.

Method as Object ("Inside the Whale")

More than any other text by Orwell, *Inside the Whale* explicitly considers
the ramifications of writing in a time of crisis. As we have seen, Orwell's
book ends by foregrounding what he calls the "impossibility" of certain
modes of writing. "History is what hurts" (102), Fredric Jameson writes in
The Political Unconscious, attempting to encapsulate the way that social conflict encroaches upon literature's efforts to sustain itself as an integral category and upon criticism's desire to preserve an essentially aesthetic concept
of the literary. This kind of hurtfulness is endemic to 1930s criticism, and
with *Inside the Whale,* Orwell very consciously jumps into a defined, and
pronounced, field of debate. All three essays reflect on and reflect back this
sense of crisis: in the face of history's destructive effect on both literature
and critical reflections on literature, how does the critic write about writing's potential impossibility? "Charles Dickens" begins by referencing other
critical efforts to "steal" Dickens for ideological purposes (Catholic, Marxist),
while "Boys' Weeklies" takes form as an implicit challenge to left-wing literary criticism concerned with working-class reality: here are the texts that
are *actually* read by the British masses. But it is in the final, eponymous essay
that Orwell's pursuit of this question—the unsettled relationship between
criticism and history—most explicitly reflects back upon *Inside the Whale*
itself. Even as "Charles Dickens" laments how "the typical modern novel is a

novel about a novelist" (54), Orwell's essay collection, in this final chapter, verges on becoming criticism about critics.

Both formally and conceptually, the self-reflexive turn of *Inside the Whale* is quite important. Indeed, rather than that eponymous leviathan, Orwell's collection, as it proceeds, risks turning into a snake that eats its own tail. While we've noted how "Charles Dickens" jumps off from contemporary debates over the nineteenth-century writer (and references a wider present-day political discourse), "Inside the Whale," in its polemic about contemporary literary criticism and historiography, comes to focus on the very genres to which the text itself belongs. Summarizing Henry Miller's passivity or acceptance, Orwell writes:

> It will be seen what this amounts to. It is a species of quietism, implying either complete unbelief or else a degree of belief amounting to mysticism. . . . But in a time like ours, is this a defensible attitude? Notice that it is almost impossible to refrain from asking this question. At the moment of writing we are still in a period in which it is taken for granted that books ought always to be positive, serious and "constructive." A dozen years ago this idea would have been greeted with titters. ("My dear aunt, one doesn't write *about* anything, one just *writes*.") Then the pendulum swung away from the frivolous notion that art is merely technique, but it swung a very long distance, to the point of asserting that a book can only be "good" if it is founded on a "true" vision of life. Naturally the people who believe this also believe that they are in possession of the truth themselves. Catholic critics, for instance, tend to claim that books are only "good" when they are of Catholic tendency. Marxist critics make the same claim more boldly for Marxist books. For instance, Mr Edward Upward ("A Marxist Interpretation of Literature," in *The Mind in Chains*): "Literary criticism which aims at being Marxist must . . . proclaim that no book written *at the present time* can be 'good' unless it is written from a Marxist or near-Marxist viewpoint." (178–179, Upward's emphasis)

To use the author's own term, we might "[n]otice" how Orwell swerves away from the question that he asks here just when he urges us to "[n]otice that it is almost impossible [for contemporary criticism] to refrain from asking" about literature's social relevance. Now, moving away from writers more generally or novelists like Henry Miller, the essay begins to discuss "Catholic critics" and "Marxist critics," and this focus continues for most of the remaining text. In other words, Orwell's focus shifts from literature to criticism and thus from an object outside of itself to writing that is analogous to itself. A "method" of analysis (asking, how relevant is a particular piece of literature?) becomes the "object" of analysis (which now asks, what does it mean that we approach literature in terms of relevance?).

Unlike the other texts that *Inside the Whale* has examined, in talking about something like Upward's hugely influential "A Marxist Interpretation of Literature," Orwell's essay is addressing a text quite similar to itself. This confusion of method and object is also a confusion of the "inside" and the "outside," to return to the governing terms of *Inside the Whale*. In one sense, a method can always internalize the "outside," acting as a frame that contains, shelters, or imprisons the object it would scrutinize. In turning to contemporary criticism, Orwell makes this framing device, itself, the object that he seeks to define or frame. But of course the particular "method" that focuses Orwell's attention—one which takes it for granted "that books ought always to be positive, serious and 'constructive'"—hinges on the priority of the "outside" (the social world that conditions and shapes the literary text) over the "inside" (the text's own autonomous, integral structure). As Louis MacNeice writes in *Modern Poetry* (one of the texts that Orwell invokes in this essay), "The primary characteristic of these poets is that they are interested in a subject *outside* themselves—or at any rate in a subject which is not merely a subject for their poetry" (17, emphasis added). Orwell troubles this stance not by elevating text over world—in a nostalgic return to purely autonomous, or self-reflective, art—but, rather, by showing how such a stance itself is embedded in a world that rests "outside" of it. (We are all, in this radically embodied and material sense, inside the whale.) For this reason, Orwell's essay is rarely understood as primarily an interpretation of Henry Miller's novel but rather as a skirmish with other practitioners of the enterprise of literary criticism. Orwell is struggling to find a horizon, or an "outside," that can provide a vantage point for examining the aesthetic stance most committed to recognizing the outside itself. Returning to the "internal criticism" that Zwerdling sees as a component part of Orwell's socialism, "Inside the Whale" functions as a polemically materialist critique of the left-wing literary intelligentsia. This critique works by attempting to "externalize" contemporary literary criticism: socially contextualizing this criticism and, more importantly, rendering it *as* visible, to the reader (or even to itself) from the outside.

Above all, "Inside the Whale" speculates about the sociological grounds for the intellectual "fashion" that has been narrowly politicizing literature. This is the core of Orwell's searing polemic. For example:

> The outstanding writers of the 'twenties were of very varied origins, few of them had passed through the ordinary English educational mill . . . and most of them had had at some point to struggle against poverty, neglect, and even downright persecution. On the other hand, nearly all the younger writers fit easily into the public-school-university-Bloomsbury pattern. The few who are of proletarian origin are of the kind that is declassed early in life, first by means of scholarships and then by the bleaching-tub of London "culture." (161–162)

> The Communist movement in Western Europe began as a movement for the violent overthrow of capitalism, and degenerated within a few years into an instrument of Russian foreign policy. . . . So far as I know, the only comprehensive history of this subject in English is Franz Borkenau's book, *The Communist International*. What Borkenau's facts even more than his deductions makes clear is that Communism could never have developed along its present lines if any real revolutionary feeling had existed in the industrialized countries. (163–164)

> Nearly all the dominant writers of the 'thirties belonged to the soft-boiled emancipated middle class and were too young to have effective memories of the Great War. To people of that kind such things as purges, secret police, summary executions, imprisonment without trial, etc., etc., are too remote to be terrifying. They can swallow totalitarianism *because* they have no experience of anything except liberalism. (168–169)

> But notice the phrase "necessary murder." It could only be written by a person to whom murder is at most a *word*. . . . Mr. Auden's brand of

amoralism is only possible if you are the kind of person who is always somewhere else when the trigger is pulled. (169–170)

To nearly all the writers who have counted during the 'thirties, what more has ever happened than Mr. Connolly records in *Enemies of Promise?* It is the same pattern all the time; public school, university, a few trips abroad, then London. Hunger, hardship, solitude, exile, war, prison, persecution, manual labour—hardly even words. (171)

These selections demonstrate how Orwell builds up a class-based critique of a Marxist literary criticism that itself revolves around class. This attack on the 1930s intelligentsia is intertwined with a critique of Communist ideology emerging out of Orwell's experience in the Spanish Civil War. Orwell's "experience" in Spain does not simply encompass the actions he undertook but also an experience or encounter with language itself, with the degraded discourse of left-wing propaganda that, because he could contrast it with real actions and events, Orwell comes to see from the outside. This sense of standing on the outside of a language system is a key to the essay and underlies its polemic against writers who are cut off from (to combine the terms from these passages) "poverty," "neglect," "purges," "secret police," "summary executions," "imprisonment without trial," "hunger," "hardship," "solitude," "exile," "war," "prison," "persecution," and "manual labour."

There is an important connection between the collapse of Orwell's own text into self-reflection (as it focuses attention on objects so much *like* itself) and the polemical insistence on what remains outside, and cut off from, writing's own interiority. It is only in the combination of these two processes that Orwell's text points us to an outside without substituting itself for the thing toward which it points. I take this pointing out (no easy thing to achieve) as the central ambition of *Inside the Whale*, or, put differently, as the central polemic (about writing) put forth inside *Inside the Whale*. In this way, we might understand Orwell's harsh rejoinder to Auden—who has such cultural prestige at that moment—as a larger admonition about writing as such. In one sense, all writing finds itself in this condition: adjacent to and at a remove from the events it describes; caught in the juncture between an "abstraction" that comprehends "the mean and actual world" and abstraction as separation *from* this world. Writing is "always somewhere else when the trigger is pulled"—and yet is nothing but the pulling of the trigger.

Conclusion: Face-to-Face (Dickens, Orwell, Williams)

Raymond Williams's 1971 *George Orwell* remains his one book-length study of a single author. In this sense, Williams's discussion of Orwell is structurally equivalent to Orwell's own most extended single-author essay. As we have seen, the initial publication of "Charles Dickens" in *Inside the Whale* (1940) accentuates this essay's length, as Orwell's consideration of Dickens is set against two briefer texts. Nor does any of Orwell's subsequent criticism in the 1940s approach the length of "Charles Dickens"; in retrospect, and in the context of Orwell's work as a whole, the essay stands out further. The question of length is often important in criticism's *formal* elaboration. What duration of critical attention is provoked or justified by specific books, objects, or authors? Why does the encounter with Dickens generate Orwell's longest essay? Why does the encounter with Orwell, in particular, generate a slender book from Williams?

Jean-Paul Sartre begins an introduction to a collection of writing by Jean Genet only to see the introduction grow and become a (substantial) book itself. Sartre's writing shifts from supplementary reflection into freestanding text. In this Borgesian transmutation, *Saint Genet* dramatizes a more ubiquitous potential, or lawlessness, within criticism. In a similar way, both Orwell's long essay "Charles Dickens" and Williams's short book *George Orwell* model a freedom—and thus also an uneasiness—that can inhere within critical writing. As we have seen, the simple lengthiness of Orwell's essay helps to elevate Dickens, underlining the significance and centrality of this writer for Orwell. But, likewise, the elevation of Dickens highlights this particular formal process. "Charles Dickens" is one of a series of works by Orwell in which duration matters, and in which length (or brevity) is tied into the dynamics of critical reflection.

Williams also draws on the specific resources of this form (i.e., the focused, single-author study) to develop his argument in *George Orwell*. In particular, I want to look at the final section of Williams's book and the way it dramatizes that "sense of an ending," which can be as important to a work

of criticism as a fictional narrative. Williams's conclusion serves to summarize and encapsulate his critical stance toward Orwell. But it is also shaped
by its position, at the climax of the book:

> We are never likely to reach a time when we can do without his frank-
> ness, his energy, his willingness to join in. These are the qualities
> we shall go on respecting in him, whatever other conclusions we may
> come to. But they are real qualities only if they are independent and
> active. The thing to do with his work, his history, is to read it, not imi-
> tate it. He is still there, tangibly, with the wound in his throat, the sad
> strong face, the plain words written in hardship and exposure. But then
> as we reach out to touch him we catch something of his hardness, a nec-
> essary hardness. We are acknowledging a presence and a distance:
> other names, other years; a history to respect, to remember, to move on
> from. (97)

This striking final paragraph has received little attention, perhaps because—
like Williams's book as a whole—it has been caught in the undertow of an
interpretive tide that it helped to generate: the diminution of Orwell, as critical object, in both left-wing and literary-theoretical discourse since the
1970s. Williams is a key figure for this, and his own polemical distance from
Orwell unquestionably hardens after this conclusion, in *New Left Review*
interviews as well as a second edition of the Orwell study.[13] But even an
added chapter in the second edition doesn't fully efface the marked, indeed
unavoidable, *rhetoric* of this ending. The tone of the conclusion draws a taut
balance between two contrasting critical impulses. Williams insists, analytically, on a distance between critic and text and works to collapse this distance, rhetorically, by means of the stark, physical terms in which he
describes it. Likewise, the passage takes conceptual leave of Orwell and,
indeed, configures the act of "reading" as nothing other *than* such leave-
taking. But it also presents reading as "touch[ing]."

　　Williams's conclusion thus superimposes two kinds of reading, or criticism: a "presence" and a "distance," as he puts it; one kind that would "imitate" (or attempt to "touch") the author, the other to "move on from" him.
Here we are back, indeed, to the "semi-sociological." And Williams chooses
quite deliberately to end his reading of Orwell at the fragile boundary

between these two impulses. To "read" here can *no longer* be equivalent to "touching" the author. But it has *not yet* become a pulling away or recoil that might occur only a bit later, once we have come to terms with that "hardness," which here is still freshly "caught." This is not an ambivalence to be decoded but rather a doubleness actively dramatized by the critical text itself.[14] Williams takes advantage of this passage's formal position to hold in place this moment of struggle, which we sense would have to resolve, just outside the frame of the analysis, in one direction or another.

The relationship between critic and criticized author here might remind us of other conclusions in British *fiction:* Moriarty and Sherlock Holmes in "The Final Problem" (caught in a tense struggle on the edge of a cliff, "reeling over, locked in each other's arms" [Doyle 505]) or Fielding and Aziz, at the very end of *Passage to India,* "half kissing" as their horses "swerved apart" (Forster 362). Like these texts, Williams's book manipulates the form—the sheer fact of ending—to freeze a dynamic process at its maximal point of internal tension. In all these cases, we sense that if only the form would extend just a *little longer,* this conflict would be resolved. But of course the form never does—and never can—extend that extra bit.

In connecting Williams's book on Orwell with an essay by Orwell, we can see a more intimate and unstable relationship between criticism and literary object, the primary and the secondary text. Williams's *George Orwell* seeks to encompass or frame Orwell's writing as a whole, but it also resembles, and can even be read through the structure of, one particular Orwell text. Inside and outside, object and frame, are thus again confused. (This confusion seems uncannily appropriate, of course, insofar as "Charles Dickens" initially appears in the middle of *Inside the Whale.* Orwell's own book also works, both conceptually and formally, to disturb a settled relationship, within writing, between inside and outside.) But the resemblances between Williams's *George Orwell* and Orwell's "Charles Dickens" extend beyond these qualities of focus and length. The attentive reader might see where I am heading here. While Williams's conclusion draws a resolute opposition between "read[ing]" and "imitat[ion]," it also inadvertently imitates the ending of Orwell's own extended piece:

When one reads any strongly individual piece of writing, one has the impression of seeing a face somewhere behind the page. It is not necessarily the actual face of the writer. I feel this very strongly with Swift, with Defoe, with Fielding, Stendhal, Thackeray, Flaubert, though in several cases I do not know what these people looked like and do not want to know. What one sees is the face that the writer *ought* to have. Well, in the case of Dickens I see a face that is not quite the face of Dickens's photographs, though it resembles it. It is the face of a man of about forty, with a small beard and a high colour. He is laughing, with a touch of anger in his laughter, but no triumph, no malignity. It is the face of a man who is always fighting against something, but who fights in the open and is not frightened, the face of a man who is generously angry—in other words, of a nineteenth-century liberal, a free-intelligence, a type hated with equal hatred by all the smelly little orthodoxies which are now contending for our souls. (85)

The association between the two endings is striking because it is so difficult to argue away this connection or to understand it as consciously intended. Williams decides to end his reflection by making Orwell "tangible." In taking leave of his study, he turns explicitly to an authorial body, defined above all by "the sad strong face." This is the same strategy that Orwell imaginatively alights upon for formulating the conclusion to *his* extended study of a single writer. And Orwell doesn't merely invoke Dickens's imagined countenance to end his essay but self-reflectively theorizes this decision ("when one reads *any* strongly individual piece of writing"). We'd be hard pressed to find a third example of a work of criticism that formulates its conclusion in these terms—that is, imagining the author's face.[15] Yet it is quite difficult to see Williams deliberately returning to Orwell's strategic choice, since such a return undermines the act of leave-taking—setting out critical distance and marking that new definition of "reading"—which drives the passage. The terms through which Williams acts to distance himself from Orwell draw from, and thus bind Williams more closely to, Orwell's own critical imagination. The proximity, the "touch," is greater than Williams realizes.[16]

And here, under the sign of such proximity, we might consider the larger significance of the distinction Williams draws between "reading" and "imitating," or "touching" and "distance." Williams's simple, transitive use of the verb "read," now distinguished sharply from imitation and proximity, emblematizes an array of intellectual energies that are developing within literary-critical thought when Williams writes. To invoke another central work of Williams, "reading" here functions as a deceptively plain keyword, and one whose central meanings—cultural, academic, philosophical, political—are, in this enunciation, changing and shifting. Williams's ending—and his transvaluation *of* ending as departure—also has a quite specific political context, as his book strives to register developments in British socialism that are intimately connected to "mov[ing] on" from Orwell. A political optimism—grounded in Williams's hopes for the New Left, and the radical youth movements of the late 1960s—suffuses the last chapter of the book and motivates this final elaboration of the relationship between Williams (as critical subject) and Orwell (as textual object). The penultimate paragraph ends:

> Beyond and past him, in and through many of the contradictions he experienced, real popular forces have continued to move, and the fight he joined and then despaired of has been renewed, has extended, and has gained important new ground. (97)

Williams writes these lines in 1971, and his final chapter invokes "the student movements of these past few years" (86) as well as a "new socialist movement . . . based on disturbance: on demonstrations, on direct action, on the politics of the streets and the localities" (87). In this sense, Williams's critique of the past is based, in an unusually explicit way, on a prophetic sense of the near future. A socialist transformation has *not yet* occurred, but its potential arrival is, Williams believes, on a closer horizon. The movement has, just in the past few years, been "renewed" and "extended." After a long period of loss or stasis, it is gaining ground. Again, Williams writes: "In other west-European countries . . . other choices were possible. But in England capitalist democracy survived with its main contradictions intact, and then the pretense or hope that it was social democracy, or was about to become so, lasted longer than was good for anybody's reason. Even after the profound disillusions of 1945–1951 and 1964–1970, the pretense or hope survived. *Yet no such illusion is static*" (95, emphasis added).

Williams's reading of Orwell (and his redefinition of what it would mean "to read") is thus intertwined with his evaluation of 1945–1951 and

1964–1970: that is, the two periods of Labour's parliamentary power. And this critique of Labour relies, in turn, on Williams's predictive sense of a different path forward, a "new socialist movement," which has not yet changed England but *has* "gained important new ground" and seems to be on the cusp of actualizing itself. In the past, Williams writes, "some sort of accommodation with capitalism . . . was at first temporarily and then habitually conceivable. . . . [T]his is the knot that was tied in the middle 1940s. And Orwell, indeed, helped to tie it" (95–96).

It is bracing to consider the way that Williams's conclusion, in *George Orwell,* draws on this sense of the near future in order to assess the literary-historical past. What is a lively optimism in 1971 looks different in the face of Thatcher's ascendancy in the late 1970s, the miners' strike of the mid-1980s, the revocation of the Labour Party's Clause 4 (on nationalization) in 1995, and the rise and fall of Tony Blair and New Labour in the 1990s and beyond. In the nearly half-century since Williams writes these lines, his picture of a new, revitalized democratic socialism in England—one that would break from its habitual "accommodation with capitalism"—has been falsified. So much new ground has been lost.

To invoke this difference—between 1971 and 2015—is not to negate Williams's effort at historicizing Orwell but to engage this effort in all of its own quite pointed historical specificity. I would want to argue, indeed, that Williams's reading of Orwell, as a figure rapidly receding into the past, could be accurate and compelling in 1971 but, ironically, gain *less* purchase as more time unfolds. Orwell, we might say—registering the force of both Williams's insights and his mistaken predictions—was further back in the past in 1971, and closer to the present in 2015 (after decades of backlash and retrenchment). And to simply repeat Williams's judgment is to negate his own historicizing ethos.

In a similar sense, part of what makes Williams's willingness to argue from his moment admirable is its sheer vulnerability. To read the past through the near future (rather than through the present itself or an unverifiable and more distant futurity) is to take a particular risk. This returns us to the issues of action, urgency, and disappointment that I discussed in the Introduction. As I argued there, Orwell's commitment to a specifically democratic socialism—as what he calls a "political position"—hinges on both the coherence and the *relative* inefficacy of socialist aspiration. To return to these opening terms: the political position has traction, for Orwell, only as long as socialism is still a viable but not an inevitable, let alone a victorious or normative, model: as long as it is a political destiny that is plausible but by no means guaranteed.[17] We could even say that Williams's optimistic 1971 socialism—which revises the past only by drawing so heavily on a *near future*—is an internally weak ideology, accruing part of its momentum from (and thus dependent on) events that are yet to come, while Orwell's less sanguine socialist position aims to sustain itself without ballast of this potentially treacherous sort. Someday, we can dream, Orwell's pessimism *will* be truly anachronistic, as Williams imagines in 1971. For now, however, this pessimism—grounded as it is in a broader, persistent sense of political commitment—can be, ironically, a source for renewal and hope.[18]

On the Threshold of Liberty

A Close Reading of "As I Please"

4

The Column as Form

Perfectly Casual

In Part Two of this book I want to make a case for the literary, and conceptual, significance of "As I Please," a weekly column that George Orwell writes for the democratic Socialist newspaper *Tribune* between 1943 and 1947. Such a claim might seem unlikely, straining not only against the uncertain status of these eighty pieces within Orwell's work but against the premises and form of this writing project itself. In fact, the significance of "As I Please" cannot be understood in contrast to, but only through, its transience as a weekly column. Its enduring quality rests in the fragility of writing that these pieces—in their ephemeral topicality—both register and crystallize. But how do you crystallize fragility? Michael Shelden has described the *Tribune* columns as a "splendid monument to [Orwell's] literary powers" (425), but "As I Please" is a form of writing that resolutely resists monumentality. Rather, Orwell's writing in "As I Please" presents itself as what we might call *perfectly casual*. Such a phrase, with just a moment's pause, invites—even as it seems to forbid—further reflection. After all, to be perfectly casual is to enter a precarious situation threatened by two kinds of loss. If the writing were any more "casual" (spontaneous, familiar, improvised), it wouldn't be so "perfect." But any more perfection (of phrasing, conception, form) would obliterate the casualness (or immediacy) upon which its distinction is founded. Orwell's column is frozen in this taut condition.

"As I Please" has had an unstable position within Orwell criticism: inviting praise but seeming to forestall analysis. Time and again, readers of Orwell have identified "As I Please" as a "quintessential" crux of his writing—as even "a perfect expression," or "the best," of his work—but then find themselves with little else to say.[1] "Viewed in their entirety," writes J. R. Hammond, "these short pieces are among the finest contributions to the English essay written in this century" (225), yet what has proven hardest for criticism's encounter with "As I Please" has been viewing the eighty "short" pieces *in* "their entirety." The overriding feature of these texts is their remarkable range and heterogeneity, or, to quote another critic on this matter, "the stunning variety of subjects" that the columns sinuously incorporate (O'Flinn 212). But this variety has a tendency to "stun" criticism itself, which has difficulty synthesizing—or conceptually recapitulating—the columns without diminishing the very "range" that is the animating source of critical interest.

Most commonly, Orwell's readers have praised the variety or diversity of the columns and then tried to convey this quality through only *several* examples, which are meant to stand in for the wider (and more radically heterogeneous) constellation of the columns as a whole. Shelden, for example, writes:

> Even in his first pieces the diversity of his interests is amazing. At one moment his thoughts are engaged with the sad fate of a long-forgotten Victorian novelist, at another he muses on the usefulness of political pamphlets, and proudly notes the large size of his collection of these works. One moment he might sketch a scene in the back streets of London, and then discuss some incredibly beautiful flower growing beside a fence in a small village. . . . One paragraph may be concerned with something as trivial as the price of tea, and the next may plunge into the difficulties of making a case for war crime trials. (423)

By wresting "diversity" into this set of antitheses—"back streets"/"beautiful flower"; something "trivial"/something "difficult"—Shelden inevitably narrows the range that has "amazed" him (a term similar to "stun"). Orwell's fragmented columns, in fact, tend to avoid this kind of binary rhetorical structure, precisely as it would become a mechanism that stalls or forecloses the effect of radical differentiation that Shelden wants to convey. But Shelden's description doesn't fall short because of some insufficient critical will. It is hard to imagine any recapitulation of Orwell's text (or perhaps *any* such varied text) that wouldn't suffer the same kind of problems.[2]

Variety—an aesthetic category that would seem to accord so happily with a politics of inclusiveness and to hold the seductive capacity of lavishing precise, even loving, attention on any version of particularity that falls within its ambit—is also, paradoxically, defined by loss of (and thus distance from) the particulars that constitute it. The varied text, to be understood *as* sufficiently various, imbues the experience of reading with more details—more differentiated particulars—than can be remembered or transmitted. Orwell's version of this variety effect in "As I Please" is particularly interesting because the self-differentiating columns are also so topically grounded. It's not merely a "stunning variety" but a "stunning variety *of subjects*" that consistently strikes readers. If the columns move the reader through a startling range of different frameworks, they also continually work to hold the reader *on* these discrete subjects. Variety rests on the movement away from any one location, but topical writing depends on locking the discourse into a relationship with its referential ground. The fundamental experience of reading "As I Please" is to be torn in this way (*between* topicality and variety). Again, we can consider a recent critical response, this one from 2007, in Frank Kermode's review of a new compilation of Orwell's writing for *Tribune:*

> Injustices large and small attracted his attention. An Indian journalist living in England needs support when he protests against being drafted into the British army. The iron railings that had protected the communal gardens of well-to-do London squares until requisitioned and torn down for munitions were now being replaced by wooden palings; so bits of London that had been liberated for the use of all were, as the war progressed, ominously returning to private use.
>
> He would comment on the quality of radio programs, on price rises, on the inadequacy of British houses, on the rudeness of shop assistants who seem to enjoy having nothing to sell, on the mysterious shortage of clocks and watches. (47–48)

This is an odd catalogue. The opening shifts unexpectedly into the present tense ("An Indian journalist . . . *needs* support"). And the final sentence—trying once more to register the essential force of Orwell's variety—devolves into a mere list, a paratactic inventory that doesn't finish but only stops. "I could go on," this structure suggests, "forever." The tense shift seems a formal response, on Kermode's part, to the category of "injustice," a particularly important horizon of topicality. It is as though the urgency of Orwell's writing—which here needs to point outside of its own presentness, *as* writing, to the presentness of its topical ground (the arrested journalist)—still encroaches on Kermode's much later recapitulation (when arrest, jail, prisoner, and the war itself have long past). Perhaps the very nature of reading about injustice (insofar as the reader understands a text in this way) renders the referenced ground in a continually present tense, both urgently unresolved and compelling outside of the discourse that refracts it. But the second case in Kermode is just the opposite. The lack of syntactical organization suggests that even in this brief list, the topics—as they are sequentially linked—cannot be understood (or certainly not dwelled upon) *as* topics. Mirroring the more widely ranging column sequence from which it is culled, Kermode's brief catalogue has meaning precisely as the terms displace one another, as we are unable to render a sufficient equivalency between the quality of radio programs *and* the rudeness of shopkeepers *and* inadequate housing *and* shortages of watches or clocks *and* rising prices.

Window Pane

The capacity of these weekly columns to "stun" or "amaze" the criticism that attempts to refract them functions, in one sense, as a perversely *non*lyric version of the "heresy of paraphrase," Cleanth Brooks's formulation for the structural dialectic between criticism and poetry. Brooks argues (in an essay written at the same historical moment as "As I Please") that any statement about what a poem "says" will, as it strives to express itself more exactly, start to bend toward the complicated shape of the poem itself: "As [the reader's] proposition approaches adequacy he will find, not only that it has increased greatly in length but it has begun to fill itself up with reservations and qualifications" (198). So, too, in a specific way, with the variety of "As I Please," which, I've suggested, eludes our grasp as we reach to articulate it. It might seem odd to frame Orwell's prose—and particularly this most quotidian instance of his writing—in terms of a critical paradigm that was developed explicitly in relationship to lyric poetry. But this frame is important because it brings out a fundamental negativity within the form—and, ultimately, the ideological texture—of these wide-ranging columns. Even as many of Orwell's columns turn upon *objects* that have been neglected, obscured, overlooked, or rendered ephemeral (like that "long-forgotten" novel Shelden mentions), the varied structure of "As I Please" creates a similar precariousness, and elusiveness, within the mode of representation itself.

This quality of (unstable) representation, grounded in the formal structure of the columns, has important political implications. The novel that Orwell touches on in his first column—*Mark Rutherford's Deliverance*—does not interest him only, as Sheldon says, because it is a "long-forgotten" book but also because it illustrates, with a particularly disturbing description, how nineteenth-century fiction encountered, but failed to adequately comprehend, urban slums. In this way, Orwell's first "As I Please" column—through the mediating prism of this other (now obscure) text—rearticulates the problem of representation in terms of an almost primal scene of structural inequality:

> "I did not know, till I came in actual contact with them, how far away the classes which lie at the bottom of great cities are from those above them.
> . . . It was an awful thought to me, ever present on those Sundays, and haunting me at other times, that men, women, and children were living in such brutish degradation, and that as they died others would take their place. Our civilization seemed nothing but a thin film or crust lying over a volcanic pit, and I often wondered whether some day the pit would not break up through it and destroy us all." (AIP 1, 16.13, quoting Rutherford)[3]

This depiction of culture as a "thin film" covering a "volcanic pit" is also a figure for representation itself, and one that resonates with the uncanny effect that is often produced, in "As I Please," by the inflection of scenes of social and historical urgency within the delimited—and often intentionally "thin"—form of the weekly column. Not just varied, Orwell's column is also—both structurally and thematically—urgent, continually manipulating the sense of immediacy generated out of its week-to-week production. The first column thus presents an overwhelming scene of inequality but only as it is mediated through an obscure and receding text.[4] As Shelden's catalogue description points out, the first "As I Please" column also contains a section on political pamphlets. Orwell identifies himself as having been a "steady collector of pamphlets" since 1935 (AIP 1, 16.13). This collection, inscribed into the opening of AIP, echoes the column's own interest in politically topical and immediate forms of writing. "A pamphlet is a short piece of polemical writing," Orwell writes in his 1948 introduction to *British Pamphleteers*:

> . . . printed in the form of a booklet and aimed at a large public. . . . A pamphlet is never written primarily to give entertainment or to make money. It is written because there is something that one wants to say *now*, and because one believes there is no other way of getting a hearing. (19.107, Orwell's emphasis)

Orwell's italicization of "now" gives point to a desire, for direct immediacy, that here has both linguistic and political dimensions. Orwell's assiduous collection of these varied efforts to "say something now" marks his own particular investment in, but also a subtle detachment from, the poetics of immediacy at stake in both forms of writing (pamphlet *and* weekly column sequence).

The inscription of this pamphlet collection into the opening column of "As I Please" is an early clue (not the only one) about the complexity and peculiarity of Orwell's writing project. Such complexity runs against a more simplified—even Manichean—logic of representation that has too often structured Orwell's cultural and critical refraction for the past thirty or forty years. We can think again of the contrasting comments from James Miller and Christopher Norris that I touched on in the Prologue. (Miller: "Must one write clearly . . . or are thinkers who are truly radical and subversive compelled to write radically and subversively—or even opaquely, as if through a glass darkly?. . . . If Orwell perfectly exemplifies the party of clarity . . . the German philosopher Theodor Adorno has come to represent the party of opacity" [34]. Norris: "Orwell's homespun empiricist outlook—his assumption that the truth was just there to be told in a straightforward, common-sense way—now seems not merely naïve but culpably self-deluding" [242]). Both sides of this argument draw on tropes—opacity, clarity, the dark glass of experimental prose— that return us, of course, to Orwell's *own* figure for politically engaged representation: "Good prose is like a window pane" (18.320). As we've seen, this comment, from the 1946 essay "Why I Write" has achieved a canonical centrality for critical reflections on Orwell's engaged writing and aesthetics.[5] The simple comment is almost inescapable in any account of Orwell and has been taken most often to frame Orwell in terms of his commitment (whether rhetorical or actual) to a kind of representation—direct, immediate, tactile, full of common sense, and naïvely empiricist—that is, in many ways, antithetical to dominant axioms of literary criticism of the past thirty or forty years. As Terry Eagleton summarizes this entrenched point of view: "Realist literature . . . helps to confirm the prejudice that there is a form of 'ordinary' language which is somehow natural. . . . In the ideology of realism or representation, words are felt to link up with their thoughts or objects in essentially . . . uncontrovertible ways. The realist or representational sign . . . is . . . essentially unhealthy. It effaces its own status as a sign, in order to foster the illusion that we are perceiving reality without its intervention" (119–120).

One further way to put pressure on this account of Orwell's best-known figure for representation is by considering some representations of window panes in his writing. Several examples occur that bear a productive, complicating relation to that governing trope for prose in "Why I Write" (though no one, to my knowledge, has read these passages in this light). "A junk shop has a fine film of dust over the window" (18.18), Orwell writes, as plainly as possible, in his brief 1948 encomium to the overlooked and discarded, "Just Junk: But Who Can Resist It?" Orwell is attracted to the image of dust on a window pane, which appears elsewhere in his work as well.[6] In this case, it's clear that Orwell is well disposed toward this dust, and doesn't want to "clean" the window. Not too much dust, though: just a "fine film" of it—an image that offers (ironically) a precise description of the dust itself. What does such a "fine film" on a window entail? Rather than simply occlude vision, this dust works in one sense to obscure our sight—which is now a bit hazy, or opaque—and in another sense to increase it, by identifying, if only negatively, the sheet of glass that would otherwise be invisible.

The thin layer of dust functions quite specifically in this sense: not enough to block our perception entirely (we can still see partially through the glass) but sufficient to make the instrument of perception, the window pane itself, noticeable. Often, Orwell's prose hovers, in this way, between observed reality and the mediating faculty of observation, holding us between the written word and the referential objects it seeks to comprehend. Consider the odd, disturbingly "plain" title of Orwell's 1946 "How the Poor Die," a brief essay that recounts his experience of falling ill in a squalid public hospital in Paris. The compacted title leads the reader in—directly, transparently—only to make us see, as we recoil against *both* the clinical circumspection of its first word ("how") and the taxonomic remoteness of its central phrase ("the poor"), that we are not seeing the things it promises to show us. Against these constraints, the unexpected last word ("die") reverberates with an almost inexhaustible dissonance. The title, despite and because of its monosyllabic bluntness, is uncompromisingly ironic.[7] Simple, urgent, and devious (because self-consciously so inadequate), the title "How the Poor Die" is significant for at once establishing a topically grounded frame of reference—another "window pane"—and putting an implacable pressure on our sense of this framework itself. James Miller talks about the "clarity" of Orwell's prose, but *neither* absolutizing nor dismissing Orwell's "clarity" will register this compact title's disorienting effect. It is a good emblem of Orwell's window-pane prose.

Another striking image from *The Road to Wigan Pier* reinforces Orwell's interest in the paradoxical qualities of window pane glass: "Which ever way you turn this curse of class-difference confronts you like a wall of stone. Or rather it is not so much like a stone wall as the plate-glass pane of an aquarium; it is so easy to pretend that it isn't there, and so impossible to get through it" (156). Here the pane of glass is conceived not just as a lens onto the world but also as a boundary and an obstacle, exactly the terms of mediation that Norris might want to invoke. The "plate-glass pane" is even more imposing a barrier than the "wall of stone," precisely because we can forget that it is there. Ten years later Orwell has recourse to a comparable—and equally tactile—image of glass, now used for a different metaphorical end. This is from AIP 68 (written in the same year as Orwell's plea for window pane prose), at the end of an ironic discussion about the inefficacy of Soviet literary censors: "They don't know what literature is, but they know that it is important, that it has prestige value, and that it is necessary for propaganda purposes, and they would like to encourage it, if only they knew how. So they continue with their purges and directives, like a fish bashing its nose against the wall of an aquarium again and again, too dim-witted to realize that glass and water are not the same thing" (68, 19.7).

I want to hold onto these two idiosyncratic images of transparent glass as they complicate the logic of Orwell's most durable metaphor for representation in "Why I Write." The glass in these examples is flat and transparent (and even mistakable for the water it contains) yet imposingly solid. In both cases, the activity of observation (empirical or conceptual) tempts the observer to elide this solidity too quickly—collapsing the actually wide distance of social class or failing to register the narrow distinction, within writing itself, between ideology and literariness. Like that dust, which can simultaneously obscure sight and heighten our awareness *of* a window, these two passages insist on an intricate mimesis that strives to see through glass and to see glass itself. Indeed, a recoil already implicit in the first example gets dramatized in that image of a fish bashing itself up against the aquarium wall. Orwell's texts are full of such recoils—complicated moments of observation that intertwine empirical perception with self-consciousness, articulating a mode of writing poised between its referential and self-reflective dimensions. "To notice" something in Orwell—a key verb in so much of his writing—often entails, in this way, not merely the direct comprehension of empirical reality but, simultaneously, the recognition of how something has been *un*seen (or pushed into invisibility) by the observer.

In one crucial example that we've seen from *Down and Out in Paris and London,* Orwell doesn't discern something that *isn't* there and then, in "a shock of surprise," recognizes the import of the absence he hadn't at first been aware of. I want to return to this passage now:

> The cell measured eight feet by five by eight high, was made of stone, and had a tiny barred window high up in the wall and a spyhole in the door, just like a cell in a prison. In it were six blankets, a chamber-pot, a hot water pipe, and nothing else whatever. I looked round the cell with a vague feeling that there was something missing. Then, with a

shock of surprise, I realized what it was and exclaimed: "But I say, damn it, where are the beds?" (146)

As the narrator is told "this is one of them spikes where you sleeps on the floor," we need to understand both his initial mistake (tellingly described as a "vague feeling") and subsequent surprise not merely in individual but paradigmatic, and epistemological, terms. This passage from *Down and Out* carefully entwines Orwell's moment of "shock" and "surprise"—at what was both missing *and* unseen—with the plain, bare language of empirical description. The description doesn't simply insist—as we might expect—that there are things the observer fails initially to see and needs more concertedly to draw into observation. Instead, more strangely, the description insists that there are things the observer cannot *not* see (and thus fails to understand as absent). We can engage key aspects of Orwell's writing (which often, famously, works to confound fiction and nonfiction) by holding onto the elusive distinction here: the distinction, in slightly different terms, between people not seeing something and people not "seeing" that they aren't seeing something (which isn't, in fact, there).[8] How do we successfully *not* see something (rather than simply work to avoid overlooking what is there)? How do we "notice" that something is absent (and thus become conscious that we are not seeing it)—and what faculties of perception does this kind of noticing entail? "It is curious how one does not notice things," Orwell writes in *Down and Out,* after walking the London streets for eight hours, "I had been in London innumerable times, and yet till that day I had never noticed one of the worst things about London—the fact that it costs money even to sit down" (154). Echoing the scene with the missing beds, this passage draws a (neglected) lack of potential shelter into startled comprehension—and makes this now-registered absence, the paucity of benches in London's public spaces, serve as the stand-in for "things," in general, that "one does not notice." Another passage, from his 1939 essay "Marrakech," offers another paradigmatic example of this:

All people who work with their hands are partly invisible, and the more important the work they do, the less visible they are. . . . I have noticed this again and again. In a tropical landscape one's eye takes in everything except the human-beings. (11.418)

What Orwell "notice[s]" here—and notices "again and again"—are *not* the human beings themselves but, rather, the way that they are invisible (or, in other words, so often, and even systematically, unnoticed). He tries to see, as there is no way of perceiving this completely, invisibility itself. The repetition ("again and again") makes clear that this is neither something that Orwell simply transcends nor projects onto other people, but a more persistent and entrenched process. "One could probably live here for years without noticing that for nine-tenths of the people the reality of life is an endless, back-breaking struggle to wring a little food out of an eroded soil" (11.419).

In attempting to grasp such a difficulty in "Marrakech," Orwell has recourse to an anecdote that situates this kind of "observation"—when we observe that we *haven't* seen somebody—in all its contingent momentariness:

> For several weeks, always at about the same time of day, the file of old women had hobbled past the house with their firewood, and though they had registered themselves on my eyeballs I cannot truly say that I had seen them. Firewood was passing—that was how I saw it. It was only that one day I happened to be walking behind them, and the curious up-and-down motion of a load of wood drew my attention to the human being underneath it. (11.419)

What I want to stress about this moment is its status *as* a moment: how Orwell suggests that a crucial process of social observation is linked to a particularly limited time frame (here, as he "happened to be walking" in such a way that the "up-and-down" movement of wood "drew [his] attention"). In this brief interval, observation and reflection meet. And the observer sustains that "shock of surprise," as Orwell puts it in *Down and Out,* which is simultaneously empirical and introspective. In other words, it is a moment (and it must be a moment that cannot last) in which an individual sees something and also, by recognizing how he doesn't fully see, glimpses his own contingent position within the world. (The fragmentary, iterative structure of "Marrakech" is one of Orwell's earlier attempts to dramatize this epistemological process—an invisibility at once contingent and occurring "again and again"—through a conspicuous manipulation of form.)

Reflection and Immediacy

In the "As I Please" columns, Orwell is able to explore—perhaps as precisely as anywhere in his work—the complicated play between immediacy and reflection at the heart of his poetics of writing. In turning to this kind of journalism, Orwell deliberately engages a discourse with a charged place in the politics-and-literature debates of the 1930s and '40s. Journalism functions, in this period, as both a threatening limit to and a point of desire for writing: a mode of expression that embodies writing's aspiration for political, and temporal, immediacy ("to say something *now*") and an "enemy of promise," in Cyril Connolly's memorable phrase, which can exhaust writing through its transience, constraints, and sheer, delimited topicality.[9] It is crucial to the columns that journalism is both of these things at once: enemy *and* promise, we might say.

The columns assiduously inflect their up-to-the-minute temporality, registering the present out of which they are composed in a variety of ways: through explicit gestures toward "current" events ("It is not my primary job to discuss the details of contemporary politics," Orwell writes in the wake of the Warsaw Uprising, "but this week there is something that cries out to be said" [AIP 40, 16.363]); suggestions about the time of composition itself ("For the last five minutes I have been gazing out of the window into the square, keeping a sharp look-out for signs of spring" [AIP 79, 19.93]); or attention to the audience, most frequently through references to the (sometimes heated) letters that previous columns have elicited from readers. These three examples suggest quite distinct ways in which AIP asserts, or reemphasizes, its underlying, week-to-week condition of production. But all these instances are still at the outer edge of "topicality" itself—flashes of content, in other words, that make the column's underlying formal relationship to contemporaneity more explicit. The crucial decision that Orwell makes in developing the structure of "As I Please" is to take the necessarily delimited temporality of the column as a whole, its breaks across each week, and reproduce this limit within individual columns. Orwell's key formal choice—and one that inconspicuously allows for the "range" and "diversity" readers so consistently note—is to fragment or truncate this *already* truncated mode of writing. The large majority of "As I Please" columns thus have more than one part, although, fittingly, even this structural decision is difficult to pin down or standardize: sometimes there is only one section; sometimes as many as five; most often two or three.[10]

In organizing the columns around these gaps, Orwell subtly moves a break that rests outside the text (that looming imperative, imposed on newspaper writing, to end according to an imminent deadline) into the column itself. The internal truncations work, in this way, to register the present, but only unsatisfactorily or incompletely so—almost grasping that exteriority *most* inexpressible within the weekly column (as these breaks limn the very contours *of* the column form) and fragmenting writerly expression in the process. Like much of Orwell's writing, the columns of "As I Please" offer various registers of irony, disruption, and displacement. But the motive for this irony here stems from, and flows back into, the fundamentally ironic structure of these truncations, as they internalize the external limit that looms over the column, creating continual, reverberating ruptures. Orwell's text, I would argue, is both *about* this effort—the effort of week-to-week writing to contain its outside—and a sustained dramatization of its difficulty.

By focusing our attention on the gap between topics in "As I Please," we can see the way that a formal choice underlies this writing project, even as the column seems oriented, both aesthetically and ideologically, toward direct, immediate, and thus ostensibly aformal representation. As we've already seen, in Chapters 2 and 3, this is not the only time that a key text of Orwell's is broken up into parts. If "As I Please" is a self-conscious and politically grounded exploration of "writing to the present," we also need to read this text as an exploration in the nature and significance of such formal splitting itself. Like the undiscussed breaks between the three essays in *Inside the Whale* or the more explicit—indeed unignorable—division between Parts One and Two in *Wigan Pier*, "As I Please," despite its tonal commitment to the politics and aesthetics of the plain style, unfolds within a form that is legible only in terms of division, in the "negative space" between the content.

This kind of formal strategy carries a cluster of potential implications. Most crucially, in the case of "As I Please," it can motivate or seem to demand a synthetic act of apprehension: the reader needs to construct a wider frame within which to comprehend the divergent parts. In this sense, formal division gestures *toward* a reflective act (hinging on that moment when, looking back across the text as a whole, we unify the seams of the object in one way or another). But it also marks a certain reticence on the part of the author. What's suggested only on the level of form (and particularly such a negative kind of form) is not fully elaborated upon, or reflected, within the text itself.[11] A degree of reflexivity is thus provoked but simultaneously frustrated by such formal division. This kind of coyness, with its combination of gesturing and reticence, is always a potential effect of formal division. But such a double tendency is dramatically heightened in the context of a weekly column, in a political newspaper, where the underlying temporality of disposability, transience, and contemporaneity—what Ian Duncan, in a different context, has called "the referential immediacy that charges the very premises of periodical publication" (29)—is never far from the surface.

My central claim is that this condition of thinking—partially emerged and partially frustrated—is embedded into the columns more generally, and has consequential aesthetic, and political, purchase. Orwell has a fear of reflecting too much, as when, in a 1933 letter to Brenda Salkeld, he breaks off from an enthusiastic consideration of *Ulysses* to apologize: "Excuse this long . . . letter. The fact is Joyce interests me so much that I can't stop talking about him once I start" (10.328).[12] We might contrast this reluctance with the intriguingly self-reflective moment in the *London Letter*s that Orwell writes for *Partisan Review:* "It is close on four years since I first wrote to you, and I have told you several times that I would like to write one letter which should be a sort of commentary on the previous ones. This seems to be a suitable moment" (16, 411). The reflective capacity that Orwell here adumbrates is a general one. Almost any text contains the potential, which is signaled in this gesture, to shift from discussing an outside topic to becoming a reflection (or "commentary") on itself. (Again, we can think of the two-part structure of *Wigan Pier* as another extended and emphatic modeling of such potential). At this point the *London Letter* becomes a letter *about* a letter, so that what Orwell gravitates toward here ("I have told you several times") resembles what he paradigmatically *repudiates* in *Inside the Whale:* "a writer nowadays is so hopelessly isolated that the typical modern novel is a novel about a novelist" ("Charles Dickens" 12.41).

Orwell hardly ever motivates or calls attention to the breaks within a column.[13] When he finally does mark a transition in "As I Please" 73—by saying, "to change the subject a bit, here is an excerpt from another letter"

(19.44)—it only accentuates how sedulously the column has neglected this kind of phrasing. Such casual links between sections would be a normal fixture of this kind of form, but Orwell is quite systematic about avoiding them (just as he refuses any "cross-talk" between the three essays in *Inside the Whale*). Often the columns do, as we've already seen, refer back to earlier weeks—including quite explicit corrections and elaborations of a topic in a previous number—but the breaks *in* a single column, even though they are obviously written more closely together, unfold as nearly absolute.[14] There is a strong tension between the often chatty, familiar tone of the column and these abrupt truncations, resolutely unsoftened by transitions that could be so easily incorporated. Once more, toward the end of the column sequence, Orwell offers another version of this same transitional principle, when the third and final section of AIP 69 begins, "looking over what I have written above, I notice that I have used the phrase a 'totally different person'" (19.20). Here the act of connecting the different sections is made overtly equivalent *to* textual self-reflectiveness: the third section still addresses an immediately present object, but this object of address is now, momentarily, the unfolding column itself (like the letter about a letter, or the "novel about a novelist"). Again, this kind of transition is new for the column. In eschewing such transitional phrases ("to change the subject a bit," "looking over what I have written above") for so long, Orwell leaves this reflective mode also unresolved—continually broached but almost never fulfilled by the columns in this way.

This precarious reflectivity (at once elicited *and* constrained by the form of Orwell's weekly columns) is, I want to argue, the key accomplishment of "As I Please"—not the expression of thoughts, however interesting many of Orwell's speculations may be, but a memorable and precise instantiation of thinking itself. Over and again (and through its content as well as its form), Orwell's column highlights a valuable—but fragile and short-lived—moment within thinking, that point at which thought, under the pressure *of* its empirical engagement, begins to become aware of itself, and thus to potentially turn away from the empirical. Just "before" this moment, we could say, thought is not sufficiently emergent, still rooted too directly in the immediate facts of the world; just "after" this moment, thought has become speculative, abstracting, conceptual, or self-conscious—and no longer observationally grounded. Orwell is interested above all in dramatizing, rather than transcending or negating, this threshold within thought, an inherently unstable one. The column works to highlight this moment within reflection both formally and substantially, as the varied topicality of "As I Please" (emerging, of course, only through the truncations in the text) *constitutes* this threshold even while many specific topics bear a thematic relation to it.

The normative opening of the columns thus presents Orwell as the observing, writing, or thinking agent who has just encountered, or been "struck" by, an experience that is, itself, often constituted in terms of observation, writing, or thought: "I was reminded once again" (4, 16.34), "Looking through the photographs in the New Year Honours List I was struck" (6, 16.55), "I note the surprise" (5, 16.45), "I was struck even more forcibly than usual" (15, 16.117), "the other day I attended a press conference" (18, 16.137), "I was struck by the automatic way in which people go on repeating certain phrases" (24, 16.182), "Arthur Koestler's recent article in *Tribune* set me wondering" (28, 16.251), "I notice" (31, 16.272), "I have just found my copy of Samuel Butler's Note-books" (34, 16.292). All of these phrases suggest a contingent balance between experience and reflection, as well as between the past (event) and the present (of writing itself). In this way, the content of Orwell's columns gravitates around a particular experience of thinking—where reflection still has an immediate relationship *to* the triggering event. ("He is always somewhere else when the trigger is pulled," Orwell writes, famously, in his polemic against what he depicts as Auden's non-experiential writing in "Inside the Whale.")

Against this precarious, situated form of thinking—both realized through and represented in the truncated columns of "As I Please"—Orwell juxtaposes an immediacy that is entirely unreflective and a mode of thinking that extends too long, lapsing into orthodoxy or abstraction, and, more essentially, forgetting its own situatedness *in* the world. These are the two extremes that Orwell's column rejects: rote, uncritical forms of speech and belief—as in that "automatic way in which people go on repeating certain phrases"— and thought (or writing) that succeeds at "breaking from" the world, as all thought must do, but eases the negation implicit within such a break by becoming unaware of (or uncritical about) itself, and thus lapsing into an equally problematic, and potentially rote, internal consistency.

Freedom, Variety, and Constraint

On one level, the breaks in "As I Please" might be understood as simply reducing the ambition and scope of the writing project. Continually dividing and circumscribing the text, the interruptions help register journalism as one of the central "enemies of promise" identified by Cyril Connolly. If they verge on reflection, the columns often seem, inversely, at risk of disintegrating into eclectic heterogeneity. This would make the truncated column sequence an exercise in trivia, like "Brains Trust," the popular BBC quiz show that Orwell satirizes at the beginning of AIP 29 as a hodgepodge of "interesting facts about birds' nest soup or the habits of porpoises, scraps of history and a smattering of philosophy" (16.258). The discussion is one of many instances in "As I Please" where Orwell—ironically underlining the risk that his own column courts—gestures at other ragged, quotidian, and ephemeral textual forms.

But even as such breaks elaborate the constrained nature of column writing, they also derive from a countervailing ambition that is registered in the title—to write how, and about what, the author "please[s]." Starting and stopping can be seen as a strong demonstration of Orwell's free subjectivity, rather than as the consequence of the limits of deadline-driven writing. Thus, just as the breaks uncannily seem to provoke *and* resist reflection, they also work to both dramatize freedom and to intensify constraint. A precarious mode of thinking is connected—through the formal logic of these columns—with an equally precarious kind of freedom (grounded in that quality of "range" or "variety," which critics always note). Free thought emerges as something fundamentally unstable, achieved only moment to moment (like that effort, on Orwell's part, to strike the posture of reflection at exactly the "suitable moment").

In this way, the inscribed breaks are bound up with a fragile but potentially "monumental" freedom that is, of course, signaled in the title of the columns. In the rest of this book, as I consider particular moments in "As I Please," I want to expand our sense that these weightless columns are, paradoxically, a telling exploration of both freedom (most essentially in their heterogeneity) and the nature of thinking (most essentially as they interweave immediacy and reflection). Largely through these formal processes, freedom and thought itself emerge as difficult, uncertain, and hard to maintain. Furthermore, this difficulty is connected with the precarious political position of *Tribune,* under Aneurin Bevan's editorship, as the major paper to support the war effort while actively opposing Churchill's unity government from the left. At least once, Orwell explicitly associates *Tribune* with a horizon of political freedom, but he casts this freedom in dialectical relationship to the explicitly socialist project of the newsweekly. This is in a retrospective column titled "As I Pleased" that Orwell writes toward the end of his stint as columnist—a moment that is somewhat akin to the "letter about a letter" that Orwell writes for *Partisan Review.* In the last paragraph of the essay, Orwell offers his most sweeping endorsement of the paper:

> For six months during the summer of 1946 I gave up being a writer in *Tribune* and became merely a reader, and no doubt from time to time I shall do the same again; but I hope that my association with it may long continue, and I hope that in 1957 I shall be writing another anniversary article. I do not even hope that by that time *Tribune* will have slaughtered all its rivals. It takes all sorts to make a world, and if one could work these things out one might discover that even the—– serves a useful purpose. Nor is *Tribune* itself perfect, as I should know, having seen it from the inside. But I do think that it is the only existing weekly paper that makes a genuine effort to be both progressive and humane— that is, to combine a radical Socialist policy with a respect for freedom of speech and a civilised attitude towards literature and the arts: and I think that its relative popularity, and even its survival in its present form for five years or more, is a hopeful symptom. (71, 19.37–38)

This "combin[ation]" is necessarily uncertain (or, as Orwell says, not "perfect"). Freedom of speech, embodied in literariness, can be neither engulfed by nor simply disjoined from that "radical Socialist policy," which defines *Tribune*'s political program. Orwell's comments thus offer a conceptual framework for the concrete negotiation, pursued by any number of texts, newspapers, and journals in the 1930s and '40s, between political journalism and literary or cultural writing, as in this description, by Cyril Connolly, in the first issue of *Horizon* (1940): "[A]nd so *Horizon* will have political articles, though it will never imitate those journals, in which, like pantomime donkeys, the political front legs kick and entangle the literary hind ones" (Connolly, "Comment" 5).

When Orwell takes up the column sequence for *Tribune* in December 1943, he also signs on as literary editor and is indeed responsible, in this capacity, for the back pages—the cultural pages—of the political weekly. The role entails not merely filling out the literary "hind [legs]" of the socialist newspaper but negotiating the shifting and unsettled relationship between the literary section and its explicitly political surroundings.[15] The dynamic intersection of *Tribune*'s literary content with its overarching socialist commitment is connected, through Orwell's *dual* roles, with the truncated elaboration of "As I Please." Although his comments in "As I Pleased" address *Tribune* in general, they also apply more specifically to Orwell's main writing project in *Tribune*. This project, too, elaborates a forceful but uneasy and "[im]perfect" sense of freedom, intermingled with (rather than seeking to transcend) constraint. The degree-zero of this combination rests in the breaks and interruptions that saturate the writing project. These breaks, I've suggested, situate the text uncertainly between form and topic. They dramatize that "threshold of reflection," registering the problematic relationship between thought and immediacy that is facilitated by the weekly format. They also help to establish the restless, dialectical boundary between literature and politics that Orwell explores in the 1930s and '40s and that he invokes in this figure of combining freedom of expression and "radical Socialist policy."

In Part Two of this book, I'll trace various ways that the topicality, formal logic, and referential dynamics of "As I Please" intertwine connection and separation. In a similar way the columns, as a whole, strive for a sustained but not overdetermined relationship to the political weekly. According to Bernard Crick, Aneurin Bevan offered this seductive gloss on Orwell's tenure at *Tribune:*

> George has alighted on our desk, as he'll be when he leaves, free as a bird. We'll be glad when he's with us. We'll accept the fact that there will be times when he will fly off. (Crick 446)

The phrasing here—coming from the political figure who embodies *Tribune*'s connection to the democratic Left in England—is significant.[16] The "free[dom]" that Bevan conjures up and relates directly and immediately to flight is linked both to the particularly literary function of Orwell's double role at *Tribune* (writer of "As I Please" and literary editor for the back pages of the journal) and to the free form of the column itself. Most obviously, Bevan's comment reflects the wide-ranging content of the weekly columns, as well as Orwell's proclivity for introducing unorthodox and idiosyncratic views from within this range. But the figure he uses also speaks to the truncated *structure* of the column. Crucially, Bevan doesn't characterize Orwell as in the air but, rather, as "alighted" upon a desk. The comment evokes an idea of freedom not constituted through an unmoored—and thus potentially pro-longed—weightlessness but only emerging at the juncture of groundedness and flight. Freedom is temporally precarious, associated with the brief moment when the bird is "alit," still poised on a surface and ready to take off into the air. In this way the penetration of experience and reflection in the columns is connected to the politically charged balance between solidarity and heterodoxy, collaboration and independence, which Orwell tries to maintain in his relationship to *Tribune* (and that *Tribune* tries to maintain with the Labor left).

The odd and simultaneous way in which the truncations of "As I Please" produce freedom *and* circumscription speaks to the role that constraint, more generally, plays within Orwell's aesthetics of expression. Freedom, for "Orwell" (beginning with this pen name itself), takes place only in and through the activity of writing, and this is an activity that is, intrinsically, mediated and limiting, always working to shock any imagination that seeks to project itself too confidently or completely—and thus "freely"—through the representation that it enacts. (From AIP 76: "A good exercise for anyone trying to improve his microphone delivery is to have one of his speeches recorded, and then listen to it. This is an astonishing and even shocking experience" [19.68]). At the simplest level, we can see this quite clearly in the columns of "As I Please": the mixture of conceit and humility, assertion and reticence is a felt quality of the prose. This tonal quality offers us a way to connect the essential formal strategies and tensions of the weekly column (the truncations that underlie its topical range, the restraint that is inter-twined with its sense of writerly freedom) and the forceful self-critique, even self-abnegation, which is a long-standing component of Orwell's artistic persona.

In "Why I Write," discussing his childhood, Orwell avers: "from the very start my literary ambitions were mixed up with the feeling of being isolated and undervalued" (18.316). Orwell leaves it deliberately open, in this fantasy of artistic origin, whether isolation drives him to write (so that it is a cause of, and perhaps something mitigated *by*, writing) or, on the contrary, whether isolation is the consequence, and perhaps the most essential effect, of writing. Cause and effect are "mixed up" here, confused from the "very start." Isolation is the negative result of, and a primary condition for, writing. The identity of the writing self originates *in* the problematic distance between itself and a world through which any sufficient freedom would necessarily be manifested. "In Moulmein, in Lower Burma, I was hated by large numbers of people—the only time in my life that I have been important enough for this to happen to me" (10.501). The remarkable opening line of "Shooting an Elephant" is more than merely biographical or topical. We can view it as an almost strictly Hegelian enactment of writing's self-generating and thus dissonant force. In this text, the writing self, "from the very start," comes into being through recording the animosity that it generates and encounters. The status of this famous opening line *as* an opening line is thus crucial.[17] What is at stake in a writer who introduces himself (or a writing voice that manifests itself) in such an abruptly self-critical way? "I was hated by large numbers of people." The very origin of the first-person voice, here, seems conditioned on a negative knowledge of itself. Subject (i.e., the writing voice, in all its own authority or "importan[ce]") and object (a perceived hatred, of the writer) arise together, intertwining self-critique and self-expression, appearance and disappearance, inflation and deflation. This formal doubleness is heightened by the stark asymmetry of the opening line. In the memory image that he conjures up, Orwell is overwhelmed by the compelling force of the "large numbers of people" who surround him, but these persons are only refracted through, and thus distorted by, Orwell's troubled, yet still foregrounded, consciousness. The mixture of aggression and reticence in such an opening flows into the formal organization of "As I Please"—and into the odd combination of ambition and constraint emerging out of that structural choice to use truncated, cross-cutting sections.

"As I Please" 2, 3, and 9

Consider the opening lines of Orwell's second and third columns of "As I Please":

> The recently-issued special supplement to the *New Republic* entitled *The Negro: His Future in America* is worth a reading, but it raises more problems than it discusses. (2, 16.23)

> So many letters have arrived, attacking me for my remarks about the American soldiers in this country, that I must return to the subject. (3, 16.25)

What I want to call attention to here is the oblique self-reflexivity that both of these openings share. The second column offers writing about reading another piece of writing (and, indeed, another weekly magazine), while the third column dramatizes itself as having to "return to" previous words from the column itself. These two kinds of reflexivity (writing that takes as its object a homologous piece of writing or writing that looks back at its own previous unfolding) are of interest not simply on their own terms but *against* the expressed casualness of the prose, signaled, for instance, by Orwell's muted praise ("worth a reading") or the passivity implied in "I must return to the subject." The slightness of these openings emerges out of the nature of the weekly column: this kind of casual discourse—loose, tentative, spontaneous, and vernacular—aims to convey a sense of being overwhelmed or swayed *by* the events that it registers, connoting, through its very familiarity, the underlying pressure of immediacy that structures such quotidian composition. But such immediacy is here strangely intertwined with the self-conscious doublings in both passages, once again instantiating that tension between transience and reflection, which rests at the formal center of AIP.[18] (It is a tension that also underlies, on a different register, the oscillation, in AIP, between columns that follow only one topic—as in the discussion of *The New Republic* and race—and columns that split up into multiple parts.)

In the opening of AIP 2, Orwell says the special issue of *The New Republic*, on race, is "worth a reading" but "raises more problems than it discusses." In a similar way, Orwell's own two openings catalyze a reflexive stance that, unfolding against the immediacy and ephemerality of the columns, cannot be fully or adequately elaborated. This sense of an excess that's provoked by but not resolved within a discourse is important to the entire project of AIP, and there is a way that this early formulation (reflecting indeed on another weekly piece of writing) anticipates the effect of Orwell's own columns— and, more to the point, anticipates a particular experience of *thinking* that is intertwined with this writing project. AIP presents us with a throttled reflectivity, in which the impulse of thought is triggered by but not substantialized through the transient prose and shifting topicality of the columns. The structure of AIP thus inevitably generates an *im*balanced writing—not least in its asymmetrical distribution of topical attention—that also seems designed to "[raise] more problems than it discusses."[19] (I'm arguing that such surface imbalance—evident to any reader of AIP—is related to the more profound, conceptual disequilibrium between reflection *provoked* and reflection fully realized.)

As an example, we could consider the particularly ephemeral constellation of four topics in the ninth column of "As I Please," which begins: "I see that Mr Suresh Vaidya, an Indian journalist living in England, has been arrested for refusing military service" (16.80). Now, by any measure, this initial topic is an urgent and disturbing one—and the centrality of unjust imprisonment haunts Orwell's work, from "A Hanging" through *Homage to Catalonia* and *1984* to some of his last fragmentary writing.[20] Despite the seriousness of this initial topic, however, AIP 9 is the first column in which Orwell seems to deliberately test the bounds of that variety, which is valorized through the form and title of his writing project—modeling, through the sense of a heterogeneity that might *go too far* (and thus crumble into overly casual minutia), the internal limits of the freedom that the column continually pursues. After condemning this form of coercion, Orwell abruptly shifts to "a correspondent [who] has sent us a letter in defence of Ezra Pound['s]" (16.80) wartime activity and briefly discusses, through the example of Pound, whether "a poet, as such, is to be forgiven his political opinions" (16.81). Following is a catalogue of pseudo-scientific aphorisms that starts, "The other night a barmaid informed me that if you pour beer into a damp glass it goes flat much more quickly" (16. 81) and then continues:

Only later did it strike me that this was probably one of these superstitions which are able to keep alive because they have the air of being scientific truths. In my notebook I have a long list of fallacies which were taught to me in my childhood. . . . I can't give the whole list but here are a few hardy favourites. (16.81)

Finally, Orwell discusses Basic English, through two rival books that he has recently reviewed that each address the utopian project of constructing and popularizing a single, international language.

Such a column hovers around a fidelity to the transient that verges on obliterating the substance of writing itself. The four quotidian topics are rendered *more* ephemeral in their abrupt juxtaposition (even as this juxtaposition simultaneously tempts the reader to connect, and thus reflect upon, these different sections). Content and form are melded together around this transience, as the fragmented column also focuses on events that all arise in a random, immediate fashion: an article that Orwell has only recently read; a letter written that week to *Tribune;* a conversation "the other night" in a bar; and, finally, these two books on internationalizing language that Orwell has just reviewed. In each case, the topic only emerges as it does because of the week-to-week structure that underlies the written composition; a less time-bound form of discourse, for example, would not be able to invoke or comprehend an event that occurred "the other night." This phrase is the most explicit gesture toward the contemporaneity of the writing itself, giving a sense that such subjects could not even get discussed, that these reflections would ironically cease to be, if Orwell were working in a more substantial form.

In this way AIP 9, more than most of the other columns, dramatizes the price that writing must pay to pursue the horizon of topical immediacy. As usual, Orwell is less interested in substantially exploring the immediate than in connoting the immediate as a potential ground for writing. But even as these four sections exemplify the way that Orwell's week-to-week writing seems to vanish before our eyes, fragmented by its contemporary topicality, AIP 9 also troubles the narrowness of the immediate. First of all, the initially disturbing focus on an unjust arrest has a discordant effect on the rest of the piece—made more disturbing, in an important sense, through the very shift to such quotidian matters. (Thus it is this section of AIP that *survives*, against all odds, as the first example of injustice in Kermode's recapitulation over 60 years later: "Injustices large and small attracted his attention. An Indian journalist living in England needs support when he protests against being drafted into the British army" [47–48]. We've seen the way that Kermode oddly shifts into the present tense here. It is also unclear in this passage whether Kermode means this event from AIP 9 as a "large" or "small" injustice: we could argue, in fact, that it is precisely our difficulty in parsing the injustice *as* large or small—when it is squeezed into this quotidian, ephemeral context—that makes it disturbing and memorable.)[21]

In the effort to "say something now," composition and topicality in AIP are at once mutually dependent and at odds, working both to generate and threaten one another. With a more extended form of writing, these everyday topics could, as we have seen, disappear altogether; at the same time, AIP 9 presents us with the spectacle of writing that seems, under the pressure of pursuing such contemporaneity, on the verge of disappearing itself, fragmenting into insubstantiality. But the fragmented form also impels us to put its pieces together, reflectively, even as each of the four topics, while anchored in its week-to-week contingency, provokes thinking that exceeds this contingent frame. Not merely in the initial, disturbingly abandoned injustice, but in its swerving between politics and literature (most conspicuously as it moves from the conscripted journalist to Ezra Pound), its meta-reflections on language (aphorisms/universal language), and its attention both to utopian desire and racial prejudice, the column broaches a dynamic constellation of topics and problems that are central to Orwell's socialist thought. It invokes an ideal of transparent or direct communication (through the project of a universal language) while also tracking a proliferating field of mistakes and "fallacies" (the falsely accused journalist, the gross political misjudgments of Pound, the trivial misinformation of popular superstitions): a thematic dichotomy that echoes the linguistic tension at the heart of Orwell's plain style (as it is torn between transparency and disruption) and the conflict, between reflection and immediacy, built into the structure of AIP.

These gestures toward conceptuality are, like the connotation of immediacy, most important as gestures: this writing isn't meant to substantively explore, but only to broach, the problems and implications of utopian language, for example. The column is designed to provoke conceptual questions that it cannot adequately substantialize—to be "thought provoking" in this precise sense. And there is another way that Orwell troubles the immediacy of these sections: even as he is trying to diminish the temporal difference between writing and reflected event (one great advantage of the column form), he also inscribes temporal disorder into the events themselves. Consider these two moments in AIP 9, each of which suggests the kind of belatedness that this weekly column—as a form—means to resist:

> Only later did it strike me that this was probably one of those superstitions which are able to keep alive. . . . (16.81)

> I wish now that I had read *Basic English versus the Artificial Languages* before and not after reviewing the interesting little book in which Professor Lancelot Hogben sets forth his own artificial language, Interglossa. For in that case I should have realized how comparatively chivalrous Professor Hogben had been towards the inventors of rival international languages. (16.81)

Despite the emphatic contemporaneity of this column, Orwell's description of what occurred "the other night" focuses on his "later" recasting of the event (and not simply the event itself). The writing of this section thus recalls his previous recollection of, and reflection upon, the initial, "strik[ing]" event.[22] Indeed, the reflective, negating dimension of language is inscribed within the experience more generally, in the form of that notebook where Orwell keeps "a long list of fallacies." The catalogue of fallacies presents a potential *mise en abyme* of reflection, as the event that merits Orwell's written reflection in AIP (so transient and fragile as a form) is constituted by another written reflection. Orwell's action, captured retrospectively in the column, already consists in a series of breaks, from the world, to record the world—breaks that are given a substantial and particular *form* in the notebook that Orwell keeps. (The notebook is thus another genre of immediate or transient writing inscribed into the varied field of AIP—like the pamphlets that we've seen in AIP 1, the radio program "Brains Trust" in AIP 29, or, to give one more early example, the war-time diary Orwell mentions in AIP 3.)[23]

The beginning of the fourth section of AIP 9 builds on this complexity by deliberately emphasizing a temporal confusion through its redundant phrasing. Substantively, nothing is gained by writing "before *and not after*" rather than merely "before." The extraneous phrase subtly heightens the disturbance within this kind of reversal—where a book that Orwell reads later in time unsettles an already formed judgment about what he has read earlier. "I wish now that I had read X before and not after Y": this is a form of thinking that hones itself through a receptivity toward, and even cultivation of, internal shocks within its own articulation. Similarly, Orwell misdirects the *reader* in this same section opening. We expect initially that the second book (the book that should have been read earlier) will belatedly correct Orwell's review of the first, not solidify it. In other words, we imagine that Orwell wants to reverse which book he read "before" and which one "after," so that he could have read the more measured language (about language) first. Instead, it is ironically the *faulty* quality of language in the later book— here as it so fervently attacks opposing viewpoints—that Orwell "now" sees more clearly, disputes, and wishes he could have seen earlier. In this way, like Orwell himself, we as readers need to put what comes after "before," modifying our own sense of Orwell's already complicated construction.

In Orwell's clotted wish to have read the second book "before and not after" the first, a reflective excess built into the structure of AIP finds a more specific form: temporal inversion. The excess of thought (structured, as in AIP 9, by the surfeit of topics crowded within this quotidian form) is linked to dilemmas within time—the way in which a "later" event can actually precede an "earlier" one (as in, for example, the Freudian model of deferred understanding). The phrasing would not be so significant if it weren't embedded in a key tendency of Orwell's prose—signaling the unrest implicit in any form of writing, no matter how quick or immediate, that seeks to catch up with its referential ground. In fact, there is a minor pathos to this moment, hinging on the way that a first book, read too early, cannot be fully understood (without benefit of that subsequent textual encounter), while the second book, read too late, reconfigures an experience that has already transpired. In the context of AIP 9, this inversion is deliberately casual, generating just a small or nagging doubt stitched into the articulation of Orwell's idea, like a hanging thread on a piece of clothing. We can understand this doubt, as I've suggested, in relation to the mistakes and slips that he records in section three of the column, and also in contrast to that desire for a universal language, which is the ostensible subject of this brief fourth section. The vexed aspiration toward such an ideal form of language structures a dialectic that runs notably through Orwell's work, from the odd conflation of experientially grounded writing with obscurity, self-negation, and pseudonymity that characterizes Orwell's initial aesthetic (in works like *Down and Out,* "A Hanging," and "Shooting an Elephant") to the parodic inflection, and even abolition, of the plain style in *1984*'s "Newspeak." In *Tribune,* discussing his policy toward book reviewing as the literary editor (an issue, also raised in AIP, that we will return to), Orwell states, dogmatically, that he doesn't want to print any prose that cannot be understood by *Tribune*'s ordinary readers (a "large, heterogeneous Left-Wing audience" ["Books and the People" 17.9]). This aspiration toward direct communication is also, crucially, intertwined with the temporality of "As I Please," as the entire project signals that effort of language to arrive, through the week-to-week format, at a greater immediacy—to close the gap between writing and the experiences that catalyze it. In this sense, both the slips of section three and the aspiration of section four (toward a universal language) are related to the column's concern with an event that occurred "the other night" and with other experiences explicitly set in the very recent past of the writer. "I wish now," Orwell begins the final section, starting once again (as in the first section) with the present tense: and we could argue that the larger "wish" of AIP, as a writing project or experiment, rests in that chimerical effort to compose the word "now," aligning discourse as closely as possible with the events that it registers—rather than having something that comes "before" (the temporally prior event) only arrive "after" (through the discourse that is composed later on and imperfectly refracts it).

Double Bind

"As a general rule," Orwell writes about Spain in *Homage to Catalonia,* "things happen too late, but just occasionally—just so that you shan't even be able to depend on their happening late—they happen too early" (13). This telling sentence, which I discussed in the Introduction, can resurface now, in connection to Orwell's casual comment in AIP 9 about reading one book too early and the other too late. The generalizing force of Orwell's statement in *Homage to Catalonia* is amplified by several passages in the memoir that link the writing of the text itself to the same double bind. On one hand, the narrative is framed, from the outset, in terms of belatedness. "This was in late December, 1936, less than seven months ago as I write," Orwell reflexively comments on the second page, "and yet it is a period that has already receded into enormous distance. Later events have obliterated it much more completely than they have obliterated 1935, or 1905, for that matter" (4). But Orwell inverts this figure at the end of the book, after he has fled across the Spanish border, writing: "The things we had seen in Spain did not recede and fall into proportion now that we were away from them; instead they rushed back upon us and were far more vivid than before. We thought, talked, dreamed incessantly of Spain" (229). Here, to stay with the terms of the original axiom, the observer or the writing itself is not "too late" but "too early." Instead of "fall[ing] into proportion," the "things [they] had seen" "rush back upon" the observers and become "more vivid" with the passage of time. These last terms are specifically spatial and sensory ones. To "recede" here is no longer negatively characterized (as it is in the first passage) but on the contrary would accommodate the compositional process of proportioning, while "vivid[ness]," which is the kind of adjective we would normally associate *with* the plain style, is now a threat to, rather than a goal of, writing. In the first passage, conversely, the recent past feels even further away than much earlier periods. Like the events in revolutionary Spain itself, the textual representation of Spain operates under a kind of pervasive misalignment: in the observation of the civil war, in "writ[ing]" about (or "as [he] write[s]") about Spain, and, again, in "[thinking], talk[ing], dream[ing]" about Spain, the discourse can be "too late," pursuing an experience that has already passed, indeed, "receded" to the point of its "obliterat[ion]," or "too early," "rushed . . . back upon" and thus wrenched out of proportion by events that only grow more vivid in their delimited, inadequate rearticulation.[24]

Before returning to "As I Please," I want to consider, once more, the passage in *Homage to Catalonia* that concerns the potentially fatal options that confront a Republican soldier carrying a grenade and now juxtapose it with an equally difficult predicament broached in *The Road to Wigan Pier*. These

scenes suggest how Orwell's work can pivot from this strictly temporal register (anchored, in my reading, to that intricate play between reflection and
immediacy) to a broader set of tensions—what we might think of as tradeoffs
or double binds—with social and political import. Orwell's engaged writing,
in fact, turns restlessly to such knotty situations, discovering them in the
experiences that he represents and within the process of representation
itself. The first scene (from *Homage*) we've looked at in the Introduction, as
part of that discussion of "early" and "late". The second (from *Wigan Pier*)
occurs in the middle of Orwell's discussion of poor housing conditions in
northern mining towns, after a series of extracts from the notes that he took
in his journal:[25]

> One afternoon Benjamin told us that he wanted fifteen volunteers. The
> attack on the Fascist redoubt which had been called off on the previous
> occasion was to be carried out tonight. . . . Bombs were served out,
> three to a man. The Spanish Government had at last succeeded in pro-
> ducing a decent bomb. It was on the principle of a Mills bomb, but with
> two pins instead of one. After you had pulled the pins out there was an
> interval of seven seconds before the bomb exploded. Its chief disadvan-
> tage was that one pin was very stiff and the other very loose, so that you
> had the choice of leaving both pins in place and being unable to pull the
> stiff one out in a moment of emergency, or pulling out the stiff one
> beforehand and being in a constant stew lest the thing should explode
> in your pocket. (*Homage to Catalonia* 86)

> And so on and so on and so on. I could multiply examples by the score—
> they could be multiplied by the hundred thousand if anyone chose to
> make a house to house inspection throughout the industrial districts.
> Meanwhile some of the expressions I have used need explaining. "One
> up, one down" means one room on each storey—i.e. a two-roomed
> house. "Back to back" houses are two houses built in one, each side of
> the house being somebody's front door, so that if you walk down a row
> of what is apparently twelve houses you are in reality seeing not twelve
> houses but twenty-four. The front houses give on the street and the back
> ones on the yard, and there is only one way out of each house. The effect
> of this is obvious. The lavatories are in the yard at the back, so that if

you live on the side facing the street, to get to the lavatory or the dust-bin
you have to go out of the front door and walk round the end of the
block—a distance that may be as much as two hundred yards; if you live
at the back, on the other hand, your outlook is on to a row of lavatories.
(*The Road to Wigan Pier* 56)

Orwell's attention is provoked by these two difficult choices, as they are
internal to the represented world. And we have seen the way that a similar
kind of double bind often informs Orwell's sense of writing and representation itself. These two passages recast such dilemmas of narrative representation in relation to pointedly situational circumstances (rather than
rehearsing them as absolute or ontological conditions).

As we have seen, Orwell's memoir of Spain is torn between recapitulating
experience that, on the one hand, "recedes" to the point of being "obliterated" and, on the other hand, far from receding, grows so "vivid" that it
"rushes back upon" the observer. We grasp the intensity of this double bind
only if we understand that it is potentially the very *same* experience that is
apprehended, simultaneously, in these two opposed ways. The bomb that
can fail in one of two ways offers a remarkably precise and external reiteration of these formal quandaries. As I pointed out in the Introduction, the
two-pinned grenade also concretizes Orwell's general aphorism about the
way that, in Spain, an event that tends to occur too late can also—"just so
that you shan't even be able to depend on [it] happening late"—take place too
early. The soldier can wait too long before taking the second pin out: the
bomb can then fail to go off on time. Or, by leaving in only the loose pin, he
risks an explosion that goes off prematurely—"rushing back upon" the soldier himself, we might say, rather than detonating away from him.

In *The Road to Wigan Pier*, Orwell's description comes to rest on another
intractable double bind. In retrospect, we realize that the image of the back-
to-back house has a significance that exceeds Orwell's putative impulse to
annotate or explain "some of the expressions" used in his shorthand notes
on housing. The predicament that erupts into *Wigan Pier* concerns the
uneasy fit of persons within the housing structures that Orwell observes.
The either/or generated by these back-to-back houses has a structural logic
akin to the passages we've seen in *Homage to Catalonia* (the axiomatic claim
about how "things happen" in Spain; the framing comments about objects

"receding" or failing to recede; and, most notably, those two disastrous outcomes potential to the Spanish grenade). Here the choice facing each individual tenant is between a house "too near" to or "too far from" the lavatory. In one case, the occupant is separated, by an uncomfortably protracted distance, from the lavatory. And in the other case, the lavatory is too close, engulfing the occupant's view. There is a striking *formal* continuity between the unforgiving dilemmas faced by the undersupplied Republican soldier and by the tenant of the back-to-back house. And in each case, Orwell doesn't only offer concrete details about the predicament but conceptualizes it as a no-win choice, so that the obstructed agency of the person, stuck within this condition, is a constitutive part *of* the condition.

Once more, the elaboration of this conspicuously imperfect choice in *Wigan Pier* is intertwined, as well, with the dilemmas or "predicaments" of the written composition itself. We arrive at the clenched intensity of this situation in the middle of Orwell's second-order reflection on his own enterprise of representation, as part of his gloss on the notes that were already a written response to his encounter with the housing projects. These notes inscribe a genre of writing into *Wigan Pier* that, as with "As I Please," derives justification strictly in relation to its immediacy. They function as both compressed, factual descriptions of the housing blight in northern England and as a dramatic marker—typographically and stylistically—*of* the compression that always can result from social reporting. They are an instrument for Orwell's depiction of the housing shortage but also an inscribed emblem of the limits of this depiction.

The tone of this passage demonstrates how Orwell pulls such a tension into the stylistic dynamics of his prose. The blunt repetition of the first sentence ("and so on and so on and so on") both underlines and strains against the epistemological problem that Orwell faces: how the social conditions that motivate the description also exceed and elude the description. "Meanwhile," Orwell writes, "some of the expressions I have used need explaining." Coming after the repetitive "and so on," this "meanwhile" suggests that such "expl[anations]"—or the proliferation of Orwell's own writing, his words about his words—take place in lieu *of* the more extensive cataloguing that is provoked by his inquiries. To linger on a specific house, or to "explain" (and thus unpack) the compressed description of a specific house, risks excluding the wider range of conditions that one is noticing.

(Those conditions that go "on and . . . on"). In particular, Orwell wants to point out the compression within his shorthand term, "back-to-back houses," which neatly contains exactly *twice* what it might be expected to. We observe twelve houses, but "in reality" we are seeing twenty-four. The difference is quantitative but *also* qualitative: how can you see the object from both sides? This same two-sided condition, of course, produces the hard choice, for the tenant, at the heart of the passage. In this way, Orwell connects trade-offs implicit within writing (and, more specifically, in the project of social representation) and double binds in the referenced world of action. "The front houses give on the street and the back ones on the yard, and there is only one way out of each house. The effect of this is obvious." This second, terse sentence is a good example of the two directions that Orwell's plain style often simultaneously takes. Proposing an "effect" as directly intelligible, the sentence also forms a beat or separation that subtly protracts the process of comprehension that it asserts should be direct, immediate, or "obvious." It leads us in and holds us back at the same time. The next sentence, in fact, offers a noticeably extended, rather than an imme-diate or obvious, explanation: "The lavatories are in the yard at the back, so that if you live on the side facing the street, to get to the lavatory or the dust-bin you have to go out of the front door and walk round the end of the block—a distance that may be as much as two hundred yards; if you live at the back, on the other hand, your outlook is on to a row of lavatories." The laborious syntax ("so that if," "to get to," "you have to go out of") reinforces the problematic relationship to distance that's being described. Orwell's own prose, too, rests suspended between immediacy and delay.[26]

Thought and World: AIP 10

Orwell's tenth column of "As I Please" begins "When Sir Walter Raleigh was imprisoned in the Tower of London, he occupied himself with writing a his-tory of the world" (10, 16.88). There is something odd in the enfolding of such a writing project within the delimited column space of "As I Please." What could be more different from the shifting, contingent topicality of this week-to-week column than a complete "history of the world"? In fact, Orwell at several points in AIP shifts to this kind of totalized frame, detailing, for example, the world-spanning disorientation of two captured Tibetan soldiers (who stray across the Soviet frontier and are conscripted, shuttled to western Russia, taken prisoner by Germany and sent to North Africa, shifted to a German army unit in France, and finally captured by British troops) in one section (44, 10.429) or considering the potential (and, intrinsically, world historical) extinction of different animal species in others (59, 17.50; 23, 16.176). The felt incongruity between such scope and the column's delimited frame is pointedly rehearsed in the Raleigh anecdote. The terms of this opening—a writer in a prison, a history of the world—radicalize the framework of Orwell's own project in "As I Please," with its acute sense of the "world" that both encircles and is inflected into the "prison" of such a delimited form. Any author, "occupy[ing] himself" with the project of writing, is simultaneously in a tower and a prison: reflecting on, and separated from, the world that forms the necessary and desired ground of the written text. In this sense, the Raleigh anecdote directly concerns the act of thinking, understood as the conceptual apprehension of a space (that "world") within which the thinker himself is also positioned. Orwell continues:

> He had finished the first volume and was at work on the second when there was a scuffle between some workmen beneath the window of his cell, and one of the men was killed. In spite of diligent inquiries, and in spite of the fact that he had actually seen the thing happen, Sir Walter was never able to discover what the quarrel was about: whereupon, so it is said—and if the story is not true it certainly ought to be—he burned what he had written and abandoned his project. (10, 16.88)

The anecdote dramatizes that threshold of such importance to Orwell. The sounds of the world penetrate through to the writer—immersed in that *Wigan Pier*–like space between the "first volume" and "the second"—and, as they penetrate, call into question the project of a total history. If "every book is a failure," Orwell here imagines the fiction of writing's destruction ("if the story is not true it certainly ought to be"), as the appropriate or fitting response by Raleigh. And this is despite Raleigh's efforts, and capacity, to peer across the threshold both empirically ("he had actually seen the thing happen") and inferentially (he makes "diligent inquiries").

Any number of elements in this brief anecdote resonate with Orwell's aesthetics (and with the unresolved crosscurrents of "As I Please"): the break between the volumes, the "window" in the cell, these two ways of "seeing" or knowing the world (inferentially and directly), the relationship between the sheer activity of writing and the encroachment of what is external to the written, and the dramatization of when writing *ends* or stops. This last is crucial. Because of the phrasing, we can't be certain where this powerful image—of writing halted—originates: whether Orwell relays an actual event ("so it is said") or gravitates, out of his own concerns, to an apocryphal story. Not only is the project "abandoned," but the manuscript is "burned." Orwell continues, signaling how this anecdote has indeed reverberated in his own thoughts: "This story has come into my head I do not know how many times during the past ten years, but always with the reflection that Raleigh was wrong." The "but" is surprising here, as though Orwell were recoiling *from* the skeptical and reflective force of the anecdote, to assert a more confident view of the writer's epistemological capacity (so that, Raleigh, in fact, *could* have written a history of the world). Almost in a parody of this, he goes on: "Allowing for all the difficulties of research at that date, and the special problem of conducting research in prison, he could probably have produced a world history which had some resemblance to the real course of events. . . . A certain degree of truthfulness was possible so long as it was admitted that a fact may be true even if you don't like it."[27]

How do we reconcile the expansion of the anecdote within Orwell's consciousness with this curtailing of its skeptical force? Orwell, in fact, elicits this tension. And we need to see a relationship between his enumeration of the story's continued reverberation—as it has "come into my head I do not know how many times"—and an endlessness *always* implicit, at least as a threat, within self-reflection: implicit, in other words, any time that a writer "occupies himself" with writing about the world. In this way, the anecdote presents a doubled, nested image of reflection or interiority: Orwell's thinking (what "come[s] into [*his*] head" countless times) about Raleigh's thoughts (how he "occupie[s] himself" in writing). But in both cases, this reflection (even as it is amplified in this way) is put under strain: in the empirical crisis that puts an end to Raleigh's writing and in Orwell's deflationary circumscription of the very anecdote that has occupied his attention. The event that disables Raleigh's history project in fact troubles the prisoner's writing in two opposed ways: not merely as it demonstrates how the world is too distant from the writer's faculties of perception (either empirical or inferential) but also, inversely, as it pulls Raleigh into the world, forcing an awareness of his own (or his *thoughts'* own) embeddedness within the world that he is attempting to describe (or think about). Too near, in other words, and too far away: once again, we can see this pattern, as the quarrel beneath the prison gates is so disruptive to the writing project only as it first interrupts and *then* eludes the writing self. If the fight had not broken out directly "beneath the window of his cell" (and broken out *as* Raleigh "was at work" on the writing project)—then its epistemological uncertainty (its remoteness) would not be so troubling. Here, once again, is a serious complication of the "window pane" as a figure for an aesthetics of transparency. The window at once makes Raleigh too vulnerable to the turmoil of the world and makes this turmoil too mediated and distant.

It is such tension within the anecdote that I think captures Orwell's notice—the animating relation between writing's vulnerability, as a (delimited) activity within the world, and the project of constructing a total "history of the world." These two dimensions of writing are made extreme in this example. Writing's vulnerability, of course, rarely results in such a literal abandonment or disruption. And the topical scope of a story is not always a "history of the world" *tout court*. But the combination of these two elements—of fragility and compass, isolation and panorama—are at the core of writing's uncanny nature for Orwell. We might consider here the two potential meanings of the column title. "As I Please" could denote the product of Orwell's composition (here we see *what* Orwell writes when he chooses to write as he pleases) or the process of the composition (here we see Orwell *as* he is in the act of writing about what he pleases). This subtle tension is important because it maps onto the difference between thought (as substance) and thinking (as process). In a pinch, at its core, does writing express thought or express thinking? The Raleigh anecdote moves from the most wide-ranging mimetic span to the fragile center of the compositional process. Thinking, here encapsulated in the necessary intensity with which Raleigh "occupie[s] himself," unfolds in this unstable space. The transience of the column—as form—is put into relief against a diametrically opposed writing project: constructing the "history of the world." And the placement of this anecdote within the column is crucial to the elaboration of this idea: its own excessive force—self-consciously both elicited *and* repudiated by

Orwell—calls attention to the same instability (within the act of thinking) that is given dramatic form in Raleigh's experience.

"Time to Think": Interiority and Delay

Orwell's sense that the elusive object (of representation) that writing attempts to comprehend can be both too near and too remote folds into a sustained and politically significant consideration of thinking itself in the columns. If several moments that I now turn to within "As I Please" foreground thinking as an explicit topic of consideration, these scenes need to be understood in relation to the column's own "thought provoking" form (its capacity, again, to "[raise] more problems than it discusses"[2, 16.23]). Put most simply, Orwell connects the precariousness inherent in the transient, truncated, and varied form of "As I Please" with a vulnerability that's lodged at the heart of thinking. Like much of Orwell's writing, "As I Please" is full of counterintuitive thinking and conceptual peripeteias, movements of thought that pivot around reversals or puncturing.[28] For instance, Orwell zeros in on the "half-conscious idea that to have aesthetic sensibilities you must be a Tory" (29, 10.259–260); or, again, in a column that addresses the equation of urban apartment buildings with noise and squalor, "the half-conscious conviction . . . that working class people must not be made too comfortable" (12, 10.101). These two comments—which point, respectively, to an internalized resistance toward beauty (on the left), and to the way in which oppressive relations can always be hidden *within* putatively ameliorative policies—both hinge on puncturing conscious or intentional thought. Thought *becomes* unaware rather than only and always resisting and negating unawareness: this is why the realm of what is "*half*-conscious," as we'll see, is quite significant (and even generative) in AIP. This kind of dangerous extension (and thus potential routinization) of thought, sympathy, representation, or language lurks everywhere in "As I Please." Another section looks at sentimental fiction about the working class and argues that narratives that insist on "the moral superiority of the poor" are, despite their ostensibly progressive intentions, one of "the deadliest forms of escapism" (35, 16.305). In other columns, Orwell considers how photographs of atrocities can become an excuse for sadism (a danger that lurks potentially within many different forms of representation); and several sections highlight how advances in technologies of transportation or communication, ironically, can serve to establish or harden rather than break down national boundaries.[29] Elsewhere Orwell contrasts state-sponsored censorship with more oblique but potentially damaging forms of cultural and psychological censoring, refusing to draw a clear boundary between external and internal coercion.[30] Such boundless coercion resonates with the problem of freedom posed by the title of the column itself: most of these topics suggest the pointed instability of free thought, highlighting how conscious tendencies—whether of representation (as in the photographs of atrocities), aesthetics, ideology, or even public policy (as in the design of working-class housing)—can so quickly become mechanical, automatic, and *un*thinking. The machines that Orwell stigmatizes as one form of such ruptured intentionality—"as it is," Orwell writes, "the aeroplane [which might have been envisioned to ease social and national boundaries] is primarily a thing for dropping bombs and the radio primarily a thing for whipping up nationalism" (57, 11.39)—also stand in for the potential mechanization of thought itself.

The reversals and counterintuitive provocations in "As I Please" are thus closely intertwined with the formal logic of the column, as it doesn't merely generate thought but shapes this particularly intensified, unstable, and temporally delimited kind of thinking. "To think" in Orwell—critically, counterintuitively, or "freely" (as the column title suggests)—is an acrobatic act, and one in which the ground and the instruments of flight may constantly shift. Reflection must not only continually produce insights that take shape against social givens but also disrupt and scrutinize its *own* insightfulness, avoiding the equally pernicious givens—the patterns and inertia—of speculation, inwardness, and formal awareness.[31] This double bind, at the core of thought itself, resonates with those two-edged predicaments that we've seen in *Homage to Catalonia* (the grenade that goes off too early or too late) and *The Road to Wigan Pier* (the back-to-back houses too near to or distant from the lavatory).

A number of times, the thought-provoking column comes to revolve around the act of thinking itself, providing topical and thematic echoes of these large conceptual stakes. There's a crucial tempo here that Orwell wants to foreground: a pause that doesn't last too long, a thought that is bound in time. In the last section of "As I Please" 12, for example, Orwell draws a distinction between two kinds of comical cartoons: one that "might take five seconds' thought" to understand, and the automatic form of comics in *Punch* magazine—an example that stands in for much larger, mechanical tendencies within a language or a culture:

> Another correspondent writes indignantly to know what I mean by saying that *Punch* is not funny. . . . But—as I always tell puzzled foreign visitors who enquire about this—*Punch* is not meant to be funny, it is meant to be reassuring. After all, where do you most frequently see it? In club lounges and in dentists' waiting rooms. In both places it has, and is meant to have, a soothing effect. You know in advance that it will never contain anything new. The jokes you were familiar with in your childhood will still be there, just the same as ever, like a circle of old friends. The nervous curate, the apoplectic colonel, the awkward recruit, the forgetful plumber—there they all are, unchangeable as the Pyramids. Glancing through those familiar pages, the clubman knows that his dividends are all right, the patient knows that the dentist will not really break his jaw. . . . Jokes that are funny usually contain that un-English thing, an idea. . . . But it might take five seconds' thought to see the joke, and as it is an axiom of the middle class—at least the golf-playing, whisky-drinking, *Punch*-reading part of the middle class—that no decent person is capable of thought, jokes of that kind are barred from *Punch*. (12, 16.102)

These "five seconds" of thinking are inscribed very precisely into an act of representation—puncturing and extending the distance between the "vehicle" and the "tenor" of the cartoon. Thought is distinctly negative here, operating to interrupt a circuit of communication that otherwise proceeds— "soothing," "familiar," and "reassuring"—to unfold in a preformed manner, one that "will never contain anything new."[32] This kind of thought relies on a scratch, pause, or stop—a moment of hesitation. (But, and this is the decisive point, such hesitation can't go on for too long). The focus on this five-second delay necessary for thought in AIP 12 finds a more dramatic elaboration in a column written several months later. The discussion, of Germany's introduction of the V-1 rocket in its air campaign against England, is one of several times that Orwell calls attention to the bombs that are dropping on London as he writes for *Tribune*. These references to the noises of war—"I write this to the tune of an electric drill" (6, 16.56); "as you probably reflected the other night when the ack-ack guns started up" (14, 16.112); "at this moment when the house still seems to be rocking from a recent explosion" (50, 16.487)—are key examples of the way that the columns mark their own immediacy. These are not just signs of the present out of which the columns take form but events that interpenetrate the act of writing itself, as made clear in the sensory vividness of these three brief asides.[33] They draw on the particular temporality afforded by "As I Please," in which the reflective capacity of writing is made pointedly simultaneous with the world it tries to comprehend. In AIP 31, Orwell's discussion of the V-1 occurs only weeks after these missiles were first launched over England (in the wake of the Normandy landing) on the night of June 13, 1944. The section does not depict the sounds of war in this same radically present tense, but its own topical focus rests directly on the (strange) intersection of sound and thought:

I notice that apart from the widespread complaint that the German pilotless planes "seem so unnatural" (a bomb dropped by a live airman is quite natural, apparently), some journalists are denouncing them as barbarous, inhumane, and "an indiscriminate attack on civilians."

After what we have been doing to the Germans over the past two years, this seems a bit thick, but it is the normal human response to every new weapon. Poison gas, the machine-gun, the submarine, gunpowder, and even the crossbow were similarly denounced in their day. Every weapon seems unfair until you have adopted it yourself. But I would not deny that the pilotless plane, flying bomb, or whatever its correct name may be, is an exceptionally unpleasant thing, because, unlike most other projectiles, it gives you time to think. What is your first reaction when you hear that droning, zooming noise? Inevitably, it is a hope that the noise *won't stop*. You want to hear the bombs pass safely overhead and die away into the distance before the engine cuts out. In other words, you are hoping it will fall on somebody else. So also when you dodge a shell or an ordinary bomb—but in that case you have only about five seconds to take cover and no time to speculate on the bottomless selfishness of the human being. (31, 16.272)

Orwell's comment about the V-1 rocket again focuses attention on a precarious interval of time in which reflection takes place. Because the bomb's impact is delayed, Orwell catches his own thought, which is to say, he thinks slightly *longer* and, in this extension, becomes aware of (and momentarily detached from) his own thought processes. The passage thus inscribes an external situation that reiterates the conceptual structure of the columns themselves.

The question that Orwell can retrospectively ask of this experience— "What is your first reaction when you hear that droning, zooming noise?"— is, in fact, a part of the experience itself. The lapsed time here is quite similar to that temporal interval, which is, in the Hegelian description, implicated into self-consciousness. Under the pressure of the immediate—the threatening noise that won't stop—the individual who has been listening to the sound of the rocket discovers himself *in* the act of listening. It is a jarring or shocking experience—a "particularly unpleasant thing." Orwell's pinpointing of how this thought arises (and his catalysis of thought in the column itself) hinges on a tightly circumscribed temporal framework. On the one hand, thinking here relies on a *slightly* prolonged interval of time, usually disallowed by the immediacy of an explosion. Thought does not come easily. (What's diabolical about the new weapon, in Orwell's account, is that it "gives you time to think" while you are experiencing it). On the other hand, as the disjunctive brevity of "As I Please" continually suggests, a thought, if it is held (or pursued) *too* long, can cease to be conceptual altogether. This is true, for Orwell, in a political sense—we might define orthodoxy as the rote extension of thought into mechanically repetitive ideology—but also in a more specific, intellectual sense. Thought, in extended duration, can lose its connection to a substantial ground, becoming a mere, potentially endless (or "bottomless[ly] selfish") reflection of itself.

This section of "As I Please" concerns a particular, temporally constrained sequence of thought. It also *produces* the typically pointed thought of these columns, the single insight or the conceptual turn that is so often the key process in AIP.[34] The writing hones in on this moment in which experience and reflection, noise and detachment, are intertwined with each other. (What's striking about the V-1 rocket is how it will first make a loud droning noise and then—when it is actually *over* its target—come to an eerie and silent stop, before issuing the decisive boom of an explosion. Orwell's innovation is to connect this uncanny, jarring sequence of noise and silence—occurring, as he wrote, over the skies of London—to the dynamics of thought.) As I've noted, this alternation between noise and silence—which might traditionally connote an opposition between experience and thought—is, on the contrary, *internal* to the experience. In a larger sense, this is what the columns as a whole intend to do—to elaborate a mode of reflection that is penetrated by, without becoming identical to, the noise of the world.

The moment in which thought catches itself in the act of hearing the sound is both a valuable and a fragile, temporally delimited one. Orwell's column, in turn, catches hold of this experience and then shifts quickly, and disjunctively, to another section and topic. The vulnerable moment of self-consciousness (because of the falling bomb, now equated with consciousness of the self's own vulnerability) is both crystallized and abandoned at its point of articulation.[35] The column continues with a quite different subject:

> So also when you dodge a shell or an ordinary bomb—but in that case you have only about five seconds to take cover and no time to speculate on the bottomless selfishness of the human being.
>
> It cannot be altogether an accident that nationalists of the more extreme and romantic kind tend not to belong to the nation that they idealise. Leaders who base their appeal on "*la patrie*," or "the fatherland" are sometime outright foreigners, or else come from the border-countries of great empires. Obvious examples are Hitler, an Austrian, and Napoleon, a Corsican, but there are many others. (31, 16.272).

This relationship between form and content continues in the montage effect of the column as a whole. After the discussion of the foreign nature of nationalism (a quarrel with the phantasmatic—or abstract—unity of nationhood that returns to the opening gesture of "As I Please"),[36] Orwell goes on to simply quote, without comment, "two samples of the English language": an ornate passage from Thomas Urquhart's seventeenth-century translation of Rabelais and an abstruse, poorly written paragraph from an unnamed American magazine. The representation of inadequate language resonates with the first section's worrying of the distinction between "natural" and "unnatural" weapons and its inscription of different terms—"pilotless plane, flying bomb, or whatever its correct name may be"—that are used to characterize the new German weapon.[37] The final section also returns with irony to this opening, beginning, "Six million books, it is said, perished in the blitz of 1940, including a thousand irreplaceable titles" (16.273). Language's insecure materiality is here couched in extreme terms, as Orwell provocatively inverts vehicle and tenor. Whereas section one conveyed the difficulty of finding language to represent the bombing campaign, section four depicts the vulnerability of words, language, culture, and actual books *to* bombs during the blitz. Words and bombs thus each contain or frame the other, twisted together like a Möbius strip.

This is a charged and unstable intermediate space—akin in some ways to the "semi-sociological" region that Orwell seeks to carve out for criticism in *Inside the Whale.* The final section of AIP 31 moves quickly from this disturbing, physical conflagration of language to a very different form of "endangered" words—focusing on the difficulty that Orwell has finding old books by Jack London. As Orwell recounts this:

> [I]t is dismaying to find how many standard works are now completely out of print. . . . Even so well-known a work of reference as Webster's dictionary is no longer obtainable unless you run across a copy secondhand. About a year ago I had to do a broadcast on Jack London. When I started to collect the material I found that those of his books that I most wanted had vanished so completely that even the London Library could not produce them. To get hold of them I should have had to go to the British Museum reading-room, which in these days is not at all easy of access. And this seems to me a disaster, for Jack London is one of those border-line writers whose works might be forgotten altogether unless somebody takes the trouble to revive them. (16.273)

Orwell is unusually interested in texts that are on such a threshold of "vanish[ing]," whether literally out of print, merely out of favor, hard to find, fading from (individual or cultural) memory, or actively suppressed. He alights on such *varied* books as Trotsky's banned *Life of Stalin,* which "had been printed and . . . the review copies had been sent out" only to be "immediately withdrawn" when the United States entered the war (AIP 50, 16.489); Tolstoy's little-read anti-Shakespeare pamphlet, of which Orwell notes that "both translations of this essay are out of print, and I had to search all over London before running one to earth in a museum" ("Literary Criticism II: Tolstoy and Shakespeare" 12.493); American children's books like *Helen's Babies, Beautiful Joe,* or Alcott's *Little Women* and *Good Wives,* which, Orwell supposes, are only "still flickeringly in print" ("Riding Down from Bangor" 18.494); or his own newly rediscovered copy of Samuel Butler's *Note-Books:* "It is twenty years old and none the better for having gone through several rainy seasons in Burma, but at any rate it exists, which is all to the good, for this is another of those well-known books which have now ceased to be procurable" (AIP 34, 16.292). These four examples suggest subtly different kinds of obscurity, drawing out a complicated threshold between permanency and transience.[38] Crucially, Orwell is not merely aiming for the recovery of content that has been forgotten or devalorized. Rather, he is drawn to the "border-line" of disposability itself, striving to foreground an intermediate space in which ephemeracy and durability are entwined. He wants to see "vanishing," rather than to render the vanished into stable visibility. This intermediate area leads Orwell, through multiple routes, to explicitly political content—connecting, for example, with the neglected status of popular culture; with disregarded perspectives and facts; with persons who are "disappeared" in totalitarian or fascist contexts (by standing out, politically) and in capitalist systems (by being submerged, economically). But it also echoes the form of reflection that "As I Please" favors, hinging on that interlace of transience and extension, immediacy and delay.

The search is important here: Orwell focuses on having "to go to the British Museum reading-room, which in these days is not at all easy of access" to find Jack London's texts (16.273) and dramatizes the "running" and "search[ing]" involved in finding Tolstoy's now-obscure pamphlet (a text that tries, ironically, to make Shakespeare himself obscure). These details work to highlight the elusiveness of the texts that interest Orwell, suggestively captured in the verbal image of books "still flickeringly in print." More than just configuring the text as a fading light or dying star, such pulsation foregrounds an unstable area in which hiding and showing are intertwined. The stretch of the adverb itself ("flickeringly"), in its quiet but unlikely phonetic extension, carries the weight of this same aesthetic sense. The word stands out from, even as it is syntactically incorporated within, Orwell's own plain style.

The *excess* of thinking in "As I Please" enters in strange places—as in this image of "simultaneity" at the opening of AIP 15:

> Reading as nearly as possible simultaneously Mr. Derrick Leon's *Life* of Tolstoy, Miss Gladys Storey's book on Dickens, Harry Levin's book on James Joyce, and the autobiography (not yet published in this country) of Salvador Dali, the surrealist painter, I was struck even more forcibly than usual by the advantage that an artist derives from being born into a relatively healthy society. (15, 16.117)

This opening sentence, unusually for the beginning of the "As I Please" columns, is cut off as a separate paragraph. Isolated and emphasized in this way, and because of the *intensity* of the activity it registers, this sentence demands our attention but also moves us quickly toward the (more delimited) argument it introduces. In this way, the opening reproduces the same overflowing process that it describes. In all of "As I Please," this might be the image that most closely echoes the column-sequence's *own* strange (conceptual) excess. There is a manic quality to the activity that's foregrounded here, a flurry of reading that must have occurred just before the column was written. It is in the nature of thought to reach beyond itself, to experience its own catalytic unfolding in this way, and the sentence inscribes the self-propelling, unfinished quality of such energetic reflection. It is, of course, *impossible* to read four books at the same time, just as there can't be a complete coincidence of thought and the experience on which it rests. Once again crystallizing the intricacy of the "plain style," the image conveys, above all, thought's frantic effort *at* simultaneity.

In the course of the sentence, however, Orwell radically narrows down the "forc[e]" of such reading to produce the single claim (about the relationship of the writer to society) that will govern the section as a whole. Orwell resists the excess that he provokes, just as he turns away from the impact of the Raleigh anecdote. The rest of the column drops any further references to the *activity* of Orwell's reading. Yet it would be a mistake to ignore the impact of Orwell's opening gesture because it has been so quickly abandoned. As we've seen, the structural logic of "As I Please" often hinges on abruptly taking leave of topics, and it could well be that the image of Orwell reading (or *trying* to read) four books simultaneously is the key movement in this number, "striking" the reader in part through its own uneasy place within the sequence of the column as a whole. (And the AIP columns, of course, echo the impossible simultaneity of Orwell's efforts—confronting the reader with two, three, or four contiguous but disconnected sections.) To be struck in this way—as Orwell is in reading the four books (and as at least one critic has been struck by this sentence within "As I Please")[39]—is precisely to experience a thought that is slightly too *big* for its moment, for its delimited temporal unfolding. This is an experience that is crucial to the very enterprise of serious or passionate thinking. This excess of intensity—these *flares* of thought—are at the hidden center of AIP.

The discussion of Jack London's texts at the end of AIP 31, like the discussion of the V-1 bomb at the beginning of the column, draws on the transient form of "As I Please" itself, linking together the vulnerability of a text that hovers on such a cultural "border-line" and that charged threshold of reflection that is foregrounded in the column's first section. Like many passages in "As I Please," these sections work to render writing neither as the (impossibly) concrete reduplication of the world or as a sealed-off system of abstraction. The shifts across these three topics—from the representation of an extremely specific and temporally delimited "thought," to a puncturing of nationalism, to this discussion of a "vanishing" and "border-line" writer—exemplify the kind of disconnections that often underlie the logic of "As I Please."

These pauses—the "five seconds' thought" in AIP 12 or the "thirty seconds" in AIP 31—suggest the way that thought needs to carve out time for itself, but, as I've been suggesting, Orwell is equally attentive to the dangers of reflection that goes on too long. It's only against each of these problematic temporal frames that the charged image of thinking that most interests Orwell emerges. Such extended reflection is also overly autonomous reflection—unmarked by interruption from or interaction with the world that forms the ground and horizon of thinking. In one section of AIP, Orwell directly quarrels with the myth of such purely independent thought, analogized to the politically powerful idea of a secret "attic." Besides standing out as another representation *of* thought, this section is notable on a political register because it emphatically connects the critique of totalitarianism—so important to Orwell's political art—with a critique (rather than a conservative apotheosizing) of individualism:

The fallacy is to believe that under a dictatorial government you can be free *inside*. Quite a number of people console themselves with this thought, now that totalitarianism in one form or another is visibly on the up-grade in every part of the world. Out in the street the loud-speakers bellow, the flags flutter from the rooftops, the police with their tommy-guns prowl to and fro, the face of the Leader, four feet wide, glares from every hoarding; but up in the attics the secret enemies of the regime can record their thoughts in perfect freedom—that is the idea, more or less. And many people are under the impression that this is going on now in Germany and other dictatorial countries. (22, 16.172)

Orwell goes on to critique this tempting but "false" idea. First of all, he suggests, "modern dictatorships don't, in fact, leave the loopholes that the old-fashioned despotisms did." And he also notes that "totalitarian methods of education" can weaken "the desire for intellectual liberty." But these are preliminary points that Orwell wants to "pass over." He continues:

The greatest mistake is to imagine that the human being is an autonomous individual. The secret freedom which you can supposedly enjoy under a despotic government is nonsense, because your thoughts are never entirely your own. Philosophers, writers, artists, even scientists, not only need encouragement and an audience, they need constant stimulation from other people. It is almost impossible to think without talking. If Defoe had really lived on a desert island he could not have written *Robinson Crusoe,* nor would he have wanted to. Take away freedom of speech, and the creative faculties dry up. . . . And when the lid is taken off Europe, I believe one of the things that will surprise us will be to find how little worthwhile writing of any kind—even such things as diaries, for instance—have been produced in secret under the dictators. (22, 16.172–173)

This is another section that reflects directly on the core project of "As I Please." By critiquing that idea of "be[ing] free inside," "record[ing] . . . thoughts in perfect freedom," the "autonomous individual," and, again, "secret freedom," Orwell also puts pressure on the political aspiration signaled by the title of the column itself. Like those diaries that Orwell here mentions (as the *formal* equivalent to, or textual product of, the "secret" "attics" of interiority), his column is designed to capture the writing self ("I") in the ephemeral and elusive act ("As") of freedom ("Please"). This section makes clear that such a project (of free writing, or thinking) can't rely simply on excavating a sheltered, protected space for a foundational or integral consciousness. Orwell's tricky example of Defoe and Crusoe works effectively to shift registers back to writing itself. Orwell invokes Defoe here as his novel, *Robinson Crusoe,* emblematically imagines the isolation that this section foregrounds as a constitutive dimension of interiority. But Defoe's canonical representation of isolation requires—quite strangely, when we think about it—that the composition itself take place in a *less* isolated context. More generally, however, we could argue that any written thought (or, in slightly different terms, any discretely crystallized moment of free thinking) entails a crucial non-identity between the represented event of thinking and the active interiority of the writer. "[B]y the time you have perfected any style of writing, you have always outgrown it" ("Why I Write" 18.320). Orwell imagines Defoe's position, as writer, collapsing into the isolated state that he represents and then *destroying* the writing project (perhaps abandoned, like Raleigh's countervailing "history of the world"). Such a collapse of positions, insofar as it signals a stabilized and complacent relationship between the thinker and the thought, doesn't only threaten this particular writing project. It is the very tendency that enables that myth of an autonomous self, with its simplified aesthetics of expression, that Orwell is here critiquing. Instead, there must always be a distance between the thinker and the thought, between writing and topic: a distance that is activated, not refused, by Orwell's seemingly transparent plain style. "I once asked him if he had ever thought of legally adopting his *nom de guerre,*" Anthony Powell writes of Orwell. "'Well I have,' he said, slowly, 'but then, of course, I'd have to *write* under another name if I did'" (Stansky and Abrahams 307).

5

Writing's Outside

"Confessions of a Book Reviewer"

We have seen how openings in "As I Please" often call attention to a threshold between experience and reflection. The column unfolds as an only *slightly* belated elaboration of the response that is motivated by or out of experience. Orwell's depiction of the conceptual "forc[e]"(16.117) or excess within the act of reading (through the crucial image of trying to "simultaneously" read four biographies in AIP 15) echoes his 1946 *Tribune* essay "Confessions of a Book Reviewer," another important piece in the sequence of essays that work to find different, oblique angles for contemplating the "inside" and "outside" of reading and writing. This essay is part of a constellation of texts—many clustered around *Tribune* and "As I Please"—in which Orwell stages writing's reflection on its own materiality. "Confessions of a Book Reviewer" intersects, from the title on, with "Are Books Too Dear?" (about the expense of books), "Books *v.* Cigarettes" (which also considers the cost of books, while simultaneously radicalizing their materiality in the comparison), "The Cost of Letters" (on how much and in what way writers should be paid), "Good Bad Books" (on books with simultaneously "high" and "low" value for readers), and "Books and the People" (his statement of policy about book reviewing for *Tribune* at the beginning of 1945).[1] The mere repetition of that talismanic term "books" in most of these titles suggests the materialist drive in Orwell's writing. In this same period, Orwell becomes immersed in pamphlet collecting (something, we've seen, he highlights in the first column of

AIP), writes a recurring piece for *Partisan Review* described as a "Letter," and, in his capacity as *Tribune*'s literary editor, organizes a short-story competition that prompts reflection on the limits and nature of this form.[2] In all these examples, Orwell's writing is both formally variegated (pamphlet, letter, essay, column, story, etc.) and continually veering toward or peering over at its own formal and material bases. One of the key effects in Orwell's mid-1940s writing is to present the spectacle of writing that tries to look at its own "outside": a process that, like the dynamics of thinking we've been considering in "As I Please," is necessarily short-lived, truncated, and dialectically charged. In fact, these two processes—the image of *precarious thought,* which grounds the formal and topical logic of "As I Please," and the materialist drive of Orwell's writing, in its sustained attention to the physicality of writing itself—are intricately conjoined. In this chapter I will consider this connection further, demonstrating how that "border-line," where writing glimpses its own materiality, is connected to the charged image of thinking that these columns both highlight and instantiate. Moving between these two frameworks, this chapter will also weave together my developing reading of "As I Please" with a slightly wider constellation of Orwell's mid-1940s writing. This constellation is centered on (but not exclusively contained by) his contributions to *Tribune,* just as these *Tribune* contributions revolve around, but are not limited to, the AIP columns.

"Confessions," which appears in *Tribune* in May 1946 (in between the two sequences of "As I Please"), begins:

> In a cold but stuffy bed-sitting room littered with cigarette ends and half-empty cups of tea, a man in a moth-eaten dressing gown sits at a rickety table, trying to find room for his typewriter among the piles of dusty papers that surround it. He cannot throw the papers away because the wastepaper basket is already overflowing, and besides, somewhere among the unanswered letters and unpaid bills it is possible that there is a cheque for two guineas which he is nearly certain he forgot to pay into the bank. There are also letters with addresses which ought to be entered in his address book. He has lost his address book, and the thought of looking for it, or indeed of looking for anything, afflicts him with acute suicidal impulses. . . . Needless to say this person is a writer.

He might be a poet, a novelist, or a writer of film scripts or radio features, for all literary people are very much alike, but let us say that he is
a book reviewer. (18.300)

We've seen how the opening of AIP 15 offers a paradigmatic image for the
self-generating excess always potential within thought, drawing on the misalignment between that manic expansiveness implicit in Orwell's effort to
read four biographies "as nearly as possible simultaneously" and the compression of the column itself. "Confessions of a Book Reviewer" marks this
excess in a different way, through the chaotic materiality that both encroaches
upon, and reflects, the charged interiority of the writer. The room is "lit-
tered" with objects, the writer "surrounded" by "dusty papers," the wastepaper basket "overflowing." The writer is vainly "trying to find room," within
this space, "for his typewriter," an instrumental extension of the writing
mind itself. At the same time, the "cigarette ends" and "half-empty cups of
tea" are peculiarly suggestive marks of the external. They constitute both a
pluralized world (not just one cigarette, or one cup of tea) and a residual one
(objects that are partially consumed, and, more specifically, stand as the
remains of their ingestion by the writer). They both surround and reflect,
threaten and extend the writer. They are half finished, like those columns of
"As I Please" that are half in and half out of abstraction, on the threshold
between the event and the reflection upon the event. And like those columns
(with their intersecting and overlapping sections), the hapless book reviewer
in Orwell's essay (who, importantly, could be any kind of writer) is subject to
interruption:

He is a man of 35, but looks 50. He is bald, has varicose veins and wears
spectacles, or would wear them if his only pair were not chronically
lost. If things are normal with him he will be suffering from malnutrition, but if he has recently had a lucky streak he will be suffering from
a hangover. At present it is half past eleven in the morning, and
according to his schedule he should have started work two hours ago;
but even if he had made any serious effort to start he would have been
frustrated by the almost continuous ringing of the telephone bell, the
yells of the baby, the rattle of an electric drill out in the street, and the

heavy boots of his creditors clumping up and down the stairs. The most recent interruption was the arrival of the second post, which brought him two circulars and an income tax demand printed in red. (18.300)

"From the very start," Orwell writes, as we've seen, in another 1946 essay, writing was "mixed up with the feeling of being isolated" ("Why I Write" 18.316). These opening paragraphs of "Confessions of a Book Reviewer" situate the sitting reviewer at the threshold of writing, both unable to and just about to "start" writing. For Orwell the "isolat[ion]" of writing is intertwined with interruption; writing veers constantly away from and toward the world, which here enters through a cacophony of markedly *different* noises. Like Walter Raleigh, the reviewer is not simply cut off from the world but also disrupted by it—just as, in a suggestively related detail, he suffers either from malnutrition (not eating enough) *or* from a hangover (ingesting too much). This image of the writer, then, suggests Orwell's view of writing itself: not just as the texts that this reviewer reads become threateningly materialized but as his own words are marked—penetrated and interrupted—by the world as well. The writing table, to pick up another detail in the description, is "rickety," so that even the surface on which he works is prone to wobble, disrupting and unbalancing the writing itself. Such an image resonates with the pervasive vulnerability of engaged writing for Orwell—a vulnerability that underlies other images in, but also the formal structure of, "As I Please." (The great example of this might be Winston Smith's tactile, secretive, half-hidden and handwritten journal writing in *1984*—though we can draw a line from Gordon Comstock in *Keep the Aspidistra Flying*, through the eponymous book reviewer, to Smith.)

"Books v. Cigarettes"

The "cigarette ends" are particularly important for Orwell, who comes to associate cigarettes and writing in a number of different ways. He's struck by the narcotic potential within both writing and cigarettes but also by the unfurling and disintegration of paper in smoking, in contrast to writing's intended projection of a thought, into permanency, when it is expressed on paper. Individuals, lodged in the cold world—here that "cold but stuffy room" (another telling contradiction)—seek narcotics, whether Orwell himself, shivering in the trenches of Spain ("beside the cold, the other discomforts seemed petty" [*Homage* 31]), or Winston Smith, heading through the glass doors of Victory Mansions on the "bright cold day" that begins *1984*, with "his chin nuzzled into his breast in an effort to escape the vile wind" (1). If both these books situate their central figures in the cold, they also both, of course, show them cadging, smoking, and hording cigarettes.

Orwell's wartime writing, crystallized in "As I Please," conjures up a wide range of different images for disintegrating paper: from books burning in the Blitz (as we have seen, in AIP 31) to newspapers used as kindling when coal is rationed ("The unspeakable depression of lighting the fires every morning with papers of a year ago, and getting glimpses of optimistic headlines as they go up in smoke" ["Wartime Diary" 12.277].) Even the celebratory confetti on V-J Day is subject to the same (pessimistic) material scrutiny:

> There was quite a bit of jubilation in the streets, and people in upstairs offices instantly began tearing up old papers and throwing them out of the window. . . . [F]or a couple of miles my bus travelled through a rain of paper fragments which glittered in the sunlight as they came down and littered the pavements ankle deep. It annoyed me rather. In England you can't get paper to print books on, but apparently there is always plenty of it for this kind of thing. ("London Letter" 17.249)

Paper can go "up," "in smoke," or come "glitter[ingly]" "down." AIP 32 opens by reaching back to a mythic, originary version of paper's destruction (originary both in history and in Orwell's own childhood formation): "When the Caliph Omar destroyed the libraries of Alexandria he is supposed to have kept the public baths warm for eighteen days with burning manuscripts, and great numbers of tragedies by Euripides and others are said to have perished, quite irrecoverably. I remember that when I read about this as a boy it simply filled me with enthusiastic approval" (16.275).[3] And the 1942 BBC radio broadcast "Paper Is Precious" climaxes with a panoramic, almost apocalyptic image of the same fragility: "It is a strange sight to go round one of the great mills where paper is repulped, and to see, apart from the huge bundles of newspaper and wrapping paper, piles of private letters, torn crackers, official documents, posters, bus tickets and streamers from Christmas trees all waiting to go into the vats together" (13.120).[4] The persistence and variety of this material drive—a striking desublimation of culture—is important. Like the word "book" that appears in that constellation of essay titles from this period, images of paper, paper rationing, the destruction of paper, and, conversely, the inundation of the writer *by* paper ("smothered under journalism")[5] recur in Orwell's war-time writing. "When anyone enters the *Tribune* office nowadays, the first thing that strikes his eyes is a huge mound of papers from beneath which a nose makes occasional and momentary appearances. This is myself dealing with the entries for the Short Story Competition" (AIP 20, 16.153).

A transformation of paper—first into (conspicuous) flame and then into ash—also has generated the cigarette ends in "Confessions of a Book Reviewer." But, crucially, for Orwell, thought (as such) is also a form of narcotic—of reflecting, dreaming, or "abstracting" the self, as we have seen with Gordon Comstock in *Keep the Aspidistra Flying,* who, "with smoke tickling his lungs . . . abstracted himself from the mean and actual world" (32).[6] This scene draws cigarette smoking specifically into the center of writing, and thinking, itself—and the way in which Gordon Comstock needs to inhale this smoke, while sitting down to reenter his long, incomplete, perhaps never-to-be-completed poem, anticipates the "cigarette ends" littering the book reviewer's room. Cigarettes are both the residue of writing—its material deposit—and a mark of how the world is swallowed up within the abstracting activity of thought. Inhaled cigarette smoke marks the center of writing's interiority, half-finished cigarette ends the residual sign of its exteriority.[7]

Another *Tribune* essay from this period, "Books *v.* Cigarettes" (from February 1946), sustains this same comparison from a different angle, ostensibly considering the relative cost or value of the two objects. In making this mock-serious calculation, the essay indulges various forms of abstraction even as the resonance of the snappy title is generated by the sheer *physical* resemblance between books and cigarettes, as two forms of paper. The blunt title is another important example of how Orwell's plain style works: starkly matter-of-fact (and pared down to these sparse noun substantives), the title remains, at the same time, off-kilter, insofar as it challenges us—playfully, perversely—to imagine books as merely material. Seeing books as akin to cigarettes, in this sense, resembles other impossible but provoking challenges, like looking at familiar words and trying *not* to see the language but merely the shape of the letters (something we'll return to).

Such hypermaterialization of words and language ironically involves a sustained effort of the mind. It takes less thought, as it were, to "see" books as only conveying thoughts and more conceptual effort to see them in their material dimensions. (We remember that the addiction to cigarettes, for Orwell, is associated with the addiction to thought itself.) Edging toward that radical (and finally unrealizable) juxtaposition of books and cigarettes thus involves a lot of active thinking by the writer. The provoking wit of the abbreviated title rests in the conflation of books and cigarettes as two forms of paper object, and this wit would collapse if the two objects *could* be simply or finally equated. The compressed phrase holds the two terms together but also suspends them, signaling, in this combination, the precarious nature of the thought experiment.[8]

An experiment it is. Like a one-man band, Orwell seems to enact the entire social project of *Mass Observation* on his own, turning himself into specimen but also authoritative expert.[9] The chatty essay reads as both a model for and parody of a reflective process in which the facts of social life can be brought to the surface through sustained, displaced attention to one's own individual patterns of consumption and behavior. The three pages thus offer a flood of figures, modifications, addendums, complications, approximations, claims, and charts, all derived out of Orwell's effort to trace how much he reads, how long it takes, how much it costs, and how this stacks up against other forms of expense. (It is a good essay, in this sense, for dramatizing the fault line between means and end, or between the act of claim-making and the claim itself.) At the beginning of this effort, Orwell avers, "Exactly what reading costs, reckoned in terms of pence per hour, is difficult to estimate, but I have made a start by inventorying my own books and adding up their total price" (18.95). On the one hand, it is "difficult" to discover how much "reading costs" because this entails a series of discrete mental steps: counting the number of books, calculating their value, and dividing this by the time it takes to read them. The reckoning will be only approximate, an "estimate" (97) that can always be further elaborated or developed. But the "difficult[y]" also suggests the larger *speculative* challenge of this essay, in which thought needs to step outside of itself, eluding its own interior nature, in order to glimpse the activity of reading in such estranged terms (as so many words per minute at so many pages per pence). Orwell makes sure to dramatize the conceptual activity entailed in the project of seeing books *as* material (rather than purely conceptual). His sentence on calculating "what reading costs" thus folds together a range of distinct *reflective* processes: "reckon[ing]," "estimat[ing]," "inventorying," "adding." Making the comparison of books to cigarettes brings the mind's restless activity to the foreground, and the essay is full of self-interrupting amplifications, caveats, and asides. This passage continues:

> The books that I have counted and priced are the ones I have here, in my flat. I have about an equal number stored in another place, so that I shall double the final figure in order to arrive at the complete amount. I have not counted oddments such as proof copies, defaced volumes, cheap paper-covered editions, pamphlets, or magazines, unless bound up into book form. Nor have I counted the kind of junky books—old school textbooks and so forth—that accumulate in the bottom of cupboards. (18.95)

Orwell again foregrounds the process of abstraction (first "counting" and "pricing" the books in his flat; then "doubling" this aggregate figure), discretely concretizing the work of thinking itself. At the same time, Orwell's preterition conspicuously dwells on the same "oddments" that it discounts. The dispersed force of physicality is here inscribed even as it is ostensibly negated, or transcended. Orwell manipulates this rhetorical effect—the way it confers a kind of intermediate status onto the putatively excluded material, leaving it half in, half out—to create, once again, a middle space between conceptuality and its material ground.

The books that he doesn't count proliferate and, specifically, are framed in terms *of* their materiality: "cheap," "defaced," "junk," "paper-covered," and, once again, at the bottom of a drawer.[10] They are unfinished ("proof copies"), in pieces (not "bound up") and "accumulat[ing]." Against this grittiness is the work of the calculating mind that can, in one quick instant, "double the final figure." This doubling—accounting for books that are elsewhere, not "here, in my flat" but in "another place" (deliberately unspecified)—suggests the core dynamics of mental replication. We duplicate the embodied particulars of the world (i.e., the "here") within the mind itself (i.e., "another place").

Orwell provokes a tension between such synthetic calculation and the unruliness of physical detail (simultaneously dismissed and dilated upon) as part of the serio-comic texture of the essay as a whole.[11] As we have seen, a clash between rationality and whimsy is built into the title of the essay as well, and Orwell maintains a complicated, uncertain tone throughout. Certainly there are specific claims that Orwell makes by the end of the essay, climaxing in the assertion that the (relative) expense of books doesn't explain their unpopularity.[12] But at the same time, Orwell emphasizes the train of thinking that leads to these conclusions—on the one hand suggesting that the conclusions are only "a rough estimate" (97), "probably a high estimate" (97), or "guesswork" (97) and, conversely, lavishing a conspicuous, unmotivated amount of attention on the twists and turns of his reflections. Consider one more movement of thought, in a paragraph that echoes both the invocation of "difficult[ty]" and the preterition that we've already seen:

> It is difficult to establish any relationship between the price of books and the value one gets out of them. "Books" includes novels, poetry, textbooks, works of reference, sociological treatises and much else, and length and price do not correspond to one another, especially if one habitually buys books secondhand. You may spend ten shillings on a poem of 500 lines, and you may spend sixpence on a dictionary which you consult at odd moments over a period of twenty years. There are books that one reads over and over again, books that become part of the furniture of one's mind and alter one's whole attitude to life, books that one dips into but never reads through, books that one reads at a single sitting and forgets a week later: and the cost, in terms of money, may be the same in each case. But if one regards reading simply as a recreation, like going to the pictures, then it is possible to make a rough estimate of what it costs. (96–97)

The half-included material of this passage—the long list of examples he invokes only to immediately "[dis]regard"—functions differently than those "oddments" that Orwell catalogues only to say that he hasn't counted. While such oddments emphasize the irreducible materiality of the book (as it underlies the governing juxtaposition in the title), these examples, on the contrary, mark the necessary limits of such a material comparison.[13] We assent to this list of four kinds of mental experience even as we can't fully synthesize such compressed variety. The different kinds of imperfect encounters that constitute "reading" are strikingly inconsonant. Orwell doesn't simply distinguish books that are remembered and books that are forgotten. He compares (in the first two examples) books that are "remembered" in quite different ways—reread "over and over again" or simply impressed, durably, upon the mind. He juxtaposes (in the first and fourth examples) two different modes of compulsion—reading the same text repeatedly or reading one text at a single sitting. And he offers (in the third and fourth examples) a subtle inversion between the reader who goes part of the way through a book and then abandons it and a book that, as it were, moves all of *itself* through the reader's mind and then leaves or abandons him. These competing, compacted images—which, intertwined, suggest the fragile and unstable nature of reading—are all lodged within the preterition, and thus unfold in a contingent and vulnerable manner themselves.

Doubling and Inverting: Thought's Microdynamics

In my reading, "Books *v.* Cigarettes" emerges—from the title on—as another exploration of the difficulty entailed in thinking about materiality and, in particular, the difficulty of comprehending (within writing itself) the materiality of texts. The essay wavers or wobbles between its object of thought and the process of thinking. But it also dramatizes the specific act of "doubl[ing]" an object, in one's mind, against the loose, accumulating oddments that would disrupt such replication. When we understand Orwell's essay in this light—in relation to the texture of thought—that act of doubling (with its intriguing replication of books in "another place") is an important afterimage of "Books *v.* Cigarettes." The essay works to isolate this thought, as a discrete "step" within consciousness. The sequence of such steps constitutes the dynamic and mercurial process of thinking. This act of doubling is "isolat[ed]" not just because it is discrete but also, as we have seen, because Orwell is so attentive to the dynamic vicissitudes of thought. Reflection can become routinized, lose the object, extend itself too far or turn, unwittingly, into a mere echo of itself.

This isolated act of "doubling" the object might remind us of those twelve back-to-back houses in *Wigan Pier* that we must, likewise, unpack (within our minds) to twenty-four. More pointed still, another section of "As I Please" foregrounds a related step within thinking: the moment of conceptual inversion, when we "reverse" something in our thoughts. Perhaps more than any other conceptual "step," this is a privileged and paradigmatic one for Orwell. This is in "As I Please" 62, in an irreverent discussion of the relationship between the relative "intelligence" of different newspapers and their "popularity":

> Below I list in two columns our nine leading national daily papers. In the first column these are ranged in order of intelligence, so far as I am able to judge it: in the other they are ranged in order of popularity, as measured by circulation. By intelligence I do not mean agreement with my own opinions. I mean a readiness to present news objectively, to give prominence to the things that really matter, to discuss serious questions even when they are dull, and to advocate policies which are at least coherent and intelligible. As to the circulation, I may have misplaced one or two papers, as I have no recent figures, but my list will not be far out. Here are the two lists: (AIP 62, 18.499)

At this point, the column shifts briefly to tabular form, with two competing lists that are placed side-by-side:

INTELLIGENCE	POPULARITY
1. Manchester Guardian.	1. Express.
2. Times.	2. Herald.
3. News-Chronicle.	3. Mirror.
4. Telegraph.	4. News-Chronicle.
5. Herald.	5. Mail.
6. Mail.	6. Graphic.
7. Mirror.	7. Telegraph.
8. Express.	8. Times.
9. Graphic.	9. Manchester Guardian.

It will be seen that the second list is very nearly—not quite, for life is never so neat as that—the first turned upside down. And even if I have not ranged these papers in quite the right order, the general relationship holds good. The paper that has the best reputation for truthfulness, the

Manchester Guardian, is the one that is not read even by those who admire it. . . . (AIP 62, 18.499)

This passage demonstrates again Orwell's interest in generating a conceptual effect that is intertwined with but not merely equivalent to the substance of the argument. I would argue that Orwell explores this topic just so that he can conjure up the sensation *of* turning a list upside down in one's mind. (It is an important sensation, as we'll continue to see, in Orwell's writing, and one central to the aesthetics of counterintuitiveness.) This action of the mind is highlighted by the unusual deployment of the two tables within AIP 62. The device first slows our reading down, as we encounter the two lists without active comprehension, and then speeds the reading up, by compressing these vertical sequences of names into one crystallized claim. The acceleration of the column's *own* conceptuality thus occurs specifically at the moment in which Orwell reframes the two lists as inversions of one another. The pseudo-scientific or empirical valence that we've seen in "Books *v.* Cigarettes" is here used, in the extreme form of these numerical tables, as the edifice for this conceptual punchline, which hinges on the instant in which the two lists are subject to ironic reversal, or, in Orwell's deliberately more tactile terms, "turned upside down." Crucially this is again an instant, as Orwell draws the fleeting feeling of turning, or being turned, upside down into the unfolding of his argument.

The passage exemplifies Orwell's interest not just in producing a thought or an insight but (as with the V-1 bomb, in AIP 31, that "gives you time to think") foregrounding the brief interval in which an insight occurs: here that point after something has been flipped "upside down" but *before* it has been fully righted or settled in its new position. The section resembles any number of counterintuitive or ironic reversals in Orwell's writing—aimed at producing a discretely striking thought—but it also offers a particularly literal version *of* this more general movement. This literalization is important. If the example we considered in "Books *v.* Cigarettes" isolated the act of conceptual doubling (as a discrete moment of, and within, reflection), this example adds one more turn of thought *to* doubling. The left-hand column is, in one sense, a replication of the right-hand column (like the two rooms full of an identical number of books). But now its spatial position is changed. The doubled object is briefly estranged from the original (both homologous to and starkly dissimilar from it), and thought arises out of the temporary disjunction between the two (and thus out of a specific, contingent play of resemblance and difference).

This sense of disjunction, or imbalance, affects our evaluative understanding of the juxtaposition. The way in which we arrive at the substantive conclusion suggests that there is something fundamentally troubling about the conclusion. Only in a world gone wrong ("turned upside down") would there be such marked discrepancy between the "intelligence" of texts and their "popularity." But if this inversion colors our judgment about the substance of the thought, it also acts as a figure for the act of thinking, here registered as wobbly and precarious. Such an effect is intensified when Orwell interrupts himself at the moment of reversal, bisecting what would be his claim that one list is "very nearly the first turned upside down" with the parenthetical clause "not quite, for life is never so neat as that." The interruption, at once forestalling and extending the moment of reversal, registers the same instability, or lack of "neatness," that it espouses. It syntactically marks that suspended moment within any fall.

All this happens very quickly, of course—indeed, the quickness of the movement (against the *stalling* of the argument by the numerical lists themselves) is part of the process I'm describing. Like many moments in "As I Please," the passage *resists* extended analysis even as it provokes (and here explicitly concerns the process of) reflection. The inverted lists physicalize the essential dynamic of counterintuitive thinking, which so often does rely on some kind of reversal. Such conceptual movement—literalized in this 180-degree inversion, but more generally standing in for any kind of judgment that builds on, tilts away from, pushes against, or establishes a distant or new perspective in relation to the initial conceptual object—is, like the mental act of reduplication, a discrete component of thought. Counterintuitiveness, central to the aspiration of free thought, is here a quite temporally unstable enterprise. This makes logical sense, as a counterintuitive insight—functioning like a lever or point of traction for critique, reframing, originality—always risks betraying itself, becoming a merely rote, instrumental or repetitive dogma once it is incorporated into a more extended, substantial sequence of thinking.

As with that discrete movement of thought in "Books *v.* Cigarettes" (when Orwell "doubles" the number of books that he owns), the larger topic of this section concerns a second-order reflection *on* writing itself. "Books *v.* Cigarettes" plays with an extreme version of materializing the written word (through the impossible equivalence provoked by the title). This section in AIP broaches the "outside" of writing as well. After all, where does Orwell's own effort to articulate his thought both intelligently *and* popularly fall within this topsy-turvy ratio? The writing that makes such an observation is also caught, imperfectly, in the throes of the observed condition. The section is an attempt—from within the folds of his own writing in *Tribune*—to account for the larger field of journalistic writing in England. The conceptual reversal that Orwell highlights (as subjective process) is intertwined with this socio-logical approach to discourse. The topical claim that Orwell makes here (on that diametric relationship between "intelligence" and "popularity") can be connected to other points in his writing that scrutinize the differentiated field of British journalism—for instance, an article on "Britain's Left-Wing Press" that he writes for a left-wing U.S. magazine (the Wisconsin *Progressive*) in 1948. This article opens with the claim that "there are in Britain only six left-wing papers of any consequence" and then offers brief descriptions of *The Daily Herald, Reynold's News, The New Statesman and Nation, Tribune, Forward,* and *The Daily Worker.* After these descriptions, Orwell writes:

> These six papers that I have enumerated are all that Britain possesses— that is, all that is of the slightest importance—in the way of a left-wing press. Beyond this there are only obscure sheets dealing with trade-union intelligence or purely local affairs, and thin little magazines which hardly pretend to be aimed at the big public, and one or two peri-odicals devoted to direct Soviet propaganda and not having much bearing on British politics. (19.297)

This passage recalls the preterition we've seen in "Books *v.* Cigarettes." The last sentence simultaneously dismisses and dwells on the writing that *isn't* important enough to be absorbed into the structural enumeration—too "slight," "obscure," "local," "thin," or "direct[ly]" propagandistic. In this way, the prose creates a threshold effect—shadowing, once again, a piece of structural-sociological analysis with the work *of* structural abstraction. And it's this kind of work, of course, which constitutes a central part of "As I

Please," Orwell's own significant contribution to, and within, the "Left-Wing Press" that this article seeks to taxonomically examine.

If the section on the "intelligence"/"popularity" ratio connects to other such moments of commentary on the British press (a connection mostly in terms of topical content), it also connects, formally, to other "upside down" moments of inversion and reversal in Orwell's work.[14] This particular detail has an afterlife, for example, in *Animal Farm,* the most extended text that Orwell conceives and writes during his work on the fragmented columns of "As I Please":

> It was very neatly written, and except that "friend" was written "freind" and one of the "S's" was the wrong way round, the spelling was correct all the way through. Snowball read it aloud for the benefit of the others. All the animals nodded in complete agreement, and the cleverer ones at once began to learn the Commandments by heart. (43)

This is an unusually literal moment within Orwell's allegory—one passage in the fable of *Animal Farm* where the points that are being made consistently *through* language coincide directly with the language itself. If Orwell's text ends by collapsing, or reversing, the meanings conveyed by the words "man" and "pig" ("the creatures outside looked from pig to man, and from man to pig, and from pig to man again; but already it was impossible to say which was which" [139]), this passage juxtaposes actual words, or letters, themselves, in that reversal of "friend" and "freind." On the other hand, *as* a detail within the referenced world of the allegory, this misspelt language punctures the abstraction implicit in the equivalencies that drive the text forward. The detail is one of many in the text that function to assert the actual difference between childlike animals and men or, to put this differently, between the material ground of representation and a system of political abstraction. The allegory in *Animal Farm* in this way "wobbles"—the animals in *Animal Farm* stand for Russian workers, but also, at times, merely stand for animals. (Wobbling—and its more consequential parallel, falling—are, in turn, defining events within the plot of *Animal Farm*.) In a similar way, the words that often stand for their abstract meanings here seem to stand for themselves. But if this is the case with the typographic inversion of "friend," it's more complicated with the description of how "one of the 'S's' was the wrong way round." Here, after all, we're not given the actual shape of the upside-down "S" (something Orwell might easily have inscribed) but rather, precisely, a *representation* of it. Drawing on one's own childhood experience most likely—one's own encounter with this very mistake—the reader must conjure up, in her head, the reversed "S" that this passage points to. Once again, a discrete and temporally limited act of cognition is provoked, a single movement in which the reduplicated "S"—"turned upside down" (as Orwell writes in "As I Please") or "the wrong way round" (as he writes in *Animal Farm*)—produces a disjunctive awareness.[15] It is as though the passage has distilled the most narrow, but essential, aspect of oppositional thinking—generating the single flash of that technically unarticulated upside-down "S," within the reader's own consciousness, without which a rudimentary understanding (let alone the more polemical implications) of the passage could not coalesce.[16]

Handwriting/Representation: AIP 75

"One thing one notices in these days when typewriters have become so scarce," Orwell begins in AIP 75, "is the astonishing badness of nearly everyone's handwriting" (19.51–52). This is clearly another example of materializing the text, another angle (like that inverted "S" in *Animal Farm*) for the almost impossible project of trying to *see* writing. The topic has force only as it unfolds within the wider, extended field of such reflections that develops over the course of AIP. (And, as with the example of V-J Day confetti, Orwell's emphasis on the surprising "badness" of handwriting underlies the negative impulse of this material drive.) Perhaps the fundamental capacity of criticism is its ability to displace itself from the most well-grooved channels of meaning within any text—to carry the implications of textual meaning one step further, or to consider them one step to the side. The discussion of handwriting is in this spirit. It highlights the way that criticism must always try—and try in various ways—to grasp the "outside" of writing, even as it assuredly *can't* do so with complete or absolute success. The sum of this disjunctive process is greater than its parts: the discussion of handwriting would not be of much interest merely as it addresses this narrow topic. Exploring the topic (as always, under the axiomatic constraints of "As

I Please"), the column also signals a more profound critical desire, and, finally, a powerful and suggestive *unease*. To consider handwriting is also to inevitably remember one's own handwriting and, thus, for writing to glimpse—from within its "interior" conceptuality—its own material, social nature. Such unease, grounded in the confrontation of writing with its outside, is subtly elaborated by the odd way that Orwell lingers on a number of examples for his point. It is another passage within the tightly constructed, quickly dispatched column that has a strange *excess*, an excess that unfolds in particular ways in this discussion:

> One thing one notices in these days when typewriters have become so scarce is the astonishing badness of nearly everyone's handwriting. . . . It would be interesting to know whether there is any connection between neat handwriting and literary ability. I must say that the modern examples I am able to think of do not seem to prove much. Miss Rebecca West has an exquisite handwriting, and so has Mr. Middleton Murry. Sir Osbert Sitwell, Mr. Stephen Spender and Mr. Evelyn Waugh all have handwritings which, to put it as politely as possible, are not good. Professor Laski writes a hand which is attractive to look at but difficult to read. Arnold Bennett wrote a beautiful tiny hand over which he took immense pains. H. G. Wells had an attractive but untidy writing. Carlyle's writing was so bad that one compositor is said to have left Edinburgh in order to get away from the job of setting it up. Mr. Bernard Shaw writes a small, clear but not very elegant hand. And as for the most famous and respected of living English novelists, his writing is such that when I was at the BBC and had the honour of putting him on the air once a month there was only one secretary in the whole department who could decipher his manuscripts. (19.52)

The excess of this discussion rests, first off, in its oddly personal nature. Orwell rarely makes such comments, in print, about his own relations with well-known cultural figures. It is peculiarly, pointedly "immodest" for Orwell. And the name-dropping here also breaks down the walls between different acquaintances that Orwell tended to construct.[17] This leads to the second notable excess in the section: it pours out more examples than are strictly necessary. As though under the spell of personal reverie, Orwell seems to list the names, and acquaintances, as they occur to him, piling together several examples for one category (Sitwell, Spender, Waugh) and also listing *more* categories than we can easily hold in our mind. There's a conflict here between the dilation of such reverie and the column's ostensible commitment to immediate expression. The excess of this list transcends the merely personal, however, since, as I've suggested, Orwell bleeds personal examples into categorical—and thus conceptual—ones. At the same time, even while the examples strain toward conceptuality, Orwell seems to diminish this topic as soon as he has raised it; his touch is very light; he makes it seem unimportant or at least casually taken up; and he ends with an obliquity that can only be taken to trivialize the entire matter ("the most famous and respected of English novelists" for E. M. Forster). He almost dares the reader to make anything of this: to linger with, criticize, or, better yet, *reflect upon* what has been written.

In all these ways, the section embodies that precariousness I've been trying to locate at the juncture of complexity and simplicity within Orwell's work. This meld is rooted in the origins and texture of Orwell's plain style (from the start connected to pseudonymity, isolation, going "down and out") and takes specific, structural form in the truncated sections of "As I Please," as they signify, or express the desire *for,* both simplicity and complexity. This meld is developed stylistically in AIP 75, in that clash between the casualness of tone and the excess of (categorical) examples. But it also emerges, as so often in "As I Please," around a related problem of representation: how, and with what consequence, does writing represent (hand)writing itself? If the section seems like a thin hook on which to hang such a heavy analytical claim, this is again part of the point. Orwell's writing continually creates disjunctures of this kind. While the tone of this section is almost glibly casual, it at times becomes unusually precise, culminating in the description of how Laski has "a hand which is attractive to look at but difficult to read." This comment betrays a careful experience of observation on Orwell's part—of both scrutinizing and thinking about the object at hand. In this way, the description brings us both close to and keeps us distant from its object of representation. Even the abundance of examples fits into this tension, as they provide us with *more* conceptual categories than we can readily synthesize. We lose sight of or forget some of the examples as they arise. But this partial "disappearance" of the hands that are being described is already apparent in the difference between seeing a specific example of actual handwriting and reading these descriptions by Orwell. It is in the nature of *this* topic, in particular, that a representation withholds and reveals simultaneously. Most generally, to notice handwriting in any context entails, at least momentarily, *not* seeing the ideas—the words, phrases, images, and stories—expressed in the writing. Handwriting is thus another vehicle for the difficult (and unsustainable) effort to stay both within and outside language, the "semi-sociological" method that Orwell advocates and that underlies the governing formal premises of the AIP column. More particularly, we cannot see handwriting fully here because this discussion is only a representation of handwriting (rather than a direct inscription or replication): as precise as Orwell's description might be, like all mimetic language, it offers us only a partial, refracted, and mediated image of what we strive—as readers—to see.

The careful effort to convey the look of other people's writing through the sense of his own dramatizes this fault line within representation. In this way the final, willed emphasis on coded language—the coy, indirect description of Forster—merely echoes a more fundamental structure of mediated representation gestured at by the column section as a whole. And, further confusing things, the precision of Orwell's observation about Laski's handwriting centers on exactly this rift between the physical nature of writing and its sense: thus the *oddity* of a handwriting that can be attractive to look at but difficult to read. Despite the ostensible narrowness of the topic, the section works through representation to the inner dynamics of solidarity—insisting on both (empirical) intimacy and (reflective) distance as it tries to comprehend, or "notice" in full detail, the particularity of written expression.

The Space of Writing: AIP 47

In "As I Please" 47, Orwell imagines "an anthology of executions," an idea that, on its face, concerns the strained relationship between (delimited) form and (absolute) event.[18] Orwell introduces the idea, of this hypothetical book, as a specific thought—he gives the context for how it arises—and as a thought that, in turn, prompts another, specific reflection:

Penguin Books have now started publishing books in French, very nicely got up, at half-a-crown each. Among those to appear shortly is the latest installment of André Gide's *Journal*, which covers a year of the German occupation. As I glanced through an old favourite, Anatole France's *Les Dieux Ont Soif* (it is a novel about the Reign of Terror during the French Revolution), the thought occurred to me: what a remarkable anthology one could make of pieces of writing describing executions! There must be hundreds of them scattered through literature, and—for a reason I think I can guess—they must be far better written on average than battle pieces. (47, 16.451)

This opening once again works to mime or enact the process of thinking itself. "The thought occurred to me," writes Orwell, and, as in many of the short pieces in this column, the writerly expression of the thought unfolds in subtle relation to its charged emergence. Here we see Orwell noting the series that "have now" started appearing, marking the latest installment of Gide's *Journal*, and "glancing through" France's novel. The terms of these catalyzing events resonate with the practice of writing "As I Please": in different ways, the appearance of a new series, the transient genre of Gide's *Journal*, and the process of skimming a book all summon up the quotidian or ephemeral practice of writing that animates the columns as a whole. Orwell's column is committed to the force of the ephemeral, to writing that is occasioned by interactions with the world, and here Orwell is drawn to reflect on forms of culture that are likewise oriented around the new or transient. (And yet, at the same time, the book which prompts this new thought, when Orwell "glance[s]" through it, is "an old favourite"—and Orwell's idea itself, of course, concerns an event defined by its dramatic relationship to finality as such.)

Orwell's columns strive to preserve the novelty of thought, of reaction— or *reflection*—that occurs, in relation to the world, before becoming overly substantialized. The columns try to preserve or represent this encounter but also, as pieces of writing (and thus forms of written reflection), to reproduce it. Another paragraph allows Orwell to expand on the examples that have occurred to him, a list that begins by saying, "Among the examples I remember at the moment" and ends only as an interruption: "Then there is Jack London's short story, *The Chinago*, Plato's account of the death of

Socrates—but one could extend the list indefinitely." At this point, Orwell leaves off the examples that have filled his mind and offers the discrete, second-order thought that has, in fact, motivated him to begin the column with this speculative topic:

> The thing that I think very striking is that no one, or no one I can remember, ever writes of an execution *with approval*. The dominant note is always horror. (16.451, Orwell's emphasis)

Here Orwell has identified a point in writing—a crystallized tendency— which is in fundamental opposition to (a particularly inexorable, and violent, expression of) the given. And it is *this* "striking" thought, about writing, enabled by conjuring up that imaginary anthology, that the section as a whole works to give discrete, emphatic form to. We might compare this to Orwell's (similarly italicized) rendition of the thought that emerges out of the noise of the V-1 bomb. Here, too, Orwell pinpoints (in that conceptual emphasis of *"with approval"*) writing's subtle distance from the event that it registers—a distance which, in this case, allows for a meaningful and substantial critique of violence (the cumulative force of the way that writing creates a field of opposition, to executions and, in fact, to the larger systems of violence and brutality in which they are implicated).

Orwell's dramatized insight here fits into a constellation of essays— mostly from this same period—that come to center, conversely, on modes of thinking that surrender to the given:

> And this attitude is defended, if at all, solely on grounds of power. The Russians are powerful in Eastern Europe, we are not: therefore we must not oppose them. This involves the principle, of its nature alien to Socialism, that you must not protest against an evil which you cannot prevent. (AIP 40, 16.365)

> It will be seen that at each point Burnham is predicting *a continuation of the thing that is happening*. Now the tendency to do this is not simply a bad habit, like inaccuracy or exaggeration, which one can correct by taking thought. . . . Power-worship blurs political judgment because it leads, almost unavoidably, to the belief that present trends will continue.

Whoever is winning at the moment will always seem to be invincible.
("Second Thoughts on James Burnham" 18.278, Orwell's emphasis)

The essay on Burnham works to equate Orwell's idea of "power-worship" with what we could call "bad mimesis": where thought automatically duplicates—and thus both accepts and comes to defend—the given. Crucially, this is a problem not merely of political judgment but also within the dynamics of thinking as such—and Orwell identifies the tendency to accept or reduplicate the given world as not merely a position that he is outside of but as a danger that's intrinsic to the process of thinking or writing. (It's in this way that Orwell wants to distinguish such a tendency from mere "inaccuracy or exaggeration.") Such transparent reduplication—which ossifies and serves to extend "the thing that is happening"—once again can trouble the aesthetics that we would associate with the "windowpane."[19]

As with the different pitfalls of abstraction, this accession to the given can intersect with, disrupt, or forestall creative thinking in many different ways. Imagination necessarily takes shape against the given, and so is oppositional in its very form—a process that both endangers imaginative writing (rendering it intrinsically unstable) and makes it a vehicle for dissent and critique. From early on in "As I Please," Orwell identifies the repudiation of originality as a fulcrum for conservative ideology, critiquing, for example, both the "stock argument of intelligent reactionaries" that "'there is nothing new under the sun'" (13, 16.104) and varieties of "neo-pessimism" with "their refusal to believe that human society can be fundamentally improved" (4, 16.35).[20] Orwell draws these seemingly straightforward political comments into the column's sustained engagement with the paradoxes and microdynamics of critical thinking, conceptual originality, and the unsatisfied aspiration (signaled again in the column title) toward writerly freedom. This section from AIP 47 offers an important version of Orwell's wider engagement with such accession to the given because of the way in which Orwell's own isolation *of* this "very striking" thought (about writing on executions) tightly echoes its negative content. The fragility of writing, implied in this insight about represented executions, gets reinforced both by the articulation of the claim within the section as a whole and in the very proposal of the imagined anthology. In Borgesian terms, we could say that the *idea* of the anthology, as a speculative act, gains priority over—and is paradoxically more substantial than—what the anthology would be itself:

> The composition of vast books is a laborious and impoverishing extravagance. To go on for five hundred pages developing an idea whose perfect oral expression is possible in a few minutes! A better course of procedure is to pretend that these books already exist, and then to offer a résumé, a commentary. (15)

Not just a cry for artistic efficiency, Borges's sly comment privileges the speculative moment in which the writer takes leave of the actual over any residual filling in or motivation of this speculation. The comment highlights, again, writing's—and thought's—negativity, but in seeking to compress such a process, it doesn't favor the flight of the speculative so much as that discrete moment when thought is "alit" upon and thus poised to ascend from its substantial ground. (The flight itself would, in its own extension, require the *same* consolidation and elaboration—the same paradoxically "impoverishing extravagance"—as the realism that Borges spurns.)

The act of writing, always potentially opposed to the world that it reflects upon, here finds a topicality (in that imagined collection of represented executions) that gives pointed form and force to this latent denial. In AIP 47, Orwell proceeds to develop or substantialize this idea, but the essential motive for the topic resides in the italicized phrase itself, as it crystallizes (both formally and ideationally) the way that writing can maintain a (tenuous) detachment from, and thus opposition to, the world it represents. The rest of this section is not uninteresting, but its interest lies partially in its very *retreat* from the fundamental point that Orwell has made. Against the striking observation of negativity, crystallized (or "clicking into place") in that italicized phrase, Orwell begins to provide various kinds of content for the thought he has provoked. The "pure" insight into negativity gets fleshed out—motivated and evaluated. Orwell speculates, for instance, on the reasons behind such opposition to executions, notes his own experience ("I watched a man hanged once"), and then satirically "corrects" himself by turning to the enthusiasm with which British papers have been representing the mass executions of quislings and collaborators in France and Italy.

Orwell's imagined anthology provides an important element for a larger idea about representation that is elaborated at various points in, and consistently through the form of, the columns. Imagination here functions as an equivalent to the precariousness—of thinking—that, as we have seen, is a consistent horizon of both the columns' form and their topicality. The section moves seamlessly from the way that Orwell imagines this mode of literary expression (the anthology) to the (negative) work such imaginative writing itself performs. This negativity forms the underlying current of several other sections in "As I Please," as when, for example, several months later, Orwell comments that "when a battle poem wins really wide popularity, it usually deals with a disaster and not a victory" (52, 16.506) or, again, when he suggests, in a *Tribune* discussion of comic writing, that "all great humorous writers show a willingness to attack the beliefs and the virtues on which society necessarily rests. . . . Some comic writers, like Dickens, have a direct political purpose, others, like Chaucer or Rabelais, accept the corruption of society as something inevitable; but no comic writer of any stature has ever suggested that society is *good* ("Funny, But Not Vulgar" 16.484, Orwell's emphasis). These generic amplifications of social resistance—in the anthology of executions, battle poetry, and comic writing—serve to substantialize the negativity, or "isolation," implicit within writing, and at stake in the weekly column's own unstable position between immediacy and reflection.

The entwining of imagination, speculative thinking, and negation in this section of AIP 47 resonates with the dramatic way that AIP 16 opens up onto the politics of language (anticipating one of Orwell's most influential essays):

> With no power to put my decrees into operation, but with as much authority as most of the exile "governments" now sheltering in various parts of the world, I pronounce sentence of death on the following words and expressions: "Achilles heel, jackboot, hydra-headed, ride roughshod over, stab in the back, petty-bourgeois, stinking corpse, liquidate, iron heel, blood-stained oppressor, cynical betrayal, lackey, flunkey, mad dog, jackal, hyena, blood bath." (16, 16.124)

Once again, a tentative form of "authority" is achieved through the writer's lack of power, by his exilic position within—or, more precisely, displacement from—the world. It is no more logical for Orwell to "pronounce sentence of death" on anyone (as this confuses the agency of a writer and a politically powerful person) than it is to sentence "words and phrases," rather than persons, to death. The sentences that writing pronounces work only indirectly, opening up the difference between *other* forms of language and the world they inadequately refract or comprehend. The words that Orwell picks apart here, of course, circle around violence—saturated by it metaphorically ("stab in the back," "stinking corpse," "blood bath") even as they occlude its actual nature (i.e., "liquidate") through their melodramatic and heightened rhetoric ("hydra-headed," "mad dog," "jackal," "hyena," "jackboot," "iron heel," etc.).[21]

Censorship, Writing, and Negation

Orwell's concern with censorship is not merely abstract. His own writing was subjected to many different kinds of pressure, distortion, and expurgation, including, most famously, the multiple rejections of *Animal Farm*[22] and, most pointedly, the exclusion on political grounds of work that he had been twice commissioned to write about Spain for *The New Statesman*.[23] Even posthumously, Orwell's work has been exposed to a range of manipulation and misappropriation.[24] These explicit instances of suppression are part of a larger continuum in which Orwell foregrounds different forms and instances of both censorship and self-censorship, as well as the flawed or problematic comprehension and refraction of writing. Orwell's concrete experiences of censorship are, in this sense, only one of the pivots for his exploration of the generally imperfect "predicament" of writing. There is no absolute version of censorship (since this would necessarily imply a transcendent version of the written), and Orwell's writing also grapples with how difficult it is to draw a precise or sufficient line between external and internal manipulation, or between work that has been literally expurgated and work that has been more subtly transformed. Writing can be banned, erased, forgotten, misrepresented, mistranslated (across language, culture, context), or simply misunderstood.

In this way, Orwell's struggle with censorship manifests itself ultimately in *the variegation of the written field itself*. The "As I Please" columns are a particularly salient example of this. In these columns, as much as any of Orwell's work, form's specificity is connected directly to the precariousness of the written text. Put differently, these columns highlight a sense of imperfection that is so often—both in Orwell's work and more generally—an intrinsic part *of* formal experiment.[25] The center of this conjunction rests in the manifest variety of the columns themselves, as they are committed, paradoxically, to both heterogeneity (difference) and contemporaneity (immediacy, convergence). Around this formal principle Orwell teases and explores the nature of topicality and shuttles back and forth between the "inside" and "outside" of writing. These slips across the "border-line" of writing are connected to other kinds of slips—a wide-ranging emphasis on errors and mistakes that emerge from the "predicament" of textuality. Thus another continuing theme in Orwell's columns is mistakes that have been frozen into print, as in a recurring typo from H. G. Wells's *The Island of Doctor Moreau,* which is carried from edition to edition (72, 19.41–42)[26] or, better yet, this example from his own work, which constitutes a brief, freestanding section in "As I Please" 58:

> A sidelight on the habits of book reviewers.
>
> Some time ago I was commissioned to write an essay for an annual scrapbook which shall be nameless. At the very last minute (and when I had had the money, I am glad to say) the publishers decided that my essay must be suppressed. By this time the book was actually in process of being bound. The essay was cut out of every copy, but for technical reasons it was impossible to remove my name from the list of contributors on the title page.
>
> Since then I have received a number of press cuttings referring to this book. In each case I am mentioned as being "among the contributors," and not one reviewer has yet spotted that the contribution attributed to me is not actually there. (58, 17.43–44)[27]

Orwell's sensibility gravitates toward this revealing example—a synecdoche aimed at grasping a more general (and conceptually elusive) process through a single instance. We can compare it, for instance, to this double image of censorship from *Homage to Catalonia:*

> *La Batalla* was still appearing, but it was censored almost out of existence, and *Solidaridad* and the other Anarchist papers were also

heavily censored. There was a new rule that censored portions of a newspaper must not be left blank but filled up with other matter; as a result it was often impossible to tell when something had been cut out. (197)

In both of these cases, Orwell's attention is caught *not* by the elision or suppression of content but by the (more unusual) suppression, or neglect, of an elision itself. Thus Orwell fixes on the erasure of that blankness that indicates where censorship has already taken place in the Spanish newspaper and, again, on the inability of book reviewers not as they fail to register something present (omitting from their discussion, for example, one of the articles in a collection) but as they "overlook" (by actually noting) something that has been cut out of the book they are reading.[28] We've seen versions of this same elusive opposition in earlier examples from *Down and Out* and "Marrakech": not neglecting a bench where homeless people sleep but failing to "see" the absence of a bench (where people, of course, *can't* sleep) or "missing" the beds that are, themselves, missing from the British spike. What is at stake in this distinction? Is there a qualitative difference between writing that elides an aspect of the object and writing—like the flawed book review in AIP 58 or the doubly censored version of *La Batalla*—that doesn't account for the way something is or has been elided?[29] I think there is a specific answer to this question, and it hinges once again on a persistent self-reflexiveness: to "see" an overlooked absence (rather than a neglected presence) entails confronting how words cover reality as much by what they represent (and thus inscribe as securely comprehended) as by what they explicitly cut out, ignore, or distort. "Noticing" the way that an absence has itself been elided, as Orwell models in these two examples, requires attention to the discourse that excludes as well as the excluded object. In the passage from *Homage to Catalonia,* erasing an erasure is clearly worse than the simple act of censorship itself. But in one important sense, the words that are rolled in over blankness in the censored Spanish newspaper simply do what language *always* does: to the degree that it convinces us of its referential function, all writing "erases"—or makes us unaware of—its erasure of, or difference from, the reality that is refracted or expressed. And again, thought is in many ways the same process as writing for Orwell: thinking also both allows us to comprehend the world and always risks not simply "erasing" aspects of the world but erasing our awareness (or mindfulness) of this erasure, of the difference between the form and the substance of a thought.

The relation between mimesis and shock in Orwell's prose (a relationship carried into the center of the "plain style" itself) is attentively focused on this process, aiming, above all, to generate representations that are not self-sufficient or complete, and to discover ways of situating the reader both inside and outside of the representation. (Thus Orwell reacts with "a shock of surprise" when he realizes that he hadn't noticed—or, more precisely, had not *not* seen—the beds that are missing from the room in *Down and Out*.) The examples from *Homage to Catalonia* and AIP 58 concern not a social encounter but the encounter with other texts, whether a doubly censored Spanish newspaper or a written review, which misconstrues the edited book collection that Orwell's piece is "cut out of." We've seen the way that AIP so often constitutes itself reflexively, as writing about other writing, and even writing about texts that refract still another text (as in this case of Orwell's "sidelight" on book reviews). Two antithetical modes structure the textual encounter in AIP—on one hand, catching hold of writing that has been forgotten or is in danger of being disposed of and, on the other hand, puncturing or destabilizing writing that has been extended too long or absorbed without friction.[30] In these two tendencies (to foreground vulnerable writing and to short-circuit or disrupt entrenched language), we can find the same dialectic between fragility and crystallization that is so prevalent in "As I Please."

In discussing the class biases that still inform the British jury system, Orwell begins AIP 62 by describing how he had thrown away a piece of paper that then proves useful:

> The query I raised two weeks ago, about the methods used in selecting jurymen, is answered authoritatively by a contributor in this week's issue. It also brought in a considerable stream of letters, nearly all of them enclosing a copy of a recently issued Government form which has to be filled in by anyone claiming exemption from jury service. I had received a copy of this myself through the usual channels, and had immediately flung it into the wastepaper basket, but actually it contains most of the information that I wanted. (62, 18.497)

This action valorizes holding on to a disposable piece of writing and equates this act with recoil from an "immedia[cy]," which is literalized here but that, more generally, is intertwined with both Orwell's plain style and the poetics of "As I Please." For Orwell, the act of catching what we might take as disposable can always imply a potential recoil: the viewer, reader, or witness doesn't merely recover the lost, or too-quickly disposed, object (here, the "Government form" that Orwell has "flung . . . into the wastepaper basket") but also confronts his or her own inability to *have* seen this object. Representation, for Orwell, almost always hinges on some degree of surprise. Seeing, at the very least, requires a care that, in its patience and circumspection, seems to work against the other thing that is required to see (in the "plain style"): immediacy, immersion, engagement.

Certainly Orwell's description means, in this case, to devalue the hollow bureaucratese of the government form even as it produces an uncanny effect by revisiting something that he had "flung" into the "wastepaper basket." Such a verb ("flung") can *only* be "immediate," and the subtle redundancy of the adverb here works to intensify this effect, bringing out terms that are resonant with the logic of the columns as a whole.[31] The paradoxical extension of this rushed or "immediate" disposal (both as it is emphasized, in the discourse, and revisited, in the story) prefigures *1984,* a novel that often hinges on distending the brief moment of time in which disposable texts are "flung" into oblivion: the "love letter" that Julia writes to Winston; Winston's own diary; and, most notably, the photograph of Aaronson, Rutherford, and Hayes that, saved for only "thirty seconds" from the memory hole, then continues to haunt Winston's consciousness:

Just once in his life he had possessed—after the event: that was what counted—concrete, unmistakable evidence of an act of falsification. He had held it between his fingers for as long as thirty seconds. In 1973, it must have been—at any rate, it was at about the time when he and Katharine had parted. But the really relevant date was seven or eight years earlier. . . . He had gone straight on working. As soon as he saw what the photograph was, and what it meant, he had covered it up with another sheet of paper. Luckily, when he unrolled it, it had been upside-down from the point of view of the telescreen. He took his scribbling pad on his knee and pushed back his chair so as to get as far away from the telescreen as possible. To keep your face expressionless was not difficult, and even your breathing could be controlled, with an effort: but you could not control the beating of your heart, and the telescreen was quite delicate enough to pick it up. He let what he judged to be ten minutes go by, tormented all the while by the fear that some accident—a sudden draught blowing across his desk, for instance—would betray him. Then, without uncovering it again, he dropped the photograph into the memory hole, along with some other waste papers. Within another minute, perhaps, it would have crumbled into ashes. That was ten–eleven years ago. (75, 78–79)

There is something odd about this particular icon for Smith. He doesn't actually *save* the photograph (which itself is a text meant to record or save a fact of the historical record) but merely holds it "for thirty seconds," and then delays its expected fate (being flung into oblivion) for "ten minutes" longer. After this it is discarded just like all the other representations of past events that are routinely thrown down the memory hole at the Ministry of Truth. Orwell juxtaposes these narrow temporal frames—thirty seconds, ten minutes—against much more extensive ones: "once in his life," "seven or eight years earlier," "ten–eleven years ago."[32] Winston doesn't preserve the photograph or fundamentally alter the process of its erasure. He only lingers slightly longer at the threshold of its destruction. Not coincidentally, the photograph itself doesn't preserve a remembered presence for Winston but rather memorializes a falsification (the erasure *of* these men's disappearance). This unstable combination of preservation and destruction, exposure and erasure, instantaneity and duration, can be related to a tension within the ontological structure of the photograph as such, that charged intersection between image and referent.[33] This is the same threshold of representation that is addressed both formally and topically in Orwell's columns.[34] "As I Please" brings attention to and seeks to intensify the effect of this threshold, highlighting the way that writing both draws on *and* potentially extinguishes its referential ground. It is a tension beautifully literalized, at the end of an AIP section on postwar fuel shortages, in a brief image of (quotidian) writing that feeds on the vanishing world: "During the last two weeks, most of the people known to me have used anything, not despising the furniture as a last resort. I kept going for a day myself on a blitzed bedstead, and wrote an article by its graceful warmth" (77, 19.76). Earlier passages in Orwell's wartime writing have dwelt on the destruction of paper and the use of books or texts as kindling (from the "optimistic headlines" that "go up in smoke" as Orwell uses old papers to heat his house ["Wartime Diary" 12.277] to the destruction of the libraries of Alexandria to provide eighteen days' worth of fuel for the public baths [AIP 32, 16.275]). This image, which correlates the act of writing a single article with the slow burn of a single piece of furniture, inverts this process: not depicting books as a source of fuel in the world but the world itself as contingent fuel for writing.

We might compare this with the waxworks of German atrocities—"grubby, unlifelike and depressing" (AIP 54, 17.18) that Orwell discusses in "As I Please" and then returns to in *1984*. For Orwell, these waxwork atrocities combine the problematic representation of violence with a form that, by calcifying itself, does violence to the transient matter on which it is based (the melted wax):

> "Where was St Martin's?" said Winston.
>
> "St Martin's? That's still standing. It's in Victory Square, alongside the picture gallery. A building with a kind of a triangular porch and pillars in front, and a big flight of steps."
>
> Winston knew the place well. It was a museum used for propaganda displays of various kinds—scale models of rocket bombs and Floating Fortresses, waxwork tableaux illustrating enemy atrocities, and the like.
>
> "St Martin's-in-the-Fields it used to be called," supplemented the old man, 'though I don't recollect any fields anywhere in those parts." (98–99)

These waxworks provoke Orwell as they embody different perils within the representation of historical trauma: that they narrow and harden our response, provide only limited comprehension of the event, and, worst of all, allow revenge fantasies to take place *within* the act of sympathetic representation. "Now, however, you can wallow in the most disgusting descriptions of torture and massacre, not only without any sensation of guilt, but with the feeling that you are performing a praiseworthy political action" (AIP 54, 17.18).

The piece of paper "flung immediately" into oblivion and these calcified waxwork representations mark two limit points of textuality in AIP—too transient and disposable, or too monumental. Orwell's representations of writing in AIP are best understood as *encounters* because he so often draws on the complicated temporalities that are intertwined and juxtaposed when one act of writing frames another. Several columns—extending the self-referential intricacy of the columns as a whole—dramatize an encounter with framed writing itself. Thus Orwell comments, for example:

> If you ever have to walk from Fleet Street to the Embankment, it is worth going into the office of the *Observer* and having a look at something that is preserved in the waiting-room. It is a framed page from the *Observer* (which is one of our oldest newspapers) for a certain day in June, 1815. In appearance it is very like a modern newspaper, though slightly worse printed, and with only five columns on the page. The largest letters used are not much more than a quarter of an inch high. (55, 17.23)

A "preserved" and "framed" daily newspaper: the image offers a simple, almost vulgar figure for the uncanny meld of disposability and duration, immediacy and reflection, in AIP. What we "see" in this now-frozen, framed transience is, again, something that has been *hidden,* as the defeat at Waterloo is only displayed "[h]alfway down the last column" of the page. ("SANGUINARY BATTLE IN FLANDERS. COMPLETE DEFEAT OF THE CORSICAN USURPER," reads the headline). This discrepancy turns out to be the only reason this newspaper, from "a certain day in June, 1815," hangs on the wall, and, of course, it is such discrepancy—provoked by this ironic monumentalizing of erroneous, quotidian language—that catches Orwell's attention.[35]

Reading and Measuring

Orwell picks up "As I Please" in November 1946, without any explicit acknowledgment of the twenty-one months that have elapsed since he last wrote the column. But the first section—a semi-sociological discussion of an unnamed "American fashion magazine"—does inscribe the passage of time:

> I do not know just how many drawings or photographs of women occur throughout the whole volume, but as there are 45 of them, all beautiful, in the first 50 pages, one can work it out roughly. (60, 18.471)

As in other passages that we've seen in Orwell, this sentence doesn't so much synthesize as dramatize the act of synthesis itself. It subtly highlights the experience of abstraction, pushing the reader to imagine Orwell's own previous counting *of* the magazine's images, rather than simply presenting the abstracted ratio of images to pages. The challenge of counting images is somewhat like the challenge of noticing handwriting. It's the active relationship to material culture—the process of thinking in these terms—that constitutes the interest of the section, more than the specific consequence of the figure that Orwell counts. This after-image of thought revolves around the repulsion of identification; the reader falls into thinking only by pulling away from a direct, sensual absorption into the (uniformly "beautiful") images. With this methodologically charged anecdote, Orwell reenters the project of "As I Please," across an unacknowledged gap in time. He begins, in other words, with a reading situated at a threshold—a representation *of* reading as it is torn between (analysis of the) image and (absorption into the) referent. The next paragraph elaborates this doubleness in terms of language itself, as Orwell notes that "[a]nother striking thing is the prose style of the advertisements, an extraordinary mixture of sheer lushness with clipped and sometimes very expressive technical jargon" (18.471). He goes on to offer a catalogue of such phrases, and, once again, we can note the charged excess in this demonstration: "Words like suave-mannered, custom-finished, contour-conforming, mitt-back, innersole, backdip, midriff, swoosh, swash, curvaceous, slenderize and pet-smooth are flung about with evident full expectation that the reader will understand them at a glance" (18.471). There's a clear pleasure in this list, so that, as in the image of thinking that precedes it, the reading is poised between being "inside" and "outside" of the phrases it comprehends. (In both cases, Orwell then lapses into a more colloquial tone—"one can work it out roughly," "flung about"—which functions, I would argue, as a way to stabilize or end this dynamic play.)

Orwell's choice of topic seems playful, obviously dismissive of the object of analysis and, in a certain sense, dismissive of its own importance. (More playful still, as Gordon Bowker points out, is the private joke that this copy of *Vogue* offered a photographic feature on Orwell himself.) But however blithe or dismissive, the column also works (in typically Orwellian fashion) in *excess* of this casualness, by placing the reading subject in an unstable, unsettled position, between connection and detachment. Analysis relies, problematically, on both of these states, lending it an unfixed quality. In particular, such unsettledness marks the vexed position of reading, or critiquing, popular culture—an explicit interest of Orwell's since at least the essay "Boys' Weeklies." "Boys' Weeklies," as we've seen, was situated in (unstable) relation to two other, quite different essays and often, in "thinking about" popular culture, Orwell stages a larger challenge to the integrity or coherence of thinking itself.[36]

The discussion of the fashion magazine inhabits the same threshold between "inside" and "outside" as the section on handwriting, though here the reader is trying to arrive at abstraction, rather than particularity. In both cases, Orwell elicits the tension between how writing must engage with and break from its referential ground. We could relate this as well to the dialectic between measurement and visualization that arises in another section of "As I Please," when Orwell discusses the metric system:

> But there is a strong case for keeping on the old measurements for use in everyday life. One reason is that the metric system does not possess, or has not succeeded in establishing, a large number of units that can be visualized. There is, for instance, effectively no unit between the metre, which is more than a yard, and the centimetre, which is less than half an inch. In English you can describe someone as being five feet three inches high, or five feet nine inches, or six feet one inch, and your hearer will know fairly accurately what you mean. But I have never heard a Frenchman say, "He is a hundred and forty-two centimetres high"; it would not convey any visual image. So also with the various other measurements. (77, 19.75)

This image of "measurement" draws a dynamic balance between (agential) mind and (calculated) world—eschewing the utopian goal of direct correspondence in favor of a structured, intermediate space in which writing, thinking, measurement, or what we could understand here as figuration can take place. Orwell is not advocating a system of measurement that merely resists abstraction—here conceived simultaneously as more detached *and* more directly connected (as a calculation) to reality—but one in which such "pulling back" would still allow a process of visualization. It is a system of measurement, then, that would remain partially outside of, and partially affiliated with, the object it seeks to measure. Frequently in Orwell we find this partial independence of mind—not simply the taking of unorthodox or independent positions but a more specific highlighting of the act of thought, in unstable play with the world it measures, comprehends, and acts within.

Reflection and Form—Book Reviewing: AIP 47

In AIP 47, Orwell shifts from the imagined "anthology of executions" that we considered above to a discussion about the structure of the book review section in *Tribune*. It's a striking jump. What is the best method of reviewing books in a weekly journal? And, in particular, how can *Tribune* satisfy the desire for adequate discussion of specific texts without excluding a large number of books that appear from week to week? "The present policy of trying to give every book a review of about a column is felt to be unsatisfactory" (16.452). Reviews can neither be too extended (since, given "the small space at [*Tribune*'s] disposal" [16.452], this would squeeze out consideration of other books) nor too brief (since this, while allowing a larger number of topics, would make each discussion too insubstantial). Such an "unsatisfactory" situation is another double bind that Orwell foregrounds—and also, in this strain between "short" (16.452) and "long" (16.452), a dilemma that mirrors the structuring tension of reflective thought in AIP. Book reviewing is, in fact, a very distilled form of reflection—perhaps that one genre of writing, in a weekly newspaper such as *Tribune*, explicitly intended as writing about writing.

As in *Enemies of Promise* (which also has much to say about the paradoxes of book reviewing), we need to note not merely the answer that Orwell formulates in response to this particular "predicament" but also how his discussion foregrounds the underlying nature of the predicament itself.[37] "The best solution seems to be to make some reviews shorter and others longer" (16.452). Surely, on one level, this is a reasonable, even bland, policy. But

Orwell's impulse to repeatedly *describe* this imperfect solution in AIP 47 (as well as in "Books and the People" two months later) stems finally from the imbalance (and not the reason or common sense) that it conveys, as another site emerges in AIP that intertwines compression, expansion, reflexivity, and form. The dynamic imbrication of short and long gets articulated in several more ways in the column: "for the rest we intend to have about nine very short notices . . . and one very long one, probably of about 1,500 words" (16.452); "[t]his will allow us to cover rather more books than at present . . . but it will have the added advantage that serious books can be seriously treated" (16.452); "[i]n every week there is at least *one* book that deserves a full-length review, even if its importance is only indirect" (16.452); "a book review is seldom of much value *as a piece of writing* if it is under 1,000 words" (16.453); "[o]ur aim is to produce leading reviews which thoroughly criticise the chosen book and at the same time are worth-while articles in themselves" (16.453). As Orwell's distinction between making "some reviews shorter" and "others longer" unfolds, the terms of the division unmistakably change: the longer reviews become valued not merely for more detailed substance but, first, as *"piece[s] of writing"* (a phrase that he italicizes for emphasis) and then (in quasi-Hegelian language) as "articles in themselves."

In this shift, "As I Please" once again crosses the threshold of reflexivity, foregrounding that moment in which writing moves from content into form or loses its motivation *vis-à-vis* the represented object (the starting point in "As I Please") to take shape in terms of its own unfolding. Part of the fascination of AIP rests in how the reflective tendency emerges in such surprising ways, at unexpected points. Orwell's interest in language, writing, and form as it is poised on the brink of reflection is obviously connected to the larger dynamics and ambition of "As I Please" as a *représentation du présent*.[38] The very instinct to discuss—or externalize—the internal policy of *Tribune*'s reviewing format is a part of this process as well. By showing the "seams" of the left-wing journal itself, this section broaches reflexivity in another way, echoing the contrast between "short" and "long". Blunt and pragmatic on the one hand and resonantly self-conscious on the other, the section is both a contained, instrumental discussion of *Tribune*'s considered policy and a thought-provoking, third-order reflection on how to reflect on textual reflections.[39]

Textual Encounters: AIP 69

"As I Please" presents a writing-saturated world, moving quickly, for instance, from "the disappearance of the facetious epitaph, once a common feature of country churchyards" (73, 19.45) to "a child's illustrated alphabet, published this year" (75, 19.50) two weeks later. The casual juxtaposition of the last words that describe a person and the first words a child might read suggests the ambition of AIP's linguistic concerns. From within its own quotidian fragmentation, AIP imagines the fantasmatic moment in which a person enters into the system of written language and the writing most directly intended to limn the end of an individual life. Both kinds of textuality—alphabet primer and epitaph—exist at the perimeter of the writing subject's grasp. They emblematize, once more, writing's effort (necessarily incomplete) to comprehend its own outside, like a snake that tries to eat its own tail.

The alphabet primer echoes a number of Orwell texts that look back to the experiences of reading and writing that form the necessary prehistory *of* the work itself. ("Boys' Weeklies" and "Such, Such Were the Joys" are perhaps the two most prominent examples.) Here, Orwell's written column briefly imagines the text through which the childhood subject enters into relationship with the written word, much like the moment in "Nausicaa" where Joyce imagines the inscription of an infant (somewhat messily) into spoken language:

And then she told him to say papa.

—Say papa, baby. Say pa pa pa pa pa pa pa.

And baby did his level best to say it for he was very intelligent for eleven months everyone said and big for his age and the picture of health, a perfect little bunch of love, and he would certainly turn out to be something great, they said.

—Haja ja ja haja.

Cissy wiped his little mouth with the dribbling bib and wanted him to sit up properly, and say pa pa pa but when she undid the strap she cried out, holy saint Denis, that he was possing wet and to double the half blanket the other way under him. Of course his infant majesty was most obstreperous at such toilet formalities and let everyone know it:

—Habaa baaaahabaaa baaaa. (*Ulysses* 292–293)

"Nausicaa" offers the most significant refraction of an imperfect, inscribed discourse within *Ulysses* (in the sentimentalized voice of Gerty McDowell). This scene within "Nausicaa" dramatizes—and generalizes—the charged entrance of the individual into a (quite-literal) patriarchal language. Orwell's brief interlude on alphabet primers also offers a problematic, historically laden version of this imaginary point of origin:

> Recently I was looking through a child's illustrated alphabet, published this year. It is what is called a "travel alphabet." Here are the rhymes accompanying three of the letters, J, N and U:
>
> J for the Junk which the Chinaman finds
> Is useful for carrying goods of all kinds.
>
> N for the Native from Africa's land.
> He looks very fierce with his spear in his hand.
>
> U for the Union Jacks Pam and John Carry
> While out on a hike with their nice Uncle Harry.
>
> The "native" in the picture is a Zulu dressed only in some bracelets and a fragment of leopard skin. As for the Junk, the detail of the picture is very small, but the "Chinamen" portrayed in it appear to be wearing pigtails. . . . (19.50)

Orwell alights on this moment ("recently I was looking through"), rests inside and outside of it, reads the way that people not only learn to read but are scripted into language: "The sad thing about this alphabet-book is that the writer obviously has no intention of insulting the 'lower' races. He is merely not quite aware that they are human beings like ourselves. A 'native' is a comic black man with very few clothes on; a 'Chinaman' wears a pigtail and travels in a junk—which is about as true as saying that an Englishman wears a top hat and travels in a hansom cab. This unconsciously patronisng attitude is learned in childhood and then, as here, passed on to a new generation of children" (19.51).[40]

Orwell's discussion of comic epitaphs also historicizes this genre—as a form of memorializing the deceased that is itself, somewhat troublingly,

"disappear[ing]." And what interests Orwell in this vanishing form of com-
memoration ("I should be astonished to see a comic epitaph dated later than
1850" [19.45]) is the way that it also works to puncture language. The example
Orwell highlights is thus one that creates its effect only through the disjunc-
ture between two textual levels (much like Orwell's own strategy of inflecting
different textual encounters within "As I Please"). "There is one in Kew, if I
remember rightly, which might be about that date. About half the tombstone
is covered with a long panegyric on his dead wife by a bereaved husband:
at the bottom of the stone is a later inscription which reads, 'Now he's gone,
too'" (19.45).

What relation can we see (aside from their temporal extremity) between
these adjacent treatments of the child's first inscription into written language and a fading genre of last words? In both cases, the column works to
render these moments incomplete, or insufficient unto themselves: larding
the entry into language with symbolic freight that necessarily exceeds the
comprehension of the child and offering another example of second-order
language, as the long-winded effort of the bereaved husband to comprehend
his wife's death is punctured by a belated, and lightning-quick, statement
that radicalizes the position *from which* he had written the panegyric that
"covered" half the tombstone. Writing's ability to grasp its outside is limited—uncertain and transient, as this example demonstrates. The comic epitaph, at its best, registers the transience of the remembered person whom it
is trying to represent by means of its own quasi-permanent language. This
example (the "long panegyric"/and the brief, cutting epigram:"now he's
gone too'") distills and disaggregates such a movement into two temporally
separated parts, a montage effect. Orwell's text often plays off imperfect
forms of discourse, as in the three-part column written a few weeks earlier,
that begins with a mislabeled photograph from the *Daily Herald:*

The *Daily Herald* for January 1, 1947, has a headline MEN WHO
SPOKE FOR HITLER HERE, and underneath this a photograph of two
Indians who are declared to be Brijlal Mukerjee and Anjit Singh, and
are described as having come "from Berlin." The news column below
the photograph goes on to say that "four Indians who might have been
shot as traitors" are staying at a London hotel, and further describes the
group of Indians who broadcast over the German radio during the war

as "collaborators." It is worth looking a bit more closely at these various statements. (69, 19.18)

Orwell's commentary about this textual moment runs in two directions: he wants to distill what is specifically inaccurate—and thus surprising—about the *Daily Herald* passage and to consider the general ideological background that would allow these particular mistakes to occur. In Orwell's view, there are several interlocked registers of error at play here. Most broadly, he goes on to argue, it is misleading to call Indian nationalists who supported Germany "collaborators." More particularly, one of the two men identified— Anjit Singh—did *not* actually broadcast in Berlin. And, most notably, the caption has misidentified the second man altogether:

> It is worth looking a bit more closely at these various statements. To begin with, there are at least two errors of fact, one of them a very serious one. Anjit Singh did not broadcast on the Nazi radio, but only from Italian stations, while the man described as "Brijlal Mukerjee" is an Indian who has been in England throughout the war and is well known to myself and many other people in London. But these inaccuracies are really the symptom of an attitude of mind which comes out more clearly in the phraseology of the report.
>
> What right have we to describe the Indians who broadcast on the German radio as "collaborators"? They were citizens of an occupied country, hitting back at the occupying power in the way that seemed to them best. I am not suggesting that the way they chose was the right one. Even from the narrow point of view which would assume that Indian independence is the only cause that matters, I think they were gravely wrong. . . . (19.18)

Orwell continues in this vein—putting more pressure on the term "collaborator" (in general), before returning to the "slovenly handling of the photographs":

> The caption "Brijlal Mukerjee" appears under the face of a totally different person. No doubt the photograph was taken at the reception

which the repatriated Indians were given by their fellow-countrymen in London, and the photographer snapped the wrong man by mistake. But suppose the person in question had been William Joyce. In that case, don't you think the *Daily Herald* would have taken good care that it *was* photographing William Joyce and not somebody else. But since it's only an Indian, a mistake of this kind doesn't matter—so runs the unspoken thought. And this happens not in the *Daily Graphic,* but in Britain's sole Labour newspaper. (19.19)

This section exemplifies Orwell's commitment to pragmatic and specific acts of "noticing." This is not merely commentary but the dramatization of a precise, time-bound empirical response that "begin[s]," as Orwell says, only through specific "facts."[41] When Orwell spends a beat writing, in the simplest language—"it is worth looking a bit more closely at these statements"—he is opening up a tiny window of time, *within* immediacy, in order to hold on to or reflectively consider something that otherwise would go unnoticed. The phrase "*a bit* more closely" is thus important here, not merely as a rhetorical or falsely modest gesture but as it underlines (like the thirty seconds in which Winston Smith holds onto the photograph) the precarious temporality of reflection. And, again, what Orwell has "noticed" here is *not* a positive fact but a negative one—the omission that is promulgated through or within another (likewise quotidian) text. Orwell highlights and analyzes the mistaken caption, connecting it both to other errors that are not as palpable but arguably more consequential (the misuse of "collaborator") and then, on returning to the specific mistake, framing it, on its own terms, within a larger, troubling context, as a product of the "unspoken thought" that Orwell unearths, and with which he ends this section. Or almost ends it. The final beat of the section elaborates his insight (first the way he has noticed this mistake at all and then the unspoken thought he has been able to unearth *by* noticing it), bringing the errors that the section has tracked (in its encounter with this passage from the *Daily Herald*) closer to the left-wing perspective that is the shared position of Orwell and his *Tribune* readers. The act of "noticing" in this way once more culminates in a partial—and necessarily short-lived and incomplete—seeing of oneself (as an agent who has both seen *and* not seen something that had been unnoticed).

Orwell gestures toward this process more explicitly in the third and final section of the column, which breaks one of the fundamental conventions of "As I Please" by referring to an earlier section:

> Looking through what I have written above, I notice that I have used the phrase "a totally different person." For the first time it occurs to me what a stupid expression this is. As though there could be such a thing as a partially different person! I shall try to cut this phrase (and also "a very different person" and "a different person altogether") out of my vocabulary for now onwards. (19.20)

We see here how quickly a reflective process can assert and expand itself within engaged thinking. Orwell first decides, from within his alert attention to the day's news, that *this* article in the *Daily Herald* was "worth looking [at] a bit more closely." (If he might have reflected slightly longer upon this article because of the weekly pressure to produce topics or content for "As I Please," we could conversely argue that "As I Please" is nothing other than a model for—or a formal enactment of—the kind of reflexive thinking that is the necessary activity of any engaged writer, intellectual, or person.) The first section of "As I Please" only emerges by "looking a bit more closely" at this newspaper article, but then the third section of the column is constituted only by "looking through what I had written above" (or reflecting upon this previous reflection *on* the newspaper that was "worth looking [at] a bit more closely").

The phrase that Orwell uses and then regrets issues from his passion about the "topic" at hand—it is part of an effort to register shock and outrage over the mistake that he has noticed in the *Daily Herald*. In other words, it's a *politically* motivated phrasing, flowing out of Orwell's own subjective sense of urgency and indignation. The newspaper's mistake is only so consequential to Orwell because of the way that it brings to a point that larger issue—"the unspoken thought," which we could equate with the "unconsciously patronizing attitude [that] is learned in childhood and then, as here, passed on to a new generation of children." These two uses of the "unconscious" each concern racial misprision that is carried on through language— language that serves to both *efface* the excluded other (the misrepresented "Chinaman" and "native" in the reading primer; the Indian dissidents who are flattened out and rendered identical in the *Daily Herald*) and, in doing so, to conceal part of the reading agent's own consciousness from him- or herself (to exclude the act *of* exclusion, in other words, from the reader's or writer's awareness). What's most terrifying, as we know from the canonical achievements of Orwell's late work, is not the brutal act of exclusion but the exclusion or hiding of these acts themselves. The form that Orwell develops and explores in "As I Please" is a response to this epistemologically challenging conception of politics (and the political "unconscious")—in its stops and starts; its cunning and frustrating intertwining of immediacy and reflection; and thus in the dynamics of variety itself (a variety that is a constitutive element of liberty). Returning to our first example, we need to see the critique of the alphabet primer in AIP 75 not merely as an attack on this particular, reactionary text but as another telling dramatization of the "outside" of language (here the ideology that is necessarily outside of the reading capacity instantiated by the alphabet primer). Writing that fails to grasp its "outside" will necessarily be unable to see *what* its representations exclude—thus not merely, like any written representation, engaging in some kind of exclusion but also systematically excluding—from its own awareness or consciousness—this act of exclusion itself.

In between the first and third sections of "As I Please" 69 (between the misidentified photograph in the *Daily Herald* and the critique of his own indignant phrase "a totally different person"), Orwell begins the middle section: "I hope everyone who can get access to a copy will take at least a glance at Victor Gollancz's recently published book, *In Darkest Germany*" (19.19). Gollancz's book is itself a montage of different forms, and it is this formal variety that Orwell focuses on. He notes that "[h]alf of Victor Gollancz's book consists of photographs," before praising, as "the best device in the book, after innumerable descriptions of people living on 'biscuit soup,' potatoes and cabbage, skim milk and ersatz coffee," the decision to "include some menus of dinners in the messes provided for the Control Commission" (19.19–20). Orwell's brief description of Gollancz's montage is interesting, as the passage continues: "Mr. Gollancz says that he slipped a menu card into his pocket whenever he could do so unobserved, and he prints half a dozen of them." This temporality might remind us of the moment in "Marrakech" when Orwell "happened to be walking behind" the firewood bearers and, through the "curious up-and-down motion of a load of wood," a "kind of

accident," came to "notice" an experience otherwise hidden from view
(11.419–420). In other words, we need to see the relationship between the
furtive, temporally contingent act of "slipp[ing]" those menu cards away and
the simple, transparent reproduction of the menus in Gollancz's text. The
menus—reproduced *directly and completely* within Gollancz's text—might
serve as a "pane of glass" onto the conditions of hunger in Germany, but first
they had to be quickly snatched away, whenever Gollancz could do so "unobserved." Like Orwell's own brief pause to reflect on the *Daily Herald* or to
look back over what he has written, Gollancz's action is a temporally contingent one, a reflection that is plucked out of the immersion in events. (Thus
Orwell highlights, conversely, the way that Gollancz "has taken the wise pre-
caution of including himself in a good many of" [19.19] the photographs in
his text, a signal of such immersion.) In this way, Orwell's brief comment
(lodged within the complicated three-part structure of "As I Please" 69) provides a figure for political representation as such—achieved through a kind
of furtive theft, an ability to reflectively grasp the salient detail, to "slip
away" from within the situation in which you have immersed yourself
enough to gain critical purchase, to formulate language both "inside" and
"outside" of the represented event. Orwell goes on to extract one of these
menus and then to juxtapose it, without comment, "with a paragraph, headed
'This Week's Hint for Dog-lovers,' which I cut out of the *Evening Standard*
just before Christmas" (19.20) that describes how to care for a dog after he's
been overfed on the holidays. We have Orwell's AIP text here, Gollancz's
book, the menus Gollancz excerpted in this book, the photographs he
included, and this verbatim passage clipped by Orwell from the *Evening
Standard*. Before the juxtaposition, furthermore, Orwell makes one of his
most programmatic statements about social representation (a comment that
Alex Zwerdling rightly emphasizes in his study *Orwell and the Left*):

> It is not a literary book, but a piece of brilliant journalism intended to
> shock the public of this country into some kind of consciousness of the
> hunger, disease, chaos and lunatic mismanagement prevailing in the
> British zone. This business of making people *conscious* of what is hap-
> pening outside their own small circle is one of the major problems of
> our time, and a new literary technique will have to be evolved to meet
> it. . . . Tales of starvation, ruined cities, concentration camps, mass

deportations, homeless refugees, persecuted Jews—all this is received with a sort of incurious surprise, as though such things had never been heard of before but at the same time were not particularly interesting. The now-familiar photographs of skeleton-like children make very little impression. As time goes on and the horrors pile up, the mind seems to secrete a sort of self-protecting ignorance which needs a harder and harder shock to pierce it, just as the body will become immunized to a drug and require bigger and bigger doses. (19.19)

This passage highlights the idea of technique, explicitly connected here to defamiliarization—or the way that technique functions as much by *interrupting* entrenched or automatic means of comprehending or understanding as it does by introducing new, more expansive ways to see or comprehend. Technique relies on shock and surprise against "familiar[ity]" and "incurios[ity]." It's worthwhile to see the continuity between the aspiration voiced here of "making people conscious" and the comments that we've seen, in other sections of "As I Please," about "the unspoken thought" behind the error in captioning and "the unconsciously patronising attitude" that is passed on, as Orwell frames it, in the very entry of the child into reading.

At first glance, the problem that is identified here—seeing outside the range of one's "own small circle"—might seem the very opposite of Orwell's well-known claim, in the 1946 *(Tribune)* essay, that "[t]o see what is in front of one's nose needs a constant struggle" ("In Front of Your Nose" 18.163). But there are two discrete and seemingly opposed meanings to this empirical claim. One, the more commonly understood sense, centers on the necessity for direct, unmediated observation. Here the struggle is with modes of abstraction, frames of interpretation that prevent us from seeing what is right "in front of" us, or what should require no conceptual framework *to* see. At the same time, Orwell suggests something quite different. First of all, the comment implies a near and a far—a system within which we *are* seeing things that are further away from us and, in the act of seeing these things, are overlooking (which is distinct from simply *not seeing*) something much closer. But what is that "nearby" thing that is constantly overlooked, ignored, not noticed or left unseen even in (or especially in) the act *of* seeing something further in the distance, or, to put this differently, further away from the self? What Orwell means here, I would argue, are things that have fallen into the ambit *of* the self, of that seeing and conceptualizing person him- or herself. In other words, that have fallen within one's "own small circle." And what is required in this instance is not further, more refined empirical observation—further instruments that would give us more detailed, precise, or textured accounts of the nearby world—but, on the contrary, a reflective awareness of our act of seeing itself. Only reflection or introspection would allow us to see these things that are, in this sense, right under our noses and, by forcing an awareness of our own means of comprehending—or of the position *from which* we comprehend—will also make it possible to glimpse what has been excluded from our "own small circle" of thinking.[42]

6

First-Person Socialism

Column and Autobiography: AIP 26

In Part Two I've been making an argument for an account of identity that is expressed through "As I Please," as the columns return us—sporadically but insistently—to the precarious position of the *columnist,* poised at the charged intersection of reflection and immediacy. But I want to now consider more explicit instances of autobiographical writing in AIP. At several points Orwell turns the projected, topical focus of AIP back upon himself—his own past actions and experiences. Like those sections in which the thought-provoking column represents the act of thinking, these autobiographical swerves in "As I Please" harden an incipient self-consciousness that is at stake, more continually, on the level of form. By bringing AIP's explicit topical drive into such close proximity with the source or originating perspective of the columns, the autobiographical mode also poses a problem for this writing project. When Orwell's column tells stories about the author himself—and there are several conspicuous examples of this—it stages a collapse of (writing) subject and (represented) object, columnist and topic.

This is perhaps one reason these episodes are rare within the column sequence—and, as we'll see, quite self-critical. This *delay* of the autobiographical register will be important to my ensuing discussion. The first conspicuous autobiographical turn occurs at the end of AIP 26, after Orwell has been writing "As I Please" for six months. This column begins, indeed, by revisiting the initial topic of AIP 1—discord between British and

American troops. Recalling the opening section of the first column, Orwell opens AIP 26 by quoting "a young American soldier, who told me—as quite a number of others have done—that anti-British feeling is completely general in the American army" (16.230). For Orwell, the topic—in both the first column and AIP 26—is a mechanism for puncturing the home-front imaginary, and betrays his skepticism about the abstract unity that is projected onto the Allied forces.[1] In AIP 26, Orwell is not so much interested in probing this question as identifying the topic as a problem for contemplation; in fact, he takes advantage of the structure of "As I Please" to *abandon* the topic at the instant that he has generalized it:

> At the same time my friend told me that anti-British feeling is not violent and there is no very clearly-defined cause of complaint. A good deal of it is probably a rationalisation of the discomfort most people feel at being away from home. But the whole subject of anti-British feeling in the United States badly needs investigation. Like anti-semitism, it is given a whole series of contradictory explanations, and again like anti-semitism, it is probably a psychological substitute for something else. *What* else is the question that needs investigating.
>
> Meanwhile, there is one department of Anglo-American relations that seems to be going well. It was announced some months ago that no less than 20,000 English girls had already married American soldiers and sailors, and the number will have increased since. (26, 16.230)

Having shifted from the relative *dis*unity of the Allied forces to these actual alliances, Orwell briefly discusses, and quotes from, a recent issue of the *Matrimonial Post and Fashionable Marriage Advertiser*, which contains "advertisements from 191 men seeking brides and over 200 women seeking husbands." In all his columns of "As I Please," Orwell only uses the term "meanwhile" as a method of transition *between* topics in this one instance, although he employs the term quite vigorously a number of times within the discussion of a particular topic. (In several cases, the force of the term—always within a particular section—derives from the way it calls attention to an activity that is taking place concurrently with the writing itself.) As we've seen, the general withholding of this sort of transitional modifier in the columns signals a displacement of variety onto the silent register of form or structure itself. Orwell refuses to soften or personalize the breaks between sections. In this example, likewise, the "meanwhile" works to underline the abruptness of the change in register, highlighting how Orwell leaves the topic (or "the question") at hand at the very moment that he articulates it. (This effect is also produced through the typically Orwellian italicization at the end of the paragraph—"*What* else is the question that needs investigating.")

The "something else" that is invoked but *not* examined by the text suggests Orwell's desire to hold onto—and thus actually not resolve or answer—questions that are generated in and through writing. As is often the case in AIP, Orwell is strategic about making shifts in register and *curtailing* perspectives as the column moves, or leaps, from topic to topic. In AIP 26, Orwell first emphasizes the force of a problem that he actually will *not* analyze (that "anti-British feeling"). He then moves on to the scrutiny and inscription of another text—the classified ads in the *Matrimonial Post*. These are the first two resting places in the column. In each case, Orwell obliquely estranges the topic of inquiry from the discourse unfolding within the column itself: first by raising an unresolved question and then by threading his discussion through another text's language. (In the first instance, Orwell's own writing is not commensurate with the topic he introduces—since he leaves the questions he poses unanswered—and, in the second instance, his writing stands apart from the language he excerpts.) The shift from topic to topic helps generate this subtle detachment of the writer, or, more exactly, the writ*ing,* from the topics that are being addressed. And this detachment (on the level of form) echoes a thematic tension between unity and disconnection foregrounded across the topics of AIP 26.

The discussion of the ads in the *Matrimonial Post* also gains significance as part of Orwell's interest in the horizons of popular culture. The choice in topic is meant to identify something that would otherwise go "unnoticed." These classified ads are a form of popular discourse that—like boys' adventure magazines or Donald McGill's comic postcards—would usually be overlooked by the language of textual criticism. The ads that now come into view, however, are themselves a form of covering, as Orwell (rather predictably) notices the distortion—and desire—that is inherent in the form: "[t]he thing that is and always has been striking in these advertisements is that nearly all the applicants are remarkably eligible" (16.231). Orwell gives two extravagant examples, one male and one female, as the column briefly cedes its own language to these instances of overly idealized, and thus mimetically hollow, language (but language, as with "As I Please" itself, that we find *in* a newspaper):

> When you consider how fatally easy it is to get married, you would not imagine a 36-year-old bachelor, 'dark hair, fair complexion, slim build, height 6 ft., well educated and of considerate, jolly and intelligent disposition, income £1,000 per annum and capital,' would need to find himself a bride through the columns of a newspaper. (16.231)

The point here is the proliferation of terms. Orwell continues:

> And ditto with "Adventurous young woman, Left-wing opinions, modern outlook" with "fairly full but shapely figure, medium colour curly hair, grey-blue eyes, fair skin, natural colouring, health exceptionally good, interested in music, art, literature, cinema, theatre, fond of walking, cycling, tennis, skating and rowing." Why does such a paragon have to advertise? (16.231)

In their misleading idealizations, the personal advertisements emerge as another markedly imperfect language system within "As I Please"—another object on which his own language reflects and, simultaneously, another mechanism for reflecting on language itself. At this point, Orwell shifts from holding these classified ads up to ridicule (of interest only in terms of their inaccurate, or willfully false, representations) to considering the ads as an emblem of social disconnection:

> What these things really demonstrate is the atrocious loneliness of people living in big towns. People meet for work and then scatter to widely separated homes. Anywhere in inner London it is probably exceptional to know even the names of the people who live next door. (16.231)

From here the column pivots toward its final topic, changing registers again (but fueled by these accumulating instances of textual slippage).

Years ago I lodged for a while in the Portobello road. This is hardly a fashionable quarter, but the landlady had been lady's maid to some woman of title and had a good opinion of herself. One day something went wrong with the front door and my landlady, her husband and myself were all locked out of the house. It was evident that we should have to get in by an upper window, and as there was a jobbing builder next door I suggested borrowing a ladder from him. My landlady looked somewhat uncomfortable.

"I wouldn't like to do that," she said finally. "You see we don't know him. We've been here fourteen years, and we've always taken care not to know the people on either side of us. It *wouldn't do,* not in a neighbourhood like this. If you once begin talking to them they get familiar, you see."

So we had to borrow a ladder from a relative of her husband's, and carry it nearly a mile with great labour and discomfort. (16.231)

This closing sentence, set off as a separate paragraph, is an important one within the writing project of AIP. There has been nothing quite like it in the first 25 columns. It is only this final sentence that stabilizes the section as a more strictly autobiographical exercise than anything the reader has seen heretofore in AIP. Once again, Orwell draws on the circumscription of AIP to catalyze the energy of his prose, as the column deliberately ends by situating the reader at the threshold of this remembered experience. It is a suggestive way for Orwell to introduce a dissonant register of writing into AIP, which here lapses from textual and cultural commentary into experientially grounded recollection, autobiography, and even confession. This shift in register constitutes one of the more noticeable surprises in the columns as a whole. Such a surprise belatedly unifies what we might have *previously* taken as already quite heterogeneous: all the varied topics that had marked the range of AIP until this point. It thus suggests, ironically, the relative lack of freedom always potential within any genre. We realize, in other words, the limits of what we had been reading in the column—and had been taking as superbly varied and diverse.

While the column's autobiographical turn works to suggest the relative *un*freedom of AIP's variety heretofore, Orwell also emphasizes his own constraint within the memory itself. Indeed, like the radicalized opening of

"Shooting an Elephant" ("I was hated by large numbers of people"), Orwell's peculiar example of *mémoire involontaire* is a distinctly negative one. The physical onerousness of the event is folded into a different kind of necessity: Orwell's own remembered complicity with the structure of class stratification. This complicity comes across as almost mechanically inevitable. Orwell's inefficacious words are registered only in indirect discourse, and the final consequence of his participation is foregrounded through a stark and fragmented result clause ("[s]o we had to borrow a ladder . . ."). On the one hand, an assertion of the self's authority is implicit in the way that Orwell's own experience becomes, suddenly, the ground for the free-writing project of "As I Please." But this is shadowed by a critique of the self, socially and epistemologically. The passage is thus marked by contradictory valences: physical and circumspect at the same time, highlighting an experience that seems both quotidian and emblematic. It is also "immodest"—introducing the author himself as the very topic of his writing, and as an agent whose past experiences are now authorized as much as any other cultural text he might encounter—at the same time as it is painfully self-critical. These contradictions—self-aggrandizement and self-critique, expression and reticence, the ephemeral and the memorable—are related to one another. And we can begin to see how a specific politics of experience is facilitated by the larger textual dynamics of AIP. This double motion is echoed, formally, as the end of the column stops short, in the abrupt and clipped last sentence, but also works to draw the reader in. The tersely described action (carrying the ladder "nearly a mile") is an intrinsically distended one. And the reverberating significance of the event is intertwined with both its disruptive generic position in "As I Please" as a whole (as the first such experientially grounded episode) and its compacted position at the end of this particular column. Even minor details contribute to this tension so that, for example, the disturbing *duration* of the implied action is also subtly compressed: consider the difference in effect if Orwell had written "more than a mile" instead of eliciting the falling-off implicit in "nearly a mile."

This reading of AIP 26 rests on the specific effect of this last sentence. It is only here, in the abbreviated depiction of Orwell's (protracted) struggle with the ladder, that the odd autobiographical effect is catalyzed, casting its shadow back over the rest of the episode. From the outside, as the section ends, we glimpse an experience that is, for the participants, both physically taxing (putting the body in uncomfortable, unfamiliar positions) and drawn out. It combines travel and effort. This combination might remind us of the "commute" that is so important, both formally and topically, in *The Road to Wigan Pier*. In both cases, the scene of the commute, conjoining temporal distension and physical intensity, emerges as a crux of representation. Representation is not directly effected through the plain style but relies on a complicated interweaving of reticence and display, concealment and exposure.

Orwell's plain style, more generally, is structured by *im*balance— interweaving emphatic and restrained tendencies, irony and urgency, gaps and excesses, distension and compression. We've seen how "As I Please" allows Orwell to elaborate these tensions and to connect them, more specifically, with the politically and aesthetically charged relationship between reflection and immediacy. AIP 26 offers an important instance of such imbalance, elevating its putatively quotidian material (by reaching back much further in time and pushing the writer's own self confessionally forward) even while ending with almost tight-lipped restraint. The commute, or that implied movement through the London streets with which the column ends, rests at the core of both this formal dynamic of representation and the thematics of autobiography that Orwell here develops. Two other explicitly autobiographical sections in the column sequence reinforce this connection. Put most simply, "As I Please" connects its rare shifts to autobiographical narrative, as the ground of material for the column, with scenes of travel. And we need to understand the unstable context in which the self emerges in these episodes (vulnerable, in flux, between destinations, subject to new experience) in relation to the disruptive modal or generic position of the autobiographical event within the columns as a whole. The columns leave us with a provocative image of selfhood that, like the formal instability of "As I Please" more generally, arises only through the uneasy intersection of immediacy and reflection.

"Just Before": "Notes on the Way"

Orwell configures traveling as both a vulnerable and an epistemologically privileged state of experience. Traveling is related, for Orwell, to a fundamental

condition of selfhood in "As I Please": where the subject leaves an ordered
and sheltered position in the world (like the writer in the tower) to become
immersed within, and disrupted by, the world. As might be clear by now,
that position of "shelter" can be equated with *thinking* itself, while the traveling state marks the penetration of thought by the world—that world that
both informs thought (as the material it draws upon) and surrounds it. It
makes sense that those moments that bring out the "I" within "As I Please"
would compensate for their potential naturalization of selfhood (if only on
the level of genre or form) through the specific (disruptive) experiences and
images that are unleashed. It is as though the very shift toward autobiography (sealing together the columnist's self as both subject *and* object) sparks
a compensatory wave of self-castigation. The surprise ending of AIP 26
anticipates the two other most overt autobiographical shifts in "As I Please"—
each of which opens a column. First, in AIP 42, Orwell describes the train
ride that he takes across France on his way to Spain in December 1936,
beginning: "About the end of 1936, as I was passing through Paris on the
way to Spain, I had to visit somebody at an address I did not know, and I
thought that the quickest way of getting there would probably be to take a
taxi" (16.402). This section of "As I Please" focuses on the transition that
Orwell makes out of England to revolutionary Spain—a transition that is
conspicuously *elided* in the opening of *Homage to Catalonia*:

> I had come to Spain with some notion of writing newspaper articles,
> but I had joined the militia *almost immediately,* because at that time
> and in that atmosphere it seemed the only conceivable thing to do. . . .
> To anyone who had been there since the beginning it probably seemed
> even in December or January that the revolutionary period was ending;
> but when one *came straight from England* the aspect of Barcelona was
> something startling and overwhelming. (*Homage to Catalonia* 4,
> emphases added)

Later, in "As I Please" 68 (January 3, 1947), Orwell reaches back further in
time, to his initial journey out of England to Burma in 1924:

> Nearly a quarter of a century ago I was traveling on a liner to Burma.
> Though not a big ship, it was a comfortable and even a luxurious one,

and when one was not asleep or playing deck games one usually seemed to be eating. (19.5)

From foot (crossing London), to train (crossing Europe), to ship (crossing continents): there's something cumulatively suggestive in these three autobiographical episodes, which function like Russian dolls nested inside one another. Always traveling but never at the same scale. The physical inflection of Orwell's own self within "As I Please" suggests a continuum that extends from the most local act of ambulation (the implied scene of Orwell and his neighbors struggling, step by step, with the ladder) to movement across nations and finally across the "world-system," from England "to Burma." In this sense, the interlinked events of travel in the autobiographical sections echo the internal dynamics of column writing itself, as it sways between specificity and abstraction, between local, circumscribed particularity (writing that refers to "the other night," or takes place "when the house still seems to be rocking from a recent explosion," or highlights that brief interval that "gives you time to think") and larger, more comprehensive scales of analysis.

Before looking at these two examples from "As I Please," I want to consider a concise encapsulation of this relationship between displacement, traveling, autobiography, the plain style, and the column form in an earlier piece of writing: Orwell's 1940 contribution to "Notes on the Way." This weekly column in *Time and Tide,* which featured a continually changing roster of writers, offers an important precedent for "As I Please," as the topics ranged freely; often crossed the lines between literature, culture, and politics; could shift between analysis and first-person narrative; and occasionally featured several different subjects within one column. Orwell's own single contribution has two distinct parts, standing as another text in his body of work with a fundamentally divided structure.[2] The whole column is interesting but my focus will be on a single clause. Orwell opens this free-writing sequence with a sentence that anticipates two of the key compositional strategies in "As I Please": the reflection that is spurred by a recent textual encounter and the long-term, experientially-grounded memory:

When the other day I read Dr Ley's statement that "inferior races, such as Poles and Jews" do not need so much to eat as Germans, I was suddenly reminded of the first sight I saw when I set foot on the soil of Asia—or rather, just before setting foot there. (12.121)

The modification that both interrupts and ends this sentence also locates the time frame of the experience quite precisely: not the "first sight" when Orwell "set foot" in Asia but an occurrence that barely precedes this seeing. The deliberately staged correction ("—or rather, just before setting foot there") is particularly conspicuous at the opening of the text. Taking advantage of the ephemerality that attaches to the weekly column (and which is foregrounded here by the reference to "the other day"), Orwell begins by intentionally preserving, and emphasizing, his compositional "mistake." He sets in stone a confusion that concerns only an instant (and highlights an error that could have been avoided altogether with different phrasing).

This would suggest that the distinction marks more than a minor, temporal difference. In fact, I take this stutter-step as a paradigmatic instance of Orwell's negotiation with the plain style. The plain style functions through directness and immediacy, qualities that are here thematized in Orwell's description of being "suddenly reminded" and provocatively substantialized with the figure of "set[ting] foot on the soil of Asia." The monosyllabic alliteration ("first sight that I saw when I set foot on") further reinforces this suddenness. But Orwell complicates all these registers of the plain style by intertwining them with that conspicuous glitch in expression—the retraction that is deliberately left in the opening sentence. The text *performs* the glitch. This retraction foregrounds the distinction between what Orwell first sees when he "set[s] foot" on Asia and a moment "just before setting foot," as though calling attention to an aspect of experience, always potentially within an act of perception (or "first sight"), that cannot be fully encompassed (or "claimed") by the observing self.[3] Part of *any* encounter might be said to occur "just before" perception—insofar as the encounter is not just observed but entails a disruption to the observing self as it seeks to cognitively organize the world that is apprehended. Rather than seeing this deliberately confused opening sentence, then, as shifting between two events, we can see it as distending the complicated temporality of one event—and, through this, modeling a more general paradigm of subjective apprehension. The ostensibly plain style works *with* its conspicuous complication to reinforce this subtle depiction of consciousness, hinging, once more, on the interplay, and dissonance, between immediacy and reflective awareness. In this sense, the staged "correction" in the first sentence (which is precisely equivalent to the displayed mistake) says something important about Orwell's plain style. And, in the almost imperceptible distinction between seeing an object and what occurs "just before" seeing, it speaks to Orwell's politically charged understanding of epistemology, representation, and perception. The unjust event (on ship) that Orwell goes on to recount in "Notes on the Way" resonates with Orwell's foundational 1930s essays, "A Hanging" and "Shooting an Elephant," as well as the next section I will turn to from "As I Please." But I'm less concerned with the actual episode than with the disjunctive frame that Orwell uses. The conflicting tendencies of Orwell's empirical style are evident here in an exemplary, and philosophically resonant, way.

"Just Time to See": AIP 68

The opening of "Notes on the Way" fuses an extended scale of travel—from England to Burma—with the narrowest form of travel: the threshold across which the observer "sets foot" on a new place, or, even more instantaneously, apprehends the external world through which he or she is moving.[4] "As I Please" 68 returns to the same ship that forms the larger background for this memory and marks another crucial inflection of autobiographically grounded experience into the column's dominant textual mode. If this section's event, as we'll see, echoes the politically fraught episode in "Notes on the Way," "As I Please," as a form of writing, also echoes the basic structure and premises of the *Time and Tide* column. In both cases there is a conjuncture between this kind of disturbing event and this *form* of writing.

> Nearly a quarter of a century ago I was traveling on a liner to Burma. Though not a big ship, it was a comfortable and even a luxurious one, and when one was not asleep or playing deck games one usually seemed to be eating. The meals were of that stupendous kind that steamship companies used to vie with one another in producing, and in between times there were snacks such as apples, ices, biscuits and cups of soup, lest anyone should find himself fainting from hunger. Moreover, the bars opened at ten in the morning, and, since we were at sea, alcohol was relatively cheap.

The ships of this line were mostly manned by Indians, but apart from the officers and the stewards they carried four European quartermasters whose job was to take the wheel. One of these quartermasters, though I suppose he was only aged forty or so, was one of those old sailors on whose back you almost expect to see barnacles growing. He was a short, powerful, rather ape-like man, with enormous forearms covered by a mat of golden hair. A blond moustache which might have belonged to Charlemagne completely hid his mouth. I was only twenty years old and very conscious of my parasitic status as a mere passenger, and I looked up to the quartermasters, especially the fair-haired one, as godlike beings on a par with the officers. It would not have occurred to me to speak to one of them without being spoken to first. (68, 19.5–6)

The reader of Orwell's columns might be slightly disoriented at this point, since the tempo and structure of this opening is so different from the usual manner of "As I Please." The leisurely description is as unfamiliar, to such a reader, as Orwell's "twenty-year old" self—and unbounded by any clear generic constraints. It is only here, in this generically suspended context, that the section hones in on a specific event:

One day, for some reason, I came up from lunch early. The deck was empty except for the fair-haired quartermaster, who was scurrying like a rat along the side of the deck-houses, with something partially concealed between his monstrous hands. I had just time to see what it was before he shot past me and vanished into a doorway. It was a pie dish containing a half-eaten baked custard pudding.

At one glance I took in the situation—indeed, the man's air of guilt made it unmistakable. The pudding was a left-over from one of the passengers' tables. It had been illicitly given to him by a steward, and he was carrying it off to the seamen's quarters to devour it at leisure. Across more than twenty years I can still faintly feel the shock of astonishment that I felt at that moment. It took me some time to see the incident in all its bearings: but do I seem to exaggerate when I say that this sudden revelation of the gap between function and reward—the revelation that a highly-skilled craftsman, who might literally hold all our lives in his hands, was glad to steal scraps of food from our table—taught me more than I could have learned from half a dozen Socialist pamphlets. (19.6)

Occupying the same intermediate zone as the event from "Notes on the Way," this anecdote offers another uncanny temporal conjunction: between a glimpse that occurs in a single instant and a memory that stretches across many years ("nearly a quarter century ago"). Only the form of the columns holds this unsettling difference in place. (Or, to put this differently, in compounding, within this anecdote, the instant of a "glimpse" and the stretch of a "quarter of a century," the column reiterates a doubled temporality that is intertwined with its own aesthetic structure, as both fleeting and reflective.) In this event, I would argue, Orwell expands the distinction that rends the opening phrase in "Notes on the Way," between the intentionally grasped "first sight" and the disruptive experience that occurs "just before." Orwell's interest in this threshold is crucial because of the way that it speaks to the dominant ideology of the "windowpane" as a structure of seeing, an ideology that is linked, famously, to the plain style itself. In ideological terms, the plain style has no room for the shock of observation, for any social encounter that disrupts (and in this way exceeds) the organizing faculties of the observer. But shock is what this passage describes; a "shock of astonishment" that is related—even phonetically—to a "shot," or to the way in which the stevedore "shot past" and "vanished into a doorway." This oddly foregrounded vanishing occurs simultaneously with an act of comprehension ("I had just time to see what it was before he shot past me and vanished into a doorway"), so that the passage compactly and painfully links together (memorable) appearance and (sudden) disappearance.

Importantly, Orwell's comprehension of this event within the story—"I had just time to see what it was"—is already quasi-reflective. The difference between "see[ing] it" and "see[ing] what it was" marks precisely the threshold between perception and reflection that is so central to "As I Please." (As with "Notes on the Way," this intricate state is articulated in the most unassuming, colloquial terms.) This unstable boundary (between perception and reflection) is now associated specifically with the charged threshold of the worker's disappearance, as the focus on that moment in which the quartermaster "shot past" eerily heightens the impression or substantialness of the vanishing itself. In this way Orwell, crucially, overlays two distinct temporal processes: that instant, within cognition, when observation crosses over into reflection (i.e., when we can move from "see[ing]" something, perceptually, to "see[ing] what" something is, conceptually) and that painful instant, within a stratified social encounter, which conjoins the conspicuously visible and the recessed or hidden. By the time Orwell "sees" the furtive act for "what it was," the quartermaster is already gone—as though any act of social comprehension must contain and confront the partial absence of the comprehended object.

The precarious moment of reflection that's at the heart of the formal logic of "As I Please" is here associated, specifically, with the complicated process of "seeing" (or "glanc[ing]") disappearance. But the quartermaster's disappearance—which motivates the painfully *incomplete* act of witnessing at the center of the scene—is also linked to a larger structure of exploitation, or what Orwell belatedly terms "the gap between function and reward."[5] The divided nature of the shock—both impressing the observer more deeply than he can intentionally comprehend and eluding the observer's very conceptual faculties—has meaning that extends beyond this particular encounter. Too early and too late: we can find the same temporal confusion in Orwell's claims that "at one glance I took in the situation" *and* that "it took me some time to see the incident in all its bearings" or, again, in how, even in the writing of the piece itself, he "can still faintly feel the shock of astonishment." What would it mean to "faintly" feel shock?[6]

This is a paradigmatic encounter. Social witnessing hinges on a form of perception that—far from the transparency and directness often associated with the "windowpane"—necessarily involves a displacement, a recognition of a contiguous and vulnerable perspective that cannot be fully seen (or replaced *by* the perceiving subject him- or herself) but, rather, "vanishes" even as he "see[s] what it was." The anecdote in "As I Please" marks out such belatedness quite explicitly. Orwell stumbles upon this experience only because—in a choice that is given no privileged cause—he breaks from the rigid social constraints of the ship, through the mere act of being somewhere slightly before he is supposed to: "One day, for some reason, I came up from lunch early. The deck was empty." These simple sentences now take on more significance. Such "mistakes"—both as real, socially grounded actions (arriving too early, tarrying too late) and also when they are understood as equivalent forms of *cognition* (seeing something from a suddenly alternative perspective, staying with a thought longer than one should)—are generative of—and, for Orwell, perhaps intrinsic to—social change. At some point, solidarity (like representation) requires this kind of "tardiness," or "precipitousness." Orwell's work ultimately insists on a relationship between this form of action within the story—coming up early enough (or, from a different perspective, *late* enough) to see the quartermaster stealing the leftover food—and that peculiar combination of delay and haste intrinsic to column writing itself.[7]

The episode, in fact, offers multiple versions of this temporal displacement, radiating out of its own elaboration within the structure of "As I Please." Orwell can replay the situation twenty-five years later, still "faintly feel[ing]" the original "shock of astonishment" and while still on board the ship, needs "some time" to "see the incident in all its bearings," even as the incident is constituted by its suddenness. But this belatedness—in one sense, as we've seen, nothing other than the time intrinsic to reflection as such—is, even earlier, a component part of the event itself. The single "glance" (in which Orwell "see[s] what it was" that he is looking at while the quartermaster "sho[o]t[s] past") strangely comprehends a retrospective chain of reasoning. Part of what Orwell "sees," in this instant, is that "the pudding *was* a left-over from one of the passenger's tables. It *had been* illicitly given to him by a steward" (emphases added). The folding of past and pluperfect into the instant of observation (the "sudden revelation") is linked, finally, to another curious temporal discontinuity hidden within the folds of this experience, when Orwell imagines the quartermaster "carrying [the pudding] off to his quarter to devour at his leisure." Does the quartermaster eat the food gradually, at his leisure, or does he "devour" it? There is a tension between these two terms (much like the contrast between "faintly" and "shock") that works to imply the perspective of the quartermaster without containing it in the written representation itself. The contradiction (which we might easily glide over) takes us into the heart of this elusive, socially charged experience; and also, by fusing together quick and slow, it echoes once again the unstable temporal dynamics of Orwell's own column form.

The other two sections in "As I Please" 68 are worth considering in relation to this opening memory image, even as they pull away, inevitably, from the mode of autobiographical reflection. It is in the second section that Orwell, explicitly discussing the relationship between politics and literature, compares Soviet officials who are unable to control and manipulate literature to "a fish bashing its nose against the wall of an aquarium again and again, too dim-witted to realize that glass and water are not the same thing" (19.7). The thin, almost unrecognizable line between glass and water—unnoticed by that stupid, painfully recoiling fish—might now be equated with the subtle difference between the represented ground and the representation that Orwell often highlights in "As I Please"—and that he draws into the episode that starts this column (as Orwell glimpses a scene that both impresses him *and* eludes him). The third, final, section of the column is a notably short one. Like many of the briefer sections in "As I Please," its very compression highlights that sense, so important within the column sequence as a whole, of language dwindling or even vanishing before our eyes:

> From *The Thoughts of the Emperor Marcus Aurelius:*
>> In the morning when thou risest unwillingly, let this thought be present—I am rising to the work of a human being. Why then am I dissatisfied if I am going to do the things for which I exist and for which I was brought into the world? Or have I been made for this, to lie in the bed-clothes and keep myself warm?—But this is more pleasant—Dost thou exist then to take thy pleasure, and not at all for action or exertion? Dost thou not see the little plants, the little birds, the ants, the spiders, the bees working together to put in order their several parts of the universe? And art thou unwilling to do the work of a human being, and dost thou not make haste to do that which is according to thy nature?
>> It is a good plan to print this well-known exhortation in large letters and hang it on the wall opposite your bed. And if that fails, as I am told it sometimes does, another good plan is to buy the loudest alarm clock you can get and place it in such a position that you have to get out of bed and go round several pieces of furniture in order to silence it. (19.7–8)

This comment also reflects back on the opening section, suggesting, in "the loudest alarm clock you can get," an instrument that will cause the kind of "shock" and "astonishment" that rests at the center of Orwell's earlier experience. At the same time, the prose dwindles down, almost trivializing itself, and even diminishing, by association, the significance *of* the earlier sections.

But characteristically, the casual section offers us a powerful image at its end—that prolonged moment of disorientation when the vulnerable self, abruptly awoken, is moving toward but hasn't yet reached the blaring alarm clock. Once again Orwell, arriving back at the ground of his own experience, configures selfhood in terms of travel, as the perceiving subject is vulnerably implicated in and penetrated by the world he struggles to apprehend. As readers, however, we glimpse such an experience (the disoriented, newly woken self, stumbling toward the source of noise) only from the outside, in an at least slightly belated inference that locates this unsettled condition underneath the strained playfulness, euphemisms, and deliberate smallness of the section. The event of waking—or of being awoken *by* the "loudest" noise we can imagine—only emerges in a partial manner, both in and against the discourse through which it is refracted, like the quartermaster who simultaneously makes an impression and "vanishes." Such partial representation is thematized in the section's juxtaposition of the exhortative language meant to be, window-like, immediately available to the self (written in "large letters" and placed directly "opposite your bed") and the alarm clock, deliberately displaced *from* the awakening sleeper, who is forced to "go round several pieces of furniture." Our own encounter with this text is, similarly, woven through the disjunctive registers of immediacy and displacement, and it is only at the very end of the sentence (as we read "in order to silence it") that the reader catches up *with* the situation, and, just as the column has ended—or is ending—that we hear, a little too late, the alarm bell ringing.

Paris/Spain: AIP 42

The inscribed scene in which we imagine Orwell moving around these pieces of furniture in order to get to the alarm clock offers another odd conjunction of autobiography, self-expression and "travel." Orwell's movement in this case is reduced to the mere span of his bedroom but still involves not one but "several" obstacles, each serving to confuse and disrupt the awakening subject. Like the close of AIP 26 (when Orwell struggles with the ladder), the represented experience here comes only at the column's end (abruptly, incompletely), generating a tension between its clipped, externalized rendition and its protracted intensity *as* an experience. These two closing passages work the same way. And their alignment extends the range of these first-person travel scenes: from moving across the world system (England to Burma), to tottering along the London streets (with the ladder), to this brief—but still tangibly extended—movement of a disoriented self in his bedroom, to, arguably, the single instant that separates the "first sight" of a new place and what occurs "just before" this sight is intentionally apprehended.

I want to look at the only other major autobiographical section of "As I Please," which takes place earlier in the column sequence but concerns a later event in Orwell's life. As we've seen, this section begins, tellingly, with Orwell attempting to project himself straight toward a destination:

> About the end of 1936, as I was passing through Paris on the way to Spain, I had to visit somebody at an address I did not know, and I thought that the quickest way of getting there would probably be to take a taxi. The taxi-driver did not know the address either. However, we drove up the street and asked the nearest policeman, whereupon it turned out that the address I was looking for was only about a hundred yards away. So I had taken the taxi-driver off the rank for a fare which in English money was about threepence. (42, 16.402)

We've already noted Orwell's interest in the process of "getting" places, and this leisurely opening mimes a tension between immediacy ("the quickest way") and delay that is at the heart of Orwell's exploration of plain style.[8] Likewise, the transience and consequent "quickness" of the column itself here runs against the *longue durée* of memory. As the weekly column casts back to "the end of 1936," it has recourse to an expansive temporal framework similar to the other autobiographical sections we have seen ("[n]early a quarter of a century ago" [19.5] and "[y]ears ago" [16.231]).

The column begins with an action that echoes, from within the story, a basic motive for autobiographical writing as such: self-projection. As so often in Orwell, this attempted self-assertion leads into temporal, spatial, and social disorientation. The column then describes their quarrel in excruciating detail:

> The taxi-driver was furiously angry. He began accusing me, in a roaring voice and with the maximum of offensiveness, of having "done it on

purpose." I protested that I had not known where the place was, and that I obviously would not have taken a taxi if I had known. "You knew very well!" he yelled back at me. He was an old, grey, thick-set man, with ragged grey moustaches and a face of quite unusual malignity. In the end I lost my temper, and, my command of French coming back to me in my rage, I shouted at him, "You think you're too old for me to smash your face in. Don't be too sure!" He backed up against the taxi, snarling and full of fight, in spite of his sixty years.

Then the moment came to pay. I had taken out a ten-franc note. "I've no change!" he yelled as soon as he saw the money. "Go and change it for yourself!"

"Where can I get change?"

"How should I know? That's your business."

So I had to cross the street, find a tobacconist's shop and get change. When I came back I gave the taxi-driver the exact fare, telling him that after his behaviour I saw no reason for giving him anything extra; and after exchanging a few more insults we parted. (16.402-403)

What's most striking about the first part of this section is its overdetermination. The conflict between Orwell and the taxi driver is loaded down with contingent, even embarrassing particulars (embarrassing—as in "Shooting an Elephant" or "A Hanging"—on both the level of story and discourse). But it is also driven by a starker, more structural and impersonal irony: that confusion of near and far in which Orwell accidentally seeks to get a taxi ride to a destination that is right next to the place from which he departs. These two registers of the anecdote are intertwined, but they do not converge smoothly. The latter kind of conflict resembles other moments in Orwell: the comment in *Homage to Catalonia* about "early" and "late"; the distinction in "Notes on the Way" between "setting foot on the soil of Asia" and the moment "just before" this event; the (absolute) claim in *The Road to Wigan Pier* that "this is the kind of point that one is *always* liable to miss" (29, emphasis added); the reversals and inversions that we've seen in "Marrakech" and *Down and Out in Paris and London;* and even the hyperformalized irony in *1984* ("Ignorance is Strength," "2+2=5") and *Animal Farm* ("some animals are more equal than others"). All of these instances ratchet up a potentially discrete tension into a more systematic double bind. In this episode, the uncertain relationship between a contingent, social conflict (Orwell arguing—fairly viciously and needlessly—with the French driver) and a much more structural, abstract contradiction (hiring a taxi to take you to the place where you already are) is significant. It mirrors a broader tension within AIP between the familiarity of the prose, informing even the title itself, and the (unmotivated) logic of the structure, which continually "breaks" the conversational tone through its varied, disconnected sections. Orwell radicalizes the mistake: "it turned out that the address I was looking for was only a hundred yards away." The destination (probably Henry Miller's studio) is not simply close by but almost on the very spot he is starting from.[9] And though this mistake is not lingered on, its absoluteness sits uneasily with the colloquial unfolding of the ensuing description (already evident in Orwell's use of a passive phrase like "it turned out that" to describe such a stark and striking mistake).

I want to suggest that the uncanny meld between these two styles of irony or tension (absolute and colloquial/contingent) mirrors some of the underlying currents of the column form that we've been considering. By this I don't mean to resolve this scene of disagreement and confusion into merely formal terms. The opening of AIP 42 also, obviously, concerns class conflict and difference. In different ways, both forms of irony in the opening are disturbing in this light: both the radically *im*personal coincidence, where Orwell's intended direction, through no fault or desire of his own, turns out to be markedly askew (so that he confuses, and almost inverts, the basic categories of "near" and "far") and the embarrassingly *personal* disagreement, the "sordid squabble" that is full of "ang[er]," "accus[ations]," "roaring voice[s]," "offensiveness," "protest[s]," "malignity," "rage," threats, "yell[ing]." In the uneven boundaries between these two scales of tension, Orwell's anecdote captures (more than either register would itself) the nature of class conflict, which is not readily legible in either purely personal or systematic terms. This unevenness intertwines irony and class tension, the structural and the contingent, once again creating that complicated form of representation within the autobiographical sections of "As I Please" that, building on the dynamics of the columns as a whole, seems to reveal and withhold simultaneously.

We've seen the way that this can lead, as well, to an intricate interweaving of two temporal registers, the compacted and the distended, delay and intensification, "devouring" something at "leisure." This same combination of the quick and the slow helps organize the second half of the section, a transition itself facilitated by geographical movement:

> This sordid squabble left me at the moment violently angry, and a little later saddened and disgusted. "Why do people have to behave like that?" I thought.
>
> But that night I left for Spain. The train, a slow one, was packed with Czechs, Germans, Frenchmen, all bound on the same mission. Up and down the train you could hear one phrase repeated over and over again, in the accents of all the languages of Europe—*là-bas* (down there). My third-class carriage was full of very young, fair-haired, underfed Germans in suits of incredible shoddiness—the first *ersatz* cloth I had seen—who rushed out at every stopping-place to buy bottles of cheap wine and later fell asleep in a sort of pyramid on the floor of the carriage. About halfway down France the ordinary passengers dropped off. There might still be a few nondescript journalists like myself, but the train was practically a troop train, and the countryside knew it. In the morning, as we crawled across southern France, every peasant working in the field turned round, stood solemnly upright and gave the anti-Fascist salute. They were like a guard of honour, greeting the train mile after mile. (16.403)

The train is "a slow one" that moves first "halfway down" France and then "crawl[s]" through southern France, where the impression of the peasants raising the anti-Fascist salute seems to unfold in slow motion. Orwell emphasizes the gradualness of the journey, which marks not just a geographical trajectory but also the more profound reversal of class position itself. At the same time, Orwell describes the German soldiers "who *rushed* out at every stopping-place to buy bottles of cheap wine," and the quickness of these soldiers is intertwined with the force of the impression they make on Orwell, who sees "ersatz" clothing for the first time (thus apprehending the materiality *of* the clothes itself) and hears the ringing echo of "là-bas" all over the train, "up and down . . . repeated over and over again." If the sight of a new object makes a categorically strong impression, this quintessentially deictic phrase ironically *surrounds* the listener on all sides. With this Orwell concludes the unusually substantial section:

> As I watched this, the behavior of the old taxi-driver gradually fell into perspective. I saw now what had made him so unnecessarily offensive. This was 1936, the year of the great strikes, and the Blum government was still in office. The wave of revolutionary feeling which had swept across France had affected people like taxi-drivers as well as factory workers. With my English accent I had appeared to him a symbol of the idle, patronizing foreign tourists who had done their best to turn France into something midway between a museum and a brothel. In his eyes an English tourist meant a bourgeois. He was getting a bit of his own back on the parasites who were normally his employers. And it struck me that the motives of the polyglot army that filled the train, and of the peasants with raised fists out there in the fields, and my own motive in going to Spain, and the motive of the old taxi-driver in insulting me, were at bottom all the same. (16.402–403)

Here, too, Orwell's concluding realization is presented as both sudden and "gradual." The swelling of the anaphoric final sentence (so uncharacteristic in AIP) emerges in paradoxical contrast to the way in which the realization "str[ikes]" the thinker. And the column section, as it reaches the delayed final clause ("the motives . . . were at bottom all the same") no sooner allows the realization—the dissolving of tension—than it ends, taking advantage of AIP's structure to shift to an unrelated topic.

This imbalance essentially inverts what we've seen at the end of AIP 26: in the earlier case, a compacted description of an extended action; in this case, the "leisurely" unfolding of a thought that (insofar as it "struck" Orwell) actually transpires in, and can only persist for, a brief moment of time. In different ways, each of the three major autobiographical sections threads such an imbalance (within the compositional dynamics of the representation itself) into *structural* ironies—arriving on deck too early (or too late), locking yourself out of your own house, seeking a destination where you already stand. And in each case, this is connected to an emphatically personal depiction of class division: Orwell's complicity, while carrying the ladder "nearly half a mile," with his landlady's hostility toward her

working-class neighbors; his troubling mixture of distance from and rever-
ence toward the quartermaster (at once "godlike" and "ape-like"); his nearly
violent disagreement with the "snarling" taxi driver.

These examples show something important about Orwell's writing. The
intricate patterns that we've seen in his prose—those alternations of quick
and slow, "leisurely" and urgent, "early" and "late"—are not merely motivated on the stylistic plane but intertwined with the stratified structure of
the social world. This is quite different from simply linking Orwell's plain
style and social commitment in a direct sense. On the contrary, it is often the
mediations in Orwell's voice, its fissures and strains, its complicated attention to the constructedness (or formal drive) of writing, and its awareness of
the "isolation" intrinsic to writing, which access the social world. We've seen
the way that Orwell's columns often turn on "discovering" the unnoticed,
neglected, forgotten, or overlooked. I put this phrase in quotes because the
columns are also attentive to perils within the act of discovery itself: the
obscuring that can take place through conceptualization or abstraction,
the potentially dangerous complacency of achieved representation, and the
negation (of elision itself) that often occurs when something only partially
visible, recognized, or respected is brought back into language and reflection. As we have seen, this preoccupation—with the disposable, peripheral,
and transient—is also connected both to the *structural* logic of "As I Please"
(as the sections create a continually precarious, and self-dividing, topicality
even while the weekly context brings out an equally pointed contemporaneity) and to the stylistic pulsations of the prose (full of those imbalances). It
also helps coordinate specific scenes of representation. The alarm clock; the
excursus on handwriting; the ladder carried nearly a mile; the disappearing
quartermaster: in these and other passages Orwell draws an oblique distance between the discourse and the represented ground we recover through
the discourse.

The representation of inequality and commonality is near the heart of the
transient poetics that informs the strategy of "As I Please." As we have seen,
"As I Please," at its core, generates representations that *can't be held onto,*
taking advantage of the temporal structure of the column, as form, to generate an internal drama within the field of representation itself. There is too
much to grasp, to remember, to hold in mind. This "flaw" of "As I Please"
(writing that disappears) is clearly one of the virtues of the form for Orwell,

even as he usually refuses to take full advantage of the more immediate temptations offered by the weekly column (direct engagement, contemporaneity, authenticity, etc.). To hold onto that "glimpse" of inequality is to misrepresent the force of stratification that has been witnessed or apprehended; similarly, Orwell is cautious about reifying or sentimentalizing the single instant in which the politically driven commonality of the working class, peasantry, and bourgeois fellow travelers is legible. These concerns—social and epistemological—find a home in the column form. We've also seen the way that Orwell draws these tensions into the fraught balancing of thought and materiality and, specifically, that moment, within reflection, when social comprehension implicates the orienting position of the thinker, writer, or observer. Grasping commonality, in AIP 68, involves precisely this unstable form of externalized self-perception. In one sense, then, AIP 48 and 68 inscribe moments that dramatize (or melodramatize) the constructive poetics of the AIP columns as a whole. Here, in the *story*, Orwell, as a passenger on the ocean liner, is "glimps[ing]" a scene of social injustice; here, on the train, in revolutionary transit, Orwell is momentarily "struck" by a provoking or generative thought. Yet what are these columns as a whole other than a mode of writing designed to generate "glimpses" and "striking" moments?

The unusual autobiographical moments thus also function to foreground the writing process more consistently at work in AIP and to establish further connections between the formal dynamics of the column and larger questions of experience, selfhood, and authenticity. By intertwining experience and style in this manner, Orwell amplifies the way in which the fundamentally *imbalanced* patterns of representation in "As I Please"—with its inversions, asymmetries, truncations, deflations, and shifts; its emphasis on "noticing," being "struck," and "glimpsing"; and its inscriptions of the overlooked and disposable—are grounded in an encounter with social stratification and inequality. The three major autobiographical sections thus come to hinge on two diametrical processes: encountering social difference (as with the quartermaster whom Orwell can glimpse only in the instant of disappearing) and a short-lived, vulnerable form of equality (as on the train ride across France, which "strikes" Orwell with the recognition of commonality). This analysis has tried to demonstrate the continuity between these two terms. While the "glimpsed" object and the "striking" event are in one sense antithetical (the "glimpsed" object is remote from and outside the reach of the self; the "striking" event encroaches on and penetrates the self's observational faculties), they share a fundamentally precarious temporality. Furthermore, we've seen how Orwell's plain style frequently works to confuse the "near" and the "far" (e.g., in the section on back-to-back houses in *Wigan Pier* or the description of Walter Raleigh in AIP). The "striking" event, by moving so quickly into—and thus disrupting, disordering, and shocking—the experiencing self, is *also* something that can only be glimpsed (by these now-disordered faculties). And the "glimpsed" object, by bringing the self so discernibly to the boundary of what it can and cannot view or comprehend—by making the observer, in other words, uncomfortably aware of his delimited bodily and social positioning—also functions as something shocking, striking, disruptive.

Conclusion: Orwell, Post-Structuralist ("Can Socialists be Happy?")

In this chapter, I've tried to connect a key pattern of experience in "As I Please" (where the narrating self, en route, is surprised, disrupted, or jammed up); the formal logic of representation in these truncated, week-to-week columns; and Orwell's political engagement with social stratification and inequality. Injustice *fuels* writing and representation but cannot be sufficiently comprehended in writing—it is accessible in "striking" moments and "glimpses" that can lead toward, without producing a stable or self-sufficient account of, justice (as elusive as complete or absolute representation). One version of the pressure that Orwell puts on any idea of pure justice is crystallized in a piece titled "Can Socialists be Happy?" that he writes, pseudonymously, for *Tribune* just as he is beginning the "As I Please" columns (and starting his position as *Tribune*'s literary editor). This simultaneity makes the brief essay an important intertext for "As I Please," particularly if we recognize the relationship between the absolute *happiness* that Orwell engages with in this essay and the potential freedom invoked by the column's title. If the "free" columns are paradoxically wedded to their transient structure, Orwell wants to insist, in this essay, on the instability of happiness: as a political state toward which we always aspire but which we can never sufficiently inhabit.

The tone of "Can Socialists be Happy?" is peculiar. In one important sense, it is a quite serious essay, and a model for Orwell's democratic-socialist position. He says, explicitly, that "[t]he inability of mankind to imagine happiness except in the form of *relief*, either from effort or pain, presents Socialists with a serious problem" (16.42) and, again, draws attention to ideological fracture when he writes, "[a]t the risk of saying something which the editors of *Tribune* may not endorse, I suggest that the real objective of Socialism is not happiness" (16.42). But the essay seems deliberately *unse-rious* in other ways: it reads as colloquial and conversational, associative, speculative, and wistful.[10] It is also a "Christmas" piece, written in late December 1943 and associating itself, rhetorically, with the holiday season. It's also a fundamentally enigmatic piece, signed under the assumed name "John Freeman" and incorporated into Orwell's complete work only through the editorial skill of Peter Davison in the 1980s.[11]

I take the essay "serious[ly]" for several reasons. First of all, the increased critical emphasis that I've put on "As I Please" can spill over into this *Tribune* piece. As we've seen, Orwell never explains his motives for writing the "As I Please" column, and he never comments explicitly—in the columns themselves or in his personal correspondence—on the logic or implications of the column structure (its variety, its truncations, its political orientation, etc.). The significance of "As I Please" must derive, of course, from an inductively grounded reading of the columns themselves. But intertextual material emerges once we foreground "As I Please" in this way. I've mentioned the retrospective column "As I Pleased," which is one obvious example: a *Tribune* column about *Tribune* itself. (And the wordplay of the title—"please" to "pleased"—cheerfully condenses the reflective movement so central to "As I Please.") As we've seen, this essay identifies *Tribune* as an ideological and cultural affiliation for Orwell ("I . . . think it is the only existing weekly paper that makes a genuine effort to be progressive and humane"[19.38]). This sense of affiliation is further registered by the *double* role that Orwell takes on at *Tribune* in late 1943: as the newsweekly's columnist and also its literary editor. There is a relationship between these two roles. While Orwell didn't take to the responsibilities of being an editor, he did, according to most of the biographical accounts we have, take to the affiliation that came *with* editing, and this sense of participation—not merely in the newspaper itself but in the socialist project that underlies

Tribune—is an important context for the weekly columns. "Can Socialists be Happy?" is written soon after Orwell begins both of these enterprises, and we can read it as a third form of engagement with *Tribune*. (One of the two sections in Orwell's column of that week reinforces this connection, as AIP 4 dwells explicitly on the need to "dissociate Socialism from Utopianism" [16.35].)

There is another way that "Can Socialists be Happy" seems like a significant and "serious" work within Orwell's writing: it synthesizes literary and political criticism to an unusual degree. As much as any of Orwell's work, this essay is difficult to identify as primarily literary or political—it deliberately feels like the equivalent of a rabbit/duck icon. In its sinuous movement between literature and politics, the essay, even while explicitly resisting the utopian, marks a certain utopianism of method itself: the possibility that writing can incorporate *both* literature and politics without subordinating or instrumentalizing one perspective in terms of the other. We can't underestimate the degree to which such a reconciliation of literature and politics is a form of *methodological* "happiness" for Orwell.

My sense of the importance of "Can Socialists be Happy?" doesn't mean to ignore or transcend the casual-familiar tone of the essay. On the contrary, I'm most interested in the tension between the casualness and the seriousness of the piece—and the significance (or we might even say seriousness) *of* this tension. It is tension, as well, that rests at the heart of this essay's diagnosis of happiness. "Happiness" Orwell writes, "derives mainly from contrast" (16.39), only out of relief from suffering, hunger, and oppression. Orwell reaches this argument in the second paragraph of the essay, and it is worth looking at the construction that takes us to this point, as well as the implications that unfold in its wake:

> The thought of Christmas raises almost automatically the thought of Charles Dickens, and for two very good reasons. To begin with, Dickens is one of the few English writers who have actually written about Christmas. Christmas is the most popular of English festivals, and yet it has produced astonishingly little literature. There are the carols, mostly medieval in origin; there is a tiny handful of poems by Robert Bridges, T. S. Eliot, and some others, and there is Dickens; but there is very little else. Secondly, Dickens is remarkable, indeed almost unique,

among modern writers in being able to give a convincing picture of
happiness. (16.39)

Like many sections of "As I Please," the start of this text compels and dilutes
our attention simultaneously. Orwell deliberately begins not with the conceptual content that the essay will reach toward but with a contingently
grounded chain of associations, or "thoughts."[12] "The thought of Christmas"
and the "thought of Dickens": neither of these are yet the "thought" of happiness, the actual subject of the piece. (Another celebrated essay in *Tribune*
is called "Some Thoughts on the Common Toad," and we've seen how
important this simple verb—"think"—is for other crucial terms in Orwell's
work: "until one stops to think about it" [*Wigan Pier*]; "it gives you time to
think" [AIP 31, 16.272]; "any thinking person"[11.168] "think[ing] too
deeply"[11.104]; "doublethink," etc.) Only gradually, and in a circuitous
path, does the opening move toward its consequential and essentially *structural* claim: its daunting proposition that what we take as "happiness" is
intertwined with—dependent on, built out of, and implicated in—suffering.
The second paragraph begins:

> Dickens dealt successfully with Christmas twice—in a well-known
> chapter of *The Pickwick Papers* and in *The Christmas Carol.* The latter
> story was read to Lenin on his deathbed and, according to his wife, he
> found its "bourgeois sentimentality" completely intolerable. Now in a
> sense Lenin was right; but if he had been in better health he would per-
> haps have noticed that the story has some interesting sociological
> implications. (16.39)

It is here, as Orwell begins to elaborate these "implications," that the argument, or grounding "thought" of his own essay, accelerates:

> To begin with, however thick Dickens may lay on the paint, however
> disgusting the "pathos" of Tiny Tim may be, the Cratchit family do give
> the impression of enjoying themselves. They sound happy as, for
> instance, the citizens of William Morris's *News from Nowhere* don't
> sound happy. Moreover—and Dickens's understanding of this is one of
> the secrets of his power—their happiness derives mainly from contrast.

They are in high spirits because for once in a way they have enough to eat. The wolf is at the door, but he is wagging his tail. The steam of the Christmas pudding drifts across a background of pawnshops and sweated labour, and. . . . [t]he Cratchits are able to enjoy their Christmas precisely because Christmas only comes once a year. Their happiness is convincing just because it is described as incomplete.

All efforts to describe *permanent* happiness, on the other hand, have been failures, from earliest history onwards. Utopias (incidentally the coined word Utopia doesn't mean "a good place," it means merely "a non-existent place") have been common in the literature of the past three or four hundred years, but the "favourable" ones are invariably unappetising, and usually lacking in vitality as well. (16.39)

I hope these excerpts convey the strangely unbalanced quality of Orwell's essay, as both light-hearted and urgent, associative (and, thus, diffuse) and conceptual (and, thus, focused). "The steam of the Christmas pudding drifts across a background of pawnshops and sweated labour." Like other points in Orwell, and in the long tradition of the literary left more generally, this image highlights the always potentially surprising and disturbing connection of well-being and social deprivation. ("Every monument of civilization is also a monument of barbarism.") The image is, itself, a powerfully "socialist" one, as it insists not only on a quantitative association here (that the world is full of suffering as well as wealth) but a qualitative one (that suffering and wealth are, in crucial ways, mutually constitutive). In this way, Orwell explicitly connects the insight with Lenin, arguing that its fundamentally "sociological" nature would have aligned with Lenin's perspective.

This insistence on contrast is part of Orwell's more general critique of "permanency," in a psychological as well as conceptual and political sense. As the essay unfolds, it becomes clear that Orwell is making a philosophical and ideological claim, but we also can read the critique of permanency here in relation to the *formal* brevity of the "As I Please" writing project: a brevity that, we've seen, is associated with Orwell's effort to articulate the unstable threshold between experience and reflection. Reflection loses itself when it becomes overextended; such "permanency" tends to turn thought into non-thought—rote, abstract, repetitive, complacent. Thought needs to continually displace itself, and this struggle, a struggle *of* self-fracturing, is part of what's at stake in Orwell's comment, in "Why I Write," that "one can write nothing readable unless one *constantly struggles* to efface one's own personality" (16.320, emphasis added). The paradoxical leeching of happiness when it is deprived of contrast—in its "permanent," transcendent state—resonates with this generative instability of thought or reflectiveness, and gives it a particularly political dimension.

The essay doesn't aim to disavow socialism by suggesting that it has a particular inability to achieve, or even imagine, a stable or contented state (as though *socialism* won't lead to happiness, but some other kind of political ideology could—or as though socialists can't experience happiness, but some other kind of person could). Rather, the state of happiness is critiqued on its own terms and redefined. (This redefinition only works, indeed, if we hold onto socialism as a valorized and privileged category.) Socialism needs to aim for happiness but, just as happiness can never stably or durably transcend the negative state out of which it arises (the state of deprivation, inequality, longing), socialism also can't escape its fundamentally oppositional nature. Socialism takes flight from the real—it is "alit," like Bevan's description of Orwell at *Tribune*—and it would not be able to permanently realize itself, as a sufficient and alternative reality. Socialism is largely constituted out of the "effort" or "struggle" to realize itself. Thus, describing H. G. Wells:

> All the evils and miseries that we now suffer from have vanished. Ignorance, war, poverty, dirt, disease, frustration, hunger, fear, overwork, superstition—all vanished. So expressed, *it is impossible to deny that that is the kind of world we all hope for.* We all want to abolish the things Wells wants to abolish. But is there anyone who actually wants to live in a Wellsian Utopia? (16.39, emphasis added)

The bulk of Orwell's essay traces out various images of permanence (political, "other-worldly" [16.40], "pagan" [16.41], and finally sensual), in each case showing how "perfection" is, in fact, misaligned with "happiness" and how the dream of happiness is, vexingly, implicated with its exterior. As we've seen, Orwell suggests that this poses a challenge ("a serious problem") to the left. But the thrust of his own reasoning is constructive, seeking to highlight the practice of solidarity (or what he terms "brotherhood" and "love") over the product of well-being (which is residual and can never be fully projected or planned):

> We want a world where Scrooge, with his dividends, and Tiny Tim, with his tuberculous leg, would both be unthinkable. But does that mean that we are aiming at some painless, effortless Utopia?
>
> At the risk of saying something which the editors of *Tribune* may not endorse, I suggest that the real objective of Socialism is not happiness. Happiness hitherto has been a by-product, and for all we know it may always remain so. The real objective of Socialism is human brother-hood. This is widely felt to be the case, though it is not usually said, or not said loudly enough. Men use up their lives in heart-breaking polit-ical struggles, or get themselves killed in civil wars, or tortured in the secret prisons of the Gestapo, not in order to establish some central-heated, air-conditioned, strip-lighted Paradise, but because they want a world in which human beings love one another instead of swindling and murdering one another. And they want that world as a first step. Where they go from there is not so certain, and the attempt to foresee it in detail merely confuses the issue. (16.42)

We can understand "Can Socialists be Happy?" as a socialist text itself only if we understand that, for Orwell, such "problems" (as those that permanent happiness "presents") are necessary to and generative of socialism. Problems are crucial. This passage combines a number of different forms of opposition and instability: the "first" tentative step, couched in "uncertain[ty]"; the "risk" of saying something that breaks from ideological orthodoxy; the con-viction that goes unsaid or spoken too softly; and martyrs of dissent, who "use up their lives in heart-breaking political struggles," "get themselves killed in civil wars," or "tortured" in "secret prisons." This paragraph—unfolding against the systematic critique of "permanent happiness" in the essay as a whole—works to inscribe opposition, and the *tentativeness* that is a consequential result of opposition, into multiple levels of the socialist project: from the enactment of political ideals in war, political action, and resistance to the subtle formulation of justice as (always) a "first" and "uncer-tain" step rather than a final, transformative crossing from one state into another.

Orwell's own inclination to define socialism negatively (and thus to raise more "problems" than he can answer) fits into this same pattern, connecting with the tentativeness of the essay as a whole. The essay's tone wavers, as in the opening, between the structural and the casual-familiar, so that the reader is never certain if the central claim is speculative or programmatic, whimsical or ideologically urgent. This methodological ambiguity is under-lined by the way the opening of the essay invokes an earlier Orwell text—his extended analysis of "Charles Dickens" in *Inside the Whale*. As we have seen, "Charles Dickens" also gravitates toward structural claims, hinging on the blend of elisions and achieved representation that constitutes the nineteenth-century novelistic imaginary: "There are large areas of the human mind that he never touches" (78); "[i]t is noticeable that Dickens hardly ever writes of war, even to denounce it" (41); "he is not mechanically minded" (59); "[o]ne can see Dickens's utter lack of an educational theory" (30). Most notably, of course, the essay comes to focus on the absence of both the proletariat and the experience of work itself, polemicizing famously: "If you look for the working classes in fiction, and especially English fiction, all you find is a hole" (11-12).

The method—but not the content—is strikingly similar to the opening procedure of "Can Socialists be Happy?" which weaves its contingent, tran-sient associations through two structural claims: that Christmas "has pro-duced *astonishingly* little literature" and that "Dickens is remarkable, *indeed almost unique,* among modern writers" for offering a convincing depiction of happiness (emphases added). I emphasize these emphases precisely because they underline the force of structure. There is a threshold between "little literature" and "astonishingly little literature" and between "remark-able" and "indeed almost unique." It marks the point where a quantitative, empirical observation shifts into a conceptual, synthetic category, like the reversal of figure and ground. Orwell's essay wants to take us to this "aston-ishing" threshold but *not* quite across it—in the same, uncanny, way as the 1940 Dickens essay follows its (already strangely tactile) image for the struc-tural "hole" that the reader "finds" with the clipped rejoinder: "This state-ment needs qualifying, perhaps" (11).[13]

Once again, I'm stressing the significance of what might seem like quite minor stylistic choices by Orwell, particularly given this essay's casual tone. But the durable effect of Orwell's work is generated only as it strains against, without transcending, this casualness. The modifiers I'm identifying—"astonishingly little," "almost unique"—are a case in point. They are important. They resemble other points in his work that use the same kind of emphatic modification: when Orwell writes that the dog in "A Hanging" rests "*just* out of reach" or when at the opening of "Notes on the Way" he distinguishes what he saw "*just* before setting foot" on Asia for the first time (emphases added). In "Can Socialists be Happy?" these modifiers align exactly with the shift to a structural perspective. In this sense, they demonstrate the stakes of such Orwellian intensification, an intensification that takes on vivid and palpable form only in relation to the casualness that it resists.

The intensification in these comments is not sensory or empirical but *structural*. Like the comments in "Charles Dickens," these sentences demonstrate how important the structural orientation is for Orwell. One way to look at such a process—against a writing practice that maintains a *steadier, more committed* relationship to structure—is that Orwell continually brings out the dynamic movement toward structure. His work is "consciousness raising" not in the sense of transmitting a valorized set of positions or perspectives but rather of enacting the dynamic movement of consciousness itself, as it moves *from* induction—immersion—to structure. In "Charles Dickens," too, what seems like a concession—"this statement needs qualifying, perhaps"—is also another form of intensification, a way of foregrounding the structural perspective as a dynamic, active mode of thinking. Of course, we can view this as a retreat from structure. The easiest critique of this comment is readily at hand: the comment can be understood as a compromise, a modulation, an eschewal of structural intensity. In the same way, the writing project "As I Please" could be understood to resist structural analysis or theoretical depth—always foregrounding pluralism, variety, locality, and the expression of "immediate" sensation or response.

I would argue instead that Orwell's essay suggests how a structural orientation is necessary *to* thinking (as the horizon of happiness is necessary *to* socialism) but can never be fully or stably realized without negating thought. (To put this formulaically: "happiness" is to "socialism" as structure is to thought.) Why is this the case? In a Platonic (or, we might say, a structural) model of structural thinking, there is inevitably the crossing of a threshold, when the pressure of an empirical pattern, produced only through contingent immersion in, and attentiveness to, discrete particulars, pushes the thinker to reorganize and reconstellate these particulars in relation to a larger, overarching totality. Thought, through inductive immersion in the particular, starts to take flight from the particular; the trees become a forest. If we understand this conceptual process in temporal terms, there must be a moment, necessarily brief, in which "trees" and "forest" coincide: a moment of maximal pressure, and of maximal range, since, at this intersection, particular and general are coextensive within a single frame.

This maximal point of pressure brings us back to the "glimpses" and "striking" moments that we've seen recurrently (in both the form and content) of "As I Please." What's crucial to note here is that these states are not presented as either preceding or turning away from the structural perspective but as registering its impact. Orwell's impressionistic register, in other words, is *post*-structural in the sense that it emerges out of the disorienting encounter with structure itself. This disorientation tracks, furthermore, to that key form of structural analysis that we can see in Marx: where a strictly contemplative knowledge is drawn to see its own shaping by, and embedding within, a larger, totalized, social system. "Can Socialists be Happy?" wants to distinguish between the *impact* of this structural horizon—as it provokes a restless political desire—and any compensatory, teleological scheme that tries to channel this impact into a fixed, stable—and thus less structurally dynamic—political or aesthetic model. As Orwell writes in the corresponding issue of AIP:

> Socialists don't claim to be able to make the world perfect: they claim to be able to make it better. And any thinking Socialist will concede to the Catholic that when economic injustice has been righted, the fundamental problem of man's place in the universe will still remain. But what the Socialist does claim is that that problem cannot be dealt with while the average human being's preoccupations are necessarily economic. It is all summed up in Marx's saying that after Socialism has arrived, human history can begin. (4, 16.35)

Orwell's topic in "Can Socialists be Happy?" resonates with this nuanced sense of synthesis, by focusing on a generalized state of contrast, or a permanent condition of impermanency. The final two paragraphs of the essay gesture at this same idea—inscribing a horizon that is both necessary to socialist thought and never fully definable or attainable:

> Socialist thought has to deal in prediction, but only in broad terms. One often has to aim at objectives which one can only very dimly see. . . . The world wants something which it is dimly aware could exist, but cannot accurately define. . . . To make that kind of [war] impossible is a good objective. But to say in detail what a peaceful world would be like is a different matter. . . . Whoever tries to imagine perfection simply reveals his own emptiness. (16.43)

"Can Socialists be Happy?" makes a connection between its puncturing of "permanent happiness," the debate between procedural and teleological forms of socialism, and the contingent nature of thinking that is explored more extensively, and formally, through the continuing experiment of "As I Please."

Conclusion
Happy Orwell

Time and again, Orwell's relationship with *Tribune* has been characterized as an unusually harmonious one. "Orwell clearly loved the freedom at *Tribune,* all the more so because it was a journal with which he could totally identify" (Keeble 101). Crick notes "the happiness of the *Tribune* days" (449) and concludes that "the *Tribune* days were in the main good days" (448). "[G]ood days," "happiness," "freedom," "love," and "identif[ication]": the sequence of terms is striking. This is a discretely *political* happiness, since Orwell's affiliation with *Tribune* is shaped by the newsweekly's status as "the leading voice of the left-wing of the Labour party" (Keeble 100). The political association reinforces Orwell's compacted assertion, in "Why I Write," about "every line" he has written since 1937. On strikingly different scales, these are both dramatic gestures of commitment to "democratic socialism" (and not simply *evidence* of such commitment). Each gesture—the years-long *Tribune* affiliation and the single-line summary—intensifies the other. The whole enterprise flies against readings that have focused on Orwell's pessimism and, most typically, have read this pessimism as a retreat from politics or from socialism. On its face, the happiness of the "*Tribune* days" (and the *Tribune* column) unsettles a pessimistic reading of Orwell. That this pleasure is forged *through* political affiliation dilutes some of the implications often derived from his pessimism.

Each week, Orwell's title reasserts that he is "please[d]" to write for *Tribune*—but pleased, as well, to write "*as* [he] please[s]." Here, it is impossible to separate freedom and happiness: doing what one pleases (freedom) and being pleased in what one does (happiness). Any pessimistic reading confronts this conspicuous *node* in Orwell's work: the affiliation with *Tribune*, the column writing that secures this affiliation, the freedom associated with column writing, and the pleasure deriving from such freedom. Yet Orwell's relation to the newspaper is only legible as an affiliation in the degree to which it is contingent and indeterminate. To write "as he pleases" also means to stray outside of any positive definition that *Tribune* would offer. "[T]here will be times when he will fly off." Crick avers that the "*Tribune* style of argument . . . suited Orwell perfectly" (441). This (perfect) "suit[ability]" echoes the sense of "totally identify[ing]." Yet "[t]he joy he felt at being Literary Editor of *Tribune* lay largely in his own writing" (443). The affiliation is purchased in terms of independence, and thus, uncertainty. It is not a natural or *given* condition, Orwell's happy relationship suggests. The gaps between sections stand out.

The question of identity that haunts Orwell's reception—the endless debate, rehearsed by my own study as well, as to whether Orwell really *is* a socialist—is not merely a matter of projections made onto the work, nor even an imprint of his essential contradictoriness. This book has argued that Orwell is *not* contradictory about his socialist position so much as he is intent on making socialism a necessarily asserted act (and thus a contingent state) rather than an organic, immediately realizable, or stable condition of political being. This is another reason Orwell's essay "Can Socialists be Happy?"— with its strangely cheerful tone—is significant. Certainly, this text denies the possibility of (absolute, permanent, contrast-free) happiness. But this very denial implies, in fact, a reaffirmation of the *other* key term in the title: "socialis[m]." We have to pause for a second to recognize this, and it requires a few steps by indirection—but the affiliation is there to be seen.[1] The effort to classify is treacherous, and a prosecutorial tone can run, as though by inversion, through Orwell's posthumous reception. This criticism would ask: "Are you *not now*—despite your claim to the contrary—a Socialist?" Or, indeed, in the more radical versions of this—"Have you *never been* a Socialist?" Scott Lucas: "Orwell was not a socialist" (2000, 49). Robert Colls: "Orwell said he belonged to the left. He may have protested too much the fact" (228). Colls reiterates, noting that "Orwell wanted to be a socialist, said he was a socialist, tried to look the part of a socialist, and never wavered in his belief that he was a socialist" (224) and yet still rejecting this identity (as, for example, "those who knew him well swore that deep down he was really a conservative" [3]).[2] There is a lot of good evidence to marshal here but also a major problem. The problem is that we are left with a quite straitened definition of politics (not just Orwell's politics) if we come to define political affiliation outside of what a writer "belie[ves]," desires, and "sa[ys]." At some point, for example, wouldn't the sustained association with *Tribune* simply constitute a writer's identity as socialist? Or risk making the whole matter of political affiliation (not just Orwell's affiliation) untenably esoteric?

Again, Colls's reading isn't unfair or unresponsive because Orwell certainly invites this suspicious response. In a certain sense, Orwell's political accomplishment feeds directly into such suspicion, or uncertainty about what constitutes the left.[3] The great freeing act of Orwell's writing is to dissociate Socialism from (what can then be redefined as) its Stalinist negation. The price of this, however, is to inject a heretical uncertainty into the core of socialist belonging. For Orwell, democratic socialism is an ideology—perhaps the ideology—that must implacably disrupt itself. This mirrors the struggle and effort that constitutes the socialist project—the "realisation," as Orwell writes in "Arthur Koestler," "that to make life livable is a much bigger problem than it recently seemed"(16.399). As long as socialism is locked within this struggle to realize itself democratically, there are no pure socialists (just as there is no adequate manifestation, by the time of Orwell's death, of socialist desire). After all, the very term "*democratic* socialism" puts socialism under the pressure of an undemocratic potential. As Empson suggests, we wouldn't qualify water with the modifier wet (because water is always wet).[4] And every adjective, in this way, is an instrument of ambiguity (and thus tension) rather than precision (and stability). This seems to me the great (and positive) significance of the double term: not synthesis but internal tension. The politics of democratic socialism hinges on the way this reverberating tension, while unstabilized, nonetheless *can* be contained by the overarching category. Either an achieved harmony—of the two terms, with each other—or an explosion, of the governing category that relates the two terms, would betray the democratic socialist position. In this sense, the ostensible strains in Orwell's politics are consistent with his "political position."

In "Can Socialists Be Happy," Orwell argues against a political thinking that projects itself too confidently, or complacently, into the permanency of

the future. "Whoever tries to imagine perfection simply reveals his own emptiness." In a similar way, Orwell gravitates toward noting the *loss* of equality—
and the pressures of inequality—rather than simply imagining equality itself.
I want to close this book with three example of this from *Homage to Catalonia,
Animal Farm,* and "As I Please." In each case, though in quite different ways,
a representation—or "imagin[ing]"—of equality is bound up in an encounter
with *in*equality. Orwell's remarkable description of such vanishing equality
in *Homage to Catalonia* establishes the terms of this. What's most important
to note about these excerpts from *Homage to Catalonia* is the strict *pattern*
that Orwell is invested in—a pattern visible both in the way that he returns to
the topic in different passages, and, more profoundly, as these passages highlight a template of experience, engulfing any one individual case:

> This was in late December, 1936, less than seven months ago as I write,
> and yet it is a period that has already receded into enormous distance. . . .
> To anyone who had been there since the beginning it probably seemed
> even in December or January that the revolutionary period was ending;
> but when one came straight from England the aspect of Barcelona was
> something startling and overwhelming. It was the first time that I had
> ever been in a town where the working class was in the saddle. (4)

> All happened so swiftly that people making successive visits to Spain at
> intervals of a few months have declared that they seemed scarcely to be
> visiting the same country; what had seemed on the surface and for a
> brief instant to be a workers' State was changing before one's eyes into
> an ordinary bourgeois republic with the normal division into rich and
> poor. (56)

> Everyone who has made two visits, at intervals of months, to Barcelona
> during the war has remarked upon the extraordinary changes that took
> place in it. And curiously enough, whether they went there first in
> August and again in January, or, like myself, first in December and
> again in April, the thing they said was always the same: that the revolu-
> tionary atmosphere had vanished. (109)

The last passage combines (once more) plainspoken familiarity of tone with
a pointedly structural orientation. More specifically, Orwell insists on privileging temporal structure over the content of experience. On the one hand,

the impression of this experience—as all three passages make clear—is extraordinarily vivid. It is "startling" and "overwhelming," and it forms a pervasive "atmosphere." It takes place "right before one's eyes." Orwell elaborates this in another crucial passage from Chapter 8 that frames his memoir as a whole in relation to a connected impression (at once sensory and political) from his time, during this same "interval," on the Republican front:

> However much one cursed at the time, one realized afterwards that one had been in contact with something strange and valuable. . . . One had breathed the air of equality. . . . This period which then seemed so futile and eventless is now of great importance to me. It is so different from the rest of my life that already it has taken on the magic quality which, as a rule, belongs only to memories that are years old. It was beastly while it was happening, but it is a good patch for my mind to browse upon. . . . The whole period stays by me with curious vividness. (104–105)

On the other hand, this politically charged substance—the "air of equality"— is *not* self-evident but determined only by structure (or, we might say, by the event structure of perception itself). Depending on the interval, what stands out as revolutionary equality and what constitutes the reemergence of inequality will change (or even, to use Orwell's favored image, turn upside-down). The month that marks the acme of this encounter with equality, for one "visit[or]," could epitomize equality's loss, for another. Orwell, coming "straight from England," puts December 1936 as the moment that underlies his impression of revolutionary Barcelona. For someone who arrived in Spain in August 1936, December would instead be the point in time that made clear how the "revolutionary period was ending." And someone who first arrived in Spain in 1937, by contrast, might think they were encountering such equality at the very moment when Orwell felt it to be unraveling. This shifting time frame is so significant because—against the "overwhelming" and "startling" impression that revolutionary Barcelona produces—it suggests that there is no period, no political moment, in which the substance (the "air") of equality is perfectly apparent or secure. Despite the impression that *everyone* takes away, there is *no* point in time that coincides absolutely with the moment of equality.

Thus, each time a visitor to Spain experiences equality, she doesn't encounter it directly. Rather such an experience is embedded within this longer, arcing trajectory: the initial contact (with equality), an "interval," an absence (of equality), a shock (in the difference between the two states), and, finally, a recognition that becomes fully activated only through the shock of this absence. This mediated encounter suggests not only the impermanence of equality (like "happiness") but also, and just as significantly, its radical *non-transparency*. And crucially, this non-transparency is itself a stable, even mundane, universal: as Orwell quietly comments, "the thing they said was always the same." Notice here how Orwell uses the plainspoken key-word "thing" to describe a *process* that, in fact, centers on unraveling the stability of things, or substances.

This universal quality, the unperturbed way in which Orwell generalizes this unsettling temporal trajectory, has important implications. Among other things, it allows us to read this passage as a wonderful, hidden representation *of* representation itself. (And certainly we can schematize that five-step process in a way that touches on representation: contact, interval, absence, contrast, recognition.) *Homage to Catalonia* isn't only "about" equality (and equality's loss) but "about" the representation of equality. In the structure that *Homage to Catalonia* adumbrates—these visits, intervals, and impressions, moving through time but "always the same"—the encounter with equality is bound up with inequality, with its negation. To use slightly more theoretical language, this encounter hinges on difference and not simply identity. Without such difference, we risk mistaking the representation for the substance and thus *losing* the profundity, the elusiveness, the fragility, and the complexity of equality. (These traits are all intrinsic to equality, above all because of its radically intersubjective nature.) This loss, or collapse of structural difference, has gone under other names in this book as well: as the loss of thought, when it is projected into permanence, as the transmutation of political desire into ideology, or as the forestalling of a democratic tension that must remain internal to the socialist project.

The combination of sensory vividness and structural irony in Orwell's descriptions of equality is remarkable, since these two approaches would seem to cancel each other out. Is equality tangible and real—anchored in an objective and actual place and time—or is it in the "eye of the beholder," a fragile projection of the visitor who happens to see things *not* as they are but only in a contingent, arbitrary time frame? Are these passages utopian or disillusioned? (Equality doesn't lend itself to anything other than these two choices.) Orwell cultivates this tension with another simple keyword in the text: "curious." He remarks how the atmosphere of equality on the front line—even once it has disappeared—"stays by me with curious vividness." *And* he notes how "curiously enough," visitors to Barcelona will experience the same process—encountering that same sense of vanishing equality—across any two intervals. The text thus insists that both the vivid impression (that instantiates equality) and the overarching structure (that unravels any absolute point of equality) are surprising. Why is this the case? The impression is surprising (or "curious") because it endures, remaining vivid (indeed becoming *more* vivid) after this period of equality has faded. (As Orwell notes, *"now,"* this period has "great importance." It is "strange and valuable;" has a "magic quality" and, not least impressively, makes "a good patch for [the] mind to browse upon.") And the structure is "curious" because it also persists, remaining uniformly consistent even though the experience, for each individual—of encountering, losing, and recognizing equality—is so singular and definite. Each surprise, in this sense, feeds almost parasitically on the other. And the effect of these passages is to lock the ironic structure and the vivid experience (equality's loss and equality's impression) together.

This is not the only time that Orwell imbricates a lingering sense of equality with the unhappy pressures of inequality. We can think immediately of the cunning aphorism at the center of *Animal Farm:* "All animals are equal but some animals are more equal than others." The taut sentence dramatizes a warping that unfolds at the very heart of egalitarian ideology. But it also establishes this same ideology as the necessary and only frame through which to conceive and thus to see this warping. The tension sharpens in juxtaposition with the sequence of passages we've been considering in *Homage to Catalonia.* Taken seriously, as it demands to be, this sentence marks both the destruction of equality (*as* a concept) and its conceptual apotheosis. Like the fable as a whole, it presses the inversion of equality to a limit point while preserving (if only by its sheer semantic mechanics) an ulterior horizon of equality, without which we couldn't register the linguistic and political unnaturalness of the statement.[5]

Let me return one last time to "As I Please." We've already seen how its fleeting *mimetic* structure is entangled with both equality (as in that instant of recognition on the train ride to Spain) and inequality (as in the encounter with the hungry quartermaster). In this text, too, Orwell returns several times to the scene of a *fading equality*—and, particularly, to the "signs" he detects, of returning social stratification, as London eases out of wartime emergency. As with the double visits to Barcelona, the solidarity of wartime London emerges, poignantly, only as it has begun to fade. Though "As I Please" generally *resists* leitmotifs—since what device more thoroughly hobbles variety?—this recurrent interest of Orwell proves an exception to the rule. It is almost as though, with this sporadic emphasis, we could understand the entire present tense in which "As I Please" is conceived—the entire writing project—as commensurate with this specific transition. As he writes, equality fades. My last quotation gives an example of this:

> I see that the railings are returning—only wooden ones, it is true, but still railings—in one London square after another. So the lawful denizens of the squares can make use of their treasured keys again, and the children of the poor can be kept out. When the railings round the parks and squares were removed, the object was partly to accumulate scrap-iron, but the removal was also felt to be a democratic gesture. Many more green spaces were now open to the public, and you could stay in the parks till all hours instead of being hounded out at closing time by grim-faced keepers. It was also discovered that these railings were not only unnecessary but hideously ugly. The parks were improved out of recognition by being laid open, acquiring a friendly, almost rural look that they had never had before. And had the railings vanished permanently, another improvement would probably have followed. The dreary shrubberies of laurel and privet . . . would probably have been grubbed up and replaced by flower beds. Like the railings, they were merely put there to keep the populace out. However, the higher-ups managed to avert this reform, like so many others, and everywhere the wooden palisades are going up, regardless of the wastage of labour and timber. (36, 16.318)

Harnessing the particular temporality of the weekly column, Orwell doesn't claim that the railings *have* returned but rather how he "see[s] that the railings are returning."[6] This is an acutely particular, intermediate state: between the moment when common land has been freed up—rendered public—and sealed back off, into privacy. The mark of this intermediateness is the wooden material of the railings—material that, like these columns themselves, is not meant to be permanent. A boundary is being demarcated—the division between inside and outside is itself open *to* observation, ready to be noticed or "see[n]." In this way, the melancholy nature of this leitmotif—equality as it fades—is only half the picture. The *seeing of* this fading—impossible when the railings were gone or once they are back in their "iron" permanence; possible, though, as they go up in this temporary wooden state—is the other half of this picture. The capacity of "As I Please" to depict this intermediate state—to see the boundary—is linked, as I've suggested, to its own intermediate status: between freedom and constraint, critique and solidarity, immediacy and reflection, the expression of thinking and the expression of thought. As with these vulnerable but "friendly" commons, there is a happiness, here, within the unhappiness. A space within the enclosure. It is a good patch, at least, for the mind to browse upon.

Notes

Prologue: Reagan and Theory

1. Buck Mulligan offers Stephen Dedalus this rejoinder in James Joyce, *Ulysses* (New York: Vintage Books, 1986 [1922]) 5.

2. See Fred Block, Richard Cloward, Francis Fox Piven, and Barbara Ehrenreich, *The Mean Season: The Attack on the Welfare State* (New York: Pantheon, 1987).

3. Looking back ten years later on his 1984 book *The Painting of Modern Life*— a critical landmark of the 1980s—T. J. Clark registers this uncanny combination of energy and distress (and marks it as not fully recognizable at the time): "[T]he book comes out of too troubled a period in my life; the task it takes on seems in retrospect (and seemed too much of the time as I pursued it) impossibly difficult; and my writing strikes me now as struggling too hard to keep demons at bay— among them, those of Margaret Thatcher and Ronald Reagan" (xxx). "To keep . . . at bay:" an apt and suggestive phrase, different from either confronting or simply ignoring these political pressures.

4. For one recent attempt to frame the contiguity of 1980s theory and Reaganism (as chiefly parallel rather than causally related), see Daniel T. Rodgers, *Age of Fracture* (Cambridge: Harvard UP, 2011). For two recent and influential critiques of symptomatic reading and the hermeneutics of suspicion—less concerned with this particular political historical context—see Rita Felski, *The Uses of Literature* (Oxford: Wiley Blackwell, 2008); and Sharon Marcus and Stephen Best, "Surface Reading: An Introduction," *Representations* 108 (2009): 1–21.

5. For example: "'My opponent hates the "L" word,' the Republican nominee said. 'You know, the word that he used to utter proudly in the Democratic primary, talk about it all the time. Well, the "L" word and the "L" has failed; liberalism

has failed because it lost faith in the people" (Gerald M. Boyd, "Bush Presses Issue of Rival's Liberalism," *New York Times* 16 Oct. 1988).

6. See Butler's discussion of Stevens's "rebuke to Scalia for restricting the fighting words doctrine" (57), which hinges on reading Stevens's distinction between "lighting a fire near an ammunition dump" and "burning trash in a vacant lot" as a racially inflected comparison: "with the vacant lot, we enter the metaphor of poverty and property, which appears to effect the unstated transition to the matter of blackness introduced in the next line, 'threatening someone because of her race or religious beliefs', unlike Scalia, (58). Of course, the "transition" to such threatening behavior, which Stevens wants to legally condemn, is also motivated by the basic terms of the decision and this opposing dissent. Butler's argument depends, however, on reading the "vacant lot" (valorized by Stevens as the much less harmful form of activity) exclusively as a synonym first for poverty, then for race. Butler concludes: "And though Stevens is *on record as endorsing* a construction of 'fighting words' that would include cross-burning as unprotected speech, the language in which he articulates this view deflects the question to that of the state's right to circumscribe conduct to protect itself against a racially motivated riot" (59, emphasis added). But in the only sentence that Butler quotes from this dissent, Stevens has written "[t]hreatening someone because of her race or religious beliefs may cause particularly severe trauma or touch off a riot" (58). There is equal emphasis here to race and to religion, something elided in Butler's account. If these kinds of "fighting words" can "touch off a riot," they also can cause (first and foremost?) "particularly severe trauma" to the individual who is threatened; this is also elided in Butler's account. Most significantly, it is not at all clear that such a "menacing riot" (Butler's term, 56) wouldn't be directed at the same vulnerable persons (rather than the "state . . . itself"): we can think of pogroms, lynch mobs, etc. Butler insists, however, on channeling these terms—the vacant lot, "touch[ing] off a riot," "social disruptions"—in only one direction, as only facilitating a shift away from "the need for protection *from racist speech* to the need for protection from *public protest against racism*" (57, Butler's emphasis). This line is the rhetorical "transition" point in Butler's own discussion, as it moves from Scalia's explicit effort to redefine "fighting words" to Stevens's explicit "rebuke." The arc of the rhetorical reading can be long, but it bends toward injustice.

Introduction

1. I offered some examples of this at the end of the Prologue. As these examples already suggest, the relation needs to be defined as much by absence—by the lack of uptake, in the theoretical and critical formations of the 1980s, 1990s, and beyond—as presence. The editors of the 1998 essay compilation *New Casebooks: George Orwell* thus can easily identify, on the opening page, "a dearth of theoretically-informed published material" on Orwell, noting that "there has not

been as much theoretical criticism of his work as one might suppose" (see Holderness, Loughrey, and Yousaf 1). The scant theoretical engagement that Orwell's writing did receive in the 1980s—particularly in two influential books, Daphne Patai's *The Orwell Mystique: A Study in Male Ideology* and Christopher Norris's *Inside the Myth: Orwell: Views from the Left*—falls squarely into the symptomatic form of political criticism that I discuss in this introduction. Conversely, two of the most important, *non*-biographical studies of Orwell of the past twenty years—John Newsinger's *Orwell's Politics* and Stephen Ingle's *The Social and Political Thought of George Orwell*—are from an intellectual historian and political scientist, respectively. (They fall well outside of the kind of textual, literary, or formal analysis that I'm concerned with.) Likewise, some of the most important work on Orwell by a literary critic, John Rodden, in this period, is grounded specifically in the reception history and "afterlife" of Orwell's writing. (I take Rodden's accomplished body of work, in this vein, as both an exception to and a confirmation of the general problem, and will discuss it briefly later in the introduction.)

2. All quotations from George Orwell, except for his book-length novels, memoirs, and essay collections, or where otherwise noted, are from *The Complete Works of George Orwell,* Ed. Peter Davison, Vols. 11–20 (London: Secker and Warburg, 2002 [1998]). Whenever I discuss an article or essay by Orwell, full citation provided in Works Cited.

3. For a suggestive consideration of this dialectical process in contemporary criticism, see Amanda Anderson's discussion of "aggrandized agency" in *The Powers of Distance: Cosmopolitanism and the Cultivation of Detachment* (Princeton: Princeton UP, 2001). See also Sean McCann and Michael Szalay, "Do You Believe in Magic? Literary Thinking After the New Left," *Yale Journal of Criticism* 18.2 (2005): 435–468, which portrays a complicated range of influences and crosscurrents running between the New Left in the late 1960s and 1970s and the poststructuralist academic left in the late 1970s and 1980s. McCann and Szalay stigmatize "a range of theories that invoke the singular, the individual, and the inassimilable against the basic elements (norms, institutions, deliberation) of the public realm" (459).

4. See "Orwell's Statement on *Nineteen-Eighty Four*" in Davison 20.134–136.

5. See "WWGOD?" *Scenes from an Afterlife: The Legacy of George Orwell* (Wilmington: ISI, 2003) 158–169 and, with John P. Rossi, "If He Had Lived, or A Counterfactual Life of George Orwell," *Prose Studies* 32.1 (2010): 1–11. More generally, see John Rodden, *George Orwell: The Politics of Literary Reputation* (New Brunswick: Transaction Publishers 2002 [1989]).

6. Christopher Norris, as we've seen, writes: "Orwell's homespun empiricist outlook—his assumption that the truth was just there to be told in a straightforward, common-sense way—now seems not merely naïve but culpably self-deluding" (242). And again, "Basically Orwell subscribes to the straightforward

empiricist view that language in a normal, healthy condition simply hands over the raw stuff of experience" (254). I return to Norris's comment briefly in Part Two. In a 2014 review essay in *New Left Review* on Orwell, Francis Mulhern dismisses Orwell's "characteristically wrong-headed, simplistic excursions on behalf of 'plain' language" (141).

7. Likewise, in "Politics and the English Language," Orwell writes: "When you think of something abstract you are more inclined to use words from the start, and unless you make a conscious *effort* to prevent it, the existing dialect will come rushing in and do the job for you. . . . This *last effort* of the mind cuts out all stale or mixed images, all prefabricated phrases, needless repetitions, and humbug and vagueness generally" (17.429–430, emphases added). The fraught and temporally distended nature of these processes—of such "struggle" or "effort"—contrasts with the immediacy and directness of the plain style that both these passages advocate.

8. See W. K. Wimsatt and Charles Beardsley, "The Intentional Fallacy," in Wimsatt, *The Verbal Icon: Studies in the Meaning of Poetry* (Lexington: U of Kentucky P, 1982 [1954]) 3–20, and Fredric Jameson, *The Political Unconscious: Narrative as a Socially Symbolic Act* (London: Routledge, 1981).

9. In October 1944 (during the major run of "As I Please" in *Tribune,* a focus of this study), Orwell reviews T. S. Eliot's *Four Quartets* in *Manchester Evening News* and singles out lines from "East Coker" that resonate with *both* of these comments from "Why I Write" two years later: "So here I am . . . trying to learn to use words, and every attempt is a wholly new start, and *a different kind of failure* because one has only learnt to get the better of words for *the thing one no longer has to say,* or the way in which one is no longer disposed to say it" (16.421, emphases added). Orwell deliberately prints this excerpt from Eliot's verse as prose (strengthening another potential connection between this quotation and the concerns of "Why I Write").

10. These registers of projection and retrospect are, as I hope to show in this study, intertwined in many ways with the dynamics of Orwell's writing (even as this writing continually aspires toward the present-tense directness implied by the figure of window pane prose). But one of the most dramatic, biographical versions of this would be the double status of "Such, Such Were the Joys," at once reaching back—iconically and polemically—to the earliest formation of Orwell's intellectual and emotional identity (as a memoir of his childhood education) and delayed indefinitely (as an intentionally posthumous publication).

11. I return to this passage and discuss how Orwell carefully frames his own composition of *Homage to Catalonia* in similar terms (as *both* too distant from and too proximate with the events that it describes) in Chapter 4.

12. I've already discussed "quick" and "slow," "up" and "down," and "early" and "late" (and will return to each of these instances—as they are refracted through other works by Orwell—later on). "Back" and "front" are destabilized in a fascinating passage from *The Road to Wigan Pier* that I will consider in Chapters 2 and

4. "Near" and "far" are intertwined in a section of "As I Please" that I discuss in Chapter 6. "Empty" and "full" (or, more exactly, "crowded" and "bare") come into play in the central passage I consider from "A Hanging," in Chapter 1. "Inside" and "outside" are most emphatically destabilized, appropriately enough, in Orwell's essay (and essay collection, of the same title) "Inside the Whale," which I discuss in Chapter 3.

13. Elsewhere I've discussed the way a similar predicament, in a radically different context, drives a key passage in Orwell's essay "Rudyard Kipling." Highlighting Kipling's unusual proximity to military life, Orwell writes: "It is an error to imagine that we might have had better books on these subjects if, for example, George Moore, or Gissing, or Thomas Hardy, had had Kipling's opportunities. That is the kind of accident that cannot happen. . . . [N]o one with sufficient sensitiveness to write such books would ever have made the appropriate contacts" (13.156–157). See Alex Woloch, "Orwell and the Essay Form: Two Case Studies," *Republics of Letters* 4.1 (2014): 1–12.

14. We'll see, in the course of this book, that Orwell also unsettles the specific opposition between "covering" and "uncovering," arguing that language (and ultimately thought itself) needs to be understood as both a means of uncovering and covering. Engaged writing aims to uncover, or to reveal, hidden and obscured facts, but Orwell also claims, in "Politics and the English Language," that the aim of writing is to choose the "phrases that will best cover the meaning" (17.430) and to find "the fewest and shortest words that will cover your meaning" (17.429). To "cover," in these instances, is to adequately encompass and, finally, to bring forth the meaning that you wish to represent. In the same essay, however, "covering" also describes a linguistic obscuration of the world: "A mass of Latin words falls upon the facts like soft snow, blurring the outlines and *covering up* all the details" (17.428, emphasis added). Here such "covering" is equated with linguistic prolixity, which seems to fit the terms of the plain style. But in *The Road to Wigan Pier* the same term is used to stigmatize concise, rather than ornate, language. Orwell thus comments on the truncated notes he has transcribed directly from the journal he kept while in northern England: "Words are such feeble things. What is the use of a brief phrase like 'roof leaks' or 'four beds for eight people'? It is the kind of thing your eyes slides over, registering nothing. And yet what a wealth of misery it can *cover!*" (57, emphasis added). I discuss this passage further in Chapter 2.

15. This doubleness extends to the palpable mixture of confidence and insecurity that Orwell expresses in these letters about *Inside the Whale,* and, as I'll argue in Chapter 3, to a methodological ambiguity ("semi-sociological") that is at the core of this essay collection. In this introduction, however, I'm trying to keep the focus on Orwell's sense of writing as such.

16. Or, again, in his 1942 review-essay "T. S. Eliot:" "What are these three poems, *Burnt Norton* and the rest, 'about'?" (14.64). The quotation marks put an

uncertain, but crucial, measure of distance between Orwell and this category. (The review, perhaps appropriately, hinges not so much on the "deterioration in Mr Eliot's subject-matter" [14.63] that Orwell notices but rather in the reverberating, internal effects of what Orwell sees as Eliot's own loss of enthusiasm *in* this subject-matter.) For another instance of this emphasis, see Orwell's comment in "Lear, Tolstoy and the Fool": "*Lear* is one of the minority of Shakespeare's plays that are unmistakably *about* something" (19.60, Orwell's emphasis).

17. See "Charles Dickens" (12.47) and "War Time Diary" (18.229). Mark Wollaeger inaugurates his study on modernism and propaganda with Orwell's ambivalent comments. See Wollaeger, *Modernism, Media and Propaganda* (Princeton: Princeton UP, 2006) xi–xii and 4–6.

18. See, for example, Peter Marks, *George Orwell the Essayist: Literature, Politics and the Periodical Culture* (London: Continuum, 2011) 8. The key texts here are Theodor Adorno, "The Essay As Form," *Notes on Literature 1,* Ed. Rolf Tiedemann (New York: Columbia UP, 1991) 3–23, and Georg Lukács, "On the Nature and Form of the Essay," *Soul and Form,* Eds. John T Sanders and Katie Terezakis (New York: Columbia UP, 2010) 16–34.

19. See Anna Vaninskaya, "The Orwell Century and After: Rethinking Reception and Reputation," *Modern Intellectual History* 5.3 (2008): 597–617. Vaninskaya is sympathetic toward this movement but also raises important and interesting questions: does this method of study (or, perhaps more narrowly, this method of study when applied to Orwell) tend to harden a "distinction between originating subject and passive object" that is problematic? And, related to this, does reception study guarantee "a missing literary center" (616), reinforcing Orwell's strangely marginal position within academic literary criticism?

20. Francis Mulhern, writing from a quite different perspective in a recent review (of Robert Colls's *George Orwell: English Rebel*) in *New Left Review,* offers a similar point: "[W]hat he resists, as a matter of non-negotiable priority, is any attempt at classification, any critical gesture that would reach for conclusion, draw a line or indicate an order, and in so doing limit the play of 'the other hand.' Colls's Orwell cannot 'really' be any of the political or cultural beings he was or appeared to be" (137).

21. The programmatic nature of "The Lion and the Unicorn" is reinforced by its position as the inaugural text of the series—Searchlight Books—that Orwell organized with Tosco Fyvel. Each short book (or long pamphlet) in this series was meant to serve as an "amplification" (to use Orwell's term in "The Lion and the Unicorn") of a particularly concrete political question, one that would play a role in the wartime and postwar democratic socialist transformation that Orwell projects and advocates for in "The Lion and the Unicorn." As he writes in the opening line to his foreword to Joyce Cary's *The Case for African Freedom,* "The Searchlight Books aim at setting forth a coherent policy, and the earlier books in the series have most of them stated in black and white 'what one can do' about the particular

problem they were tackling" (12.521). The essay's own functional place in the series—as a text that Orwell writes to inaugurate this larger editorial project—reinforces its programmatic drive as well.

22. In the August 1945 "London Letter" we can find an echo of this passage, when Orwell writes, "A Labor government may be said to mean business if it (a) nationalizes land, coal mines, railways, public utilities and banks, (b) offers India immediate Dominion Status (this is a minimum), and (c) purges the bureaucracy, the army, the Diplomatic Service etc., so thoroughly as to forestall sabotage from the Right" (17.246). In "Catastrophic Gradualism" (1945), Orwell writes, "Social-ism used to be defined as 'common ownership of the means of production,' but it is now seen that if common ownership means no more than centralized control, it merely paves the way for a new form of oligarchy. Centralised control is a neces-sary pre-condition of Socialism, but it no more produces Socialism than my type-writer would of itself produce this article I am writing" (17.344). While this certainly puts pressure on his view on nationalization (the first item in both "The Lion and the Unicorn" and "London Letter"), Orwell is quite precise here: nation-alization is still necessary to Socialism, a "pre-condition," just not sufficient.

23. Wheatcroft of course says that Orwell has *transmuted* these Tory qualities, pressing them into the service of a radical politics. But by the mid-1940s, Orwell self-consciously understands himself in affiliation with the Labour Party, and, moreover, understands the electoral battle between Labour and the Tories as the definitive fault line in British politics. In "The Labour Government After Three Years" (1948), Orwell writes: "At present, although [the Labour Party] has ene-mies, it has no ideological rival. There is only the Conservative party, which is bankrupt of ideas and can only squeal about grievances which are essentially middle-class or upper-class, and the opposition on the Left, the Communists and 'cryptos' and the disgruntled Labor supporters who might follow them. . . . *One must remember that between them the Labor party and the Conservative party ade-quately represent the bulk of the population, and unless they disintegrate it is diffi-cult for any other mass party to arise.* . . . Electorally, it is only the Conservatives that the Labor party has to fear, and there is no sign that they are making much headway. . . . The mass of the manual workers are not likely ever again to vote for the Conservative party, which is identified in their minds with class privilege and, above all, with unemployment" (19.441, emphasis added).

24. See, for example, Daphne Patai, "Third Thoughts on Orwell?" *George Orwell: Into the Twenty-First Century,* Ed. Thomas Cushman and John Rodden (Boulder: Paradigm Publishers, 2004) 200–214.

25. There has been some ambiguity about the nature of this proposal in Orwell scholarship. Thus Bernard Crick writes: "Alas, if most of this is a pretty good syn-thesis of Labour Left-wing policy, yet the idea of a ten to one differential of *tax-free* income shows that his amateur economics did not match his amateur sociology—this would have been a far more stratified society than the one he lived in" (407).

But Orwell's discussion of this throughout "The Lion and the Unicorn" makes it clear that he is envisioning an absolute limit on income (so that "tax-free" refers simply to *some* portion of income, within the 10 to 1 ratio, that would be free of taxation while implying that incomes above the tenfold ratio would be prohibited altogether). Thus Orwell elaborates: "It is no use at this stage of the world's history to suggest that all human beings should have *exactly* equal incomes. It has been shown over and over again that without some kind of money reward there is no incentive to undertake certain jobs. On the other hand the money reward need not be very large. . . . [T]here is no reason why ten to one should not be the maximum normal variation. And within those limits some sense of equality is possible. A man with £3 a week and a man with £1500 a year can feel themselves fellow-creatures, which the Duke of Westminster and the sleepers on the Embankment benches cannot" (423–424, Orwell's emphasis). That Orwell is arguing for an absolute limit on income (rather than merely minimal taxation of higher incomes) is made clear at other points as well. We've seen that he refers explicitly to "limitation of incomes" (426) and he, analogously, discusses land-holding in the same absolute terms: "Nationalization of agricultural land implies cutting out the landlord and the tithe-drawer, but not necessarily interfering with the farmer. It is difficult to imagine any reorganization of English agriculture that would not retain most of the existing farms as units, at any rate at the beginning. . . . But the State will *certainly impose an upward limit* to the ownership of land (probably fifteen acres at the very most), and will never permit any ownership of land in town areas" (423, emphasis added).

26. See also Orwell's fantasy of repetition in his 1945 review of Herbert Read:

"If a thing is beautiful you do not diminish that beauty by reproducing it." I suppose that "Whether on Ida's shady brow" is beautiful. (If you don't care for that particular poem, substitute some other that you do care for.) Well, would you like to hear it read aloud five thousand times running? Would it still be beautiful at the end of such a process? On the contrary, it would seem the most hideous collection of words that has ever existed. Any shape, any sound, any colour, any smell becomes odious through too much repetition, because repetition fatigues the senses to which beauty must makes it appeal. (17.404)

Orwell then zooms in on the paradox of *remaining current,* or (permanently) affiliating with the young:

He is always on the side of the young against the old. . . . It is probably a mistake for any kind of artist, even a critic, to endeavor to "keep up" beyond a certain point. This does not mean that one has to accept the normal academic assumption that literature and art came to an end about forty years ago. . . . But one ought also to recognize that one's aesthetic judgment is only fully valid between fairly well-defined dates. Not to admit this is to throw away the advantage that one derives from being born into one's particular time. (17.404–405)

Here Orwell rejects repetition as well as its immediate antithesis—an easy, continual rapprochement with what is new. That willfully conjured nightmare of a beautiful phrase, through the force of repetition, turning into "the most hideous collection of words" is not easily avoided by what would seem to be a countervailing commitment to the new. The pervasiveness and consequences of repetition are more challenging than that.

27. Its thus no coincidence that Bernard Crick singles out this passage in his introduction to a new edition of "The Lion and the Unicorn," noting the particular "importance" of "the actual six-point programme he advocated. For all its vagueness, it was very much the kind of programme that the *Tribune* group and later the Bevanites espoused. There is no essential mystery about Orwell's politics after he left the I.L.P. in 1939 . . . he was a '*Tribune* socialist', and such he remained until his death" (Crick, "Introduction," 23–24). I obviously agree with Crick's biographical conclusion: I think it is possible, and productive, to argue for the coherence of Orwell's politics and, like Crick, I see this coherence as dramatically encapsulated in the passage. But I'm more interested than Crick in what we could take as the second-order significance of this encapsulation—in the (formal) drama of such a clarifying, yet isolated, gesture.

28. Does he repeat the *ideas* in "The Lion and the Unicorn"? In one sense, of course, yes: Orwell's 1941 essay, subtitled "Socialism and the English Genius," informs his political position more generally and is reiterated in numerous texts. But "The Lion and the Unicorn" is clearly Orwell's major statement about nationalism and patriotism, his most realized effort to reconcile these terms in relation to the left. And even this basic description of "The Lion and the Unicorn"—as a "major" statement—indicates a certain formal movement. It is typical of Orwell's compositional practice to emphatically foreground, in a particular text, topics or issues that have been moving dynamically under the surface in his writing. The key formal movement here is (simply) extension: the text accommodates, and indeed valorizes, a new question through its deliberate expansion into an entire textual structure. The force of the question motivates the length of the text (quite conspicuous, for example, in "The Lion and the Unicorn"). And the length of the text elevates and justifies the topic at hand. This two-way movement is often at work in Orwell's writing. We sense the topic arising, coming into the foreground, into ideational clarity and even validity, only in relation to the unfolding and actualization of the writing as extended text. In this way, as well, none of Orwell's other major writing on nationalism simply repeats the ideas of "The Lion and the Unicorn"; on the contrary, "Notes on Nationalism," for example, pushes in quite

different directions. Here, too, we can only speak of a dynamic, unfolding interaction between the various texts.

29. At the same time, and again unsurprisingly, both texts themselves constitute an act of positioning. Orwell's insistence on his socialism, in the Ukrainian preface, contrasts with his emphasis, in the unpublished preface to the British edition of *Animal Farm* (entitled "Freedom of the Press"), on forms of British censorship and self-censorship. Addressing a British left-wing audience, Orwell feels less inclined to emphasize his own socialism; addressing political refugees from the Soviet Union, Orwell makes sure to distinguish his critique of Stalin from the democratic socialism that he explicitly affiliates with. And the act of positioning, as I will discuss in the next section, is still more central to "Arthur Koestler." Orwell's unpublished British preface concentrates on different ways that free speech can be abridged or resisted: by direct government intervention (such as the "official censorship" during the war [17.254]); by "vested interests" (his examples are the *Catholic Herald* and the *Daily Worker* [256]); by economic elites (the daily British press, "most of it . . . owned by wealthy men who have every motive to be dishonest on certain important topics" [254]); and, what truly interests him, by unofficial orthodoxies that are voluntarily but not consciously accepted and internalized, and the resultant heterodoxies that are "not exactly forbidden"(255) but effectively shut out. "The sinister fact about literary censorship in England is that it is largely voluntary"(254). Orwell doesn't use the word "socialism" in this preface (unlike the Ukrainian preface, where he explicitly states that he is "pro-Socialist"), but he does signal his "political position" in various ways. Thus at one crucial point Orwell makes clear that what he otherwise identifies as a universal orthodoxy—"[a]ny serious criticism of the Soviet regime . . . is next door to unprintable" (255)—has a major exception: "Throughout that time, criticism of the Soviet regime *from the left* could only obtain a hearing with difficulty. There was a huge output of anti-Russian literature, but nearly all of it was from the Conservative angle and manifestly dishonest, out of date and actuated by sordid motives" (256, Orwell's emphasis). (Orwell's disdain for the right-wing critique of the Soviet Union is clear. He makes a similar distinction in his August 1945 "London Letter," arguing that the Labour Party is "involved, as the Tories are not, in the ideological struggle between the eastern and western conceptions of Socialism, and if they choose to stand up to Russia public opinion will support them, whereas Tory motives for opposing Russia were always justly suspect" [17.248]).

30. Already this *Wigan Pier* association is complicated. Part Two of *Wigan Pier* includes a major autobiographical "digress[ion]" that spends some of *its* time focusing on the composition of *Down and Out*. The association with *Homage to Catalonia* is just as obvious, but the references to Burma, snaking back even to "I was born in India in 1903" are also embedded in his 1930s texts—"A Hanging," "Shooting an Elephant," and Part Two of *Wigan Pier*.

31. This introduction has stressed a consideration of Orwell's politics in terms of desire, as much as ideology. Political ideology might be fueled by, but can never *fully* account for, political desire. For this sense of the excess of political desire, see also Orwell's discussion, in *The Road to Wigan Pier*, of how his hatred for imperialism built up in Burma: "All over India there are Englishmen who secretly loathe the system of which they are part; and just occasionally, when they are quite certain of being in the right company, their hidden bitterness overflows" (145). This passage conjoins contingency ("just occasionally") and excess (the bitterness that "overflows") and soon shifts to a more overt depiction of political intimacy: of politics *as* intimacy, and intimacy through politics. Orwell continues: "I remember a night I spent on the train with a man in the Educational Service, a stranger to myself whose name I never discovered. It was too hot to sleep and we spent the night in talking. Half an hour's cautious questioning decided each of us that the other was 'safe'; and then for hours, while the train jolted slowly through the pitch-black night . . . we damned the British Empire—damned it from the inside, intelligently and intimately. . . . [I]n the haggard morning light when the train crawled into Mandalay, we parted as guiltily as any adulterous couple" (145). As much as anywhere in Orwell's work, this passage makes the affective nature of political commitment explicit. This passage also anticipates the furtive, outlawed relationship of Winston and Julia in *1984*. Orwell's stress on this intimacy with someone who remains a stranger ("whose name I never discovered") also resembles the focus on his brief but "utter intimacy" (4) with the Italian militiaman at the opening of *Homage to Catalonia*. Here, too, such intimacy is built on contingency (we might even think of the oxymoronic description of how the train, in *Wigan Pier*, "jolted slowly"): "But I also knew that to retain my first impression of him I must not see him again; and needless to say I never did see him again. One was always making contacts of that kind in Spain" (4).

32. Or, again, in "Writers and Leviathan": "Until well within living memory the forces of the left in all countries were fighting against a tyranny which appeared to be invincible, and it was easy to assume that if only *that* particular tyranny—capitalism—could be overthrown, Socialism would follow" (19.289).

33. We might juxtapose this sense of protracted temporality—the time of democratic politics, as such—with Orwell's polemic in "Lear, Tolstoy, and the Fool" (19.54–66). In this essay, Orwell critiques Tolstoy's religiously driven (or religiously justified) desire to escape from the *distension* of history: "If only, Tolstoy says in effect, we would stop breeding, fighting, struggling and enjoying, if we could get rid not only of our sins but of everything else that binds us to the surface of the earth—including love, in the ordinary sense of caring more for one human being than another—then *the whole painful process would be over* and the Kingdom of Heaven would arrive" (63-64, emphasis added). Orwell explicitly connects this resistance to time with an ironically undemocratic will-to-power

that is implicit in any "creed [like pacifism or anarchism] which appears to be free from the ordinary dirtiness of politics" (66).

34. For a polemical critique of Orwell's anti-intellectualism, see Stefan Collini, "Other People: George Orwell," in *Absent Minds: Intellectuals in Britain* (Oxford: Oxford UP, 2006) 350–374.

35. On the 1920s modernists in "Inside the Whale": "And even the best writers of the time can be convicted of a too Olympian attitude, a too great readiness to wash their hands of the immediate practical problem. They see life very comprehensively, much more so than those who come immediately before or after them, but they see it through the wrong end of the telescope" (12.99). On the middle-class targets of his polemic in Part Two of *The Road to Wigan Pier*: they "are all for a classless society so long as they see the proletariat through the wrong end of the telescope; force them into any *real* contact with a proletarian—let them get into a fight with a drunken fish-porter on Saturday night, for instance—and they are capable of swinging back to the most ordinary middle-class snobbishness" (163, Orwell's emphasis). In "English Writing in Total War": "If one is looking through the wrong end of the telescope it is easy to see this war as simply a repetition or continuation of the last" (12.528). And from *Keep the Aspidistra Flying*: "He saw as something far, far away, like something seen through the wrong end of the telescope, his thirty years, his wasted life, the blank future, Julia's five pounds, Rosemary" (172).

36. Most emphatically: "Even if I had the power, I would not wish to interfere in Soviet domestic affairs. . . . It is quite possible that, even with the best intentions, they could not have acted otherwise under the conditions prevailing there. But on the other hand it was of the utmost importance to me that people in Western Europe should see the Soviet regime for what it really was. . . . Indeed, in my opinion, nothing has contributed so much to the corruption of the original idea of Socialism as the belief that Russia is a Socialist country" ("Preface to Ukrainian Edition of *Animal Farm*" 19.87) and, several years earlier, in a letter to Dwight Macdonald: "I think the fact that the Germans have failed to conquer Russia has given prestige to the idea of Socialism. For that reason I wouldn't want to see the USSR destroyed and think it ought to be defended if necessary. But I want people to become disillusioned about it and to realise that they must build their own Socialist movement without Russian interference, and I want the existence of democratic Socialism in the West to exert a regenerative influence upon Russia" (16.381). In "London Letter" from June 1945 Orwell writes, "I have always held that pro-Russian sentiment in England during the past ten years has been due much more to the need for an external paradise than to any real interest in the Soviet regime" (17.163).

37. Orwell discusses this kind of instability, for example, in "Notes on Nationalism" (where he casts it alongside "obsession" and "ignoring reality" as the three major maladies of nationalism [17.145–147]). He famously encapsulates this

process in the set piece in *1984* that describes the sudden shift between Eastasia and Eurasia as the enemy of Oceania.

38. For another emblematic instance of this, see the opening to "Notes on Nationalism," which, by way of a striking reference to Byron's ironic comment on the French term *longeur* (as Orwell paraphrases, "though in England we happen not to have the *word,* we have the *thing* in considerable profusion") puts immediate pressure on its own key term, "nationalism," as *not* exactly "equivalent" to what it seeks to represent (17.141).

39. I will discuss Orwell's recourse to imagine dust on windows later in the book, in Chapters 2 and, particularly, 4.

1. "Quite Bare"

1. In all these cases, the force or power of Orwell's prose is not a starting point but the end point of the analysis, the innate quality of the text that secures its political impact. On "A Hanging," for example, Ingle is very brief, writing: "The whole exercise, in short, provided a sordid example of the exploiter/exploited relationship that characterized imperialism and it is told with a force and an economy of style that arouses our sympathy but, more importantly, helps us experience at first hand, as it were, the real nature of the imperial relationship" (36). "Force," linked here with "economy of style," generates various effects: arousing sympathy, exposing the "real nature" of society, immersing the reader in the events of the text ("at first hand, as it were"). But, again, Ingle avoids offering a specific description of this "force," or further scrutiny of what it might mean to write a text "with . . . force." The question is important because the distinctive quality, and political impact, of Orwell's work rests, in all of these assertions by Ingle, in the "force" or "power" of the writing.

2. This paradoxical sense that the spare lucidity of the plain style might also leave it *in*accessible, sealed off from any extrapolation or amplification, is anticipated in a piece that Orwell writes for *Adelphi,* in May 1930, a review of Lewis Mumford's critical biography *Herman Melville* (10.182–184). This is, in fact, the first text that Orwell publishes in English, and the first of several reviews that precede his earliest *literary* works, "The Spike" and "A Hanging." Orwell's writing begins in this doubly-mediated form: with a review, rather than an experientially grounded text like "A Hanging" or "The Spike," and a review *of* Mumford's own critical study of Melville. In this sense, simply as a "third-order" composition, (writing about Mumford's writing about Melville's writing), this initial text would stand as a rebuke to the plain style. At the core of this review, however, Orwell inscribes a challenge to such critical rearticulation, one that resonates with both the stylistic dynamics and the topical concerns of "A Hanging." Within his generally admiring discussion, Orwell reserves one major criticism of Mumford:

Mr Mumford does not allow this background of poverty to be forgotten; but his declared aim is to expound, criticize, and—unpleasant but necessary word—interpret.

It is just this aim which is responsible for the only large fault of the book. The criticism which sets out to interpret—to be at the deepest meaning and cause of every act—is very well when applied to a man, but it is a dangerous method of approaching a work of art. Done with absolute thoroughness, it would cause art itself to vanish. . . . It follows that Mr. Mumford is least happy when he is dealing with *Moby Dick*. He is justly appreciative and nobly enthusiastic, but he has altogether too keen an eye for the inner meaning. . . . It were much better to have discoursed simply on the form, which is the stuff of poetry, and left the "meaning" alone. (10.182-183)

The crucial turn here is Orwell's oddly Hegelian intensification, in "absolute thoroughness" and "art itself." These terms make the comment both reflective and antireflective. Orwell imagines art ("itself") not only as something immediate or self-evident but also something fragile and endangered, at risk of "vanish[ing]." This sense of a categorical, and thus "absolute," "vanish[ing]" reemerges, as I'll suggest, in "A Hanging." At the same time this subsequent text—particularly in the opening paragraph—exemplifies that transparent but paradoxically sealed, anti-interpretive language that Orwell gestures at in the Mumford review.

3. The term *bare* would thus be the first in a chain of subsequent redescriptions that would run through Ingle's words about these words in *The Social and Political Thought of George Orwell*. In the Introduction I have called this tendency (a crucial, but unstable tendency within Orwell's work) second-order meaning, and it is striking that the first strong example of this in his writing is so closely tied in *with* the plain style.

4. This is quite a paradox: "bare" becomes reflective only insofar as it is an accurate description of the opening style; but insofar as the text *is* reflective, in this way, it has ceased to be so bare.

5. The severity of the opening description in "A Hanging"—its own quality of bareness—is fundamentally unstable. On the one hand, these terms are so stark because the text aims to directly, efficiently, or adequately bear witness to the scene of these prison cells. On the other hand, such starkness emerges as a disturbing echo of, rather than a means of analytically comprehending, urgency and deprivation. The language itself is stunted and corroded. This effect, quite important to the opening of "A Hanging," crystallizes a tension that occurs often in realist aesthetics. The *stylistic* "grittiness" of so much realist description can be strangely intertwined with the deprivations that the realist text wants to abjure or contest. Thus, for example, a hyperrealist film like *La Promesse,* by Jean-Pierre Dardenne and Luc Dardenne, uses a series of formal strategies, including cramped framing, handheld cameras, natural lighting, and extreme close-ups, which bring

the viewer close to the scenes of poverty that they convey *and* often work to disorient the viewer, blocking our comprehension. In both the opening to "A Hanging" and the austere technique of a film like *La Promesse,* the realist medium sets itself over and against the referenced world (in its sheer power of comprehension) and catches the blight of this world; the *same* "bare" devices striving at once for a lucidity (which would allow deprivation to be registered) and exhibiting a hollowness that seems forged out of such deprivation itself.

6. This "reveal" of the first-person narrator is only partial, since the narrative voice remains, noticeably, in the first-person plural for eight paragraphs, before gradually shifting into first-person singular (with the possessive "my" and then, in the following paragraph, the "I" finally emergent). I'm emphasizing the partial elision of the first-person narrator less than the partial elision of the prisoners (as objects of narrative), but these two processes are linked. We might juxtapose this emergence of the narrative "I," initially *obscured* in the plain-style opening, with Orwell's admonition in "Why I Write" (in the sentence preceding his figure of window pane prose): "And yet it is also true that one can write nothing readable unless one constantly struggles to efface one's own personality." Here such "efface[ment]" is valorized. At the start of "A Hanging," however, this "efface[ment]" of the narrator's personality, or personhood—so clearly linked *to* the "bare" opening—is the *problem* and not just the solution.

7. As we'll see in other examples in this book, Orwell often links shock to the confrontation with absence, or the absence of an object. The "shock of surprise" over the missing beds in *Down and Out* is a crucial scene for my understanding of Orwell and something I will return to when discussing "As I Please" in Part Two.

8. This is a notoriously difficult question to answer. Bernard Crick is one of many biographers to question whether Orwell actually witnessed an execution of this sort. He concludes that "A Hanging," like a number of Orwell's other works, is "a compound of fact and fiction, honest in intent, true to experience, but not necessarily truthful in detail" (318). These details could include not just embellishments of what Orwell saw but whether he saw any such execution directly. The complexity or "compound" nature of the work militates, however, against the tonal qualities that critics have repeatedly singled out in this text, and indeed in Orwell's writing more generally: vividness, lucidity, precision, succinctness, and, above all, "forcefulness" or "power." It is also important to note how the biographical uncertainty of this—whether Orwell, while serving as an MP in Burma, took part in such an execution—is mirrored by the text's own (more immanent) stylistic instability. The sheer formal deliberateness of the text, in other words, strains against its asserted veracity. I tend to agree, above all, with Peter Marks's observations here about the carefully wrought depiction of the dog. Marks remarks, "Understanding the dog's profoundly symbolic significance challenges readings of 'A Hanging' founded simply on its being an autobiographical account" (30) and, again, "the *crafted* symbolism of the dog calls the purely autobiographical

reading into question" (31, emphasis added). Marks does not elaborate on this, but one important sign of such craft is the precisely timed emergence of the first-person narrative voice around the arrival and restraining of the dog. The narrative bridges the transition from first-person plural ("[w]e were waiting outside" [207]) to first-person singular ("I watched the bare brown back of the prisoner marching in front of me" [208]) with this strangely passive first-person possessive: "[. . .] someone managed to catch the dog. Then *we put my handkerchief* through its collar and moved off once more, with the dog still straining and whimpering" (208, emphasis added). This "my" is the first grammatical inflection of a first-person singular in the text. It is another sign of the carefully sequenced and only *gradual* emergence of the narrating "I" in "A Hanging." In this first instance, the "my" is still, strangely and unsettlingly, coordinated by that lingering first-person plural ("*we* put"). On top of the "crafted symbolism" of the dog, the formal coincidence here—the calibrated emergence of the first-person singular *at* this particular juncture, during this scene—also "calls the purely autobiographical reading into question."

9. By confusion of subject and object, I mean a blurring of what is momentarily absented in the opening paragraph: whether the prisoners themselves (as an object of representation, in the world) or their point of view (and thus the way each of them makes a representation of the world).

10. And because of this, ironically, there is a sense in which the *temporary* form of disappearance is "permanent"—etched stably into our subjective comprehension—while the *permanent* form of disappearance is only "temporary," impossible to durably understand or keep in mind.

11. I've noted the strangely passive way in which the narrator signals that he has first leashed the dog: "Then we put my handkerchief through its collar and moved off once more"(208). This "my," which is the text's first hint of a first-person singular, is still coordinated by a collective "we." The narrator himself is subtly dissociated from the restraining action. It is only *after* the execution, when the narrator writes, "I let go of the dog"(209) that we realize he alone has been holding the dog this entire time. This action of restraint, in part because of the way it is belatedly inferred but never directly stated, ties the narrator more closely into the violent proceedings.

12. As Robert Colls writes, "Blair was part of a civil force of 13,000 police officers supported by 10,000 soldiers responsible for thirty-six districts and 13 million people . . . an entire global project [was] bearing down on his shoulders" (21). And: "Orwell and his constables . . . held the front line in a gradually deteriorating situation which included over 700 judicial hangings over the period of his stay" (23).

13. *Wigan Pier* has recourse to confusing "back" and "front" more literally, in its striking discussion of "back-to-back" houses, which I will discuss in Chapter Four.

14. See also "Shame as Form," Timothy Bewes's stirring discussion of writing and imperialism in *The Event of Postcolonial Shame* (Princeton: Princeton UP, 2010) 11–48.

Interlude: Between Texts

1. Like "dwelling" (which can also be a verb or a noun), "hanging" is not just a participle but a word that points to the ongoing temporality *of* the participle mode. Orwell's title plays on this fact. "Depend" (like "suspend") derives from the root form *pendere*, "to hang." An enigmatic suspension is provoked by the title "A Hanging" (with its indefinite article and the conspicuously verbal noun), even as this brief title *also* emblematizes a topical plainspokenness at odds with such suspension.

2. For Orwell's discussion of *Down and Out*, see Chapter 9 in *The Road to Wigan Pier*, particularly pp. 148–153. *Down and Out* is, of course, Orwell's first *book*, just as "A Hanging" and "The Spike" are his first published texts. It is with this book that Orwell takes his pseudonym. He emerges into an identity (but a disguised identity) by means of plainly recording an experience (but an experience of anonymity). *Down and Out* intertwines self-assertion, in the generative act of writing itself, and self-effacement, in that submersion into temporary poverty. It is not quite memoir, not quite novel. In all these ways, it helps to establish both the intimacy and the tension between writing and experience that is so important to Orwell's work.

3. As we've seen, for example, in both the Preface to the Ukrainian edition of *Animal Farm* and "Why I Write," Orwell highlights the pivotal role of Spain in his self-conception as a writer. In 1942, Orwell writes an essay titled, paradigmatically, "Looking Back on the Spanish War" (13.497–511). That we might not always be able to distinguish, in these retrospective pieces, between his primary experience in Spain and his initial representation of this experience, in *Homage to Catalonia*, is part of the complexity that I'm trying to foreground. In this sense, the 1942 essay "look[s] back," in part, on the way Orwell first "look[ed] back on" the Spanish Civil War.

4. At the end of Part Two, I'll consider several further examples of such autobiographical returns in "As I Please" (each of which is also intertwined with earlier acts of writing). These are much smaller, almost micro-autobiographical, units. "Such, Such Were the Joys," Orwell's posthumously published memoir of his childhood education, is another key text for this "coiled" effect, as the release of this text takes place after all of Orwell's other work has been published, while the content goes back to some of his earliest experience.

5. It is thus a pattern in many studies of Orwell to divide chapters in the break between Orwell's trip to northern England and trip to Spain—at once a

chronological *and* a compositional division. See, for example, Crick, Chapters 9 and 10 ("The crucial journey to Wigan Pier and home to Wallington"/"Spain and 'necessary murder'"); Newsinger, Chapters 2 and 3 ("Down Among the Oppressed"/"Spilling the Spanish Beans"); Colls, Chapters 2 and 3 ("North Road"/"Eye Witness in Barcelona 1937"); and Bowker, Chapters 10 and 11 ("Journeys of Discovery"/"The Spanish Betrayal"). This is overdetermined. The division is motivated by the two separate books (registering their integrity, their ballast *as* books, as discrete acts of writing) and by the two phases of life (that have significance and legibility apart from the texts that are produced during, and reflect on, these periods). The two memoirs thus represent this break (when we see it in terms of action, experience and event) and *constitute* this break (when we see it in terms of texts, writing, bibliography).

6. We can see this, for example, in the various temporal marks that Orwell places in the opening lines of many chapters: "When I had been three weeks in the line a contingent of twenty or thirty men . . . arrived at Alcubierre" (38, Chapter 4); "On the eastern side of Huesca, until late March, nothing happened—almost literally nothing (46, Chapter 5); "The days grew hotter and even the nights grew tolerably warm" (101, Chapter 8); "About midday on 3 May a friend crossing the lounge of the hotel said casually: 'There's been some kind of trouble at the Telephone Exchange, I hear'"(121, Chapter 10); "It must have been three days after the Barcelona fighting ended that we returned to the front"(180, Chapter 12). These examples (which are not uniform but each of which carefully places the chapter in an unfolding arc of time) all stand in contrast to the atemporal opening of Chapter 9 that I discuss in this section.

7. Orwell's epigram also manifests this dissonance in a more obviously *tonal* sense, as it shifts, jarringly, from a whimsical, literary register ("disposal of the body" marks the generic conventions of the murder mystery) to the actuality of suicide. For Orwell's interest in crime fiction, as genre, see "Decline of the English Murder" (18.108–110) and "Raffles and Miss Blandish" (16.346–358).

8. In one entry Orwell simply writes, "Anything is untrue when said by a parrot" (19.500). There are two ways to take this aphorism, which speak to the divide between first- and second-order writing. In the colloquial sense, of course, a parrot says things that aren't "true" because they are derivative and repetitive. The parrot thus provides a metaphor with which to judge and distinguish the *relative* truth-value of real statements in the world. (Sometimes people, like parrots, only imitate language or ideology promulgated by another.) In another sense, however, we confront a starker divide, whenever a parrot "speaks," between the semantic meaning we invest in any language (whether true *or* false) and the semantically-void, phonetic and material substrate of this language. There is an "untruth" hidden in even the most accurate or sincere statement (because of that inner, purely material dimension of the language). In the first sense of his epigram, Orwell naturalizes language by distinguishing between truthful and hollow

(parrot-like) propositions. In the second sense, Orwell denaturalizes language, by pointing to a material (parrot-like) dimension intrinsic to *all* speech. In another montage effect, the rest of this page in Orwell's notebook contains only a catalogue list of "Nationalist leaders & nationalist romantics of non-foreign origin," juxtaposed against the much longer list, on the preceding page, of nationalists "of foreign origin" (19.499-500). Orwell's interest in a foreignness, and alienation, lodged at the center *of* twentieth-century nationalisms—a topic repeated, as we'll later see, in AIP 31—resonates suggestively with this epigram about the parrot. Each of the two entries encompasses a critique of authenticity, either linguistic or political.

9. Perhaps the most significant set piece in *The Road to Wigan Pier* enacts this same phenomenological movement, when Orwell, at the end of Chapter 1, dramatizes the shift from focusing on the oppressive conditions that another person experiences to focusing on the other person's own perspective about these conditions:

> The train bore me away. . . . As we moved slowly through the outskirts of the town we passed row after row of little grey slum houses running at right angles to the embankment. At the back of one of the houses a young woman was kneeling on the stones, poking a stick up the leaden waste-pipe which ran from the sink inside and which I suppose was blocked. I had time to see everything about her—her sacking apron, her clumsy clogs, her arms reddened by the cold. She looked up as the train passed, and I was almost near enough to catch her eye. She had a round pale face, the usual exhausted face of the slum girl who is twenty-five and looks forty, thanks to miscarriages and drudgery; and it wore, for the second in which I saw it, the most desolate, hopeless expression I have ever seen. It struck me then that we are mistaken when we say that "It isn't the same for them as it would be for us," and that people bred in the slums can imagine nothing but the slums. For what I saw in her face was not the ignorant suffering of an animal. She knew well enough what was happening to her—understood as well as I did how dreadful a destiny it was to be kneeling there in the bitter cold, on the slimy stones of a slum backyard, poking a stick up a foul drain-pipe.
> But quite soon the train drew away into open country. . . . (18)

This passage is structured around an inversion, from seeing another person to "seeing" ("what I *saw* in her face") what that person herself sees or knows ("[s]he knew well enough what was happening to her"). Orwell is deliberately confusing about time and space here. The train "moved slowly," but "quite soon the train drew away." Orwell "had time to see everything about her," but the crucial expression is only manifest "for the second in which [he] saw it." This expression occurs "as the train passed," and Orwell is "almost near enough" (and thus technically *not* near enough) "to catch her eye." Does this mean he narrowly *doesn't* "catch her eye"? Does an encounter take place or not? And does this phrase ("to catch her eye") mean to see the woman looking—and thus to "catch," or capture, her own point of view—or to be seen *by* her as she looks? (And, if the latter, is this then only for a "second," and not quite "near enough," because her look would, of course, *change* as she, in turn, sees Orwell, looking at her?) These tensions and displacements all occur around the inversion that structures the description, in the unstable movement from the writer's governing perspective to the young woman's perspective—on herself and the world.

10. For another suggestive reading of the stakes and complexity of this metaphor in Orwell, see Michael Clune's recent essay on Orwell, "Big Brother Stops Time" in *Writing Against Time* (Stanford: Stanford UP, 2013) 87–114, in particular 99–101. Clune's reading is an unusual, literary-theoretical account of Orwell (unusual, that is, both within Orwell studies, which rarely embraces the philosophical and conceptual vocabulary or perspectives that Clune is committed to, and within theoretical work, that so rarely touches on, let alone lingers on, Orwell's writing).

11. To focus on the means *as* an end: this is no easy or simple process. We sense the reverberating strangeness here, how the act of taking aim becomes the focus—i.e., the aim—of Orwell's own descriptions. In passage #13, in another turn of this same irony, the gun, itself, becomes "[t]he thing I was after" (rather than the thing he would point *at* the thing he is after) and, in its absence, the source of "bitter disappointment."

12. This double condition obviously connects to the two-pinned grenade that I discussed in the Introduction, which can either go off too late, missing its target, or too early, causing once more a self-inflicted wound. I will return to this in Chapter 4.

13. Likewise, the ostensible error in passage #9—that the Fascists, "tiny as ants," and with heads that look like dots, are impossible to hit "at that range and with these rifles"—is shadowed by the converse possibility: that when the "dot disappeared," Orwell actually *had* hit a "human being," grotesquely misperceived as an "ant" or a "dot." This potential reversal is further amplified by the sweeping inversion that emerges much later in the text, when Orwell focuses, at last, on his own wounding in the throat by an enemy sniper. (Orwell's remarkable description of his injury, in turn, is driven by another inversion, when he memorably confuses inside and outside: "The whole experience of being hit by a bullet is very interesting and I think it is worth describing in detail . . . Roughly speaking it was the sensation of being *at the centre* of an explosion"[185], Orwell's emphasis. Rather than the bullet that explodes within him, the gunshot feels as though *he* is inside—"at the centre"—of an explosion).

2. "Getting to Work"

1. This is a book that has famously divided readers and elicited colliding responses and reactions. Yet there is no disagreement about the text's own conspicuous structure, hinging itself on a division. Whatever readers might have to say about *Wigan Pier,* the two-part form rests at the center of its reception. That this division takes place near the *literal* center of the book is merely a reinforcement of this structural quality. There are thirteen chapters in *Wigan Pier*—seven before the split, six after. The Left Book Club edition allots 118 pages to Part One and 111 to Part Two. These exact numbers are incidental. Any reader will remember not just the two parts but a roughly proportionate, symmetrical pairing—not just two parts, in other words, but two halves. The rough equality between Parts One and Two ratchets up their intimacy with one another and amplifies the import of the division (by situating it so near the textual center).

2. In his influential interpretation of Orwell, Richard Rorty, in *Contingency, Irony and Solidarity,* makes a claim for Orwell's centrality to modern culture and politics while also drawing a line of demarcation between Orwell and a skeptical tradition of "ironist theorizing" (101), including Hegel, Nietzsche, Heidegger, and Derrida, which grounds the postmodern critique of an authoritative language system. For Rorty, this division between different intellectual traditions speaks to a wider, and inevitable, bifurcation within liberal culture. As Rorty puts it, we need to "give up . . . [on] the attempt to unite one's private ways of dealing with one's finitude and one's sense of obligation to other human beings" (63–64). While Rorty's analysis is driven (from the title on) by the rigorous separation of irony and solidarity, I will attempt to show how we must consider irony as implicated in—perhaps necessary to—Orwell's solidarity.

3. Orwell never discusses the two-part division of *Wigan Pier* in his extant correspondence. We don't know how or when he conceptualizes this structure. This biographical detail is significant because it is one of a number of ways in which Orwell leaves the division in *Wigan Pier* more *glaring.* (We'll find a similar reluctance—to explain or motivate their formal breaks—with *Inside the Whale* and "As I Please.") Likewise, there is no paratextual frame for *Wigan Pier,* nor any hint of Part Two within Part One. We could contrast this with other 1930s texts that have a divided structure. For example, Stephen Spender's *Forward from Liberalism* (another Left Book Club selection from 1937) and Cyril Connolly's *Enemies of Promise* (1938) each contains an introduction that discusses the text's ensuing parts and divisions. (In Connolly's case this is added to the second edition, in 1948.) In one sense, Connolly and Spender thus show themselves to be more at home with such formal experiment—ready to avow, and to reflect upon, it. But at the same time, these introductions work to motivate, and thus *soften,* the event of form. *Wigan Pier* begins differently: there is no suggestion of the division that will later occur. By the end, as we've seen, this division looms large; it is, indeed, the

controlling feature of the book. The eschewal of such paratextual devices in a divided work has some specific implications. It makes the structure more enigmatic, for example—not simply through the lack of positive explanation but also as it provokes the reader to begin absorbing, and thus seeking to understand, the split only as it occurs, dramatically, in "the middle of the journey." We scramble to explain, once we have discovered, this formal rupture—rather than the other way around (as with a preface in which explanation would precede and shape such formal discovery). This enigma—the sense of a kind of thinking that is provoked *by* but not contained (or even fully acknowledged) *within* the text—resonates, of course, with the text's problematic turn toward self-reflection at its hinge.

4. See, for example, Valentine Cunningham's influential *British Writers of the Thirties,* with its wonderful compendium of different thematic and cultural clusters. A whole series of these at the core of the book—"Going Over," "Notes from the Underground," "Movements of Masses," "Mass Observations," "Seedy Margins" (211–376)—encapsulate different manifestations of the cross-class movement, real or imagined, that is so important to 1930s British literary culture.

5. I consider a similar emphasis on the perils of thinking *as such* in Orwell's ambivalent discussion of H. G. Wells and what he tellingly calls "a lifelong habit of thought" (538) associated with Wells's perhaps "too sane" (540) rationalism. See Woloch, "Orwell and the Essay Form: Two Case Studies."

6. And not just reckless or lazy thought; this is a key. In one crucial passage, Orwell resurrects "an interesting passage" from Lissagaray's *History of the Commune* as a way of discussing how entrenched bourgeois privilege can be:

> Even when I am on the verge of starvation I have certain rights attaching to my bourgeois status. . . . A thousand influences constantly press a working man down into a *passive* rôle. . . . A person of bourgeois origin goes through life with some expectations of getting what he wants, within reasonable limits. Hence the fact that in times of stress "educated" people tend to come to the front; they are no more gifted than the others, and their "education" is generally quite useless in itself, but they are accustomed to a certain amount of deference and consequently have the cheek necessary to a commander. That they *will* come to the front seems to be taken for granted, always and everywhere. In Lissagaray's *History of the Commune* there is an interesting passage describing the shootings that took place after the Commune had been suppressed. The authorities were shooting the ringleaders, and as they did not know who the ringleaders were, they were picking them out on the principle that those of better class would be the ringleaders. An officer walked down a line of prisoners, picking out likely-looking types. One man was shot because he was wearing a watch, another because he 'had an intelligent face.' I should not like to be shot for having an intelligent face, but I

do agree that in almost any revolt the leaders would tend to be people who could pronounce their aitches. (49–50)

This is a remarkable and a shocking passage, not least for the sheer intelligence with which Orwell extracts this telling, but quite subordinated detail, from Lissagaray's actual account. Orwell's brooding concern that "intelligence" itself would have a face—and that these social differences would emerge in such a charged moment, in the violent suppression of a truly revolutionary struggle for equality—is an emblem of my more general argument, about Orwell's persistent efforts to "externalize" the conceptual, reflective activity of writing. We can think here, instantly, as well, of the "pale face" of the young woman that Orwell sees at the end of Chapter 1 in *Wigan Pier* (18); his disquisition on "innumerable remembered faces" in Burma (147); the famous, ironic line, in the same section, "unfortunately I had not trained myself to be indifferent to the expression of the human face" (147); or the end of "Charles Dickens": "When one reads any strongly individual piece of writing, one has the impression of seeing a face somewhere behind the page" (12.55).

7. These are two of the passages I have in mind:

In order to symbolize the class war, there has been set up the more or less mythical figure of a "proletarian," a muscular but downtrodden man in greasy overalls, in contradistinction to a "capitalist," a fat, wicked man in a top hat and fur coat. It is tacitly assumed that there is no one in between; the truth being, of course, that in a country like England about a quarter of the population is in between. (226)

Literary London now teems with young men who are of proletarian origin and have been educated by means of scholarships. Many of them are very disagreeable people, quite unrepresentative of their class, and it is most unfortunate that when a person of bourgeois origin does succeed in meeting a proletarian face to face on equal terms, this is the type of person he most commonly meets. For the result is to drive the bourgeois, who has idealized the proletariat so long as he knew nothing about them, back into frenzies of snobbishness. . . . It is of course true that plenty of people of working-class *origin* are Socialists of the theoretical bookish type. But they are never people who have *remained* working men; they don't work with their hands, that is. (164, 177)

Orwell's polemics about literary London are remarkably bitter and harsh—on one register, indefensible—but I think it is important to hold onto the core structural point that emerges through them, which I see as this double resistance to neutralizing, or cleansing, writing (and above all writing's encounter with class) through either a legitimating *object* of representation (that "mythical figure") or a purified subject of representation (the writer who would also remain authentically or absolutely proletarian). It is limiting to read the irony in *Wigan Pier* as merely stigmatizing middle-class perception (or only Orwell's "lower-upper-middle class" perception [121]), both because of Orwell's distrust of authenticity and also because this irony, as I've tried to demonstrate, has distinct epistemological value. On the second page, Orwell already offers a subtle, and *structurally* grounded, critique of a purely "inside" perspective (and we can note here, as well, another, quite different, representation of the windowpane). Describing the cramped conditions of the Brookers' rundown lodging house, Orwell writes: "All the windows were kept tight shut, with a red sandbag jammed in the bottom, and in the morning the room stank like a ferret's cage. You did not notice it when you got up, but if you went out of the room and came back, the smell hit you in the face with a smack" (6). This passage suggests how a longer immersion in poor conditions can ironically block perception, once again troubling any simple equation of experience and knowledge. Likewise, the brilliantly ironic response that Orwell records from an anonymous miner (subject *to* an outside writer's questions): "Talking once with a miner I asked him when the housing shortage first became acute in his district; he answered, 'When we were told about it,' meaning that till recently people's standards were so low that they took almost any degree of overcrowding for granted" (64).

3. "Semi-Sociological"

1. Peter Marks, in his recent study of Orwell's essayistic writing, says merely, "All three essays deal with literature in the broad sense" (88). Marks's book, which chronologically traces Orwell's essayistic writing from the early *Adelphi* texts to the end of his life, is a powerful demonstration of the contingency of Orwell's work. Above all, Marks foregrounds this contingency by trying to recover the initial contexts of publication of various essays, in order to register the dynamic, always temporally embedded, movement of Orwell's essayistic production across a range of generic and political contexts. *Inside the Whale* is unusual, in this respect, since a heightened attention to the original publication of these three pieces doesn't only bring out their temporal contingency (as Marks does to fine effect with many of Orwell's essays) but also, paradoxically, their enigmatic collocation within a larger, and presumably more durable, textual structure. As Orwell writes in his own review of a book of essays (by Herbert Read), "the multiplicity of subjects is in itself a point to be noticed" (17.402). For further analysis of Orwell's essays in this vein, see my discussion of two 1940 pieces—"Rudyard Kipling" and "Hitler, Wells and the World State"—in Woloch, "Orwell and the Essay Form: Two Case Studies."

2. All quotations from "Charles Dickens," "Boys' Weeklies," and "Inside the Whale" taken from the first edition of *Inside the Whale* (London: Victor Gollancz, 1940) rather than Davison.

3. In one of the few overt repetitions in this book, Orwell twice comments on the difficulty inherent to his critical project, nearly repeating the same line:

> Actually, nearly everyone who read it saw at once that it was nothing of the kind, but a very remarkable book. How or why remarkable? *That question is never easy to answer.* It is better to begin by describing the impression that *Tropic of Cancer* has left on my own mind. (133–134, emphasis added)

> By this time anyone who is a lover of Dickens, and who has read as far as this, will probably be angry with me.
>
> I have been discussing Dickens simply in terms of his "message," and almost ignoring his literary qualities. But every writer, especially every novelist, *has* a message, whether he admits it or not, and the minutest details of his work are influenced by it. All art is propaganda. . . . On the other hand, not all propaganda is art. As I said earlier, Dickens is one of those writers who are felt to be worth stealing. . . . The question is, What is there to steal? Why does anyone care about Dickens? Why do *I* care about Dickens? That kind of question is never easy to answer. (66)

What a simple phrase with which to express difficulty! Indeed, the sentence suggests, once again, the way in which we need to engage the often *invisible difficulty* of Orwell. And the repetition of this comment bridges two distinct kinds of difficulty. In both essays, the comment focuses on the problematic relationship of aesthetics and history. In this sense, we are confronting the chief "difficulty" of the book as a whole, and (as Orwell continually suggests) the chief difficulty for literary criticism at the time of its writing—as Peter Marks puts it, "the fraught and immensely complex interactions between literature and politics" (131). How do we understand the relationship between the "inside" and the "outside" of literature: between the freedom of aesthetic form (when a literary text is viewed from the "inside") and the constraints of ideology, politics, and history (when that same text gets contextualized in relation to the things outside itself)? Simultaneously, of course, the *repetition* of this comment points to the challenge of putting these three essays in relation to one another.

4. See Crick: "plain speaking always meant to him clear writing . . . even if plain style sometimes limited the kind of literature he could enjoy as well as the development of his own more theoretical ideas" (xiv).

5. For example: "Serious essays on popular culture are common today, but 'Boys' Weeklies' was the first important essay of its kind written in England" (Shelden 45–46); "in an essay on 'Boys' Weeklies' (included in *Inside the Whale*),

Orwell had opened up the realm of 'popular culture' to serious scrutiny" (Lucas 70); "[h]is essay on 'Boys' Weeklies' studied the politics of popular culture, a pioneering essay" (Crick 260).

6. This is also evident in Orwell's decision to use this essay, of all possible choices, in the March 1940 *Horizon*, when his friend Cyril Connolly solicited a contribution. Orwell's first piece of writing for *Horizon* thus immediately strains against the limits of this journal, subtitled "A Review of Literature and Art."

7. As Michael Shelden writes in his study of Connolly's journal, *Friends of Promise*, "[I]ts subject hardly seemed appropriate for *Horizon*'s 'highbrow' readership. Why would sophisticated readers of a literary monthly want to read about popular boys' papers like the twopenny *Gem* and *Magnet?*" (45).

8. For a memorable recent example of realism's attentive focus on the doorway as threshold (and vice versa), see the opening scene in the "Old Cases" episode of *The Wire* (Season 1, Episode 4). The investigative squad clusters around both sides of a passageway and, with great effort, tries to push an old desk inside *and* outside an office (the group on either side of the door in effect pushing against the other) until realizing their mistake.

9. In a similar way, Orwell italicizes "impossibility" in the closing sentence of the book and italicizes "rubber stamp" in that passage from *Wigan Pier*—there to highlight, as here, what he calls "the significant detail."

10. Taken far enough, such questions can lead to extreme versions of anarchy and authoritarianism—either each text fighting for itself (in a war of all against all) or all texts slavishly adhering to external protocol. (Taken far enough, this formal question is necessarily revealed as a political and existential one.)

11. For a related analysis of this idea in Orwell's essay, see my comments in *The One vs. the Many: Minor Characters and the Space of the Protagonist* (Princeton: Princeton UP, 2003) 155–159 and 359.

12. See "Flaubert, Analysis of Flaubert: A reading of *Sentimental Education*," in Bourdieu, 1–46.

13. See Raymond Williams, *"Orwell,"* in *Politics and Letters: Interviews with New Left Review* (London: Verso, 1981) 361–384.

14. Other critics have noted how Williams's very proximity to Orwell might account for some of the rhetorical and analytical distance he feels impelled to take. For a thoughtful and detailed account of Williams's complicated, shifting relationship to Orwell, see John Rodden, "'An Ex-Socialist': Raymond Williams and the British Marxists' Orwell," in *The Politics of Literary Reputation* 188–200. See also David Lloyd and Paul Thomas, "Raymond Williams and George Orwell," in *Culture and the State* 163–188, which considers Williams's anxious relationship as "a touchstone for the left at large in its uncomfortable dismissal of Orwell" (181).

15. We might pause here to ask: What does it mean for these critics to envision the face of a writer? Why would they each invoke this image as their conclusion?

And why does Orwell emphasize, simultaneously, that this *often* happens and that it is *not* the real author's face that he is speaking of? The most obvious way to account for Orwell's ending is as part of an intuitive humanism, animated, above all, by the investment in (a now naturalized) individuality. As Orwell writes, the process is only set off by "any strongly individual piece of writing." In this desire to meld writing and face, we can see the closing image in "Charles Dickens" as a striking equivalent to Orwell's sense of plain-style prose itself. It is an image, after all, about the closure of image: the collapse of writing into writer and text into body. But then Orwell goes out of his way to *mediate* this seemingly closed image, stressing that what he has in mind "is not necessarily the face of the actual writer" (and that sometimes he doesn't even "want to know" about this actual face). Once again, an emphatic instance of the plain style is entwined with its subversion. This image of a face—pointedly *not* the "actual" thing—also tells us something important about the dynamics of image (as such). A face is not only the mark of individuality. It can also be a privileged vehicle for recognition. We might even say that human faces, along with our capacities for perceiving the face, have evolved over time as a means of facilitating recognition. One often can't *help* but recognize a person on encountering his or her face. This is a less ideological and a more strictly pragmatic sense of the image: faces don't mark an internal, sealed-off, individualized essence but rather facilitate an external and social process. The face, in this context, is a privileged object of perception. It is *the* object that we most readily recognize as something *more* than an object—that is, as also a subject. As Orwell writes, with biting sarcasm, in *Wigan Pier:* "And unfortunately I had not trained myself to be indifferent to the expression of the human face" (147). The comment underlines how we would, ironically, have to "train" ourselves *not* to recognize—but merely to see—faces, as simply objects in the perceived world. This process of recognition connects to the dynamics of reading and criticism we have been considering. Criticism, from a necessarily "outside" position, strives to recognize something "inside" the writing—to be moved (in a technical, not just emotional, sense) by qualities internal to the text. The author's "face," in both Williams and Orwell, registers this pole of the dialectic, the inevitable way that some qualities of the object will help to shape and condition the object's apprehension—or, in other words, how some qualities of the *text* help to shape and condition any reading of the text. We don't always see the writer's face, of course (and "[i]t is not necessarily the actual face"); but always, when we read, we are cast into this mingled state of projection and induction. The closing image of the face functions, in these two texts, as a dramatic embodiment of this larger principle—it is, in some sense, simply the mark of *any* intrinsic quality of the text that leaves its imprint on our own critical recognition.

16. Both Lloyd and Rodden (see note 14) take Williams's vividly ambivalent relationship to Orwell as emblematic of a more general dynamic of Orwell's left-wing reception. This section is calling attention to the ways in which this (vivid)

ambivalence itself reproduces the "half in" and "half out" threshold position which is so important to Orwell's own "semi-sociological literary criticism." It is fascinating, in this sense, how often an intricately ambivalent reception of Orwell has recourse to name its own ambivalence *through* Orwell's language. Few writers have coined so many seductively appropriate terms for a *skeptical* reading of themselves. Thus, for example, one of Orwell's most talismanic phrases—reapplied so frequently *to* the author himself—is the opening line of "Reflections on Gandhi": "Saints should always be judged guilty until they are proved innocent" (20.5). Few readers of Orwell can resist the temptation to direct these words back at their source. The punch of this epigram relies, of course, on its own inversion of the common saying ("innocent until proven guilty"). When critics read Orwell through this counterintuitive phrase, they mean, in turn, to reverse his hagiographic elevation as truth-teller (to make him "guilty" rather than "innocent"). But they also, paradoxically, endorse the truth value of the phrase that facilitates this reversal. This example is not unique. Orwell critics frequently stage their argument with recourse to such talismanic phrases, many of which are from "Charles Dickens" (as with this Williams example about the writer's face, or, again, with the famous opening on Dickens as a "writer well-worth stealing") or *Inside the Whale*. The title itself is, quite wonderfully, the grounds for *two* different "inversions" that encompass three of the most influential left-wing refusals of Orwell: *Inside the Myth* (by Christopher Norris) and "Outside the Whale" (used by both E. P. Thompson and Salman Rushdie). Both phrases neatly enact this same paradox, increasing intimacy (with Orwell's own words) in the very assertion of distance (from Orwell). The punning titles are at once earnest and parodic. In their necessary semantic doubleness, they highlight—much like *Inside the Whale* itself—the threshold that rests between (and constitutes) "inside" and "outside." At one point in his work, Orwell, now discussing this very question *of* the memorable phrase, even anticipates such persistence through inversion. He writes in "Rudyard Kipling": "Kipling is the only English writer of our time who has added phrases to the language. . . . The fact is that Kipling . . . is generally talking about things that are of urgent interest. It does not matter, from this point of view, that thinking and decent people generally find themselves on the other side of the fence from him. 'White man's burden' instantly conjures up a real problem, *even if one feels that it ought to be altered to 'black man's burden'*" (13.157, emphasis added).

17. One version of this, and another important "late" statement of his socialist affiliation is in "Toward European Unity": "Our activities as socialists only have meaning if we assume that socialism *can* be established, but if we stop to consider what probably *will* happen, then we must admit, I think, that the chances are against us" (19.163, Orwell's emphases). Rather than take the obvious pessimism here as the end—or as the final meaning of the passage—I want to suggest that this pessimism is a means of accessing the distinction—so crucial to Orwell—between the two italicized terms, what "can" and what "will" happen. Arguably,

political intention as such depends on suspending these two terms (and thus on at least a shadow of pessimism). Democratic socialism needs to be uncertain about what's to come.

18. For another dialectical account of Orwell's pessimism, see David Weisberg's unusual comparison of "commitment and autonomy" in Orwell and Samuel Beckett (*Chronicles of Disorder* 124–160).

4. The Column as Form

1. "The columns were, indeed, a perfect expression of Orwell's interests and personality, of his moral seriousness and quirky humour, and deserve reprinting in full" (Crick 446); "Orwell, it seems to me, had always been at his best, not in the novels or political articles, but in casual pieces of the kind he wrote for the London *Tribune* in his column 'As I Please'" (Isaac Rosenfeld, quoted in Meyers, *Critical Heritage* 170). Both descriptions—whether combining "perfect" and "quirky" or "best" and "casual"—bring into relief the same problem of the column's deliberately *anti*-monumental ambition. For "quintessential," see following note. Keeble, in his thoughtful essay on AIP, also notes that the columns "have received almost unanimous praise from critics" but that "there has been no major critical assessment of their literary elements" (7).

2. Gordon Bowker's brief description also opts to convey "range" through a binary opposition of the trivial and the serious: "Orwell was given his own column, called 'As I Please,' enabling him to *range* across a wide spectrum of topics—from racism and neo-Fascism to solar topi and the Woolworth's rose" (Bowker 306, emphasis added).

Again, Paul Anderson: "Orwell's columns for *Tribune* are justly feted. The *range* of subjects he covered is extraordinary: it is difficult to think of anyone before or since who could write about so many different things" (2, emphasis added).

Again, Julian Symons: "He discussed a hundred subjects, *ranging* from the comparative amounts he spent on books and cigarettes or lamenting the decline of the English murder from the days of Crippen to a casual wartime killing to the spawning of toads in spring" (329, emphasis added, see note in Anderson 40).

Again, John Newsinger: "His 1000-word 'As I Please' columns, each one dealing with three or four topics, are generally regarded as quintessential Orwell. Here he was free to write about whatever he wanted and his subject matter *ranged* from the lighthearted to the deadly serious. The discussion *varied* from consideration of war crimes to an attack on the honours system, from discussion of popular superstitions to the politics of Ezra Pound, from a defense of clothes rationing as egalitarian to a discussion of the nature of Fascism, from the beneficial effect of the war on geographical knowledge to the military effectiveness of the V-bombs, from the need to oppose the colour bar to a defence of the bombing of German cities, from the problem of housework to the theories of James Burnham" (Newsinger 105–106, emphasis added).

Newsinger's 2002 comment obviously absorbs this history of critical response, building on the "binary" strategy of recapitulation by placing these oppositions, now stretched in a sequential chain themselves, into yet a new paratactic list. It's a fairly effective dramatization of the columns' heterogeneity (though again, of course, extremely compressed), and it foregrounds the paradox of how such radical variety could be understood *as* "quintessential" ("the purest, most typical, or refined of its kind," *Oxford English Dictionary*). George Woodcock characterizes the writing itself in AIP (rather than the topics) as "a prose that, for all its ease and apparent casualness, was penetrating and direct" (199, quoted in Anderson 2). If Woodcock understands the casualness of AIP as only "apparent," he still preserves a tension between the column's ease and its penetrating directness: a tension that demands and rewards detailed consideration.

Peter Marks notes that "while [the AIP columns] provide a detailed catalogue of Orwell's interests and responses to events . . . they are not essays" (127) and so, for his purposes, not part of Orwell's essayistic production. But Marks's synthetic account of Orwell's essays returns again and again to their own quality of variety and range; this is clearly an organizing aesthetic horizon of Orwell's *entire* writerly corpus and one that is uniquely dramatized, or staged, in "As I Please." Here are some of Marks's terms for this aesthetic effect (linked at various points to other aesthetic qualities): "broad-ranging" (1), "an array of subjects" (1), "a variegated palate" (10), "vigour and pliability" (85), "diverse" (85), "eclectic" (122), "a rich miscellany" (131), "flexibility" (136), "variety and excellence" (136), "an array of modes, moods and perspectives" (183), "a range of interrelated interests"(183), "diversity and vitality" (184), "breadth and variety" (187), "powerful assortment" (188), "multifaceted, multidimensional and flexible" (189), "clarity, range and subtlety" (189), "the diversity and quality . . . were unprecedented" (191), "variety and quality" (195), "readability, variety of tone and diversity of topic" (195). There is in this way, running through Marks's important study, an ironic *repetition* of variety, as modifier, because it is such a key aesthetic category for Orwell's work. My discussion of AIP can be understood, largely, as an effort to pause on this repetition and develop its implications more thoroughly.

3. All subsequent references to "As I Please" columns in Part Two will first list the number of the column and then the volume and page number from Davison; i.e. 1, 16.13. Each of these columns was originally published in *Tribune*.

4. Orwell further complicates this image of inequality by insisting that this kind of suffering is in fact a distinctly *historical* phenomenon, overlaying the "awful thought" that centers this passage with a radically different kind of "impossible" thought: "Actually, such an improvement in the standard of living has taken place as Mark Rutherford and his contemporaries would have considered quite

impossible. The London slums are still bad enough, but they are nothing to those of the nineteenth-century"(1, 16.14).

5. Just as a brief example of this, consider four major articles on Orwell that have recently appeared in *The New Yorker* and *The New York Review of Books*—by Julian Barnes, Frank Kermode, James Wood, and Louis Menand:

> He warned us against the corrupting effect on politics and public life of the misuse of language, which pleases almost everyone. He said that "good prose is like a window pane," which pleases those who, despite living in the land of Shakespeare and Dickens, mistrust "fancy" writing. . . . "Good prose is like a windowpane." As an instruction to cub reporters and old hacks—also as a self-instruction of the kind writer-critics issue to the world while actually describing their own procedures—it sounds reasonable enough. . . . But does anyone, even Orwell, actually write like that? And are words glass? (Barnes 18-19)

> His solicitude about the English language is a recurring topic. He admires Samuel Butler's style, of which Butler said he never thought about it, and believed that to do so would be a loss to himself and his readers. Orwell thought the best style would be as transparent as a windowpane. Then the thought could be unambiguously conveyed. The cliché smears the pane and is the enemy of truth. Secondhand language was dishonest, and honesty, he believed, was the best policy. "The advantage of a lie is always short-lived." (Kermode 48)

> Orwell is famous for his frank and easy style, and for his determination that good prose should be as transparent as a windowpane. But his style, though superbly colloquial, is much more like a lens than like a window. (Wood 58)

> One of the effects of the tone Orwell achieved—the tone of a reasonable, modest, supremely undogmatic man, hoping for the best but resigned to the worst—was the impression of transparency, something that Orwell himself, in an essay called "Why I Write," identified as the ideal of good prose. It was therefore a shock when Bernard Crick, in the first major biography of Orwell . . . confessed that he had found it difficult to corroborate some of the incidents in Orwell's autobiographical writings. . . . The point is not that Orwell made things up. The point is that he used writing in a literary, not a documentary, way: he wrote in order to make you see what he wanted you to see, to persuade. (Menand 87)

6. This image of dust *on* a window reoccurs immediately after the famous opening line of *1984,* as the second sentence reads: "Winston Smith, his chin

nuzzled into his breast in an effort to escape the vile wind, slipped quickly through the glass doors of Victory Mansions, though not quickly enough to prevent a swirl of gritty dust from entering along with him"(1). The odd interaction of dust and glass here suggests the larger, generic tension between "gritty" naturalism and projective fantasy that animates *1984* (a novel which reads oddly and simultaneously as a work of social realism and science fiction).

7. The fraught combination of obscurity and transparency that is triggered by this short title is elaborated in the essay as well, full of mistaken frames of reference, suffused with half-lit spaces, and centered on a death that goes conspicuously *un*witnessed. But even as a freestanding phrase, or, more specifically, a title that acts as a "window" onto the essay itself, "How the Poor Die" both announces and displaces the topical ground of the writing that will proceed. I've come to see this title as a key example of Orwell's devious plain style.

8. For more on the relationship between this complicated empirical stance and Orwell's challenges to the distinction between fiction and nonfiction, see my discussion of "A Hanging" in Chapter 1.

9. I take Cyril Connolly's 1938 *Enemies of Promise* as a crucial intertext for, and a suggestive phrase for thinking *about,* Orwell's self-conscious attention to the problematic limits of any form of writing. Orwell, of course, is mentioned a number of times in Connolly's book. He, in turn, polemicizes against the third section of *Enemies* in "Inside the Whale," and conceives of "Such, Such Were the Joys," his posthumously published essay about St. Cyprian's boarding school, as a "pendant" to Connolly's own memoir. While Orwell thus twice acknowledges a—markedly ambivalent—relationship to the third, autobiographical section of the book ("A Georgian Boyhood"), I am more interested in the strong, implicit connection of Orwell's work and Connolly's emphasis, in Part One ("Predicament"), on the tension between endurance and immediacy and, in Part Two ("The Charlock's Shade"), on the tension between promise and failure, as constitutive dimensions of modern writing. For further details on this analysis of Connolly's text, see Alex Woloch, "A New Foreword," *Enemies of Promise* (Chicago: U of Chicago P, 2008 [1938]), vii–xviii. For Connolly's discussion of journalism, see *Enemies of Promise, passim,* and in particular, the chapter "The Blue Bugloss," 91–95. For Orwell's discussion of "Such, Such Were the Joys" as "a sort of pendant to Cyril Connolly's *Enemies of Promise,*" see letter to Fredric Warburg (19.149).

10. Nine of the eighty columns are unmarked by breaks, though one of these (AIP 7) in fact shifts topics quite clearly within the section, and one (AIP 71) stands out, as a retrospective account for *Tribune's* tenth anniversary, titled "As I Pleased." The other seven one-section columns, though, are more explicitly focused on a single topic: AIP 2 (on race and *The New Republic*), 16 (on hackneyed political language), 17 (on fascism as a term and a category), 18 (on political revenge in France), 19 (on old newspapers), 40 (on the Warsaw uprising), and 66

(on Christmas and overeating). In my view, the cumulative effect of these single-topic versions of "As I Please" is to gesture at a more sustained or elaborated version of reflection that the column-sequence as a whole refuses. Otherwise, thirty-eight of the columns have three sections—this is just around half of the total, and so the modal standard; fifteen columns have two sections (though Orwell moves away from this later in the column sequence); twelve columns have four sections, and three columns (AIP 5, 50, and 77) "max out" with five sections each.

11. We can recognize these two, countervailing tendencies on an essential level. Very often, a textual object with multiple, disjunctive parts seems to cry out for us to "put it all together." The divided object might be said to generate and thus contain this impulse, even as it proves itself, through its seams and fragmentation, unable to produce such unity intrinsically.

12. This is, in fact, the second apology; earlier in the letter, Orwell interrupts himself to write: "I hope you will forgive me for lecturing you at this enormous length. After all you can always stop reading." (Quite odd—as though securing a way that the reflection is really for the thinker or writer himself.) It *is* a long letter. We can see the ambivalence about this, as well, right at the beginning, where Orwell writes: "Many thanks for your letter of some time back. I have at last a few instants in which I can sit down to reply. I am so glad you got hold of and read 'Ulysses' at last. When you say 'What do you think Joyce is after?' I should say several things, which it is not very easy to define shortly" (10.326). The length of Orwell's response is grounded in this wish to say several things at the same time, and set against the compression of a "few instants."

13. By "motivate," I mean provide some discussion *outside* the columns themselves—an introductory note, another piece in *Tribune,* or a discussion in any of his private correspondence—concerning the internal structure of the columns, his feelings about the form, what topics he is interested in writing about, etc. I understand Orwell's reluctance to discuss the significance, origin, organization, or meaning of the column in any outside text as a counterpoint to the systematic withholding of textual transitions between sections, or other kinds of meta-commentary, *within* the columns.

14. One particular example illustrates both these principles. In AIP 56, Orwell turns back to the previous week's column (AIP 55), which had ended, after a discussion of the public fame of Edgar Wallace: "It is queer to think that London could commemorate Wallace in Fleet Street and Barrie in Kensington Gardens, but has never yet got round to giving Blake a monument in Lambeth" (55, 17.24). (I will consider this column, as a whole, again in Chapter 5.) The question of writing's monumentality can be redirected toward AIP itself, as we've seen in Shelden's intriguing description of AIP as "a splendid monument to" Orwell's "literary powers" (425). So it is worth marking this passage in which the column focuses on an actual "monument" to a writer (or, indeed, the absence of one). A week later,

Orwell amends this comment, as the second out of three sections in AIP 56 is devoted *entirely* to reflecting back on the previous column. It reads in full: "I want to correct an error that I made in this column last week. It seems that there *is* a plaque to William Blake, and that it is somewhere near St. George's church in Lambeth. I had looked for one in that area and had failed to find it. My apologies to the L.C.C." (56, 17.31). What's striking here is Orwell's decision to inscribe this correction—by far the briefest of the three sections—into the *middle* of his column. (It is quite unusual for Orwell to use this pattern in AIP: long, very short, long). Almost working simply as a larger version of those asterisks that always denote the divisions of AIP in *Tribune,* Orwell's correction bisects the rest of the column. So even as it forms a bridge with the earlier column, it creates further fragmentation in the current one. The correction thus establishes continuity and discontinuity simultaneously, echoing the changing fortune of the monument (presented not *directly* but only as the negation of a previously imputed absence).

15. For one suggestive reading of the relationship between socialist politics and literariness in the context of U.S. radical periodicals, see Harvey Teres, *Renewing the Left: Politics, Imagination and the New York Intellectuals* (New York: Oxford UP, 1996). For a discussion of Orwell's writing in the context of periodical publication, see Peter Marks, "Where he wrote: periodicals and the essays of George Orwell," *Twentieth Century Literature,* 41.4 (1995): 266–283.

16. John Campbell discusses Bevan's relationship with Orwell in *Nye Bevan and the Mirage of British Socialism* (London: Weidenfeld and Nicolson, 1987) 106–107. As I've suggested, Orwell's own heterodoxy *within Tribune* can't be dissociated from the heterodox position of *Tribune* within British coalition politics during the war, and Bevan's own sustained position "on the outside left of the [Labour] party" (Campbell 150) during the war (and then as the Minister of Health under Clement Atlee). Kenneth Morgan, writing an appreciative portrait in 1987, suggests that Bevan "remains, perhaps, the most attractive figure that the British socialist movement has produced in its eighty-odd years of fitful life" (218). Arguably no figure has emerged in the 30 years *since* Morgan's comment to change this assessment.

17. The charged sense of origin that bridges story and discourse is reinforced when we recall that "Shooting an Elephant"—as a text solicited by John Lehmann for *New Writing,* a prestigious and ambitious journal that had only recently started—serves to introduce Orwell, as a new voice, to an important literary audience. (In 1941, Orwell will call *New Writing,* "the bi-yearly publication which used to be the rallying point of the left-wing intelligentsia" [12.527]). This context adds to the striking tension between assertion and effacement in the opening line of "Shooting an Elephant," since the composition and publication of the text is itself a form of action that secures, or certainly intensifies, Orwell's still emergent position as a writer. In turn, Orwell is typically modest about the ambitious piece in his correspondence with Lehmann. Note how he critiques both himself and Lehmann

here, and simultaneously distances himself from the journal even while conferring agency onto Lehmann for the piece he intends to write and submit: "What I was going to say was, I am writing a book at present and the only other thing I have in mind is a sketch, (it would be about 2000–3000 words), describing the shooting of an elephant. It all came back to me very vividly the other day & I would like to write it, but it maybe that it is quite out of your line. I mean it might be too lowbrow for your paper & I doubt whether there is anything anti-fascist in the shooting of an elephant! Of course you can't say in advance that you would like it, but perhaps you could say tentatively whether it is at all likely to be in your line or not. If not, *then I won't write it;* if you think it might interest you I will do it & send it along for you to consider" ("Letter to John Lehmann" 10.483, emphasis added). For further details on the composition and publication of "Shooting an Elephant," in relation to Orwell's emergent authorial identity, see Stansky and Abrahams 182–185. To connect the opening of "Shooting an Elephant" with Orwell's comment in "Why I Write" is to see this conjoining of isolation and writing's origin across four separate points in time. "Shooting an Elephant" is written in late 1936 but set in the mid-1920s."Why I Write" is written nearly ten years *later* (1946) but speaks of Orwell's isolation at a much *earlier* date (around 1908 or 1909 perhaps).

18. Or consider the similarly reflective openings of AIP 43 and 44, now well into the column sequence that Orwell is just embarking on with AIP 2 and 3:

> By permission of a correspondent, I quote passages from a letter of instruction which she recently received from a well-known school of journalism. (43, 16.423)

> Sir Osbert Sitwell's little book, and my remarks on it, brought in an unusually large amount of correspondence, and some of the points that were raised seem to need further comment. (44, 16.427)

These openings are both *doubly* mediated. In the first example, Orwell quotes back not merely a reader but this correspondent's own extract from a letter she received, and this letter is in turn a text centrally concerned with (journalistic) writing. In the second example, an "unusually large amount" of writing is generated by (and reflects back on) a previous section of "As I Please," which had focused on a book itself concerned with writers (and how they should or should not receive economic support). We could chart the forms of writing that are folded into one another in these openings as follows:

1. "As I Please" 43 (as a text)
2. The letter from a correspondent to *Tribune* (mentioned in AIP 43)
3. The "letter of instruction" she received (mentioned in her correspondence)
4. The modes of writing discussed in this "letter of instruction"

1. "As I Please" 44 (as a text)
2. Letters in response to AIP 40 sent to *Tribune* (mentioned in AIP 44)
3. AIP 40 (as a text, mentioned in the letters sent to *Tribune*)
4. Osbert Sitwell's book (mentioned in AIP 40)
5. The writing discussed in Osbert Sitwell's book

These two sentences, then, contain nine textual registers. Yet the rhetoric of the openings seems deliberately limited, or "light," generating a tension between the complexity of these reflective, embedded levels and the casualness of the prose. (We can see such imbalance echoed on *another* register in the second opening, as it distinguishes between Sitwell's "little book" and the "large amount" of textual response that it elicits.) At the same time, both this book and the "school of journalism" that raises Orwell's ire open up fundamental and ultimately social questions about writing. How does *any* writing stand back from the various modes of "instruction"—example, precedent, or internalized expectations—that define its limits and possibilities? And how does any writer engage, or scrutinize, the relationship between her goals in writing and the specific modes of economic support that she must inevitably rely upon? These are the "large" questions that are introduced at the start of these two "little" columns. These questions intersect with the (still more general) relationship between writing and freedom provoked by the title of Orwell's column. The project of writing "as one pleases" leads to such dilemmas: whether the forms of "instruction" that precede (and potentially constrain) a writer's own free practice or the external, social position of the writer, with its specific privileges, burdens and blinders. These are horizons that form the "outside" of writing toward which Orwell's own writerly attention gravitates (as we'll see in more detail in Chapter 5).

19. Orwell's attention to a "special supplement" of the weekly periodical is also significant in this light: it again frames topicality as a contested process, requiring *im*balance, in much the same way as the columns of AIP themselves. *Some* topics deserve extension, or supplementation. When a weekly magazine like *The New Republic* issues such an extraneous, freestanding supplement, it implicitly raises important questions. What topics bear thinking about in this "special" way? What topics should motivate this more considered, and indeed self-conscious, reflection: one which disrupts the magazine's regular temporal form? Does the supplement merge smoothly into the magazine's regularized flow of writing, or does its extraneousness challenge the (now relatively *more* bounded) discourse of the journal?

Orwell begins by saying that this special issue is "worth a reading." This claim reiterates the implicit distinction that underlies the special supplement (some *topics* are "worth" particular, extended focus) in new terms (some texts are more or less worth reading and discussing). Orwell's own meditation on both the problem of race and on *The New Republic*'s reflection on this problem unfolds in the emphatically transient form of the weekly column, even as this discussion stands out against the other early columns of AIP by attending to only one, rather than several, topics. If the second column highlights the form of a "special supplement" (just as the first column inflects the pamphlet form, and the third column begins with a reader's letter), it also, obviously, foregrounds the topic of race. The political problem of racial difference is an important concern of the columns. See, for example, Orwell's discussion of "colour prejudice" (52, 16.507), of segregation in a London dance hall (37, 16.328-29), of Scottish Nationalism (73, 19.43-44), of racism in children's alphabet books (75A, 19.50-51); of imperialism and fantasies of biological difference (45, 16.434-436).

20. For "A Hanging," arguably Orwell's first crucial exercise in the plain style, see my discussion in Chapter 1. *Homage to Catalonia* moves toward a harrowing series of narrow escapes and failed escapes during the liquidation of POUM following the May 1937 fighting in Barcelona, including, on different scales of significance and detail, the imprisonment and death of the British soldier Bob Smillie (182–183, 216–217); the imprisonment of Orwell's battalion leader, George Kopp, whom Orwell and Eileen Blair visit in jail and try unsuccessfully to help (217–222); the arrest and disappearance of the POUM leader Andrés Nin, who was, as Orwell correctly speculates, executed in prison (206–207); and, finally, Orwell's own flight out of Spain with Eileen Blair (226–229). The plot of *1984* hinges on the arrest of Winston Smith and Julia at the threshold between Parts Two and Three. Part Three is set primarily inside the prison of The Ministry of Love and then the "prison within a prison" of Room 101. From Orwell's last notebook, "No guilty person is ever punished. So far as subjective feelings go, a person who is in a position to be punished has become the victim, & has therefore become innocent. This is perfectly well understood, internally, by everyone concerned. When a murderer is hanged, there is only one person present at the ceremony who is not guilty of murder. The hangman, the warders, the governor, the doctor, the chaplain—they are all guilty: but the man standing on the drop is innocent" (20.213). The entry echoes a much earlier comment in *The Road to Wigan Pier*, where, interestingly, Orwell already emphasizes the persistence of this rebellious judgment: "I never went into a jail without feeling (most visitors to jails feel the same) that my place was on the other side of the bars. I thought then—I think now, for that matter—that the worst criminal who ever walked is morally superior to a hanging judge" (146). The parenthetical interjection ("I think now, for that matter") is significant in this instance because Orwell is explicitly constructing a *retrospective* account in this section of *Wigan Pier*. In this way, the interjection disrupts the fundamental logic of the narration.

21. These tensions, moreover, are already inscribed into the tense shift in Orwell's opening line: "I see that Mr Suresh Vaidya . . . has been arrested." Here an imperfect verb ("has been") lodges, as it were, within the act of present-tense witnessing ("I see"), even as these verbal actions—"to see" and "to be

arrested"—emblematize, respectively, the immediacy of the observing faculty and the recessive belatedness of the observation. In its own shifts of attention, furthermore, the column exerts a writerly freedom in contrast to the incarceration that it notes and opens with.

22. Orwell even has time to go home, as the opening paragraph continues: "She added that to dip your moustache into your beer also turns it flat. I immediately accepted this without further inquiry; in fact, as soon as I got home I clipped my moustache, which I had forgotten to do for some days."(16.81). Notice the emphasis here on immediacy—equated now with the lack of reflective "inquiry"! The next paragraph begins, as we've seen, "Only later did it strike me . . ." (16.81).

23. The final section of AIP 3 begins: "One way of feeling infallible is not to keep a diary. Looking back through the diary I kept in 1940 and 1941 I find that I was usually wrong when it was possible to be wrong. Yet I was not so wrong as the Military Experts" (3, 16.27). Orwell here suggests a specific epistemological purchase that is gained through transient writing—one of self-reflection. However, this gain does not occur through the transient writing itself but precisely in the *discordant* activity of "looking back" over writing that is initially elaborated in a more immediate, contingent, and transient context. The epistemological traction here is thus not only obviously negative (seeing how you are wrong) but generated by a conjunction of transience and reflection: "say[ing] something now" and "[l]ooking back through." This is the uneasy conjunction that rests at the heart of AIP.

24. These three phrases anchor the book but are far from exceptional. *Homage to Catalonia* continually invokes a crooked temporal structure. Thus at certain points, echoing writing that comes "late," Orwell holds off recounting events, in the discourse, that have occurred earlier in the story ("As a matter of fact there were things in this period that interested me greatly, and I will describe some of them later" [46]). Conversely, on other occasions, he registers an "early" awareness, as narrator, that he would only belatedly gain in the story: "Yet this mob of eager children, who were going to be thrown into the front line in a few days' time, were not even taught how to fire a rifle or pull the pin out of a bomb. At the time I did not grasp that this was because there were no weapons to be had" (10); or, again, "I remember with peculiar vividness the spectacle of that train passing in the yellow evening light; window after window full of dark, smiling faces, the long tilted barrels of the guns, the scarlet scarves fluttering—all this gliding slowly past us against a turquoise-coloured sea. . . . Most of them, I am afraid, were killed at Huesca only a few weeks later" (191–192). The cognate "later" ("I will describe some of them later," "only a few weeks later") is important in these phrases and builds on that structuring dichotomy with which Orwell characterizes Spain.

25. This passage makes explicit the sense of imperfect choice that's implicit in Orwell's aphorism about Spain: its suggestion that, in warding off one kind of mistake or danger (being too early), both the actor and the observer can open themselves to another, different trap (being too late). This idea is crucial to the

composition of "As I Please" not merely as that stream of topical choices which constitutes the text's "freedom" always unfolds in terms of fragmentation and interruption but also because of the column's insistent awareness of the internal instability of free thinking—the way that thought, necessarily seeking to substantialize itself, can often be thrown off-course through its very "success." Orwell's focus as a political writer, and his sense of writing itself, often gravitates toward situations that present an uneasy, and, in fact, irreconcilable choice, as in these two passages.

26. In both cases, the pressure of describing (or experiencing) this choice shifts the prose into second person: "[t]he lavatories are in the yard at the back, so that if *you* live on the side facing the street" and "so that *you* had the choice of leaving both pins in place," ending indeed with the second-person possessive ("your outlook," "your pocket").

27. The passage continues, "No such thing would be possible now. A Nazi and a non-Nazi version of the present war would have no resemblance to one another, and which of them finally gets into the history books will be decided not by evidential methods but on the battlefield" (16.88).

28. For one of the best discussions of Orwell's counterintuitiveness, see William Cain, "Orwell's Perversity: An Approach to the Collected Essays." (The rebarbative dimension of this is brought out strikingly in Stevie Smith's depiction of Orwell in her *roman à clef The Holiday.*)

29. Orwell discusses photographs of French collaborators and "corpses of the Germans hanged by Russians in Kharkov" in AIP 41 (16.386). This connects to the important 1945 *Tribune* essay "Revenge Is Sour" (17.361–363), which develops Orwell's engagement with conceptual abstraction through the specific, politically charged terms of the postwar treatment of Axis soldiers, collaborators, and war criminals. Orwell discusses the representation of atrocities again in AIP 54 (17.18–19) and again in AIP 61. In AIP 24, Orwell first argues that "the effect of modern inventions has been to increase nationalism, to make travel enormously more difficult, to cut down the means of communication between one country and another, and to make the various parts of the world *less,* not more dependent on one another for food and manufactured goods" (16.182). In AIP 57, he self-consciously *returns* to this earlier discussion, noting "some months ago, in this column, I pointed out that modern scientific inventions have tended to prevent rather than increase international communication" (17.39). The critique of technology in Orwell can at times resonate strongly with a Frankfurt School–style skepticism about instrumental reason. As Orwell writes, for example, in an unusual comment about Guernica, in 1938: "the little town was . . . systematically destroyed from the air, out of sheer, wanton brutality. Guernica was not even of much importance as a military objective. And the most horrible thought of all is that this blotting-out of an open town was simply the correct and logical use of a modern weapon" (11.112).

30. "One of the most extraordinary things about England is that there is almost no official censorship, and yet nothing that is acutely offensive to the governing class gets into print, at least in any place where large numbers of people are likely to read it. . . . Nowadays this kind of veiled censorship even extends to books. . . . Circus dogs jump when the trainer cracks his whip, but the really well-trained dog is the one that turns his somersault when there is no whip" (AIP 32, 16.276–277). This passage suggests not only that the more tractable dog doesn't need the whip but that the most intrusive kinds of censorship might be the least acknowledged.

31. This double game might remind us most of Theodor Adorno, and, particularly, *Minima Moralia,* another short-form, and fragmentary, text that hinges, like Orwell's columns, as much on producing (*and* short-circuiting) the uncanny *feeling* of thought as on substantially developing its conceptual content. Adorno's text is certainly concerned with the inevitable, catalyzing difference between thought and its object: "[W]hat is is never quite as thought expresses it. Essential to [thought] is an element of exaggeration, of over-shooting the object, of self-detachment from the weight of the factual"(126). But, like AIP, it is also concerned with how this very detachment, while intrinsic *to* thinking, must be resisted and destabilized by the committed thinker: "every thought which is not idle . . . bears branded on it the impossibility of its full legitimation"(81). Adorno thus repeatedly returns to the *varied* ways that "[t]hought . . . forgets to be thought"(69), not just by over-immediacy (though this is certainly the case) but, more paradoxically, in its detachment ("[o]nce the last trace of emotion has been eradicated, nothing remains of thought but absolute tautology"[123]), disinterestedness ("[p]eople thinking in the forms of free, detached, disinterested appraisal were unable to accommodate within those forms the experience of violence which in reality annuls such thinking"[57]), or sheer extension ("thought . . . in its very willingness still to be a thought," in its "contemplative leisureliness," bears "a trace of connivance at the world"[99]).

32. In this way, Orwell depicts this recalcitrant form of thinking, despite its obvious brevity, as fundamental to much more substantial trajectories of history and change. The next "As I Please," for example, picks up this idea of "new[ness]" on a quite different temporal register:

Looking through Chesterton's introduction to *Hard Times* in the Everyman Edition (incidentally, Chesterton's introductions to Dickens are about the best thing he ever wrote), I note the typically sweeping statement: "There are no new ideas." . . . [T]he claim that "there is nothing new under the sun" is one of the stock arguments of intelligent reactionaries . . . It is not very difficult to see that this idea is rooted in the fear of progress. If there is nothing new under the sun, if the past in some shape or another always returns, then the future when it comes will be something familiar. At any rate what will never come—since it has never come before—is that hated, dreaded thing, a

world of free and equal human beings. . . . In fact, there *are* new ideas. . . .
(AIP 13, 16.104)

Between these two weeks, Orwell creates an audacious interlace between the
originality, or "newness," that is generated out of those precarious five seconds of
thought and the underlying political originality of the left, as it strives to create
new modes of equality, freedom, and human dignity. AIP 13 has only two sections, and it is split in half around two different topics. Before commenting on
Chesterton, Orwell discusses a short story in the *Home Companion and Family
Journal* that bleeds culture into advertising by glamorizing the work of its heroine,
a telephone exchange operator named Lucy Fallows. The magazine story ends
with a "little note" that Orwell then extracts and reproduces in his column: "'Any
of our young readers themselves interested in the work of the Long Distance
Telephone Exchange (such work as Lucy Fallows was doing) should apply to the
Staff Controller, L.T.R., London, who will inform them as to the opportunities
open'" (16.103). What captures Orwell's attention here is this little note, which
belatedly turns the short story into an overt advertisement. As is so often the case
in these columns, Orwell's writing is built on a differentiated relationship to
another text: "I note with interest," he writes, "the direct correlation between a
Government recruiting advertisement and a piece of commercial fiction" (16.103).
The form of writing that Orwell critiques here, on the other hand, erases difference: it marks the (unacknowledged) corrosion of fiction by advertising, and the
coercion of the audience's own thinking by propaganda. (A number of times
Orwell's column comments on the collapse of clear boundaries between writing
and advertisement, as in AIP 28's discussion of "the blurring of the distinction
between advertisement and criticism" [28, 16.252].) Against this collapse of textual levels, Orwell's column asserts the independence of critical reflection by
holding up a piece of writing and pausing to reflect upon it. But such reflection is
short-lived: elaborated only in this one thought piece. Like so many sections of
"As I Please," this section stays with the experience of being "struck," of noticing
(or "not[ing] with interest") something about another text. From here, Orwell
moves on to his discussion of Chesterton's introduction. Once again, we have a
careful representation of the encounter with (or reading of) a piece of writing that
reflects on *another* piece of writing. Chesterton's introductions to Dickens's own
texts "are about the best thing he ever wrote" (16.104). The previous column of "As
I Please" had distinguished between a text that mechanically prompts the reader's
response and one that elicits, or allows for, "five seconds of thought." Here Orwell
expands the temporal stasis implicit to the culture of familiarity embodied by
Punch magazine. It is only in these "five seconds of thought"—the same delay that
allows Orwell to reflect upon the line between advertising and fiction—that "new
ideas" are created. Orwell's writing continually rebels against the given, insisting
on a space of thought—of imagination and critical reflection—that can resist, by

reflecting on, the given state of the world. Writing is a struggle *for* reflection, but this reflection is also necessarily short-lived, rooted to the moment in which it breaks from the given.

33. The "electric drill" Orwell mentions in the opening sentence of AIP 6 is being used to construct a bomb shelter, so that this example connects to the other instances of aerial war and, ironically, involves a penetrating sound that emerges in the construction of a *barrier* meant to protect civilians from air invasion. See also Orwell's opening contribution to "Story by Five Authors" (14.89–93), which begins with two embedded descriptions of bomb explosions during the Blitz. From the "dusty pile of rubble" full of "splinters of glass" (14.90) to the "barking of the guns [which] rose and fell, sometimes bursting forth into an ear-splitting volley," the piece echoes many of Orwell's most persistent tropes. One description stands out, in particular, in relation to the play of vulnerability and shelter, as conditions of writing—or thought—in "As I Please": "The whole house would be on fire before long, but in the mean time it gave a certain amount of protection" (14.90).

34. George Packer recently makes these two comments about Orwell's essays: "On every subject he took up, Orwell quickly hit the target of something essential, making an insight that would occur to no other writer and would still resonate over half a century later" (xii), and, "Orwell's essays demonstrate how to be interesting line after line" (xi). I don't want to dispute the sensitivity of these two claims, but it seems—as always—very important to put a bit of meta-critical pressure on them. After all, Packer says only a few pages later that "'Shooting an Elephant' is probably Orwell's most perfect essay" (xx), and this text hinges, from the title forward, on troubling and distending the very act of "hitting a target." Such distension and fracturing is, as we've seen, ubiquitous in "As I Please," and in the structure and texture of Orwell's prose more generally. The pieces in "As I Please" do tend to "hit the target," precisely in that sense of articulating a distilled conceptual claim (or "insight," as Packer puts it), but they also foreground the intricacy and precariousness of this process. And, as we'll see in Chapter 6, the experience at the center of the columns (as it emerges out of those unusual but important points when Orwell narrativizes his own self) is often one of being *jammed up,* mistaken, shocked, or surprised—of stutter-steps, missteps, and paralysis.

35. The V-2 bomb, introduced several months later, in September 1944, also configures the relationship between noise and explosion in a way that resonates with the dynamics of reflection: while the V-1 bomb makes this "droning, zooming noise" before it draws to a halt, the V-2 would go entirely unheard until the explosion. As Orwell begins AIP 50 on December 1, 1944: "V2 (I am told that you can now mention it in print so long as you just call it V2 and don't describe it too minutely) supplies another instance of the contrariness of human nature. People are complaining of the sudden unexpected wallop with which these things go off. 'It wouldn't be so bad if you got a bit of warning,' is the usual formula. There

is even a tendency to talk nostalgically of the days of V1. The good old doodle-bug did at least give you time to get under the table, etc., etc. Whereas, in fact, when the doodle-bugs were actually dropping, the usual subject of complaint was the uncomfortable waiting period before they went off. Some people are never satisfied. Personally, I am no lover of V2, especially at this moment when the house still seems to be rocking from a recent explosion. . . ." (16.487). Here Orwell alludes, once more, to that protracted period of time ("uncomfortable waiting"), now contrasted with the abruptness of the V-2 where, as with shock, we hear the explosion only after it has occurred. And the response to this shows a commensurate "contrariness" not only in the bombs but in "human nature."

36. The first section of AIP 1 focuses on tensions in the Anglo-American military alliance.

37. This is one of the cases where the specific historical context—and not only the formal temporality—of the column adds to its essential effect. The problem of naming these new kinds of planes—and comprehending this new kind of destructive force—is pervasive in English journalism and culture at this moment.

38. Similarly, several of these examples, in and of themselves, interlace more than one kind of disposability: Children's books can fall out of print but *also* function, generically, as a kind of writing that is formative but often forgotten. Butler's book is both culturally out of date *and* materially worn down. The "immediate" withdrawal of Trotsky's book is different than the mere suppression or banning of a book, as it enacts the sharp wrenching of a book from one side of the "borderline" back onto the other. This withdrawal obscures Trotsky, of course, but, more specifically, suppresses his attempt to render Stalinism visible, an attempt that hinges, in turn, on showing how Stalin himself suppressed the authentic history of the Russian revolution.

39. Kermode notes this specific sentence in his review of AIP: he comments that "One week [Orwell] reports that he's reading a life of Tolstoy, a book on Dickens, Harry Levin's on Joyce, and the autobiography of Dalí" (48), and then has nothing further to say about the column.

5. Writing's Outside

1. "Are Books Too Dear?" *Manchester Evening News* 1 June 1944 (16.241–244); "Books *v.* Cigarettes," *Tribune* 8 Feb. 1946 (18.94–97); "The Cost of Letters," *Horizon* Sept. 1946 (18.382–384); "Good Bad Books," *Tribune* 2 Nov. 1945 (17.347–350); "Books and the People: A New Year Message," *Tribune* 5 Jan. 1945 (17.7–11).

2. Orwell was invited to contribute the London Letter in December 1940 and his first letter was dated 3 Jan. 1941 (and appeared in the March–April edition of *Partisan Review*). He wrote letters, during the first run of AIP columns or in between the two runs of the column, in January 1944 (16.64–70), April 1944 (16.156–161), July 1944 (16.300–303), October 1944 (16.411–416), June 1945

(17.161–166), August 1945 (17.245–249), and May 1946 (18.285–289). As we've seen, Orwell inscribes his interest in the pamphlet form into the first column of "As I Please," and he connects both modes of writing through the desire for (political and temporal) immediacy. Like the truncated sections that make up "As I Please," the form of the pamphlet is also constituted, for Orwell, in terms of its brevity: "A pamphlet is a short piece of polemical writing, printed in the form of a booklet and aimed at a large public" (19.107). And again: "All that is required of it is that it shall be topical, polemical and short" (19.114). Orwell bleeds his judgment of short stories, in his capacity as *Tribune*'s literary editor, into the framework of the column in AIP 20 (16.153), AIP 23 (16.176–177), and AIP 27, which begins its second section thus: "Wading through the entries for the Short Story Competition, I was struck once again by the disability that English short stories suffer under in being all cut to a uniform length" (16.245). See also Orwell's contemporaneous 1944 piece "How Long is a Short Story" in the *Manchester Evening News* (16.382–384).

3. Garden of forking paths: This opening *also* has a striking resonance with the Walter Raleigh section—not merely as two uncanny moments in which AIP imagines, and inscribes, the destruction of writing, but also in the way that writing's end, in both cases, is connected with an intensification of thought (so that the Raleigh story has "come into my head I don't know how many times," and this story, when read, "filled [the young Orwell] with enthusiastic approval").

4. This text, more generally, offers an interesting version of Orwell's attraction to the shortage of paper. As he writes early on, "So for some months past we have been faced with a shortage of paper—not desperate, but acute enough to make itself felt at almost every moment of the day. Paper is more important than you realize until you are short of it. I want to tell you something about the results of this shortage—and it is a curious fact that though most of them are bad, some of them are good" (118). The next few paragraphs, in fact, focus on the "good"—from the decline of poster advertisements ("before the war, every available wall was defaced with enormous posters . . . and the bare walls look much nicer without them" [118]) to the transformation of "terribly commercialized" prewar newspapers (119) which were "filled up not only with advertisements for useless luxuries, but with imbecilities of every kind" (119). It is a profusion that Orwell can't help but dilate on himself: "silly news items about burglaries and the private lives of film stars, gossip about lipstick and silk stockings, enormous articles on sport, pages and pages of horse-racing results, even columns of astrology and fortune-telling—any and every kind of cheap sensation calculated to push the real news out of the reader's attention" (119). Finally, even the elimination of billboard announcements *for* the newspapers' own headlines yields a "good" result: "Gone also are the newsposters that used to appear in the streets, advertising successive editions of the evening papers. Nowadays the men who sell the papers have little blackboards on which they write their own selection of the news, and these are

much more informative and responsible than the printed posters used to be" (119). Despite claiming that "most of [the results] are bad," Orwell devotes only one paragraph, after this, to detailing the negative consequences for periodicals, literary reviews, and new books. Both in prioritizing the "positive" results and in his expansive description of the "imbecilities" of prewar newspapers (notice how he inscribes not just the content but the *forms* of this imbecility: "silly news items," "enormous articles," "pages and pages," "columns"), Orwell's piece is striking for its own latent animosity toward paper. And in the strange emphasis on the contingent, moment-to-moment skill of the paperless newspaper vendors as well as in that final, haunted image of paper products "waiting to go into" the giant recycling mills, the essay reaches still more creative—and moving—expressions of the same desire: that desire so akin to the "enormous approval" that Orwell claims to have felt, as a boy, when he read of the destruction of the library of Alexandria, burnt for eighteen days of fuel. On the one hand, this ambition marks the more general desire of the plain style, as that paradoxical form of language which seeks to overcome its own linguistic nature, its own mediatedness, in order to serve the purpose of direct, transparent, and immediate communication. The posters are taken down, the "bare" walls "look much nicer without them." But turning back to the opening of "Paper Is Precious," what's most striking is the emphasis on consciousness itself. The paper shortage is not "good" because it eliminates paper but because it forces us to *notice* the paper that we might otherwise be unaware of. We see its "importance" only when we are "short of it," and our deprivation does not manifest itself in terms of "desperate" external consequence but precisely on an interior level, as we sense or "feel" this deprivation—generally and continually. I would argue that it is this generalized, continual awareness—ultimately an awareness by the writer of the material that he writes with, on, and through—that motivates and underlies the positive results that Orwell immediately mentions as a "curious fact" of the paper shortage and goes on, in the rest of the essay, to foreground. As one final example of this subtle inflection of consciousness, we could consider the scene of discovery which Orwell puts right before the apocalyptic image of paper heading to the recycling mill: "Now and again in a second hand bookshop you will come on an old book printed on very grey paper, and you can tell at a glance that it dates from the final years of the last war, when the paper shortage was as acute as it is now"(120).

5. This is the title that Davison chooses for Volume 18 of *The Complete Works of George Orwell*, covering 1946. The phrase comes from a letter to Dorothy Plowman that I discussed in the Introduction.

6. For a more extended discussion of this passage, see Chapter 3.

7. Winston Smith, in composing his secret diary, is another reflective (and day-to-day) writer; and, like both Comstock and the unnamed reviewer in "Confessions," he is explicitly described at his writing "desk." In *1984,* this is the cramped alcove that Winston (wrongly) assumes is shielded from the telescreen;

when he finishes writing each day, he covers his diary with a single grain of dust. Writing takes place in an ill-fitting world, although at the moment when he is shot, in *Homage to Catalonia*, Orwell pointedly laments, "My second [thought] was a violent resentment at having to leave this world which, when all is said and done, suits me so well" (186). In "Why I Write," as we've seen, he strikes a similarly affirmative note: "So long as I remain alive and well I shall continue to feel strongly about prose style, to love the surface of the earth, and to take pleasure in solid objects and scraps of useless information" (18.319–320). Here the ideology of "plain speech" is linked explicitly to the physical relationship of the writer to the world: prose style is connected to the "surface of the earth," while, somehow, "information"—"useless" and "in scraps"—gets equated with exactly the thing that it is, intrinsically, distinct from: a "solid object." What—other than Orwell's "and"—connects "solid objects" to "scraps of useless information"? We can see here how Orwell's prose tries to materialize writing, reanimating the dialectical tension between thought and its material ground. "Scraps of useless information" should remind us of the writing project of "As I Please," with all of its different parts, its tendency toward fragmentation, and the way this fragmentation is linked to the desire for presentness. "Scraps of . . . information" signals the animating desire—never fully accomplished—for writing to register the specificity, and particularity, of the world it mimetically comprehends. But "scraps of useless information" also returns us to the more dangerous materiality of writing, its literal—and threatening—"surface," to paper scraps, shredded paper—turned into confetti, furniture lining, fuel or kindling (all images which occur in AIP)—and, again, the disintegrating cigarette. For another related description, see Orwell's unusual contribution to a short-story sequence he coordinates while at the BBC: "He sat down again and drew the cigarette smoke deep into his lungs" (14.92).

8. Here again we can find an interesting connection to the later works, as the taut, unstable equivalency between books and cigarettes, provoked by the title, might connect to Orwell's exploration of identity and equality in those unstable paradoxes from *Animal Farm* and *1984* ("some animals are more equal than others," "freedom=slavery," etc.).

9. *Mass Observation* is, of course, a crucial generic horizon for socially engaged British writing in the 1930s and 1940s. Orwell touches on the enterprise explicitly in "As I Please" 79 (19.91–92). He has already discussed a volume of *Mass Observation* in 1940 ("Review of *War Begins at Home*," 12.17–18), where he avers, after several points of contention with the project, "Now even more than at other times it is of the most vital importance that something of the kind should be attempted and brought to as many people's notice as possible" (12.18).

10. "Sometimes, on top of a cupboard or at the bottom of a drawer, you come on a pre-war newspaper, and when you have got over your astonishment at its

enormous size, you find yourself marveling at its almost unbelievable stupidity" (AIP 19, 16.145).

11. In his study of Orwell's essays, Peter Marks notes this same tone in the essay, commenting on both its "semi-comic seriousness" and "pseudo-sociological conclusion" (149).

12. "I have said enough to show that reading is one of the cheaper recreations. . . . And if our book-consumption remains as low as it has been, at least let us admit that it is because reading is a less exciting pastime than going to the dogs, the pictures or the pub, and not because books, whether bought or borrowed, are too expensive" (18.97).

13. We can find *both* of these moments of preterition anticipated in one passage from Orwell's 1936 essay "Bookshop Memories," when he writes in the last paragraph (with my emphasis added on relevant phrases): "But the real reason why I should not like to be in the book trade for life is that while I was in it I lost my love of books. . . . There was a time when I really did love books—loved the *sight and smell and feel of them,* I mean, at least if they were *fifty or more years old.* Nothing pleased me quite so much as to buy *a job lot of them* for a shilling at a country auction. There is a peculiar flavour about the *battered unexpected* books you pick up in that kind of collection: *minor* eighteenth-century poets, *out of date* gazeteers, *odd volumes* of *forgotten* novels, *bound* numbers of ladies' magazines of the 'sixties. For casual reading—*in your bath, for instance,* or *late at night* when you are too tired to go to bed, or in the *odd quarter of an hour* before lunch—there is nothing to touch a back number of the Girl's Own Paper" (10.513, all emphases added). Notice how this passage shifts from one list, recounting *types* of books (and the various ways they can be "battered"—out of date, minor, forgotten, with odd volumes or with bound numbers) to a second list, recounting types of reading (once again idiosyncratic and varied—such as the strange moment when we are *too* tired to go to sleep, or the odd quarter of an hour when we wait, perhaps hungrily, for lunch). The two lists map onto these two passages in "Books *v.* Cigarettes." Furthermore, just as with the preterition in "Books *v.* Cigarettes," all of these affectionate details in "Bookshop Memories" are *negatively* couched—"there was a time" when Orwell "loved" books in this way, but, he continues, "as soon as I went to work in the bookshop I stopped buying books. *Seen in the mass,* five or ten thousand at a time, books were *boring* and even *slightly sickening*" (513, emphases added). Orwell's abiding interest in the tactile nature of books belies this disavowal—or suggests that the interest and the repulsion (in books as such material objects) are enduring, and related, aspects of Orwell's relationship to writing.

14. At least once the impulse toward reversal takes biographical form, as Jacintha Buddicom's account of first meeting Orwell begins with the description of "a boy rather bigger than Prosper [Buddicom's brother] . . . standing on his head." Buddicom continues:

This was a feat we had not observed before, and we found it intriguing. So after a while, Nors asked him:

"Why are you standing on your head?"

To which he replied:

"You are noticed more if you stand on your head than if you are right way up." (11)

15. Another choice in this complicated passage: as though in a gesture toward that act of doubling—and displacement—which underlies this conceptual event, Orwell clots up the passage by use of the possessive ("one of the 'S's'"), creating an odd echo of the literal, referenced "S" (in uppercase) with the purely syntactic, discursive "s" (in lowercase). In AIP itself, Orwell has recourse to an identical image, discussing the practice of newspaper vendors writing headlines on slate, by hand, because of the paper shortage: "The paper-sellers, who frequently did not know which way round a capital "S" goes, had a better idea of what is news, and more sense of responsibility towards the public, than their millionaire employers" (21, 16.165). This passage works to rescale its reversal of the press-boss and the newspaper vendor, as sources of cultural authority, through the implied inversion of the letter.

16. Later in *Animal Farm,* Orwell repeats the same gesture, now inscribing a more dramatic moment—within the storied world—of being "turned upside-down" and once again linking the readerly comprehension *of* this event to a crucial, but discrete, conceptual inference (rather than a direct representation). This is the moment when Squealer (himself in the act of reversing one of the animals' seven "commandments," which, in the course of the narrative, are also all turned upside down, from signs of equality to instruments of coercion and oppression) plunges off the ladder on which he writes (or, from a different perspective, rewrites and even erases):

About this time there occurred a strange incident which hardly anyone was able to understand. One night at about twelve o'clock there was a loud crash in the yard, and the animals rushed out of their stalls. It was a moonlit night. At the foot of the end wall of the big barn, where the Seven Commandments were written, there lay a ladder broken in two pieces. Squealer, temporarily stunned, was sprawling beside it, and near at hand there lay a lantern, a paint-brush, and an overturned pot of white paint. The dogs immediately made a ring round Squealer, and escorted him back to the farmhouse as soon as he was able to walk. (112)

This is a particularly powerful example. Squealer is caught here, as I've suggested, in the middle of one of the reversals that structure the logic of the narrative as a whole. As Orwell writes in the next paragraph: "But a few days later

Muriel, reading over the Seven Commandments to herself, noticed that there was yet another of them which the animals had remembered wrong. They had thought the Fifth Commandment was 'No animal shall drink alcohol,' but there were two words that they had forgotten. Actually the Commandment read: 'No animal shall drink alcohol TO EXCESS'" (112–113). The depiction of Squealer's fall can offer solace to every reader of *Animal Farm*: a bracing exposure of authority's vulnerability from within the very workings of its assertion. It is a crack in the system—an imaged moment that can inspire resistance, courage, or hope. At the same time, Orwell carefully limits our access to the event. The fall is something which—like that discretely inverted "S"—can occur only in the reader's head; something which the narrative discourse *just misses* (like the animals who "rushed out of their stalls") and which we must reconstruct each time out of the loud crash, the broken ladder, the spilt paint. The activity of the reader is distilled to a single conceptual "step," linked to the fundamental precariousness of inversion itself: Squealer is only "temporarily stunned," and the signs of the event point as closely as possible to, but don't actually converge with, the sudden fall. The reconstruction is itself "tempora[ry]"—an imaginative act that also operates precariously, cued out of but distinct from the external signification of the event in language. Here, in our head, where Squealer once again falls, is the very resource of disobedience.

Animal Farm is, needless to say, full of other slips, falls, and moments of imbalance, all of which resonate with its fundamental narrative, and sociopolitical, premises: the narrative "wobbling" between violent history and childlike fable, the complicated and (dynamically unstable) analogy of beasts to men, and, most importantly, the gradual transmutation of equality (a relationship that could, itself, be formally structured as replication) into inequality (which could be structured as inversion, or turning upside-down). At the crux of this transformation, Orwell generates the famous phrase which is so starkly and poignantly suspended between these two formal principles: "'ALL ANIMALS ARE EQUAL, BUT SOME ANIMALS ARE MORE EQUAL THAN OTHERS'" (133).

17. See John Rodden, *The Politics of Literary Reputation*, particularly "'Permanent Outsider' Among Friends: Orwell's Compartmentalized Life" (134–141).

18. As with the Walter Raleigh episode, the relationship here is starkly imbalanced—the intrinsic contingency, and limits, of the anthology as *form* grating against the absoluteness, and finality, of the execution as *event*.

19. Orwell reaches toward the same problem in another essay from this period, "Raffles and Miss Blandish," explaining the rise of hyperviolent mass culture as another version of "realism" and "power worship":

Until recently the characteristic adventure stories of the English-speaking peoples have been stories in which the hero fights *against odds*. This is true all the way from Robin Hood to Popeye the Sailor. Perhaps the basic myth of the Western world is Jack the Giant Killer. But to be brought up to date this should be renamed Jack the Dwarf Killer, and there already exists a considerable literature which teaches, either overtly or implicitly, that one should side with the big man against the little man . . . People worship power in the form in which they are able to understand it. A twelve-year-old boy worships Jack Dempsey. An adolescent in a Glasgow slum worships Al Capone. An aspiring pupil at a business college worships Lord Nuffield. A *New Statesman* reader worships Stalin. There is a difference in intellectual maturity, but none in moral outlook. Thirty years ago the heroes of popular fiction had nothing in common with Mr. Chase's gangsters and detectives, and the idols of the English liberal intelligentsia were also comparatively sympathetic figures. Between Holmes and Fenner on the one hand, and between Abraham Lincoln and Stalin on the other, there is a similar gulf. (16.354–355)

In these different versions of accepting, and valorizing, the given, Orwell's essay invents a remarkably original valence for connecting literary and political culture. For Orwell's critique of yet another version of pessimism that tilts toward accession to the political given (and "quasi-mystical belief" in a spiritual renewal), see the September 1944 essay "Arthur Koestler" (16.392–400).

20. See note 32, chapter 4 for a further discussion of Orwell's rejoinder, in AIP 13, to G. K. Chesterton's assertion that "there are no new ideas" and its connection to the preceding column, AIP 12, on how the jokes in *Punch* magazine, "unchangeable as the Pyramids," can "never contain anything new" (12, 16.102). Orwell discusses the "neo-pessimist" belief in the "alleged immutability of 'human nature'" again in AIP 34 (16.294).

21. While this section of AIP is certainly a preliminary working-through of "Politics and the English Language," which in turn formulates the language politics so crucial to *1984,* it is important to note that this initial list hinges less on technical or clinical language (what is most often taken as the target of "Politics and the English Language") than its opposite—overly direct, tactile, impassioned language. Orwell's critique, in fact, relies on a dialectical analysis of both these kinds of language, again complicating the nature of his own commitment to plain style.

22. See, in particular, the memorable correspondence with Victor Gollancz, who had the right of first refusal. On March 23, 1944, Gollancz replies to Orwell's initial, pessimistic inquiry: "Frankly I don't begin to understand you when you say 'I must tell you that it is—I think—completely unacceptable from your point of view as it is anti-Stalin.' I haven't the faintest idea what 'anti-Stalin' means. The Communists, as I should have thought you were aware, regard me as violently anti-Stalinist, because I was wholly and openly opposed to Soviet foreign policy from the Nazi-Soviet pact until Russia came into the war, because I have been

highly critical of illiberal trends in Soviet internal policy, and because the last two issues of 'Left News' have been largely devoted to compromising criticism of the Soviet proposals about East Prussia, Pomerania and Silesia. . . . I suppose I ought to pat myself on the back that you apparently regard me as a Stalinist stooge, whereas I have been banned from the Soviet Embassy for three years as an 'anti-Stalinist.'" This was quickly followed by a brief note, after Gollancz had seen the manuscript, on April 4, "My Dear Blair, You were right and I was wrong. I am so sorry. I have returned the manuscript to Moore" (Crick 452–454).

23. "As soon as I got out of Spain I wired from France asking if they would like an article and of course they said yes, but when they saw my article was on the suppression of the P.O.U.M. they said they couldn't print it. To sugar the pill they sent me to review a very good book which appeared recently, 'The Spanish Cockpit,' which blows the gaff pretty well on what has been happening. But once again when they saw my review they couldn't print it as it was 'against editorial policy,' but they actually offered to pay for the review all the same—practically hush-money" ("Letter to Rayner Heppenstall" 11.53). The article appeared as "Eye-Witness in Barcelona" in *Controversy: The Socialist Forum* (1.11 (1937); see Davison 11.54–60), and an abridged version of the review of *The Spanish Cockpit* appeared in *Time and Tide* (31 July 1937; see Davison 11.51–52). See also Orwell's rejected review of Harold Laski's *Faith, Reason and Civilization* for *Manchester Evening News* (16.122–123) and correspondence about this with Dwight MacDonald (16.298–299). Strikingly, Orwell's first published article in French is also on this topic (see "La Censure en Angleterre" 10.148).

24. One example is the infamous elision in C. M. Woodhouse's influential 1954 introduction to *Animal Farm*. Consider Woodhouse's quotation from "Why I Write" against the original:

> Every line of serious work that I have written since 1396 has been written, directly or indirectly, *against* totalitarianism. . . . *Animal Farm* was the first book in which I tried, with full consciousness of what I was doing, to fuse political purpose and artistic purpose into one whole ("Introduction" to *Animal Farm* xvi)

> Every line of serious work that I have written since 1936 has been written, directly or indirectly, *against* totalitarianism and *for* democratic Socialism, as I understand it. (Davison 18.319)

25. Too often we can take form, or formal variety, as fundamentally happy: but why have recourse to more than one form, except that none of them are sufficient? *The Road to Wigan Pier*, as I suggested in chapter 2, stands out for conspicuously highlighting—and viscerally dramatizing—this *pathos* of form.

26. "When H. G. Wells's *The Island of Doctor Moreau* was reprinted in the Penguin Library, I looked to see whether the slips and misprints which I remembered in earlier editions had been repeated in it. Sure enough, they were still there. One of them is a particularly stupid misprint, of a kind to make most writers squirm. . . . It had persisted through edition after edition ever since 1896" (72, 19.41). How strange to focus on errors and misprints in relation to reprinting and rereading a text: another uncanny mixture of contingency and extension or repetition. Wells is, more generally, an important site of ambivalence and interest for Orwell—in his subliterary cultural status; his prolific production (in the same column Orwell asks, "what writer of Wells's gifts, if he had any power of self-criticism or regard for his own reputation, would have poured out in fifty years a total of ninety-five books . . . ?" [19.42]); his combination of political interest with counterfactual, speculative science fiction; his faith in progress and rational thinking; and, not least of all, as an iconic figure in Orwell's youth. Thus, in a letter from 10 May 1948, to Julian Symons: "I have a great admiration for Wells, ie. as a writer, and he was a very early influence on me. I think I was ten or eleven when Cyril Connolly and I got hold of a copy of Wells's "The Country of the Blind" (short stories) and were so fascinated by it that we kept stealing it from one another. I can still remember at 4 o'clock on a midsummer morning, with the school fast asleep and the sun slanting through the window, creeping down a passage to Connolly's dormitory where I knew the book would be beside his bed" (19.336). In this image of furtive anticipation and charged stillness, Orwell dramatizes the absorption and illicitness of childhood "fascinat[ion]" with writing.

27. Orwell is discussing here his essay "Benefit of Clergy: Some Notes on Salvador Dali," cut from its original publication in the *Saturday Book* (see Davison 16.233–241). Against this idea of an unnoticed cut, we could contrast the potential of active mistranslation, as in Orwell's admonition, at the end of his list of "reprintable works": "NB. *Not* to be reprinted: an essay called 'Culture & Democracy' in 'Victory or Vested Interest?' This was transcribed from shorthand notes of a lecture, & was grossly altered without my knowledge" (19.244). Transcription, shorthand notation, and reprinting are arguably three *different* modes of textual replication that could all work together to compound this "gross" distortion.

28. Previously, in AIP 28, Orwell offers a simpler version of this same process, so that this time it is an actual mistake in writing—rather than the *lack* of a text— that goes unnoticed: "In America even the pretence that hack-reviewers read the books they are paid to criticize has been partially abandoned. Publishers, or some publishers, send out with review copies a short synopsis telling the reviewer what to say. Once, in the case of a novel of my own, they misspelt the name of one of the characters. The same misspelling turned up in review after review" (16.252). The further turning of the screw in AIP 58 is revealing, as it suggests a still more

complicated intertwining of absence and presence within Orwell's poetics of representation and misrepresentation.

29. From AIP 59, in a brief section on the shrinking population of grey seals, another striking comment gestures at this same dialectical play: "'When asked, "Which is the wisest of the animals?" a Japanese sage replied, "The one that man has not yet discovered"'" (59, 17.50). For me, this epigram's compounding of absence, discovery, and surprise strikes close to the aesthetic heart (or peculiar "wis[dom]") of "As I Please."

30. We've already seen several versions of this often paradoxical and intricate effort at foregrounding the obscured, which ranges from Orwell's proclivity to imagine paper as it is being destroyed, to his interest in actual secondhand stores ("Just Junk—But Who Can Resist It?" 18.17–19), to his argument that the "scraps" ("Oysters and Brown Stout," 16.498) or "unnecessary detail[s]" ("Charles Dickens" 12.48) of different writers can stand out *as* their enduring achievement, to his focus on that "border-line" (16.273) where half-forgotten writers or "good bad books" (17.347–350) are "still flickeringly in print" (18.494). In AIP 59 (the last column before an extended hiatus from the project), even the radically different topic of animal extinction yields the same dynamic. After the bleak discussion of endangered grey seals, Orwell notes, "However, we are not quite such persistent slaughterers of rare animals as we used to be. Two species of birds, the bittern and the spoonbill, extinct for many years, have recently succeeded in reestablishing themselves in Britain. . . . Thirty years ago, any bittern that dared to show its beak in this county would have been shot and stuffed immediately" (59, 17.50).

31. This uncanny effect—freezing the immediate—is tied to a very concrete social observation in the column: Orwell's inquiry, at the end of AIP 60 and then the beginning of AIP 62, into a long-standing but surprisingly underdiscussed property requirement for British juries. This residual trace of class inequality was not changed until 1972 (see Davison 18.475), and Orwell's discussion of this exemplifies the column's ability to find (or "notice") unexpected and contingent, but still structurally significant, sites of social and political inequality. Foregrounding this "detail," which so often had gone unobserved, Orwell's column elicited an unusual amount of response and feedback. (The topic was also then taken up in the main pages of *Tribune*). These occasional, pointed sites of engagement with concrete instances of social injustice, and concrete social policies, are an important component of AIP—again, not in the sense that they transform the writing into a fully realized form of action but as they gesture toward or *connote* this action potential as (a vital) part of the column's sustained engagement with the poetics of immediacy. Other examples of such contemporary, politically-charged events discussed in AIP include the conscription of non-British soldiers (as we have seen in AIP 9, 16.80); a newly segregated dance hall in London (AIP 37, 16.328–329); the uncertain—and undiscussed—political status of Burma as it is reconquered by

Allied forces (AIP 59, 17.49–50); or unnecessary difficulties of public transportation in London, particularly for internally displaced wartime evacuees (AIP 43,
16.425).

32. When O'Brien reintroduces the photograph, after Winston has been
detained in the Ministry of Love, he also, once again, enacts its destruction: "An
oblong slip of newspaper had appeared between O'Brien's fingers. For perhaps five
seconds it was within the angle of Winston's vision. It was a photograph, and there
was no question of its identity. It was THE photograph. It was another copy of the
photograph of Jones, Aaronson, and Rutherford at the party function in New
York, which he had chanced upon eleven years ago and promptly destroyed. For
only an instant it was before his eyes, then it was out of sight again. But he had
seen it, unquestionably he had seen it! He made a desperate, agonizing effort to
wrench the top half of his body free. . . . [O'Brien] stepped across the room. There
was a memory hole in the opposite wall. O'Brien lifted the grating. Unseen, the
frail slip of paper was whirling away on the current of warm air; it was vanishing
in a flash of flame. O'Brien turned away from the wall."

33. See André Bazin's canonical discussion of this dialectical relationship
between preservation and loss in "The Ontology of the Photographic Image,"
What Is Cinema? Volume 1, Trans. Hugh Gray (Berkeley: U of California P, 2005
[1967]) 9–16.

34. It's also worth noting that Winston hides the photograph initially by "cover[ing] it up with another sheet of paper," just as the erasure of the text in *La
Batalla* is accomplished most effectively when it is covered up by another text, or
"filled up by other matter." In *1984,* Orwell stresses this detail, noting how, even as
Winston disposes the piece of paper in the memory hole, "along with some other
waste papers," he makes sure to do so "without uncovering it again." The double
negative ("without uncovering") suggests the conflicting valences that Orwell will
draw out of the term "cover" (as well as "recover," "discover," and "uncover") in
relation to writing, representation, and language.

35. This four-section AIP column is worth briefly pausing on more generally,
beginning with the way that it juxtaposes four different kinds of misleading, or
only partially accurate, discourse. Right after this depiction of the framed 1815
newspaper, Orwell swerves toward contemporary politics in a very brief, two-
sentence section that merely extracts a single falsehood from a conservative MP:
"'Today there are only eighty people in the United Kingdom with net incomes of
over six thousand pounds a year'" (55, 17.23). (Orwell then goes on, in the second
sentence, to list colloquial English phrases that might serve as a response to this
comment.) This is followed by a consideration of the popular writer Edgar Wallace,
focusing on his maniacal prolificacy (always an ambivalent topic for Orwell, and
one which links back into the core formal impulses of "As I Please"): "His output
was enormous. In his later years he was turning out eight books a year, besides
plays, radio scripts and much journalism. He thought nothing of composing a

full-length book in less than a week. He took no exercise, worked behind a glass screen in a super-heated room, smoked incessantly and drank vast quantities of sweetened tea. . . . The curious thing is that this utterly wasted life—a life of sitting almost continuously in a stuffy room and covering acres of paper with slightly pernicious nonsense—is what is called, or would have been called a few years ago, 'an inspiring story'" (17.24). And the column begins with a discussion of the French journalist and collaborator Henri Beraud (sentenced to death in the week that Orwell writes) and the Fascist paper *Gringoire*. Orwell singles out one cartoon from this newspaper: "I have seldom been so angered by anything in the Press as by its cartoon when the wretched Spanish refugees streamed into France with Italian aeroplanes machine-gunning them all the way. The Spaniards were pictured as a procession of villainous-looking men, each pushing a handcart piled with jewellery and bags of gold" (17.22–23). So: a fascist cartoon that vilifies the victims of aerial bombardment, the strangely imbalanced distribution of headlines in the 1815 *Observer*, a brief (but revealing) snippet of propaganda about income inequality in the United Kingdom, and Wallace's relentless production of words—"covering acres of paper"—without clear value or purpose. It is important to note that these four sections aren't simply critical, tending instead to create a wavering or balance between skeptical and approbational comments. Orwell takes the example of Beraud in order to underline the general valor of French writers under occupation (and then to question, in turn, how British writers might have fared): "It is significant that it was mostly people of this type, who had made no secret of their Fascist sympathies for years beforehand, that the Germans had to make use of for Press propaganda in France. . . . When one pieces these [several different articles] together, it becomes clear that the French literary intelligentsia has behaved extremely well under the German occupation" (17.23). The account of Wallace is self-consciously ambivalent; Orwell seems intrigued by the sheer activity, even as he deplores the product, of his writing. And, most importantly, Orwell doesn't call attention to the underemphasized recounting of Waterloo in order to criticize the newspaper but as a sign "that our ancestors were better at remaining sane in war time than we are" (17.23). This is certainly somewhat tongue in cheek, but the effect is to neither praise nor stigmatize the *Observer*, so much as simply to foreground the uncanniness of the strangely diminished headline and story. And this uncanniness, I would argue, is linked to the act of framing (or monumentalizing) a transient, quotidian edition of the newspaper.

This foregrounding of framed transience, in and of itself, is related to the way that Orwell refuses, in this AIP column, to fully stabilize his own position vis-à-vis the other texts. It's necessary to point to two more passages within the brief column to elaborate this, as twice more Orwell explicitly reverses, or "turns," his own argument. In section one, as I said, the attack on Béraud revolves into a *valorization* of French writers more generally, but this praise, in turn, becomes a lever or point of traction for criticizing the British. Orwell ends the section by making this shift only to "turn" once more in the final sentence: "I wish I could feel certain that the English literary intelligentsia as a whole would have behaved equally well if we had had the Nazis here. But it is true that if Britain had also been overrun, the situation would have been hopeless and the temptation to accept the New Order very much stronger" (17.23). In section two, similarly, Orwell arrives at the discussion of the "framed page of the *Observer*" through a revolving argument: "I think I owe a small apology to the twentieth century," the section begins. "Apropos of my remarks about the *Quarterly Review* for 1810—in which I pointed out that French books could get favourable reviews in England at the height of the war with France—two correspondents have written to tell me that during the present war German scientific publications have had fair treatment in the scientific Press in this country. So perhaps we aren't such barbarians after all. But I still feel that our ancestors were better at remaining sane in war time than we are. If you ever walk from Fleet Street to the Embankment. . . ." (17.23).

36. We can see this in the position of "Boys' Weeklies" within *Inside the Whale;* in the shift from Orwell's comments on "The Matrimonial News" to his anecdote about carrying the ladder (examined in the next chapter) or in the pointed trajectory of "The Postcard Art of Donald McGill," as it comes to dwell on the idiosyncrasy of writing itself—from the perspective of mass culture. These three examples all end up confronting a horizon of class stratification, and, in AIP 60 Orwell notes that "work" (along with "grey hair," "middle age or fatness," and "birth or death") is systematically excluded from the images he is considering (18.471). Likewise, in the final section of AIP 60, discussing the surprising homogeneity of British juries, Orwell says: "I have a strong impression . . . that no one strictly describable as a working-man normally finds his way on to a jury" (473).

37. Connolly dwells at length on the radically imperfect enterprise of reviewing books: in some sense it is the paradigmatic "enemy" of writing that he discusses. See Connolly 93–95.

38. See Paul de Man's discussion of this phrase in Charles Baudelaire, in "Literary History and Literary Modernity," *Blindness and Insight* (Minneapolis: U of Minnesota P, 1983) 166–186.

39. The general title for those reviews that will be "somewhat longer" (or "of value as a piece of writing," or "worthwhile . . . in themselves") is "Books and the People"—a phrase that of course reinflects so many of these issues. Orwell pens the first of these columns and then, a few weeks later, writes a column, at the start of 1945, titled "Books and the People: A New Year's Message" (17.7–11). This, in some ways, is an echo of that Christmas message "Can Socialists be Happy?" which Orwell pseudonymously published, at the end of 1943, as he began the dual role of columnist and literary editor for *Tribune*. "Books and the People: A New Year's Message" also begins by discussing the question of the length of book reviews, again opting for a "balanced" solution that, in fact, hinges on *dis*proportionality. It then shifts from this discussion of short and long to the larger, but still

dialectical, relationship between form and mass culture. Orwell rejects an entrenched opposition between modernist experiment—or "art for art's sake"—on the one hand and political instrumentality on the other: "[t]he first school accuses us of being lowbrow, vulgar, ignorant, obsessed with politics, hostile to the arts . . . the other school accuses us of being highbrow, arty, bourgeois, indifferent to politics and constantly wasting space on material that can be of no interest to a working man and of no direct use to the Socialist movement'" (17.9) What's striking about this essay is the way that Orwell connects such a fundamental, overarching question—how can politically engaged writing negotiate the Scylla and Charybdis of formalism and propaganda?—with the much more pointed, specific tension between those short and long reviews. Of course, as we have seen, the uneasy, unfinished relationship between "short" and "long"—which takes particular shape in these two discussions of book-reviewing policy in *Tribune*—is also related to the core, formal dynamics of AIP, as a writing project which explores the possibility of synthesizing immediacy and reflection. The seemingly peripheral discussion of book reviewing in AIP 47 is thus, in one important sense, a crux of the column sequence.

40. Orwell finishes this section with one final sentence: "And sometimes it pops up in quite enlightened people, with disconcerting results; as for instance at the end of 1941, when China officially became our Ally, and at the first important anniversary the B.B.C. celebrated the occasion by flying the Chinese flag over Broadcasting House, and flying it upside-down" (19.51). The section—and column—ends with this image of inversion, an image, as we've already seen, that is crucial to the form and logic of AIP. To end on this image of reversal necessarily creates a gap between the reader's conceptual processing of the column and the limit of the column itself: if the flag is "upside-down" as the column ends, the reader is struggling to catch up with this, imagining the flag right-side up (if only as a point of contrast) and grappling with the consequences of the inversion. If the mistake obviously indicts the B.B.C. (and through the Broadcasting House the more generalized state of "enlightened" England as such), it also points to the essential conventionality of a flag, as symbol, and thus as something which can—like the graphic mark of "S" in *Animal Farm*—be so easily and arbitrarily reversed.

41. The identification of this specific, limited, but also appalling mistake models another version of concrete political engagement, which we might compare with Orwell's focus, in AIP 60 and 62, on discovering the surprising property restrictions in British jury selection. (See note 31 in this chapter.) Again, these moments in which AIP touches on a specific instance of injustice are *not* the dominant register of the column. Nor are they simply ornamental, as though we could understand the writing project fully outside of these occasional examples. Instead, they have a structurally subordinate but still insistent presence in the column sequence. This is another way that the columns retain a poised balance, "alit" on the ground of politics without ever collapsing the text into the world (so that the essential

motive or ground of the columns could be reduced to a purely propagandistic intention) or estranging the text stably and completely from the world.

42. Orwell's invocation of a "constant struggle" might remind us of his deployment of the terms "effort" and "struggle" at key points in his articulation of "plain style" in "Why I Write" and "Politics and the English Language." See note 7 in the Introduction. Orwell's phrase from "In Front of Your Nose" (repeated in "Why I Write") might also suggestively connect to the refrain in Auden's "Spain": "But today the struggle" (Auden 210–211).

6. First-Person Socialism

1. We've already discussed several other sections of the first column. It opens, in fact, with another dramatic inroad toward immediacy—clipped, present-tense sentence fragments that putatively set the "stage" for a dialogue: "Scene in a tobacconist's shop. Two American soldiers sprawling across the counter, one of them just sober enough to make unwanted love to the two young women who run the shop, the other at the stage known as 'fighting drunk.' Enter Orwell in search of matches" (1, 16.12).

2. In fact, both sections of his "Notes on the Way" column are connected to larger trajectories in his work, even as the seam or division between the two sections connects, less obviously, to the formal tendency I've been discussing.

3. See Cathy Caruth, *Unclaimed Experience: Trauma, Narrative and History* (Baltimore: The Johns Hopkins University Press, 1996).

4. In "A Hanging" and "Shooting an Elephant," Orwell had already articulated the deep and abiding relationship between witnessing violence (rooted specifically in racially oppressive systems) and the act of writing itself. This anecdote from "Notes on the Way" reinforces the same connection and also offers an exemplary instant of Orwell's complicated plain style. What Orwell sees "just before" arriving or seeing his "first sight" in Asia is, in fact, a scene of brutal injustice, one that stays with him long enough that it can surge up, "suddenly," as he is reading a statement about the oppression of Jews and Poles in Germany. What shocks Orwell—then and now—about this scene of violence is its noncomprehension, the acquiescence of the European passengers to it:

> The liner I was travelling in was docking at Colombo, and the usual swarm of coolies had come aboard to deal with the luggage. Some policemen, including a white sergeant, were superintending them. One of the coolies had got hold of a long tin uniform-case and was carrying it so clumsily as to endanger people's heads. Someone cursed at him for his carelessness. The police sergeant looked around, saw what the man was doing, and caught him a terrific kick on the bottom that sent him staggering across the deck. Several passengers, including women, murmured their approval.

Now transfer this scene to Paddington Station or Liverpool Docks. It simply could not happen. An English luggage-porter who was kicked would hit back, or at least there would be a chance of his doing so. The policeman would not kick him on such small provocation, and certainly not in front of witnesses. Above all, the onlookers would be disgusted. The most selfish millionaire in England, if he saw a fellow-Englishman kicked in that manner, would feel at least a momentary resentment. And yet here were ordinary, decent, middling people, people with incomes of about £500 a year, watching the scene with no emotion whatever except a mild approval. They were white, and the coolie was black. In other words he was sub-human, a different kind of animal. (12.121)

Like the early essays/stories "A Hanging" and "Shooting an Elephant," this passage refuses to stably locate the writing subject himself in relation to what has been (so imperfectly) witnessed. The narrator's own description of "the usual swarm of coolies" already carries with it the very violence that will then be depicted. The disturbing characterization of these men as "coolies" (and the workers as a swarm) seems to precede the narration in much the same way as the men themselves might bring the luggage aboard. I don't want to examine the scene as a whole, however, but to keep a focus on the crafted structure of the text's opening line.

5. Early on in *English Journey,* J. B. Priestly makes a similar point about the deprivation and, specifically, the hunger of the stewards aboard the "great liners" (20), with one "smoke room steward" complaining: "no proper food and nowhere to eat it. If you're a steward, you've got to stand up and snatch a bite when you can" (20–21). Priestly continues: "He went on to talk very bitterly about the conditions of service in these ships, with the Louis Quinze drawing-rooms and Tudor smoke-rooms. . . . It is not pleasant, to say the least of it, to remember that the poor devil who is waiting upon you may have been washed out of his quarters the night before and has not sat down to a decent square meal since the voyage began" (21). Orwell was working on an unfinished novella, called "A Smoking-Room Story," at his death: it was set aboard the same kind of ship that we see in "Notes on the Way" and AIP 68.

6. It's a phrase that echoes a key line in Wordsworth's *The Prelude.* The "gentle shock of mild surprise" also describes an event which, by the time it is grasped *as* a perception, has already "penetrated" the observing subject:

. . . [W]hile he hung
Listening, a gentle shock of mild surprise
Has carried far into his heart the voice
Of mountain torrents; or the visible scene

Would enter unawares into his mind,
With all its solemn imagery . . . (V, 381–386, emphasis added)

7. This sense of the way that delay, or mistiming, connects to epistemological opportunities might remind us of a number of other moments we've been considering in Orwell, such as the photograph that Winston holds on to for thirty extra seconds in *1984* or the fugitive moment of perception that Orwell represents in "Marrakech" (two examples that can also be linked to the compositional form of "As I Please").

8. As I suggested, this scene of transportation works to extend Orwell's seemingly immediate transition, from writing to action, at the beginning of *Homage to Catalonia*. In fact, this is the third text within a sequential chain. After Orwell writes the opening of *Homage to Catalonia*, which depicts him as coming "straight from England" and "almost immediately" joining the militia, he describes his meeting with Henry Miller en route to Spain in "Inside the Whale": "I first met Miller at the end of 1936, when I was passing through Paris on my way to Spain. What most intrigued me about him was to find that he felt no interest in the Spanish war whatever. He merely told me in forcible terms that to go to Spain at that moment was the act of an idiot" (12.106). This scene, written three years after *Homage to Catalonia*, links the time that must pass while Orwell travels to Spain with a more profound disagreement about the nature of his action. This suggests that the directness and quickness of the opening to *Homage* is something of an overcompensation—or, in any case, that the tension between thinking and action, latent in the qualified sense of abandoning writing (and joining the POUM) "*almost* immediately," is important to Orwell. The belated narrative of his conversation with Miller also echoes the opening gesture of *Homage to Catalonia*: Miller remonstrates against Orwell's intention "to go to Spain *at that moment,*" while Orwell notes that he "had joined the militia almost immediately, because *at that time* and *in that atmosphere* it seemed the only conceivable thing to do." The opening of AIP 42, following the logic of displacement that we've seen in *The Road to Wigan Pier,* appears to distend Orwell's journey to war further: if we can assume that Miller is himself the person whom Orwell "had to visit" in Paris, then he is now travelling *to* the intermediate station that, in turn, prolongs his movement "straight from England" to Spain. Orwell's accordion-like expansion of this prehistory to arriving in Barcelona (first in "Inside the Whale" and then in "As I Please") fits into the retrospection that not only informs *Homage to Catalonia* but also generates later writing, including, most explicitly, the 1942 essay "Looking Back on the Spanish War."

9. Bowker says Orwell is on his way to Miller when "he had a violent altercation with a taxi driver"(201). Bowker adds: "Later he felt ashamed of how he had behaved and could hardly bring himself to write about it"(201). A strange comment, since the only evidence we have *for* this altercation—or for Orwell's

shame—is the AIP column he writes. It is a good example of how Orwell biography can efface the writerly as such: here Orwell's writing is not only treated as the factual ground for his life (rather than as a text), but testifies, even, to a resistance to writing.

10. For a consideration, alternatively, of how pervasive humor is in so much of Orwell's most "serious" and urgent writing, see Kenneth Ligda, "Orwellian Comedy."

11. See Davison's definitive discussion of this "special and unusual instance" in 16.37–38. Davison also notes *Tribune*'s announcement of the "cheerful Christmas" piece, as "something of the spirit of the season" that "will make a change from the hurly-burly of controversy" (38).

12. The essay—like Dickens's own annual writing—is written as a product of the holiday season, but rather than imagining a story in relation to or inspired by Christmas, Orwell begins—both more directly and more reflectively—with the "thought of Christmas" itself, which leads, in an associative process, to "the thought of Charles Dickens."

13. The second paragraph of "Can Socialists be Happy?" modulates this play between social-structural analysis and the casual familiar. Lenin, invoked here just as he is at the opening of "Charles Dickens," doesn't stand (in either case) as merely a political villain for Orwell. He inscribes a mode of seeing—or thinking—that Orwell doesn't mean to simply renounce: the challenge is not to drive Lenin into the grave but to imagine what "sociological implications" the revolutionary could see if he were "in better health." Certainly the image of Lenin on his "deathbed" gives an early, implicit answer to the title's question. But Orwell calls here for *more* sociological analysis, not less. Ironically, if Lenin's suffering were less acute, if he were "happier," he could recognize the way that Dickens intertwines happiness with suffering—rendering it "incomplete" because of its contingent dependency on "contrast."

Conclusion

1. The essay wants readers to give up on being "happy," and thus to *not* give up on being "socialists." Pressure on the one term serves, unexpectedly, as consolidation of the other. And that we don't need to give up this political affiliation is itself, ironically, a source of happiness.

2. Some of those who knew him best, perhaps. Would Eileen Blair have said this? Cyril Connolly writes in 1973, "Orwell was a political animal. He reduced everything to politics; he was also unalterably of the Left" (*The Evening Colonnade* 382). Any particular comment, of course, could be seen as "too early" or "too late."

3. It is important to note that Colls balances this skeptical approach to Orwell's political identity against a countervailing framework that his book, as a whole, means to stabilize: national identity. Orwell is *not* (consistently) Socialist but *is*

(consistently) British: Colls's study, at its heart, involves a dialectical relationship between these two categories. (Ultimately, in his study, one of these two terms has to give.) In my reading, Orwell's commitment to the nation-state is always an intermediate and not a final position. For one interesting meditation on intermediateness—in relation both to the British nation-state and socialist politics—see Orwell's 1948 "The Labour Government after Three Years" (19.435–444).

4. For example: "In general, an adjective by showing where it is to be applied, and assuming it makes a general distinction, can always imply its opposite elsewhere. . . . all that can be strictly deduced from the use of an adjective with a noun is that the author believes that, at some place and some time, some one might *not* have used the same adjective with the same noun"(Empson, 203).

5. Likewise, at the end of *Animal Farm*, Orwell presents us with a spectacular version of the strange, jarring moment when identity and difference collapse into one another. "The creatures outside looked from pig to man, and from man to pig, and from pig to man again; but already it was impossible to say which was which"(139). When, exactly, does it become "impossible" to see "which was which"? (Is it when the animals first look "from pig to man"? Or when they look "from man to pig"? Or when they turn to look from "pig to man again"?) In this way, the end of *Animal Farm* freezes in place a very fleeting instant, *after* these two categories have collapsed but *before* their tension has been fully dissolved. There must still be enough difference, between pig and man, for us to register the shock of their sudden identity. The interest of the plain style, in this case, is to preserve this very brief moment of categorical confusion.

6. Reinforcing its connection to the longer series of "As I Please" columns that have emphasized such "sign[s]" of returning inequality, this section concludes swiftly after its discussion of the railings: "When I was in the Home Guard we used to say that the bad sign would be when flogging was introduced. That has not happened yet, I believe, but all minor social symptoms point in the same direction. The worst sign of all—and I should expect this to happen almost immediately if the Tories win the General Election—will be the reappearance in the London streets of top-hats not worn by either undertakers or bank messengers" (16.318). In previous examples, Orwell regrets (in the same column as the story about Walter Raleigh) the end of clothes rationing—"if the poor are not much better dressed, at least the rich are shabbier"(AIP 10, 16.89)—and the return of commercial advertising, "in all its silliness and snobbishness"(AIP 33, 16.286). In a subsequent column he returns—with more vivid detail—to the reappearance of the "top hat" in London (AIP 43, 16.425). This column also protests against "the First Class nonsense" in the railway system (16.425). In other columns, Orwell dwells on various, unpredictable consequences of paper rationing.

Works Cited

Epigraph Sources

Orwell, George. *Down and Out in Paris and London*. New York: Harcourt, 1961 (1933).

———. "Literary Criticism 1: The Frontiers of Art and Propaganda." *The Listener* 29 May 1941. Rpt. in *The Complete Works of George Orwell*. Ed. Peter Davison. 12.483–486.

———. "Review of *The Novel To-Day*." *New English Weekly* 31 Dec. 1936. Rpt. in *The Complete Works of George Orwell*. Ed. Peter Davison. 10.532–534.

Other Sources

Aaronovitch, David. "The Reluctant Patriot: How George Orwell Reconciled Himself with England." *The New Statesman* 6 Jan. 2014.

Abrams, M. H. *A Glossary of Literary Terms*. 5th ed. New York: Holt, Rinehart and Winston, 1985.

Adorno, Theodor. *Minima Moralia: Reflections on Damaged Life*. Trans. E.F.N. Jephcott. London: Verso, 2006 (1951).

Anderson, Amanda. *The Powers of Distance: Cosmopolitanism and the Cultivation of Detachment*. Princeton: Princeton UP, 2001.

Anderson, Paul, "Introduction," *Orwell in Tribune: "As I Please" and Other Writings 1943–7*. Ed. Paul Anderson. London: Politico's Publishing Ltd, 2006.

Auden, W. H. *The English Auden*. Ed. Edward Mendelson. London: Faber and Faber, 1986 (1977).

Barnes, Julian. "Such, Such Was Eric Blair." *The New York Review of Books* 12 Mar. 2009: 17–19.

Barthes, Roland. *Mythologies*. Trans. Annette Lavers. New York: Hill and Wang, 1972 (1957).

Bewes, Timothy. *The Event of Postcolonial Shame*. Princeton: Princeton UP, 2010.

Booth, Wayne. *A Rhetoric of Irony*. Chicago: U of Chicago P, 1974.

Borges, Jorge Luis. *Ficciones*. Ed. Anthony Kerrigan. New York: Grove, 1962 (1956).

Bounds, Philip. *Orwell and Marxism: The Political and Cultural Thinking of George Orwell*. London: I. B. Tauris. 2009.

Bourdieu, Pierre. *The Rules of Art: Genesis and Structure of the Literary Field*. Trans. Susan Emanuel. Stanford: Stanford UP, 1996.

Bowker, Gordon. *George Orwell*. London: Abacus, 2003.

Brennan, Timothy. *Wars of Position: The Cultural Politics of Left and Right*. New York: Columbia UP, 2006.

Bromwich, David. *Politics by Other Means: Higher Education and Group Thinking*. New Haven: Yale UP, 1992.

Brooks, Cleanth. *The Well Wrought Urn: Studies in the Structure of Poetry*. New York: Harcourt Brace, 1947.

Buddicom, Jacintha. *Eric and Us: A Remembrance of George Orwell*. London: Leslie Frewin Publishers, 1974.

Butler, Judith. *Excitable Speech: A Politics of the Performative*. New York: Routledge, 1997.

Cain, William. "Orwell's Perversity: An Approach to the Collected Essays." *George Orwell: Into the Twenty-First Century*. Ed. John Rodden and Thomas Cushman. Boulder: Paradigm Publishers, 2005. 215–228.

Campbell, John. *Nye Bevan and the Mirage of British Socialism*. London: Weidenfeld and Nicolson, 1987.

Caruth, Cathy. *Unclaimed Experience: Trauma, Narrative and History*. Baltimore: The Johns Hopkins UP, 1996.

Clark, T. J. *The Painting of Modern Life: Paris in the Art of Manet and His Followers*. Rev. ed. Princeton: Princeton UP, 1999 (1984).

Clune, Michael. *Writing Against Time*. Stanford: Stanford UP, 2013.

Colls, Robert. *George Orwell: English Rebel*. Oxford: Oxford UP, 2013.

Connolly, Cyril. "Comment." *Horizon* Jan. 1940: 5–6.

———. *Enemies of Promise*. Chicago: U of Chicago P, 2008 (1938).

———. *The Evening Colonnade*. New York: Harcourt Brace, 1973.

Crick, Bernard. *George Orwell: A Life*. New York: Penguin Books, 1980.

———. "Introduction" to *The Lion and the Unicorn*. George Orwell. London: Penguin Books, 1982 [1941]: 7–30.

Cunningham, Valentine. *British Writers of the Thirties*. Oxford: Oxford UP, 1989.

Denning, Michael. *The Cultural Front*. London: Verso, 1998.

Dickens, Charles. *Sketches by Boz*. London: Penguin Books, 1995 (1839).

———. *Bleak House*. London: Penguin Books, 1996 (1853).

Doyle, Arthur Conan. *The Adventures and Memoirs of Sherlock Holmes*. London: Penguin Classics, 2001.

Duncan, Ian. *Scott's Shadow: The Novel in Romantic Edinburgh*. Princeton: Princeton UP, 2007.

Empson, William. *Seven Types of Ambiguity*. New York: New Directions, 1966 (1930).

Eagleton, Terry. *Literary Theory: An Introduction*. Minnesota: U of Minnesota P, 1996 (1983).

Forster, E. M. *A Passage to India*. New York: Harcourt, Brace and World, 1952 (1924).

Gilroy, Paul. *Postcolonial Melancholia*. New York: Columbia UP, 2005.

Gollancz, Victor. "Foreword." *The Road to Wigan Pier*. New York: Harcourt Brace & Company, 1958 (1937). ix–xxii.

Hammond, J. R. *A George Orwell Companion*. New York: St. Martins, 1982.

Hatch, Robert. Review of *The Road to Wigan Pier*, *Nation* 30 August 1958: 97–98, rpt in *George Orwell: The Critical Heritage*. Ed. Jeffrey Meyers: 113–115.

Hartman, Geoffrey. *Wordsworth's Poetry 1787–1814*. Cambridge: Harvard UP, 1987.

Holderness, Graham, Bryan Loughrey, and Nahem Yousaf, eds. *New Casebooks: George Orwell*. New York: St. Martin's, 1998.

Hynes, Samuel. *The Auden Generation: Literature and Politics in England in the 1930s*. New York: Viking, 1976.

Ingle, Stephen. *The Social and Political Thought of George Orwell*. New York: Routledge, 2008.

Jameson, Fredric. *The Political Unconscious: Narrative as a Socially Symbolic Act*. London: Routledge, 1981.

Joyce, James. *Ulysses*. Gabler ed. New York: Vintage Books, 1986 (1922).

Keeble, Richard. "The lasting in the ephemeral: assessing George Orwell's As I Please columns." *The Journalistic Imagination*. Ed. Richard Keeble and Sharon Wheeler. London: Routledge, 2007. 100–115.

Kermode, Frank. "The Sharpest Thorn." *The New York Review of Books* 14 June 2007: 46–48.

Ligda, Kenneth. "Orwellian Comedy." *Twentieth Century Literature* 60.4 (2014): 513–538.

Lloyd, David and Thomas, Paul. *Culture and the State*. London: Routledge, 1997.

Lott, Eric. "After Identity, Politics: The Return of Universalism." *New Literary History* 31.4 (2000): 665–678.

Lucas, Scott. *Orwell*. London: Haus Publishing, 2003.

———. "The Socialist Fallacy." *The New Statesman* 29 May 2000: 47–50.

MacNeice, Louis. *Modern Poetry: A Personal Essay*. Oxford: Clarendon, 1968 (1938).

de Man, Paul. *Blindness and Insight: Essays in the Rhetoric of Contemporary Criticism*. Minneapolis: U of Minnesota P, 1983.

Marks, Peter. *George Orwell the Essayist: Literature, Politics and the Periodical Culture*. London: Continuum, 2011.

———. "Where he wrote: periodicals and the essays of George Orwell." *Twentieth Century Literature* 41.4 (1995): 266–283.

McCann, Sean and Szalay, Michael. "Do You Believe in Magic? Literary Thinking After the New Left." *Yale Journal of Criticism* 18.2 (2005): 435–468

Menand, Louis. "Honest, Decent, Wrong: The Invention of George Orwell." *The New Yorker* 27 Jan. 2003: 84–91.

Meyers, Jeffrey. *Orwell: Wintry Conscious of a Generation.* New York: W. W. Norton, 2001.

Meyers, Jeffrey, ed. *George Orwell: The Critical Heritage.* London: Routledge & Kegan Paul, 1975.

Miller, James. "Is Bad Writing Necessary? George Orwell, Theodor Adorno, and the Politics of Language." *Lingua Franca* 9.9 (2000): 33–44.

Moretti, Franco. *Signs Taken for Wonders.* 2nd ed. New York: Verso, 1997.

Morgan, Kenneth O. *Labour People: Leaders and Lieutenants: Hardie to Kinnock.* Oxford: Oxford UP, 1987.

Mulhern, Francis. "Forever Orwell." *New Left Review* 87 (2014): 132–142.

Newsinger, John. *Orwell's Politics.* London: Palgrave Macmillan, 2002.

Norris, Christopher. "Language, Truth and Ideology: Orwell and the Post-War Left." *Inside the Myth: Orwell: Views from the Left.* Ed. Christopher Norris. London: Lawrence and Wishart, 1984. 242–262.

O'Flinn, Paul. "Orwell and *Tribune.*" *Literature and History* 6.2 (1980), 201-218.

Orwell, George. *The Complete Works of George Orwell.* Ed. Peter Davison. Vols. 10–20. London: Secker and Warburg, 2002 (1998).

———. "A Hanging." *The Adelphi* Aug. 1931. Rpt. in *The Complete Works of George Orwell.* Ed. Peter Davison. 10.207–210.

———. *Animal Farm.* New York: Signet Classic, 1996 (1946).

———. "Are Books Too Dear?" *Manchester Evening News* 1 June 1944. Rpt. in *The Complete Works of George Orwell.* Ed. Peter Davison. 16.242–244.

———. "The Art of Donald McGill." *Horizon* Sept. 1941. Rpt. in *The Complete Works of George Orwell.* Ed. Peter Davison. 13.23–30.

———. "Arthur Koestler." 11 Sept. 1944. Typescript. Rpt. in *The Complete Works of George Orwell.* Ed. Peter Davison. 16.391–400.

———. "As I Please" 1. *Tribune* 3 Dec. 1943. Rpt. in *The Complete Works of George Orwell.* Ed. Peter Davison. 16.12–14.

———. "As I Please" 2. *Tribune* 10 Dec. 1943. Rpt. in *The Complete Works of George Orwell.* Ed. Peter Davison. 16.23–24.

———. "As I Please" 3. *Tribune* 17 Dec. 1943. Rpt. in *The Complete Works of George Orwell.* Ed. Peter Davison. 16.25–28.

———. "As I Please" 4. *Tribune* 24 Dec. 1943. Rpt. in *The Complete Works of George Orwell.* Ed. Peter Davison. 16.34–36.

———. "As I Please" 5. *Tribune* 31 Dec. 1943. Rpt. in *The Complete Works of George Orwell.* Ed. Peter Davison. 16.45–47.

———. "As I Please" 6. *Tribune* 7 Jan. 1944. Rpt. in *The Complete Works of George Orwell*. Ed. Peter Davison. 16.55–58.

———. "As I Please" 7. *Tribune* 14 Jan. 1944. Rpt. in *The Complete Works of George Orwell*. Ed. Peter Davison. 16.60–61.

———. "As I Please" 9. *Tribune* 28 Jan. 1944. Rpt. in *The Complete Works of George Orwell*. Ed. Peter Davison. 16.80–82.

———. "As I Please" 10. *Tribune* 4 Feb. 1944. Rpt. in *The Complete Works of George Orwell*. Ed. Peter Davison. 16.88–90.

———. "As I Please" 12. *Tribune* 18 Feb. 1944. Rpt. in *The Complete Works of George Orwell*. Ed. Peter Davison. 16.100–102.

———. "As I Please" 13. *Tribune* 25 Feb. 1944. Rpt. in *The Complete Works of George Orwell*. Ed. Peter Davison. 16.103–105.

———. "As I Please" 14. *Tribune* 3 Mar. 1944. Rpt. in *The Complete Works of George Orwell*. Ed. Peter Davison. 16.111–113.

———. "As I Please" 15. *Tribune* 10 Mar. 1944. Rpt. in *The Complete Works of George Orwell*. Ed. Peter Davison. 16.117–119.

———. "As I Please" 16. *Tribune* 17 Mar. 1944. Rpt. in *The Complete Works of George Orwell*. Ed. Peter Davison. 16.124–126.

———. "As I Please" 17. *Tribune* 24 Mar. 1944. Rpt. in *The Complete Works of George Orwell*. Ed. Peter Davison. 16.131–133.

———. "As I Please" 18. *Tribune* 31 Mar. 1944. Rpt. in *The Complete Works of George Orwell*. Ed. Peter Davison. 16.137–139.

———. "As I Please" 19. *Tribune* 7 Apr. 1944. Rpt. in *The Complete Works of George Orwell*. Ed. Peter Davison. 16.145–147.

———. "As I Please" 20. *Tribune* 14 Apr. 1944. Rpt. in *The Complete Works of George Orwell*. Ed. Peter Davison. 16.151–153.

———. "As I Please" 21. *Tribune* 21 Apr. 1944. Rpt. in *The Complete Works of George Orwell*. Ed. Peter Davison. 16.164–166.

———. "As I Please" 22. *Tribune* 28 Apr. 1944. Rpt. in *The Complete Works of George Orwell*. Ed. Peter Davison. 16.171–174.

———. "As I Please" 23. *Tribune* 5 May 1944. Rpt. in *The Complete Works of George Orwell*. Ed. Peter Davison. 16.175–177.

———. "As I Please" 24. *Tribune* 12 May 1944. Rpt. in *The Complete Works of George Orwell*. Ed. Peter Davison. 16.182–185.

———. "As I Please" 26. *Tribune* 26 May 1944. Rpt. in *The Complete Works of George Orwell*. Ed. Peter Davison. 16.230–231.

———. "As I Please" 27. *Tribune* 2 June 1944. Rpt. in *The Complete Works of George Orwell*. Ed. Peter Davison. 16.244–247.

———. "As I Please" 28. *Tribune* 9 June 1944. Rpt. in *The Complete Works of George Orwell*. Ed. Peter Davison. 16.251–253.

———. "As I Please" 29. *Tribune* 16 June 1944. Rpt. in *The Complete Works of George Orwell*. Ed. Peter Davison. 16.258–260.

———. "As I Please" 31. *Tribune* 30 June 1944. Rpt. in *The Complete Works of George Orwell*. Ed. Peter Davison. 16.272–274.

———. "As I Please" 32. *Tribune* 7 July 1944. Rpt. in *The Complete Works of George Orwell*. Ed. Peter Davison. 16.275–277.

———. "As I Please" 33. *Tribune* 14 July 1944. Rpt. in *The Complete Works of George Orwell*. Ed. Peter Davison. 16.284–287.

———. "As I Please" 34. *Tribune* 21 July 1944. Rpt. in *The Complete Works of George Orwell*. Ed. Peter Davison. 16.292–294.

———. "As I Please" 35. *Tribune* 28 July 1944. Rpt. in *The Complete Works of George Orwell*. Ed. Peter Davison. 16.304–306.

———. "As I Please" 36. *Tribune* 4 Aug. 1944. Rpt. in *The Complete Works of George Orwell*. Ed. Peter Davison. 16.317–319.

———. "As I Please" 37. *Tribune* 11 Aug. 1944. Rpt. in *The Complete Works of George Orwell*. Ed. Peter Davison. 16.328–330.

———. "As I Please" 40. *Tribune* 1 Sept. 1944. Rpt. in *The Complete Works of George Orwell*. Ed. Peter Davison. 16.362–366.

———. "As I Please" 41. *Tribune* 8 Sept. 1944. Rpt. in *The Complete Works of George Orwell*. Ed. Peter Davison. 16.385–387.

———. "As I Please" 42. *Tribune* 15 Sept. 1944. Rpt. in *The Complete Works of George Orwell*. Ed. Peter Davison. 16.402–404.

———. "As I Please" 43. *Tribune* 6 Oct. 1944. Rpt. in *The Complete Works of George Orwell*. Ed. Peter Davison. 16.423–426.

———. "As I Please" 44. *Tribune* 13 Oct. 1944. Rpt. in *The Complete Works of George Orwell*. Ed. Peter Davison. 16.427–429.

———. "As I Please" 47. *Tribune* 3 Nov. 1944. Rpt. in *The Complete Works of George Orwell*. Ed. Peter Davison. 16.451–453.

———. "As I Please" 50. *Tribune* 1 Dec. 1944. Rpt. in *The Complete Works of George Orwell*. Ed. Peter Davison. 16.487–489.

———. "As I Please" 52. *Tribune* 29 Dec. 1944. Rpt. in *The Complete Works of George Orwell*. Ed. Peter Davison. 16.505–508.

———. "As I Please" 54. *Tribune* 12 Jan. 1945. Rpt. in *The Complete Works of George Orwell*. Ed. Peter Davison. 17.18–20.

———. "As I Please" 55. *Tribune* 19 Jan. 1945. Rpt. in *The Complete Works of George Orwell*. Ed. Peter Davison. 17.22–24.

———. "As I Please" 56. *Tribune* 26 Jan. 1945. Rpt. in *The Complete Works of George Orwell*. Ed. Peter Davison. 17.29–31.

———. "As I Please" 57. *Tribune* 2 Feb. 1945. Rpt. in *The Complete Works of George Orwell*. Ed. Peter Davison. 17.37–39.

———. "As I Please" 58. *Tribune* 9 Feb. 1945. Rpt. in *The Complete Works of George Orwell*. Ed. Peter Davison. 17.42–44.

———. "As I Please" 59. *Tribune* 16 Feb. 1945. Rpt. in *The Complete Works of George Orwell*. Ed. Peter Davison. 17.49–51.

———. "As I Please" 60. *Tribune* 8 Nov. 1946. Rpt. in *The Complete Works of George Orwell*. Ed. Peter Davison. 18.471–473.

———. "As I Please" 61. *Tribune* 15 Nov. 1946. Rpt. in *The Complete Works of George Orwell*. Ed. Peter Davison. 18.481–484.

———. "As I Please" 62. *Tribune* 22 Nov. 1946. Rpt. in *The Complete Works of George Orwell*. Ed. Peter Davison. 18.497–500.

———. "As I Please" 64. *Tribune* 6 Dec. 1946. Rpt. in *The Complete Works of George Orwell*. Ed. Peter Davison. 18.509–512.

———. "As I Please" 66. *Tribune* 20 Dec. 1946. Rpt. in *The Complete Works of George Orwell*. Ed. Peter Davison. 18.517–519.

———. "As I Please" 68. *Tribune* 3 Jan. 1947. Rpt. in *The Complete Works of George Orwell*. Ed. Peter Davison. 19.5–8.

———. "As I Please" 69. *Tribune* 17 Jan. 1947. Rpt. in *The Complete Works of George Orwell*. Ed. Peter Davison. 19.18–21.

———. "As I Please" 72. *Tribune* 7 Feb. 1947. Rpt. in *The Complete Works of George Orwell*. Ed. Peter Davison. 19.39–42.

———. "As I Please" 73. *Tribune* 14 Feb. 1947. Rpt. in *The Complete Works of George Orwell*. Ed. Peter Davison. 19.43–45.

———. "As I Please" 75A. *Manchester Evening News* 21 Feb. 1947. Rpt. in *The Complete Works of George Orwell*. Ed. Peter Davison. 19.50–51.

———. "As I Please" 75B. *Manchester Evening News* 28 Feb. 1947. Rpt. in *The Complete Works of George Orwell*. Ed. Peter Davison. 19.51–52.

———. "As I Please" 76. *Tribune* 7 Mar. 1946. Rpt. in *The Complete Works of George Orwell*. Ed. Peter Davison. 19.67–69.

———. "As I Please" 77. *Tribune* 14 Mar. 1947. Rpt. in *The Complete Works of George Orwell*. Ed. Peter Davison. 19.74–77.

———. "As I Please" 79. *Tribune* 28 Mar. 1947. Rpt. in *The Complete Works of George Orwell*. Ed. Peter Davison. 19.91–93.

———. "As I Pleased." *Tribune* 31 Jan. 1947. Davison, Rpt. in *The Complete Works of George Orwell*. Ed. Peter Davison. 19.35–38.

———. "Books and the People: A New Year Message." *Tribune* 5 Jan. 1945. Rpt. in *The Complete Works of George Orwell*. Ed. Peter Davison. 17.7–11.

———. "Books v. Cigarettes." *Tribune* 8 Feb. 1946. Rpt. in *The Complete Works of George Orwell*. Ed. Peter Davison. 18.94–97.

———. "Bookshop Memories." *Fortnightly* Nov. 1936. Rpt. in *The Complete Works of George Orwell*. Ed. Peter Davison. 10.510–513.

———. "Boys' Weeklies." *Inside the Whale and Other Essays*. London: Victor Gollancz, 1940. 89–128.

———. "Britain's Left-Wing Press." *Progressive* June 1948. Rpt. in *The Complete Works of George Orwell*. Ed. Peter Davison. 19.294–298.

———. "Can Socialists be Happy?" [by "John Freeman"]. *Tribune* 24 Dec. 1943. Rpt. in *The Complete Works of George Orwell*. Ed. Peter Davison. 16.39–43.

———. "Catastrophic Gradualism." *C. W. Review* Nov. 1945. Rpt. in *The Complete Works of George Orwell*. Ed. Peter Davison. 17.342–444.

———. "La Censure en Angleterre." *Monde* 6 Oct 1928. Rpt. in *The Complete Works of George Orwell*. Ed. Peter Davison. 10.148-150.

———. "Charles Dickens." *Inside the Whale and Other Essays*. London: Victor Gollancz, 1940. 9–85.

———. "Confessions of a Book Reviewer." *Tribune* 3 May 1946. Rpt. in *The Complete Works of George Orwell*. Ed. Peter Davison. 18.300–303.

———. "The Cost of Letters." *Horizon* Sept. 1946. Rpt. in *The Complete Works of George Orwell*. Ed. Peter Davison. 18.382–384.

———. "Decline of the English Murder." *Tribune* 15 Feb. 1946. Rpt. in *The Complete Works of George Orwell*. Ed. Peter Davison. 18.108–110.

———. *Down and Out in Paris and London*. New York: Harcourt, Inc., 1961 (1933).

———. "English Writing in Total War." *The New Republic* 14 July 1941. Rpt. in *The Complete Works of George Orwell*. Ed. Peter Davison. 12.527–530.

———. "Foreword." *The Case for African Freedom*. Ed. Joyce Cary. London: Searchlight Books, 1941. Rpt. in *The Complete Works of George Orwell*. Ed. Peter Davison. 12.521–522.

———. "Freedom of the Press." August 1945. Rpt. in *The Complete Works of George Orwell*. Ed. Peter Davison. 17. 253–260.

———. "Funny, But Not Vulgar." *Leader Magazine* 28 July 1945. Rpt. in *The Complete Works of George Orwell*. Ed. Peter Davison. 16.482–486.

———. "Good Bad Books." *Tribune* 2 Nov. 1945. Rpt. in *The Complete Works of George Orwell*. Ed. Peter Davison. 17.347–350.

———. *Homage to Catalonia*. New York: Harcourt Brace & Company, 1980 (1938).

———. "How Long is a Short Story." *Manchester Evening News* 7 Sept. 1944. Rpt. in *The Complete Works of George Orwell*. Ed. Peter Davison. 16.382–384.

———. "How the Poor Die." *Now* 6 Nov. 1946. Rpt. in *The Complete Works of George Orwell*. Ed. Peter Davison. 18.459–466.

———. "In Front of Your Nose." *Tribune* 22 Mar. 1946. Rpt. in *The Complete Works of George Orwell*. Ed. Peter Davison. 18.161–164.

———. *Inside the Whale and Other Essays*. London: Victor Gollancz, 1940.

———. "Inside the Whale." *Inside the Whale and Other Essays*. London: Victor Gollancz, 1940. 131–188.

———. "Introduction." *British Pamphleteers* 15 Nov. 1948. Rpt. in *The Complete Works of George Orwell*. Ed. Peter Davison. 19.106–115.

———. "Just Junk—But Who Could Resist It?" *Evening Standard* 5 Jan. 1946. Rpt. in *The Complete Works of George Orwell*. Ed. Peter Davison. 18.17–19.

———. *Keep the Aspidistra Flying*. New York: Harcourt Brace & Company, 1956 (1936).

———. "The Labour Government After Three Years." *Commentary* Oct. 1948. Rpt. in *The Complete Works of George Orwell*. Ed. Peter Davison. 19.435–443.

———. "Lear, Tolstoy and the Fool." *Polemic* 7 Mar. 1947. Rpt. in *The Complete Works of George Orwell*. Ed. Peter Davison. 19.54–66.

———. Letter to Brenda Salkeld, Dec. 1933. Rpt. in *The Complete Works of George Orwell*. Ed. Peter Davison. 10.326–329.

———. Letter to Dorothy Plowman, 19 Feb. 1946. Rpt. in *The Complete Works of George Orwell*. Ed. Peter Davison. 18.115–116.

———. Letter to Dwight Macdonald, 23 July 1944. Rpt. in *The Complete Works of George Orwell*. Ed. Peter Davison. 16.298–293.

———. Letter to Dwight Macdonald. 5 September 1944. Rpt. in *The Complete Works of George Orwell*. Ed. Peter Davison. 16.381–382.

———. Letter to Fredric Warburg, 31 May 1947. Rpt. in *The Complete Works of George Orwell*. Ed. Peter Davison. 19.149–150.

———. Letter to Geoffrey Gorer, 10 Jan. 1940. Rpt. in *The Complete Works of George Orwell*. Ed. Peter Davison. 12.6–7.

———. Letter to Geoffrey Gorer, 3 Apr. 1940. Rpt. in *The Complete Works of George Orwell*. Ed. Peter Davison. 12.137–138.

———. Letter to John Lehmann, 27 May 1936. Rpt. in *The Complete Works of George Orwell*. Ed. Peter Davison. 10.483.

———. Letter to Julian Symons, 10 May 1948. Rpt. in *The Complete Works of George Orwell*. Ed. Peter Davison. 19.335–336.

———. Letter to Rayner Heppenstall, 31 July 1937. Rpt. in *The Complete Works of George Orwell*. Ed. Peter Davison. 11.53–54.

———. *The Lion and the Unicorn: Socialism and the English Genius*. London: Secker and Warburg, 1941. Rpt. in *The Complete Works of George Orwell*. Ed. Peter Davison. 12.391–432.

———. "List of Reprintable and Not Reprintable Works, 1947[?]." Rpt. in *The Complete Works of George Orwell*. Ed. Peter Davison. 19.241–244.

———. "Literary Criticism I: The Frontiers of Art and Propaganda." *The Listener* 29 May 1941. Rpt. in *The Complete Works of George Orwell*. Ed. Peter Davison. 12.483–486.

———. "Literary Criticism II: Tolstoy and Shakespeare." *The Listener* 5 June 1941. Rpt. in *The Complete Works of George Orwell*. Ed. Peter Davison. 12.491–493.

———. "London Letter." *Partisan Review* Winter 1944–45. Rpt. in *The Complete Works of George Orwell*. Ed. Peter Davison. 16.411–416.

———. "London Letter, 5 June 1945." *Partisan Review* Summer 1945. Rpt. in *The Complete Works of George Orwell*. Ed. Peter Davison. 17.161–165.

———. "London Letter, 15–16 August 1945." *Partisan Review* Fall 1945. Rpt. in *The Complete Works of George Orwell*. Ed. Peter Davison. 17.245–249.

———. "Looking Back on the Spanish War." [1942?]. Rpt. in *The Complete Works of George Orwell*. Ed. Peter Davison. 13.497–511.

————. "The Lure of Profundity." *New English Weekly* 30 Dec. 1937. Rpt. in *The Complete Works of George Orwell*. Ed. Peter Davison. 11.104–105.

————. "Marrakech." *New Writing* Dec. 1939. Rpt. in *The Complete Works of George Orwell*. Ed. Peter Davison. 11.416–420.

————. *1984*. New York: Harcourt, Brace and Company, Inc., 1949.

————. "Notes from Orwell's Last Literary Notebook." 1949. Rpt. in *The Complete Works of George Orwell*. Ed. Peter Davison. 20.200–217.

————. "Notes on Nationalism." *Polemic* 1 Oct. 1945. Rpt. in *The Complete Works of George Orwell*. Ed. Peter Davison. 17.141–155.

————. "Notes on the Way." *Time and Tide* 30 Mar. 1940. Rpt. in *The Complete Works of George Orwell*. Ed. Peter Davison. 12.121–126.

————. "Oysters and Brown Stout." *Tribune* 22 Dec. 1944. Rpt. in *The Complete Works of George Orwell*. Ed. Peter Davison. 16.498–501.

————. "Paper Is Precious." *Through Eastern Eyes*. BBC. 8 Jan. 1942. Rpt. in *The Complete Works of George Orwell*. Ed. Peter Davison. 13.118–120.

————. "Politics and the English Language." *Horizon* Apr. 1946. Rpt. in *The Complete Works of George Orwell*. Ed. Peter Davison. 17.421–430.

————. "Politics vs. Literature: An Examination of *Gulliver's Travels*." *Polemic* Sept.–Oct. 1946. Rpt. in *The Complete Works of George Orwell*. Ed. Peter Davison. 18.417–431.

————. "Preface to the Ukrainian Edition of *Animal Farm*" Mar. 1947. Rpt. in *The Complete Works of George Orwell*. Ed. Peter Davison. 19.86–89.

————. "The Prevention of Literature." *Polemic* Jan. 1946. Rpt. in *The Complete Works of George Orwell*. Ed. Peter Davison. 17.369–380.

————. "Raffles and Miss Blandish." *Horizon* Oct. 1944. Rpt. in *The Complete Works of George Orwell*. Ed. Peter Davison. 16.346–356.

————. "Reflections on Gandhi." *Partisan Review* Jan. 1949. Rpt. in *The Complete Works of George Orwell*. Ed. Peter Davison. 20.5–10.

————. "Revenge Is Sour." *Tribune* 9 Nov. 1945. Rpt. in *The Complete Works of George Orwell*. Ed. Peter Davison. 17.361–363.

————. "Review of *A Coat of Many Colours: Occasional Essays* by Herbert Read." *Poetry Quarterly* Winter 1945. Rpt. in *The Complete Works of George Orwell*. Ed. Peter Davison. 17.402–405.

————. "Review of *Faith, Reason and Civilisation* by Harold J. Laski." Unpublished. 1944. Rpt. in *The Complete Works of George Orwell*. Ed. Peter Davison. 16.122–123.

————. "Review of *Four Quartets* by T. S. Eliot." *Manchester Evening News* 5 Oct. 1944. Rpt. in *The Complete Works of George Orwell*. Ed. Peter Davison. 16.420–422.

————. "Review of *Herman Melville* by Lewis Mumford." *The New Adelphi* Mar.–May 1930. Rpt. in *The Complete Works of George Orwell*. Ed. Peter Davison. 10.182–184.

———. "Review of *The Novel To-Day*." *New English Weekly* 31 Dec. 1936. Rpt. in *The Complete Works of George Orwell*. Ed. Peter Davison. 10.532–534.

———. "Review of *Quick Service* by P. G. Wodehouse; *Cheerfulness Breaks In* by Angela Thirkell; *Passenger List* by Olga L. Rosmanith; *Miss Hargreaves* by Frank Baker; *Just as I Feared* by Damaris Arklow." *The New Statesman and Nation* 19 Oct. 1940. Rpt. in *The Complete Works of George Orwell*. Ed. Peter Davison. 12.274–276.

———. "Review of *The Tree of Gernika* by G. L. Steer and *Spanish Testament* by Arthur Koestler." *Time and Tide* 5 Feb. 1938. Rpt. in *The Complete Works of George Orwell*. Ed. Peter Davison. 11.112–113.

———. "Review of *War Begins at Home,* edited by Tom Harrison and Charles Madge." *Time and Tide* 2 Mar. 1940. Rpt. in *The Complete Works of George Orwell*. Ed. Peter Davison. 12.17–18.

———. "Riding Down from Bangor." *Tribune* 22 Nov. 1946. Rpt. in *The Complete Works of George Orwell*. Ed. Peter Davison. 18.493–497.

———. *The Road to Wigan Pier.* New York: Harcourt Brace & Company, 1958 (1937).

———. "Rudyard Kipling." *Horizon* Feb. 1942. Rpt. in *The Complete Works of George Orwell*. Ed. Peter Davison. 13.150–160.

———. "Second Thoughts on James Burnham." *Polemic* May 1946. Rpt. in *The Complete Works of George Orwell*. Ed. Peter Davison. 18.268–284.

———. "Shooting an Elephant." *New Writing* Autumn 1936. Rpt. in *The Complete Works of George Orwell*. Ed. Peter Davison. 18.501–506.

———. "Some Thoughts on the Common Toad." *Tribune* 12 Apr. 1946. Rpt. in *The Complete Works of George Orwell*. Ed. Peter Davison. 18.238–241.

———. Statement on *Nineteen-Eighteen Four.* July 1949. Rpt. in *The Complete Works of George Orwell*. Ed. Peter Davison. 20.134–136.

———. "Story by Five Authors, Part 1." *Through Eastern Eyes*. BBC. 9 Oct. 1942. Rpt. in *The Complete Works of George Orwell*. Ed. Peter Davison. 14.89–93.

———. "Such, Such Were the Joys." [1939?–1948?]. Rpt. in *The Complete Works of George Orwell*. Ed. Peter Davison. 19.356–386.

———. "Toward European Unity." *Partisan Review* Jul.–Aug. 1947. Rpt. in *The Complete Works of George Orwell*. Ed. Peter Davison. 19.163–167.

———. "T. S. Eliot." *Poetry* Oct.–Nov. 1942. Rpt. in *The Complete Works of George Orwell*. Ed. Peter Davison. 14.63–67.

———. "War-Time Diary." Oct. 1940. Rpt. in *The Complete Works of George Orwell*. Ed. Peter Davison. 12.277.

———. "Wells, Hitler and the World State." *Horizon* Aug. 1941. Rpt. in *The Complete Works of George Orwell*. Ed. Peter Davison. 12.536–540.

———. "Why I Join the I.L.P." *New Leader* 24 June 1938. Rpt. in *The Complete Works of George Orwell*. Ed. Peter Davison. 11.167–169.

———. Why I Write." *Gangrel* 4 (1946). Rpt. in *The Complete Works of George Orwell*. Ed. Peter Davison. 18.316–320.

————. "Writers and Leviathan." *Politics and Letters* Summer 1948. Rpt. in *The Complete Works of George Orwell*. Ed. Peter Davison. 19.288–293.

Packer, George. "Foreword." *Facing Unpleasant Facts: Narrative Essays*. George Orwell. Orlando: Harcourt Inc., 2008.

Patai, Daphne. *The Orwell Mystique: A Study in Male Ideology*. Amherst: U of Massachusetts P, 1984.

Perec, Georges. *W, or The Memory of Childhood*. Trans. David Bellos. Jaffrey: David R. Godine, 1988 (1975).

Priestly, J. B. *English Journey: Jubilee Edition*. Chicago: U of Chicago P, 1984 (1934).

Rodden, John. *The Politics of Literary Reputation: The Making and Claiming of St George Orwell*. Oxford: Oxford UP, 1991.

Rorty, Richard. *Contingency, Irony and Solidarity*. Cambridge: Cambridge UP, 1989.

Shelden, Michael. *Friends of Promise: Cyril Connolly and the World of Horizon*. New York: Harper & Row, 1989.

————. *Orwell: The Authorized Biography*. New York: Harper Perennial, 1991.

Shklovsky, Victor. *Theory of Prose*. Trans. Benjamin Sher. Normal: Dalkey Archive, 1991 (1929).

Spender, Stephen. *Forward from Liberalism*. London: Victor Gollancz Ltd., 1937.

Stansky, Peter, and Abrahams, William. *The Unknown Orwell/Orwell: The Transformation*. Stanford: Stanford UP, 1994 (1972, 1979).

Symons, Julian. "An Appreciation," in George Orwell, *Nineteen Eighty-Four* (London: Heron, 1970 [1949]). 315–344.

Teres, Harvey. *Renewing the Left: Politics, Imagination and the New York Intellectuals*. Oxford: Oxford UP, 1996.

Vaninskaya, Anna. "The Orwell Century and After: Rethinking Reception and Reputation." *Modern Intellectual History* 5.3 (2008): 597–617.

Weisberg, David. *Chronicles of Disorder: Samuel Beckett and the Cultural Politics of the Modern Novel*. New York: State U of New York P, 2000.

Wheatcroft, Geoffrey. "Why Orwell Endures." *New York Times* 14 Feb. 2010: 27.

Williams, Raymond. *George Orwell*. New York: Viking, 1971.

Woloch, Alex, "Orwell and the Essay Form: Two Case Studies." *Republics of Letters* 4.1 (2014): 1–12.

Wood, James. "A Fine Rage: George Orwell's Revolutions." *The New Yorker* 13 Apr. 2009: 54–63.

Woodcock, George. "Recollections of George Orwell," *Northern Review*, August-September 1953, in Audrey Coppard and Bernard Crick (eds), *Orwell Remembered* (London: Ariel, 1984).

Wordsworth, William. *The Prelude: 1799, 1805, 1850*. Ed. Jonathan Wordsworth, M. H. Abrams, and Stephen Gill. New York: Norton & Company, 1979.

Zwerdling, Alex. *Orwell and the Left*. New Haven: Yale UP, 1974.

Acknowledgments

There are *some* benefits when a book is a long time coming. I want to express my gratitude to many current and former students at Stanford who I worked with while developing *Or Orwell*. In the last few years, I've drawn energy and inspiration from the graduate student community in Stanford's English department. Writing this book also took long enough that several students, whom I first met in graduate seminars, ended up, years later, as valued interlocutors. To Ulka Anjaria, Matthew Garrett, Kenneth Ligda and Zena Meadowsong, who all read extensive sections of this book: thanks for being as fearless as you are brilliant, and for your thoughtful, detailed engagement with this work.

At Stanford, many colleagues took time from their own work to engage with mine. For this and for friendship and intellectual engagement, my thanks to John Bender, Terry Castle, Margaret Cohen, Michele Elam, Denise Gigante, Claire Jarvis, Nick Jenkins, Michelle Karnes, Mark McGurl, Paula Moya, Stephen Orgel, Rob Polhemus, David Riggs, Nancy Ruttenburg, Ramon Saldivar, Peter Stansky, Blakey Vermeule. In meaningful ways, Gavin Jones, Franco Moretti and Sianne Ngai have been valued friends to this work and its author. I'd also like to thank all of the remarkable administrative team of the English department—particularly Alyce Boster and Judy Candell. Teaching "Literature of the 1930s" with Nick Jenkins was an important moment for this book. My thanks to Kenneth Ligda and Abigail Droge for their valuable help, at different points, as research assistants.

I want to thank my editor at Harvard University Press, Lindsay Waters, for his support of the project, and also for a generative, long-running dialogue about the aims and structure of this book. I'd also like to thank Amanda Peery, my copy editor Kitty Wilson, and project manager Katrina Ostler, for their diligent work on the manuscript. Like all Orwell scholars, I am indebted to Peter Davison's magisterial edition of Orwell: the vectors of my study were enabled by his work.

Over the years, this work has benefitted from many conversations with, and often careful readings by, other scholars and friends. I am grateful, among others, to Amanda Anderson, Ilya Bernstein, John Bowen, Peter Brooks, Frances Ferguson, Phil Fisher, Benjamin Kahan, Rob Kaufman, David Kurnick, Sean O'Sullivan, John Plotz, Leah Price, Stephen Rachman, Chris Rovee, Stephen Schwartz, Hannah Sullivan, Emily Sun, Michael Szalay, Jennifer Terni, Elaine Auyoung, and Mike Benveniste for their intelligence and example. An exchange of work with Eyal Peretz proved invaluable. Jed Esty and Aidan Wasley read this book in manuscript and gave beautifully engaged and helpful responses. For their sustaining friendship in CA thanks to Paul Delehanty, Andrew Dimock, Elisabeth Hansot (in memorium), and all the other Green Belt denizens, Sharon Palmer, and Antonio Romero. Family and friends on the East Coast—David Woloch, Dana Goldberg, Lewis and Benjamin, Elizabeth Oeler, Kimberly Benson, Ivan Kolodny, and my wonderful parents, Isser and Nancy Woloch—have always been there.

Charles Baraw has also been with this book since its inception—he is a living presence in the work, having blurred the line between friendship and editing. D. A. Miller's writing, by its daring example, made this book more difficult to complete; his friendship made it easier. This book is dedicated with love, affection, and—not least of all—gratitude to Karla Oeler.

Index

"Newness," 225, 366n32
The New Republic, 208–209, 372n19
Newsinger, John, 5, 328n1, 355n2
Newspapers, 239, 266, 370n4, 372n10, 380n35
1984 (Orwell), 5–6, 126, 238–239, 263–264,
    337n31, 338n37, 363n20, 371n7, 380n32,
    380n34
1949 notebook. *See* "Literary Notebook"
Norris, Christopher, xvi, 192–193, 328n1,
    329n6, 353n16
"Notes on Nationalism" (Orwell), 46–47,
    335n28, 338n37, 339n38
"Notes on the Way" (Orwell), 289–291,
    384n2, 384n4
Noticing, 195–197, 261–262; difficulty of,
    105–106, 128, 196, 274–275, 383n41; the
    unnoticed, 56, 66
Nye Bevan and the Mirage of British Socialism
    (Campbell), 360n16

Observer (1815), 266, 380n35
Opening lines: in AIP, 202, 207, 219–220;
    of AIP 47, 254; of AIP 62, 262–263; in
    "Confessions of a Book Reviewer," 236–
    237; of "Notes on the Way," 289–291; of
    "Shooting an Elephant," 82, 101, 207,
    360n17
Openings, 152–153; of *Homage to Catalonia*,
    288, 386n8
Orwell, George. *See specific topics*
Orwell, George, works of: *Animal Farm*,
    5–6, 11, 38–41, 43, 249–250, 323, 336n29,
    374nn15–16, 377n24, 388n5; "Arthur
    Koestler," 38–39, 43–45, 47–52, 107, 319,
    336n29; "The Art of Donald McGill,"
    55–57, 151–152, 382n36; "As I Please," xvii,
    16–18, 27–29, 187–192, 198–215, 219–222,
    224, 233–234, 239–240, 244–253, 259–305,
    308, 313–314, 323–325, 330n12, 355nn1–2,
    356n4, 358n10, 359n11, 359nn13–14,
    361n18, 362n19, 363nn20–21, 364nn22–25,
    365n27, 365n29, 366n30–32, 372n19,
    378nn27–28, 379n31, 380n35, 382n36,
    382n39, 383n41, 383nn40–42, 385n5,
    385n7, 386nn8–9, 388n6; "Books and the
    People: A New Year's Message," 382n39;
    "Bookshop Memories," 373n13; "Books *v.*
    Cigarettes," 235, 238–244, 372n8, 372–
    373nn10–13; "Boys' Weeklies," 143, 148–
    157, 351n4, 351n5, 352n6, 352n7, 382n36;

"Britain's Left-Wing Press," 248–249;
    "Can Socialists be Happy?," 167, 306–320,
    382n39, 387n1, 387nn10–13; "Catastrophic
    Gradualism," 333n22; "Charles Dickens,"
    16–18, 54, 143, 157–173, 307–308, 312–313,
    348n6, 351n3, 352n9, 352n10, 352n15,
    387n13; "Confessions of a Book Reviewer,"
    235–241, 369n2; "Decline of the English
    Murder," 344n7; *Down and Out in Paris
    and London*, 20, 23, 41, 67–68, 72–73, 99,
    195–197, 336n30, 341n7, 343n2; "English
    Writing in Total War," 338n35; "Freedom
    of the Press," 336n29; "Funny, But Not
    Vulgar," 258; "Good Bad Books," 235;
    "A Hanging," 61–98, 101–102, 106, 108,
    330n12, 339–340nn1–5, 341n6, 341n8,
    342n9, 342n11, 342n12; *Homage to
    Catalonia*, 13–14, 72–73, 91–92, 100, 108–
    109, 112–117, 214–219, 260–261, 288, 321–
    323, 330n11, 336n30, 337n31, 341n7, 345n9,
    346nn11–13, 363n20, 364nn24–25, 365n26,
    378n28, 386n8; "How the Poor Die," 21,
    194, 358n7; "In Front of Your Nose," 279,
    384n42; "Inside the Whale," 25–26, 143,
    147–148, 173–176, 330n12, 338n35, 358n9;
    Inside the Whale and Other Essays, 28,
    143–177, 350n1, 351n3; "Just Junk-But Who
    Could Resist It?," 193–194, 357n6, 379n30;
    Keep the Aspidistra Flying, 170–172, 240,
    338n35; "The Labour Government After
    Three Years," 333n23; "Lear, Tolstoy and
    the Fool," 331n16, 337n33; *The Lion and the
    Unicorn: Socialism and the English Genius*,
    34–38, 332n21, 333n25, 334n26, 335nn27–
    28; "Literary Criticism 1: The Frontiers of
    Art and Propaganda," 1; "Literary Criti-
    cism II: Tolstoy and Shakespeare," 229–
    230; "Literary Notebook," 12–13, 104–105,
    108–109; "London Letter," 200, 333n22,
    336n29, 338n36, 369n2; "Looking Back on
    the Spanish War," 46, 343n3, 386n8; "The
    Lure of Profundity," 46–47, 140, 308;
    "Marrakech," 196–197; *1984*, 5–6, 126,
    238–239, 263–264, 337n31, 338n37, 363n20,
    371n7, 380n32, 380n34; "Notes on National-
    ism," 46–47, 335n28, 338n37, 339n38;
    "Notes on the Way," 289–291, 384n2,
    384n4; "Paper Is Precious," 239, 370n4;
    "Politics and the English Language," 8,
    330n7, 331n14, 376n21; "Politics vs.